Power, Voting, and Voting Power

Power, Voting, and Voting Power

Edited by
Manfred J. Holler

Physica-Verlag · Würzburg–Wien
1982
ISBN 978-3-662-00413-5

CIP-Kurztitelaufnahme der Deutschen Bibliothek

Power, voting, and voting power / ed. by Manfred J. Holler. – Würzburg ; Wien : Physica-Verlag, 1982

ISBN 978-3-662-00413-5 ISBN 978-3-662-00411-1 (eBook)
DOI 10.1007/978-3-662-00411-1

NE: Holler, Manfred J. [Hrsg.]

Composed and printed by repro-druck „Journalfranz" Arnulf Liebing GmbH + Co., Würzburg

Foreword

Any normative theory of democracy involves notions of equity, which are supposed to guide collective decisions. On the other hand, a descriptive theory of any decision-making body must take into account the distribution of power in that body. The development of collective decision theory along two different paths reflects these two foci of interest in the theory of democracy.

One direction can be subsumed under the theory of social choice, the other under the theory of games. In the theory of social choice, the participants are characterized only by their preferences among a set of alternatives (candidates, courses of action, etc.). They do not choose among these alternatives. They only submit their preferences to some central authority ("the Society"), which then chooses among the alternatives in accordance with some fixed rule of aggregating the preferences. On the other hand, the point of departure in the theory of games is a set of actors, each of whom can choose between alternative courses of action (strategies). The totality of choices results in an outcome, which generally has different utilities for the different actors. In this book, both approaches are presented in selected papers, from which the reader can get an excellent overview of the state of the art.

Both branches of formal decision theory, the theory of social choice and the theory of games, were developed in mathematical language, but very little technical mathematical knowledge is required to follow the arguments. What is required to *appreciate* the arguments is willingness to think rigorously (as a mathematician thinks), both in the context of definitions and in the context of logical deduction.

Since the theory of social choice deals with "democratic" decisions, it must begin with a rigorous definition of such a decision. This involves listing a set of criteria, which a "democratic" (or "equitable") decision must satisfy. The criteria are meant to reflect some commonly held intuitive notions about democratic decisions. They cannot capture the full concept of "democracy" or of "equity" in collective decision-making, but that is the price one must pay for being able to reason clearly about the *implications* of these concepts. It turns out, for example, that an apparently "minimal" set of criteria of "democratic decision" can never be realized, because the criteria are logically incompatible with each other. Since collective decision procedures purporting to be "democratic" do operate, the question arises which of these "minimal" criteria are violated and how. It is shown that if the criterion of unrestricted preference orderings of the alternatives is dropped, as when the alternatives (or candidates) can be represented by positions on a one-dimensional political scale, say from "left" to "right", a social choice rule satisfying the remaining criteria can be defined. Again, it the criterion called "independence from irrelevant alternatives" is dropped, rules of social choice satisfying the remaining criteria can be devised. In this case, the crucial importance of the "agenda" (the order of pairwise presentation of alternatives in sequential voting procedures) becomes apparent.

In the theory of non-cooperative games, the problem is that of finding optimal strategies for each actor individually, assuming that each strives to maximize his utility of the outcome under the constraint of the situation and with awareness that all the other actors are striving to do the same. If a voting procedure is conceived as a non-cooperative game, this model leads to distinctions between *voting strategies* in sequential voting on a set of alternatives and reveals the contexts, well known to politicians, where the "agenda" can decide the outcome. Here a link is provided between the theory of social choice and the theory of non-cooperative games.

In the theory of cooperative games, actors are assumed to be able to join in coalitions to pursue common goals. In particular, they can join in a grand coalition of all and, by properly coordinating their strategies, maximize their joint utility. They then face the problem of apportioning this amount among themselves. The connection between this problem and that of the distribution of power is via the circumstance that in forming coalitions, different players or groups of players have different bargaining leverages. Thus, the distribution of utility can be regarded as a reflection of the distribution of power.

To assess the distribution of power in a decision-making body such as a parliament, a committee, or the UN Security Council, a precise definition of "amount of power" is required. The theory of games provides several such definitions, based on the possible coalitions empowered to effect a decision, and the distribution of power is deduced from each such definition.

Resort to mathematical models developed in formal decision theory speaks for the maturation of political science as a *science*, if "science" is understood as a mode of cognition rather than as specific content-oriented methods of investigation. The scientific mode of cognition rests on two cognitive procedures, induction and deduction. Induction entails generalizations from particular observations to conclusions in the form "if . . . then . . . ", i.e., to the establishment of regularities, which (the scientist hopes) reflect some aspect of objective reality. Deduction entails reasoning from general assumptions to conclusions about particular cases. Modern science emerged from the integration of the two procedures in the so called hypothetico-deductive method, where observations lead to hypotheses and deductions to implications of the hypotheses to be tested by further observations.

In this book, the hypothetico-deductive method is applied primarily to testing various models of power distribution. For example, if the power of a political party is defined in terms of one of the indices based on possible coalition alignments, the distribution of power so deduced is compared with the extent of participation of the various parties in governments over a historical period. However, the integration of theoretical and empirical approaches is not confined to testing predictions (or postdictions) deduced from a theory. The primacy of explanatory potential (which some social scientists regard as independent of the predictive potential of a theory) is *also* served when various procedures of collective decision are examined in the light of the formal models of power distribution or of social choice. The former shed some light on the implications of changes of electoral procedures, especially in representative systems of government, on "log rolling" in legislative bodies, etc. The latter provide insights into the implications of pairwise presentations of issues (control of the "agenda") and, perhaps into the tendency of issues or programmes to become "linearized" over a political spectrum.

It is tempting to regard the distribution of power as a principal concern of political science, analogous to the distribution of commodities or of their surrogates as a primary concern of political economy. The analogy would have some force if "power" were defined as explicitly as economic variables (production and trade volumes, prices, interest, etc.). This book puts this fundamental problem into focus. The circumstance that "power" can be defined in a variety of ways, each with different implications, reveals the formidable complexity of the problem but also enables the political scientist to grapple with it rigorously and systematically, above all to separate the various denotations of the term "power" from its often obfuscating emotional or ideological connotations.

Vienna, June 27, 1981 A. Rapoport

Contents

5. The Empirical Approach

Author Index

Dr. H. Behrens
Geschwister-Scholl-Institut, Ludwigstraße 10, D–8000 München 22, Germany

Prof. R.F. Bensel
Prof. M.E. Sanders
Dept. of Political Science, Texas A & M University, College Station, Texas 77843, U.S.A.

Dr. E. Bomsdorf
Seminar für Wirtschafts- und Sozialstatistik der Universität Köln, Albertus-Magnus-Platz, D–5000 Köln 41

Prof. B.H. Bjurulf
Prof. R.G. Niemi
Statsvetenskapliga Institutionen, Lunds Universitet, Fack, 22005 Lund, Sweden

Prof. P.S. Goodrich
Dept. of Economics, The University of Leeds, Leeds LS 9JT, U.K.

Dr. M.J. Holler
Volkswirtschaftliches Institut der Universität München, Ludwigstraße 28, D–8000 München, Germany

Prof. R.J. Johnston
Dept. of Geography, University of Sheffield, Sheffield, U.K.

Dr. H. Kliemt
Gaußstraße 16, D–6000 Frankfurt 1, Germany

Prof. M. Laakso
Prof. R. Taagepera
Mustikkatie 23 B 3, 70280 Kuopio 28, Finland

Prof. S. Merrill III.
Dept. of Mathematics and Computer Science, Wilkes College, Wilkes-Barre, Pennsylvania 18766, U.S.A.

Prof. N.R. Miller
Dept. of Political Science, University of Maryland, Baltimore County, Baltimore, Maryland 21228, U.S.A.

Prof. D.C. Mueller
Wissenschaftszentrum Berlin, IMV, Platz der Luftbrücke 1–3, D–1000 Berlin 42, Germany

Prof. H. Nurmi
Dept. of Philosophy, University of Turku, 20500 Turku 50, Finland

Prof. G. Owen
Dept. of Mathematics, Naval Postgraduate School, Monterey, California 93940, U.S.A.

Prof. E.W. Packel
Prof. J. Deegan, Jr.
Dept. of Mathematics, Lake Forest College, Lake Forest, Illinois 60045, U.S.A.

Prof. H. Rattinger
Seminar für Wissenschaftliche Politik, Albert-Ludwig-Universität, Werderring 18, D–7800 Freiburg, Germany

Dr. H.-D. Schneider
Abteilung Sozialpsychologie der Universität Zürich, Näglistraße 7, 8044 Zürich, Switzerland

Prof. N. Schofield
Dept. of Economics, University of Essex, Colchester, U.K.

Prof. A. Schotter
Dept. of Economics, New York University, 8 Washington Place, New York, N.Y. 10003, U.S.A.

Prof. P.D. Straffin, Jr.
Prof. M.D. Davis
Prof. S.J. Brams
Beloit College, Beloit, Wisconsin 53511, U.S.A.

Prof. E.M. Uslaner
Dept. of Government and Politics, University of Maryland, College Park, Maryland 20742, U.S.A.

Prof. D. Wittman
University of California, Merrill College, Santa Cruz, California 95064, U.S.A.

1. Introduction

Holler, M.J. (Ed.): Power, Voting, and Voting Power ©Physica-Verlag, Würzburg (Germany) 1981

An Introduction to the Analysis of Power, Voting, and Voting Power

M.J. Holler, München

In the following I will outline the central ideas of this book by presenting the various contributions and by analyzing the basic concepts and their relevance. This introduction is certainly no substitute for the book. Any summary of the articles herein which exceeds the level of enumeration inevitably turns into a discussion.

1. On the Nature and Problems of Democracy

Democracy is considered by many people living in dictatorship, ideocracy, oligarchy, aristocracy, and democracy, as the best political system. This may be so, but democracy is indeed a very complex and complicated governmental system. The motto "of the people, by the people, for the people" implicates a multitude of imperatives as regards the realization of a democratic system. Since the ruling "of the people" is to be "for the people", it does not suffice to define what the people are; the ruler must also know what the people want, i.e., he must recognize their preferences.

This not only raises the question of whether ruling people can mean fulfilling the people's will; one needs also to ask what the people's will actually is and how the ruler can identify it. This is the benevolent dictator's problem. History reveals that dictators rarely tried to solve this problem, instead they themselves decided what be good for the people, for God, or for the world and hence ruled the people in accordance with an autocraticly set maxim. One way of avoiding this third-person stand of the ruler with respect to the people and the people's will, certainly is to make the ruler identical with the people. This is the fundamental idea of the classical doctrine of democracy. If the ruler is identical with the people, necessarily the preferences coincide. In consequence, there is no problem for the ruler identifying the people's will for this will be his own. Thus, individual freedom and the strive for happiness become a collective aim. Rivalry amongst individuals is possible but by definition the targets of the ruler and the ruled must harmonize.

The question of whether the people can rule themselves still remains. Do (or to what extent do) democratic institutions ensure the identity of the ruler and the ruled, i.e., the coincidence of their wills? How can democratic systems solve this problem of congruence? These are fundamental questions within the following contributions to this book on **Power, Voting, and Voting Power**.

We could take *Schumpeter's* view [1947, pp. 284f.] that "democracy does not mean and cannot mean that the people actually rule in any obvious sense of the terms 'people' and 'rule' ". Democracy, in this sense, "means only that the people have the opportunity of accepting or refusing the men who are to rule them." However, a political system which does not aim at installing the congruence of the will of the ruler and the ruled cannot be called democratic. But "aiming" needs not necessarily mean that a system actually succeeds in setting up democratic institutions. Some governmental systems seem to be caught in a suboptimal trade-off between the efficiency of ruling and the participation of the people, i.e., the representation of the ruled. In some constituencies of the U.K. the individual voter has not had any chance of influencing the outcome of the elections for the last hundred years. There has always been a clear winner, and the individual voter could neither contribute to his winning nor could the voter's decision for the loser have any impact on the ruling.

The British parliamentary system is said to be a symbol of democracy because of its functioning. It creates clear majorities for the Parliament, even when, according to the sum of votes, there aren't any. The plurality voting system has a very high factual threshold to win seats in Parliament, as Laakso and Taagepera point out in their contribution to this book. Nationwide minorities, therefore, have little possibility of expressing their political will within the parliamentary system. Instead of experiencing a large consensus, due to the minority suppressing impact of the plurality rule, the U.K. is confronted with a growing tendency of disintegration. The suppressed minority spirit expresses itself either in non-parliamentarian political radicalism as the North-Irish terrorism, or in parliamentary radicalism as implied in the Scottish and Welsh nationalist parties. Since in a plurality voting system, political ideas can be victorious and expressed within the system only by winning at least one constituency, only national (or regional) "minorities" which hold a strong regional position have a chance to defeat the monopoly of the nation-wide dominant parties. This tends to lead to regional decomposition as discussed by Goodrich (in this book) under the label of regional attitude on devolution.

I have focused on the U.K. in order to demonstrate the dilemma of efficiency and participation through representation which is inherent to representational democratic systems, since this dilemma seems to be an urgent problem to this country, as the constitutional discussion indicates. An interim result could be that the overemphasis on efficiency at the expense of representation leads to dysfunctions and inefficiency. We may conclude that there is no democratic efficiency without adequate representation. To answer the question of adequacy presupposes that we know what is meant by representation and efficiency. Yet, these terms do need clarification, as we shall see from many of the contributions in this book.

It remains to append that the more or less hypothetical decision for a representational and against a direct democracy is primarily interpreted as decision for efficiency. Laakso and Taagepera point out in their contribution "Proportional Representation and Effective Number of Parties in Finland" (in this book) that the dilemma of efficient legislature and representation of the voter (or votes) is a topic of constitutional discussion in Finland as well. Contrary to the British experience the problem seems to be how to win or regain efficiency through a minimal reduction of representation. The authors' analysis elucidates that the answer to this problem depends on the empirical vote distribution and will therefore change in the course of time.

This result and the British experience indicate that the revision of the constitution (or the legislative procedure) is a potential need to any real democracy. This is also due to the fact that the weighting of the efficiency target and the representation target might change in the course of history and induce, for instance, a demand for "more democracy" in the sense of larger and more immediate participation of the voters in the legislative procedure. We hereby find ourselves appropriate to analyze various voting schemes and representation procedures in order to be able to evaluate the effects of any changes.

A specific form of change is the implementation of a democratic constitution. This could be brought about by the formation of new states through, for example, decolonisation or by the abolition of a non-democratic political system. The formation of international organisations like the U.N.O. and the E.E.C. is another example.

2. The Quest for Research and the Knowledge We Have

The question of what democratic procedure to use also gains in importance as more democratic principles are applied to our everyday life, such as running a firm, an university, or a kindergarten, or organizing the family picnic or deciding on the family's budget. The board of directors, the school board, and the sport club's annual members' meeting are already so much integrated as democratic decision making bodies that we are hardly aware of them. As a matter of fact, this does not guarantee the effectiveness of democratic principles; on the contrary, the unawareness supports the survival of ossified non-democratic hierarchies or the creation of oligarchical leadership.

On the other hand, the extension of democratic principles beyond the government level meets, even in traditionally democratic countries, strong resistance. The opponents generally claim that the democratic principle is inefficient. Especially in the economic sector it is considered as contradicting economic principles. In consequence, this view is often introduced as an argument against the participation of employees in the firm's decision making. However, indeed never is it argued that we do not know how the proposed democratic procedures work, how they influence the outcome, how they transform the participants' preferences towards the social outcome, whether there always is an outcome, and whether the outcome is a reliable consequence of the participants' judgements. This book will point out that we are at the very beginning when we ask these questions and that we know but few answers.

An inexperienced reader in this field will probably be shocked by the little knowledge we have. This might be due to the taboos which are still valid for public discussion of democracy and its alternatives. Even today it seems to be a short step to having this discussion banned as an enemy of democracy. As we all know, Galileo also had his trouble when he pointed his telescope to the stars and told the people what he had seen (and how this was to be explained). However, it might be an exaggeration and thus misleading to compare the situation of a social scientist of today discussing democracy to Galileo's; Galileo had *seen* stars and planets.

The contributions of this book clearly show what extensive work has to be done to shed light on the discussed procedures and measures. Although I think that banning the problem had some regressive effects on the analysis of democratic principles and their realization, I would like to claim that our problem is more difficult to solve than Galileo's and that, therefore, a sufficient answer, if there is any at all, will incorporate more research, more time and more energy. I cannot, of course, prove this hypothesis, but I would like to point to the fact that the stars and planets did not revise their orbit because Galileo watched them and explained their route. However, social systems might change their behavior, for individuals react to the results presented by analyses of the system and its elements.

Given the inherent difficulties of gaining knowledge and the little knowledge we have on the functioning of democratic procedures, it is certainly incorrect to judge from defects in existing democratic systems that the principle itself is a failure. The theoretical analyses as presented in some of the contributions in this book show that only little modifications in voting procedures or in the distribution of the voters' preferences can change the outcome into its contrary. Hence, the introduction of democratic principles as well as the revision of existing procedures need careful reasoning if the proposed effects are to be attained. There is no general mechanism ensuring the proposed outcome. A radical monism in the choice of procedures will inevitably lead to unacceptable outcomes. An extension of the democratic principle, therefore, implies an unavoidable trial-and-error process. The duty of the promoters should thereby be to minimize the errors by using the available knowledge. This, of course, also holds for the revision of democratic procedures. *Shapley/Shubik* [1954, p. 787] claimed that "the effect of a revision usually cannot be gauged in advance except in the roughest terms; it can easily happen that the mathematical structure of a voting system conceals a bias in power distribution unsuspected and unintended by the authors of the revision."

3. The Frame and Aim of the Book

Although the above statement refers to an already specified problem, it points to some of the aims underlying this book; this book intends

(1) to summarize the knowledge we have on the functioning of democratic procedures and thereby to provide information for people who influence the formulation of the corresponding rules; they should know what theorists can say about the effects of various procedures and at what point trial-and-error starts;
(2) to check the frame of research and to clarify and standardize the concepts and problems with which the scholars of this field work; this should help to intensify communication and exchange and reception of results;
(3) to find a larger audience for these vital questions; this *might* result in support for the research by ideas and resources and to enlarge the group of scholars and students who dedicate their efforts and energy to research in this field; this *will* result in more tolerance for people who think of alternatives and creative support for the democratic principle.

The book can be read as a presentation of partial problems and partial solutions with reference to the fundamental idea presented in a book entitled "Social Choice and Individual Values". The latter has already been written by *Arrow* [1951, 1963]. Its quintessence says that under very general conditions collective decision making, regardless of the type of non-dictatorial aggregation rule employed, inevitably leads to inconsistency, i.e., to intransitive social choice. In other words, only dictatorship guarantees consistent social outcomes. This Impossibility Theorem weighs heavily on any theory of collective decision making and challenges the democratic principle. And indeed *Samuelson* [1972] commented in his laudation to the nobel prize winner Arrow, "Aristotle must be turning over in his grave. The theory of democracy can never be the same (actually, it never was!) since Arrow."

Arrow's result is compelling, however, it is built on very general conditions which do not necessarily conform to reality. E.g., the condition of unrestricted domain requires that there be at least three alternatives which individuals are free to rate in any way, i.e., there is no limitation on the profile of preferences. Even if we do not rely on the aid of Rousseau's "volonté général", there might be some consensus or bipolarization implying that there are no *three* alternatives which are favored within the voting community.

Or, maybe the voters will see the alternatives related to a single left-right continuum on which they can identify their first, second and third choice. This assumption, which *Black* [1968] labeled "single-peakedness", ensures transitive social choice when majority voting is applied to determine the winner.

In real voting systems, a series of norms, rules, and regulations can actually be found which exclude the occurrence of the above paradox by either limiting the domain, i.e., the set of possible preference orderings, or by reducing the alternatives to a set of two elements. A second of Arrow's general conditions, the independence of irrelevant alternatives, requires that the social orderings of any two alternatives be neither influenced nor affected by the presence of any other alternative in the set to be ordered.[1]) It, therefore, excludes the possibility of individuals relating the evaluation of a third alternative to the ranking of the other two. However, should they do this, the paradox is no longer deducible. As *Hillinger* [1979, p. 81f.] pointed out there have never been human beings climbing barricades to fight for a decision rule which is invulnerable to independent alternatives.

This might suffice to illustrate what Arrow's problem and solution are and what has to be done when we turn to more concrete questions on democratic decision making. For reorientation we must forgo the general conceptual frame and formal elegance of Arrow's approach. Instead we will grope our way from the individual preferences to social choice, picking up the problems one by one and trying to formulate a solution for them. Since the available instruments are indeed different for different questions, it should not be disturbing that the analyses are presented by different authors.

4. Contributions on the Problem of Representation

As a first operationalisation of the analysis of democratic procedure, its implications and preconditions, we can refer to the conceptual doublet of "power and support". One of the basic tenets of democracy is the representation of the will of the people. If this will could be identified through the electorate's support and if this support could be

---

[1]) This interpretation corresponds with *Arrow's* example [1963, p. 27] and is as such often presented in literature [e.g., *Winch*, p. 178] although I have to admit that it is a misinterpretation of *Arrow's* own definition [1963, p. 27] as, e.g., *Richelson* [1977, pp. 85f.] pointed out.

measured by the number of votes, the representation problem would partly be solved. However, the consideration of the voters' preferences is just one tenet, another is the ruling. The requirements of efficient ruling generally lead to a reduction of the number of preferences represented, e.g., by political parties in the legislature. This reduction can be imposed by the introduction of explicit numerical thresholds. An example is the German Bundestag, where only parties which obtain a minimum of 5 % of all votes are represented. The number of parties in the legislature can also be implicitly reduced by using, e.g., simple majority (plurality) rule with single-seat districts, as is practiced in the U.K. Various transformation formulas ("from votes to seats") are a third device to reduce the effective number of parties. Laakso and Taagepera (in this book) analyze the impact of the most widely used methods, such as the d'Hondt, the Sainte Laguë and the quota (the largest remainder) procedures, on the effective number of parties in Finland. They show that this number varies according to the selected procedure.

In his contribution to this book, Schofield presents a class of measures of both bias in representation and governmental stability. The presented measures give precision to the relationship between these two targets, and define a particular trade off between them. It might be argued that in order to ascertain the support, we could circumvent the bias of representation by referring to the original votes and their distribution on the various alternatives. These votes, however, might strongly be influenced by the bias on representation as well as by the number and presentation of the alternatives. For voting can be seen having at least two functions. First, a vote might express the voter's preference with respect to the candidates. Here the election is interpreted to be the outcome of people's will. Second, the selection of the winning candidate occurs through voting, hence a vote can be seen as a means of influencing this selection.

In a two-candidate system these two interpretations of voting provide no inconsistency. If a voter votes for the candidate who represents his preferences the best, he decreases the second candidate's chance of winning.

In a three-party system, however, a voter might face the dilemma of either supporting a candidate who is less preferred by him, but has a chance of beating his least preferred candidate, or voting for his favorite candidate and seeing the least preferred win the laurel instead of the candidate who ranked second in the voter's preferences.

If voters do cast their ballot for their most preferred *viable* candidates, this can imply casting one's vote for a second-best candidate, which is labeled "sophisticated" or "strategic" voting. Hence, vote shares can no longer be interpreted without restrictions as an expression of the voters' preferences. Viability depends both on the electoral rules and the distribution of preferences, and since it is in a way self-fulfilling, for a comparably high likelihood of being elected strengthens the viability outlook and in general attracts votes within multicandidate voting, an extraction of the people's will from the voting outcome is to a certain extent ambiguous. If strategic voting cannot be excluded, the detection of preferences from voting results presupposes knowledge of the preferences and therefore can not be successful.

In their contribution to this volume, Bensel and Sanders have investigated the drop off in the actual proportion of the final vote won by a third candidate. They analyze the 1968 US presidential elections with the three candidates Richard Nixon, Hubert Humphrey, and George Wallace. In order to test the influence of the electoral rules on the translation of preferences, the authors refer to a nation-wide opinion survey (conducted by the Institute for Social Research) which had the respondents identify their preferences by ranking the three candidates. This polling material, though rather limited, represents the available information on the distribution of the voters' preferences, It can be accepted as being unbiased because the respondents' answers had certainly no direct impact on the election outcome.

One of the findings of Bensel's and Sanders' analysis is that the tendency of supporters of the third candidate, George Wallace, to shift their voting decisions was affected by the degree of viability of Wallace within the voters' resident states. Although the authors find little evidence of shift voting, they claim that George Wallace was aware of the self-fulfilling non-viability forecasts. This was illustrated by his negative attitude towards nation-wide prognoses, which did not consider him as potential winner, and towards the media, which distributed the information.

The blocking of information, propaganda, demagogy, and related means might help ban strategic voting to a certain extent. Yet in small voting bodies such as parliaments, committees, and clubs, strategic voting does not seem to be avoidable if voters decide individually and rationally. Merrill analyzes strategic voting in multi-candidate elections under uncertainty and under risk. His result clearly points out that the occurrence of strategic voting depends on the procedure, (i.e., the kind of numerical voting system, such as plurality voting, approval voting, Borda voting, or cardinal measure voting) and on the assumptions concerning the voters' knowledge of the likely outcome of the election. For the model and voting systems considered in Merrill's study, "the optimal strategies under uncertainty are in most cases sincere reflections of the voter's rankings of the candidates. For decisions under risk, however, this need not be the case."

A specific form of strategic voting related to agenda manipulation is discussed by Uslaner as well as by Bjurulf and Niemi. The analysis of cyclical majorities, which imply the so called Voting Paradox, shows that the outcome of voting is determined by the sequence in which the alternatives are presented [see e.g., *Downs*, pp. 59f.]. Uslaner points out that even when there are no cyclical majorities and there is a Condorcet winner (an alternative which defeats every other in pairwise voting), the Condorcet winner may not result if the preferences, as regards various issues, are nonseparable and the voting is sincere and simultaneous issue-by-issue. In other words, if the voters cast their votes according to their preferences, and do not speculate on the outcome, the outcome may not be the Condorcet winner, even though one of the alternatives is a Condorcet winner.

This result supports the hypothesis that the voting outcome cannot be interpreted as the representation of the voters' preferences without further inquiries. On the other hand, Uslaner points out that, if the voters swerve from voting sincerely, the Condorcet winner might be the voting outcome under otherwise identical conditions. Loosely speaking, we can rely on the outcome but not on the votes if strategic voting is possible. The preferences might then be nonseparable.

Bjurulf and Niemi analyze the influence of the agenda on the voting outcome under an amendment procedure as well as under a successive procedure. The starting point of their analysis is not, however, given by the individual preferences but rather by social preferences which result from pairwise comparison of alternatives (e.g., through majority voting) which are introduced into the decision making. They thereby abstract from the problems involved in the formulation of social preference orderings. This leaves space to determine necessary and sufficient conditions for a given alternative to win under the proposed voting procedures if there is no socially undominated alternative. From their analysis we can deduce that sophisticated, i.e., strategic voting favors alternatives which are strong as measured by the relative numbers of socially dominated alternatives.

The discussion suggests that we can rely on the outcome but not on the vote ratios if strategic voting occurs. This could be a strong argument for a direct democracy, where voters themselves decide upon the actions of the collectivity. Hence, it challenges the idea of a representational system. The discussion also suggests that we take a closer look at the assumptions of the models and, therefore, at the conditions as they are in reality. Any modification or deviation can produce a different result. So, indeed, we are compelled to look at each specific case to find out whether the voting result can be interpreted as the people's will or not. This is just another way of saying that so far we do not have any justification for taking the voting outcome as a measure of support, if there are more than two alternatives.

5. The Philosophy of Voting Power

We could waive the problem of representation if we were to take the stand that only the majority matters, although we have seen that majority voting will not always produce the Condorcet winner. Grotius, the Father of Law, attempted to make the right of majorities a natural law [see *Gough*, p. 81]. Representation then occurs exclusively through the majority in every decision-making body on every level of decision-making. Minorities would have to be prevented from influencing the outcome of law-making and governing. Whatever representation procedure is used, the majority must remain a majority and the decisions must be made by majorities.

The criticisms of the "natural law of the majority" culminated in *Schumpeter's* statement [1947, p. 272] that "evidently the will of the majority is the will of the majority and not the will of the people". Nevertheless, the will of a majority has an outstanding quality in collective decision-making. For the outcome of majority voting is justified in the sense that it is agreed upon by more people than any other presented alternative. A larger number of voters might come closer to choosing the best of a limited set of alternatives than a smaller number or an individual. However, in order to use the statistical law of large numbers to justify majority voting there has to be a best, a "true" political decision that can be found or at least approximated by following the majority's decision. Furthermore, the voters have to be interested in finding the true political decision. They have to be impartial in order to form a sample from which the "truest" political decision can be deduced by statistical inference. This follows from the condorcet-criterion [see *Black*, p. 66]. David Hume and Adam Smith assumed "that if men were to take up a certain point of view, that of the impartial spectator, they would be led to similar convictions. . . . For the most part the philosophical tradition. . . has assumed that there exists some appropriate perspective from which unanimity on moral questions may be hoped for, at least among rational persons with relevantly similar and sufficient information" [*Rawls*, pp. 263f.].

If, however, the voters are not impartial, if the voter does not vote for the true proposition but for a proposition which promises a maximum of individual benefits for himself, we can see from a specific outcome that, e.g., a majority prefers a proposition *A* to a proposition *B* and *C*, and that a minority prefers *C* to *A* and perhaps another minority is in favour of *B* compared to *A* and *C*. From the outcome we know that *A* is preferred by more voters than *B* and *C*. Even this might depend on whether *B* and *C* are both represented in competition to *A* or whether propositions *B* or *C* challenge *A* in sequence.

When a majority prefers *A* to *B* in a two-proposition voting system we cannot deduce from the outcome that *A* is preferred to *B* by "the people". Even if there is an accepted interpersonal utility aggregation procedure (there is, however, no such thing) *B* might be preferred to *A* from a social point of view if the minority's longing for *B* is much stronger than the majority's longing towards *A*. Since there is no a priori logical and/or ideological basis in an ideal democracy which says that an individual *X* will benefit from the political system whereas individual *Y* might not, the will of both individuals should enter into the political choice if we cannot assume that *X* and *Y* strive impartially for political truism.

How and to what extent individual wills determine the political choice depends largely on their representation in the decision-making body.

The waiving of the above discussed principle of efficiency for the sake of purity (or simplicity), often lets the claim for proportional representation arise. Moreover proportionality with respect to seat distribution is in general thought to coincide with proportionality as regards to power. To illustrate the problem and the path to its solution, let us assume that the votes for parties *X, Y*, and *Z* are distributed as follows: 40 %, 30 %, and 30 %. The seats in parliament are distributed according to these vote shares. Now, if simple majority voting is used for decision-making in parliament, and if there is no ideological restriction of preference to coalition formation, the likelihood for each party to be in a winning coalition is the same. Equal (a priori) voting power can thus be deduced, notwithstanding the fact that the vote and seat distribution is unequal. Proportionality with respect to voting power is not fulfilled. This might call forth our "democratic remorse". On the other hand, if the seat distribution is changed to introduce a power distribution proportional to the vote distribution 40 %, 30 %, 30 % it would certainly violate the proportionality of representation with respect to the seat distribution.

Apart from this distortion, numerical reasoning shows that the seat distribution of three parties will never fulfill a power relation 40 %, 30 %, 30 %, given simple majority voting. Either one party has an absolute majority and therefore an a priori voting power of 100 %, or a winning coalition has to be formed out of two parties at minimum, giving equal chance to each of the three parties to be essential for power exertion through majority formation.

We see that there can be no such seat distribution that implicates a voting power relation 40 %, 30 %, 30 % given three parties and simple majority voting. This dilemma could be solved by introducing a combination of decision rules. If, for instance, 3 out of 5 (i.e. 60 %) of all decisions are made by simple majority, and 2 out of 5 (i.e. 40 %) of all decisions require a 2/3 majority, then the a priori voting power of partied based on a 40 %, 30 %, 30 % seat distribution is equal to the seat distribution.

This can be illustrated as follows:

	X	Y	Z
Seat share:	40 %	30 %	30 %
Power indices:			
(1) simple majority:	1/3	1/3	1/3
(2) simple majority:	1/3	1/3	1/3
(3) simple majority:	1/3	1/3	1/3
(4) 2/3 majority:	1/2	1/4	1/4
(5) 2/3 majority:	1/2	1/4	1/4
Total	2.0	1.5	1.5
Power ratio	40 %	30 %	30 %

The above indices are calculated with respect to minimum winning coalitions in the sense that the winning coalitions considered do not include parties unnecessary for the formation of a winning coalition. (This corresponds to Packel's and Deegan's concept as discussed in their contribution to this volume.) There are two possible minimum winning coalitions fulfilling the 2/3 majority rule: $\{X, Y\}$ and $\{X, Z\}$. Therefore, the power ratio of X is 1/2 and the power ratio of Y (respectively Z) is equal to 1/4. The problem of proportionality of votes, seat, and power seems at last solved: 40 % of the votes are represented by 40 % of the seats which represents a 40 % voting power share if the combination of simple majority and 2/3 majority rule is imposed on the parliamentary procedure.

According to the calculated voting power indices, the expected impact on the political outcome is 40 % for party X, 30 % for party Y and 30 % for party Z. If there is a true political decision which is best approximated by the majority of (impartial) voters, the power representation scheme 40 %, 30 %, 30 % leads to a 60 % expectation of an inferior outcome in comparison with the will of the majority given by the 40 % votes for party X if the voters are impartial. Thus, before discussing representation it actually should be clarified whether there might be a "true" political decision for the question to be decided upon in parliament (or in government) and whether the voters are impartially striving for the truth. If the voters are not expected to be impartial and if, therefore, it cannot be thought of as a true political decision (because, e.g., the issue constitutes a pure conflict of interest among the voters, such as a redistribution on income, wealth, etc.) then the will of the majority is not qualified sui generis.

This question is, however, not discussed in detail in the contributions in this book. Given that the problem of representation can be reduced to mapping the vote distribution into the distribution of power which shall be exerted by the elected representatives in the legislative (and governmental) process, the following questions remain to be answered: (1) What is the power to be represented? (2) How can we measure this power? (3) How can we impose a specific power distribution, what means do we have, and how do we have to apply them?

The fundamental idea applied in several contributions to answer the latter question has already been outlined in the above three-party example: Specific power distributions can be imposed (1) by choosing an adequate voting weight distribution, given a constant decision rule, which, however, might violate the proportionality of the vote-seat-transformation; or (2) given a constant voting weight distribution, by mixing various decision rules which might, however, be considered as arbitrary. In order to minimize the drawbacks, a policy mix of the two can be proposed. First, however, we have to understand the quality of the power which is to be represented.

Apart from the contributions to the introductory discussion of power, to which I shall refer below, power is identified with voting power in this book. Although this seems a very strong limitation, it covers a wide range of social decision making when not limited to explicit voting. The model of implicit voting and of different voting weights seems applicable to all non-dictatorial procedures of social choice as an analytical tool.

6. Trends in Voting Power Measures

The measurement concept presented by Nurmi is of general interest to the analyses of collective decision making, and so are the various indices which are presented in subsequent contributions. Since it is of no use to summarize the intensive discussion of the various indices in a few words, let me instead point out trends which characterize the theoretical contemporary work. There is a tendency to substitute the equal-likelihood assumption which underlies the traditional indices of Shapley-Shubik, Banzhaf, Coleman, and Deegan-Packel with respect to coalition formation by a variable weight approach. This is the tenor of Owen's article in this volume, and also characterizes Packel and Deegan's contribution. The latter reformulate their index, which refers to the minimum winning coalition, by rating the possible coalitions of that subclass with weights according to the probability of their occurrence.

Rattinger's contribution provides a theoretical frame for the different likelihoods with which the coalitions can be weighted. Starting with Axelrod's concept of the ideological neighborhood of coalition members and the one-dimensional constraints on coalition formation therein implied, he proposes the minimum connected winning coalition to be an appropriate concept of measuring an a priori voting power, that is if the assumption of a one-dimensional ordinal policy space is acceptable. The conflict of interest is minimized within a coalition if potential coalitions consist only of adjacent voting blocs. This gives a weight of zero to all coalitions which are not minimum connected winning coalitions and equal weights to the others. The adjacency between voting blocs is however based upon the dichotomy of a more general concept of policy distance in a multi-dimensional space. In his contribution, Rattinger develops a formal frame, which enables us to consider a more general mutual acceptability of voting blocs than implied in the one-dimensional policy space assumption. Rattinger's examples illustrate that his concepts are operational. They can be enriched by empirical data.

7. Power, Satisfaction, and Various Power Concepts

The ideological division of a voting body not only introduces the question as to which coalitions are more likely to be formed, it also leads us to ask what the satisfaction of a voter (or voting bloc) will be, and how this satisfaction is related to power. In this book, Straffin et al. consider the probability that the voting body's decision will agree with the voter's decision to be a measure of the voter's satisfaction. One of their essential findings is that, as the voting body becomes more ideologically diverse, but partitioned in ideologically homogeneous groups, the members of the largest group gain satisfaction; yet the group loses power. This finding points out that, at least according to the underlying definitions, satisfaction and power are of different quality. This is of importance to the fundamental discussion of power. The analysis of Straffin et al. contributes further to the discussion in using non-standardized indices which indicate that the over-all power in a system might not be constant.

On the other hand, Wittman (in this book) succeeds in formulating a simple measure for power in an ideological space, by defining power as the ability to increase one's own utility. Power and satisfaction are thereby seen to be closely related concepts: "power being the ability to change an outcome and satisfaction being the utility derived from an outcome".

The differentiation of power and satisfaction, as implied in the analysis of Straffin et al., corresponds to Miller's axiomatic presentation of power (in this book) as "the ability to bring about or to preclude certain outcomes". By this definition, the concept of power is set free from assumptions on the preferences of the considered actor. The use of game forms, i.e., "games minus any specification of the preferences", is therefore consequent. It puts emphasis on the outcomes and not on payoffs: Miller's power concept is an outcome concept. By applying it to abstract choice problems, Miller proves that "every game form involving three or more outcomes that assures, for all strict preferences, the existence of a unique undominated outcome is dictatorial". In a way, this result parallels Arrow's Impossibility Theorem. However, its relevance to the measurement of power is as yet not scrutinized in detail.

Miller's concept of outcome power contrasts Kliemt's "all-including" concept of power, which is also presented in the first chapter of this book. Kliemt's concept starts from the premise that power is the ability to get what one "wants", regardless of the various means used to achieve purpose ("including all"). Kliemt constructs the concept of power within a general framework that leaves room for diverse approaches to power measurement showing how they might all be viewed as approaching the same "thing". He also analyzes their relation to fundamental normative problems. Miller's power concept as well as the power indices may, according to Kliemt's analysis, be considered to implicitly take care of preferences, and may thus be incorporated into more general power analysis frameworks.

From this follows that the power of an individual depends on the individual's preferences: complete satisfaction therefore implies complete power. Although Miller's and Kliemt's power concepts seem to be extremely contrary, they obviously converge if satisfaction is bound to an outcome which is exclusive. If, for instance, the voters are only interested in winning the election, i.e., in forming a winning coalition, this is exclusive to the non-winners. They cannot exert power and, therefore, do not gain satisfaction. If we introduce (as in the analysis of Straffin et al.) an ideology or assume "parties as utility maximizers" [*Wittmann*] being interested in policy goals, the divergence between the two concepts cannot be denied.

Miller's concept has the advantage of formal operationality. It implies the preconditions for the analysis of the structure of measurement problems to which the various indices are dedicated. The extraction of these preconditions may help to formulate (minimum) characteristics, which useful measures have to fulfill, and to reveal problems which cannot be solved by the various other measures. Kliemt's concept of all-including power, on the other hand, can be applied to the discussion of normative problems, such as distributive justice, which lays the foundation for *Rawls'* philosophical analyses [1972], from which it actually has its impetus. (I would like to point out that Gibbard's game form as used by Miller is the counterpart to Rawls' well-known "veil of ignorance". In the game form, we do not know (or consider) the preferences of the individuals, whereas the veil of ignorance hides which individual will attain which outcome.)

In a note on the discussion on different concepts of power, Wittman demonstrates that various approaches create identical results. The problematique of power as an analytical concept is illustrated by three more contributions to this book. Mueller develops an analogy between power and profits. He thereby comes to the conclusion that the differences between profit and non-profit institutions may be far less than is widely believed. Yet, in the United States, business size growth has not been treated with the same amount of alarm as the growth of the public sector.

Schneider uses the psychological hypothesis that with regard to power relations only those resources as perceived by the other partner(s) can act as decisive variables. By taking into account the distinction between objective and phenomenal qualities, attributions as interpretations of the relations between cause and effect become essential for power recognition as well as power exertion. Schneider's exemplification of the attribution implication to power, especially the examples with respect to voting assemblies, elucidate an aspect which is neglected by the a priori measurement concepts underlying the power indices. On the other hand, Schneider's attribution analyses of the voting examples make clear that an a priori power measure, which takes account of facts like voting weights and the decision rule, can be a necessity for the extraction of psychological and other factors which have influence on the power relation but are not registered by the aprioristic power measures.

Behrens' article in this book is an inventory of the traditional concepts of power as used in political science and political sociology. The various aspects of power which are to be observed in reality are transformed by these concepts in different frames. These are used as instruments to shape qualitative data and experiences, which are more or less intensely linked to politics and its implications of power. Because of the resulting variety of power concepts, the view of power as an amorphous term suggests itself. From this basis of traditional analysis, we can evaluate the undertaking of formulating an acceptable measure of power, which was started by the pioneering work of Shapley and Shubik twenty-five years ago.

8. The Empirical Aspect of Measuring Voting Power

There is, however, another reason why a general discussion of power and the application of the various concepts is necessary as an introduction to the more specific presentation of measurement concepts. The empirical and pseudo-empirical applications of power indices often point out phenomena which are classified as paradoxes. In a contribution to this book, Schotter, for instance, identifies the "Paradox of Redistribution" when he analyzes the effects of a revision of the seat distribution of the committees of the International Monetary Fund. He demonstrate that some national representations gained power as measured by the Banzhaf index although their voting weights were decreased through the revision. This is clearly counter-intuitive if we consider vote distribution a good proxy for voting power. If not, we could expect such defections. Since the Banzhaf index measures the relative numbers of swings, its value changes when the relative number of coalitions, to which the different voters are critical, changes. Therefore, the values will change if there is change in the coalitions and their critical members. Whether a member is critical or not generally depends not only on his voting weights but also in the voting weights of all other players within the voting game.

From the general discussion we could suspect that there might be more or less over-all power in the voting body. Since, however, the Banzhaf index as used by Schotter (as well as the Shapley-Shubik index) is standardized, it is focused entirely in the distribution of power and is insensitive to variations in the structure or amount of power, and hence to the precise nature of power relations. Therefore, counterintuitive results will not be an exception.

Future research will have to distinguish between the "power of an actor" and the "power within the social system" [see, e.g., *Tannenbaum*, p. 12]. An actor might have absolute power, but this might parallel a close to zero power in the social system. The analyses of Straffin et al. point out that, for the chosen numerical examples, the non-standardized "partial-homogeneity" power index is small when the voting power of one group of voters is absolute, i.e., if the voting weights of all other voters are zero. All members of a specific voting body tend to lose power, as the ideological imbalance increases in the proposed models.

Whether a result is considered paradoxical or not depends on the various underlying images that we have of power. These could be all-including as in Kliemt's power concept or outcome-oriented as in Miller's concept, or perhaps we believe that power increases with successful actions "despite resistance", as *Weber's* [1947] well-known power definition implies.

These considerations are essential because empirical analyses are used as tests for the applied power measurement indices. Schotter's contribution to this book might be classified to a certain extent under this heading. Holler tries to show that the standardized Coleman index is a better descriptive instrument for government formation in Finland than the seat distribution. In his analysis, he compares the power values which correspond to the nine seat distributions of the Finnish Parliament during the last thirty years, to the participation of the various parties in more than thirty governmental cabinets formed during this time span. Although the therein involved weighting problems with respect to time periods and representation in government are somewhat ambiguous, the power values do allow a better description than the seat ratios.

The analyses of Schotter and Holler both reveal empirical facts which could not be seen clearly without the calculation of power indices. Schotter points out that the relative number of potential winning coalitions in thirty-eight national blocs has increased, although their voting weights decreased. Holler's analysis shows that some of the characteristics of government formation in Finland, which are thought to be due to an ideological bias, can also be explained by the relevant vote weights and decision rule as expressed by the power indices: two parties, a left-wing and a right-wing party, which had average voting weights of about 20 % and 17 % respectively, seem to have been the victims of the numerical structure of the Finnish Parliament. This does not preclude that they were (also) ideologically "discriminated against" from participating in government.

It appears that a straightforward application of power indices to historical vote distributions and decision rules could produce interesting results. For instance, Bomsdorf (in this book) has pointed out that a Shapley power index of more than 50 % corresponded to Hitler's party NSDAP in the 6th Reichstag of July 1932 under the simple majority rule, although the voting weight of the NSDAP was less than 40 %. The Shapley power index of the NSDAP increased to 60 % in the 8th Reichstag of March 1933, whereas the party's seat share was still less than 45 %. The parliamentary power of the NSDAP might indeed have been underestimated, for historical analyses generally refer to its seat share. It is, however, naive to conclude that the contemporary political parties and institutions were unaware of the NSDAP's voting strength and were therefore not alert to prevent Hitler's rise. Nevertheless, as history proves, at least some of the non-Nazi politicians at that time thought themselves strong enough, inspite of their comparatively weak a priori voting power, to play the parliamentary game of forming coalitions with the NSDAP faction.

In the final contribution to this book, Johnston outlines a formal framework for empirical power analysis, which allows us to look at the power of individual voters and groups within single territories. He develops an algebra enabling us to analyze the power of voters who are elements of two interrelated sets. In order to demonstrate the capacity of the "two-level analysis", Johnston refers to the European Parliament, "where each party's votes can be cast individually although they are distributed among parties." In fact, one can think of many voting situations in which a voter is bound to more than one dimension, e.g., to a social class as well as to a political party, or to an ethnic group or a region. In cases where the two affiliations conflict or can conflict in voting, Johnston's approach can be used at the outset for analyses of voting power as well as for measuring the a priori cross-dimensional influence.

9. Concluding Remarks

I would like to apologize to those scholars who have done outstanding work in the field of voting analysis and power measurement but who are not represented in this book. We had, however, a limit on time and space. For this reason, contributions on the analysis of party strategy under the vote maximizing hypothesis could not be published here. We also had to refrain from discussion of voter abstention and other problems which are certainly of importance to the topics in this book. We have also not discussed the more fundamental question of whether (or why) an individual should get what he (or she) wants and what (or who) determines what he (or she) wants.

Analyzing voting power is highly relevant to our political and social life. It should be more than symbolic that the Banzhaf power index has been accepted by New York State courts as a basis for judging the constitutionality of weighted voting schemes.

References

Arrow, K.J.: Social Choice and Individual Values. New Haven–London (1st ed. 1951), 2nd ed. 1963.
Black, D.: The Theory of Committees and Elections. Cambridge 1968.
Downs, A.: An Economic Theory of Democracy. New York 1957.
Gough, J.W.: The Social Contract. Oxford, 2nd ed. 1957.
Hillinger, C.: Die Bedeutung normativer Postulate in der ökonomischen Theorie der Politik. Ökonomische Theorie der Politik. Ed. by C. Hillinger and M.J. Holler. München 1979, 75–84.
Rawls, J.: A Theory of Justice. London–Oxford–New York 1972.
Richelson, J.: Conditions on Social Choice Functions. Public Choice **XXXI**, 1977, 79–110.
Samuelson, P.A.: The 1972 Nobel Prize of Economic Science. Science **178** (4060), 1972, 487–489.
Schumpeter, J.A.: Capitalism, Socialism, and Democracy. New York–London, 2nd ed. 1947.
Shapley, L.S., and *M. Shubik*: A Method for Evaluating the Distribution of Power in a Committee System. American Political Science Review **48**, 1954, 787–792.
Tannenbaum, A.S.: Control in Organizations. New York 1968.
Weber, M.: The Theory of Social and Economic Organization. Ed. by T. Parsons. New York 1947.
Winch, D.M.: Analytical Welfare Economics. Harmondsworth 1971.
Wittman, D.A.: Parties as Utility Maximizers. American Political Science Review **67**, 1973, 490–498.

2. The Idea of Power

Holler, M.J. (Ed.): Power, Voting, and Voting Power ©Physica-Verlag, Würzburg (Germany) 1981

Power in Game Forms[1])

N.R. Miller, Baltimore

1. Introduction

Power is often identified as the central concept in political science. Yet there is little scholarly consensus on how to define power, how to observe and measure it, or even how to think about it. Indeed, *March* [1966, p. 70] has concluded that "on the whole . . . power is a disappointing concept."

Here we shall conceive of power as the capacity of an actor, alone or (more likely) in combination with others, to bring about or preclude certain outcomes. The subsequent technical sections of this essay are devoted to formalizing this notion and examining some of its properties and implications. But first, I will point out how this concept differs from some other looser notions of power, and also from the various "power indices," and I will try to provide some justification for this concept.

2. Power and Political Analysis

Often (especially in more empirically-oriented studies) what is estimated and identified as power is, at least implicitly and roughly, the relative success of political actors in getting decisions they like. This simple notion – that the politically powerful are precisely those who are most successful in getting desired outcomes – is certainly straightforward and appeals, at least at first glance, to common sense. Moreover, it is methodologically convenient for empirical research, since we can usually ascertain the preference of actors in political situations, observe the decisions, and match the former with the latter.

However, this approach really does not bear theoretical scrutiny.[2]) It suggests that all factors that make for political success are components of power and that measured power is simply a summary of these advantages. To say that "A got what he wanted, because he

---

[1]) Much of this essay is drawn from a paper presented to the 1978 Annual Meeting of the Public Choice Society, New Orleans, Louisiana. For helpful suggestions, I am indebted to several participants at that meeting, to my colleagues Louis Cantori, David Jacobs, and Christopher Kelly, and to the editor of this volume.

[2]) Indeed power has been explicitly distinguished from "success" or "satisfaction" in some recent formal analyses; see especially *Brams/Lake* [1978] and the essay by Straffin et al. in this volume; also see *Barry* [1974, pp. 195ff.; 1980].

is powerful" then becomes an *a priori* (and vacuous) truth. It is more useful to have a concept of power that allows us to say that "A failed to get what he wanted, although he is powerful" or "A got what he wanted, although he is not powerful."

In a particular decision, or typically over a sequence of decisions, advantages that make for success may include, among others, the following. An actor may be successful because:

(i) he has preferences similar to those of one or a few other actors who are powerful;
(ii) he has preferences similar to those of most other actors;
(iii) he has preference that are, in some sense, about "average";
(iv) he holds, in some sense, the "balance of power" between two opposing groups and he can tip the decision as he prefers; or
(v) in any other way his preferences are related to the overall distribution of preferences in such a way that he derives advantages.

Such circumstances are certainly advantageous to the actor in question, but they may not be enduring since they depend on fortuitous, and perhaps shortlived, configurations in the distribution of preferences. If his preferences were different, or if the preferences of (some) other actors were different, his advantage would likely evaporate. In any case, we certainly want to distinguish systematically between such *preference-based advantages* in political decision making (contingent upon particular preference distributions) and other *non-preference-based advantages* (invariant under changes in the distribution of preferences). I believe that most people, upon reflection, would agree that the concept of power should be confined to non-preference based advantages in decision making, and perhaps to a subset thereof. But it bears emphasis that the success of an actor in getting decisions he likes, or his expected satisfaction with political outcomes, will depend in large part – in fact primarily (especially in large systems) – on his preference-based advantages and only in part – perhaps only in small part and sometimes not at all – on other non-preference-based advantages, including power.[3])

What further (non-preference-based) advantages may an actor have? He may be successful because:

(vi) he is strategically skillful, while (some) others are not;
(vii) he has information that (some) others do not have;
(viii) he can cooperate freely with other actors, while (some) others are hindered from doing the same; or
(ix) he is active and exploits all opportunities available to him, while (some) others are relatively inert.

I am inclined to think it redundant to say that a given decision was reached because actor *A* wanted it and is powerful, and *A* is powerful because (for example) he is more strategically skillful than others. It is more direct to say that the decision was reached be-

[3]) Probably "pluralist" and "elitist" analyses of the political process really disagree about the characteristic distribution of preferences or interests in society more than about the distribution and structure of power.

cause A wanted it and A is more skillful than others. In any case, I shall keep such non-preference-based advantages as (vi)–(ix) conceptually distinct from power.

Finally, an actor may be successful because:

(x) he is able to modify the preferences of other actors and thus also their actions;
(xi) he is able to modify the actions of other actors without changing their preferences (e.g., by means of threats or promises); or
(xii) he is able (perhaps in combination with others) to bring about outcomes he likes or preclude outcomes he dislikes, regardless of the preferences or actions of others (or those outside the combination).

In the event of (x), I say that an actor exercises *persuasive influence*; in the event of (xi), I say that the actor exercises *coercive influence*.[4]) But in either event, I distinguish *influence* – the ability to modify the actions of others (which is accordingly an *interpersonal relation*) – from *power* – the ability of an actor, or a combination of actors, to bring about or preclude outcomes (which is accordingly a *relation between actors and outcomes*) – as manifested in the event of (xii). (Coercive influence, however, is based in large part on power, viz. on the ability to bring about or preclude outcomes desired or undesired by other actors. But coercive influence is in part preference-based, for "to destroy it, nothing more is required than to be indifferent to its threats, and to prefer other goods to those which it promises" [*Tawney*, p. 176].)

It follows from this understanding that power is a *capacity* or *potential*. [Cf. *Barry*, 1976, 71, 96–97.] In any particular case, a powerful actor (or combination) may not exercise his (its) power – because of inattention, forebearance, because he will get what he wants anyway, because to do so would not accomplish what he wants (or, in the case of a combination, because of disunity, lack of coordination, etc.).

This view suggests that power may be conceived of as a generalization of "voting power." That is, a group in a voting body can succeed when it can outvote (or "overpower") its opposition – and this is true regardless of how preferences are distributed or how skillful the opposition is, whether or not the group exercises influence, and so forth. At the same time, a group that "has the power" to impose its will on a voting body may fail to do so – out of forebearance, because of internal disunity, lack of mobilization, etc. Conversely, groups that might be outvoted (or even those entirely lacking voting power, e.g., non-voting delegates) often succeed, i.e., get outcomes they like, but they succeed for reasons such as (i)–(xi) above; the fact remains that such actors or groups can always be outvoted – they can neither secure nor preclude any outcome.

Many voting bodies are *majoritarian* and are characterized by very simple *power relations*, viz. any group constituting a majority of the body is all-powerful and can secure or preclude any outcome (e.g., any bill or package of bills), while any other group (constituting less than a majority) is powerless and can neither secure nor preclude any outcome. But if we want to understand decision making in a voting body – or in a larger and less formally structured political system – it is not sufficient to look only at power relations. Power may be the first thing to look at to understand who wins and who loses, "who

[4]) Perhaps this label really is appropriate only for influence based on threats, and we might dub influence based on promises "inducive" influence. But since our concern here is with power, not influence, there is no present need to introduce or maintain such a terminological distinction.

gets, what, when, how," but it certainly is not the last or only thing to look at. We need to look also at the ideological structure or distribution of preferences or interests in the body, the distribution of information and skills, communications patterns, opportunities for influence, and so forth. Indeed, power relations in most voting bodies are so relatively simple (even if not strictly majoritarian) that analyses of the legislative process typically focus almost exclusively on other variables.

The various measures of voting power – i.e., the power indices due to *Shapley/Shubik* [1954], *Banzhaf* [1965], *Coleman* [1971], and *Deegan/Packel* [1979] – with which formal theorists are familiar are (when properly used and interpreted[5])) indeed measures of power (or, more precisely, of what we will call "power in the general sense") as we conceive it here. Precisely for this reason, they are rather uninteresting when applied to majoritarian or other unicameral "one man, one vote" bodies, since they tell us only that all members have an equal fraction of the power. (They become more interesting when applied to bicameral systems, weighted voting systems, etc.)

Furthermore, most of these indices are *normalized* – that is, defined in such a way that the power values of all actors always sum to unity. Accordingly, they focus entirely on the *distribution* of power and are insensitive to variations in the structure of power or the precise nature of power relations, which may significantly affect the nature of political decision making. For example, according to either the Shapley-Shubik or Banzhaf index, each of the members of a majoritarian voting body has a power index value of $1/n$. The same is true of each member in a "universal veto" or "pure bargaining" (*liberum veto*) system in which unanimous consent is required to bring about any change in the status quo. Yet clearly the structure of power, the nature of power relations, and the character of decision making are very different in the two cases.

The Coleman index and the non-normalized variant of the Banzhaf index [cf. *Straffin*] do distinguish between the two cases, because their power values do not automatically sum to unity (or any other constant) and do reflect the fact that power relations are (as we shall say) "stronger" in the first case. Yet the fact remains that two actors in two different voting bodies characterized by quite different power relations may nevertheless have the same power value (on any of these indices). Indeed, this defect inevitably characterizes any measure that attempts to summarize the power position of an actor by means of a single numerical value. Power relations may be sufficiently complex and varied that a single index value cannot adequately indicate the power position of an actor.

And finally we should note that these power indices do not apply at all to more complex and varied situations. They apply only to those voting or "voting-like" situations that are formally characterizable as "simple games" [cf. *Shapley*, 1962]. Voting or "voting-like" situations – and simple games – are characterized by a kind of neutrality among outcomes – if an actor or coalition can secure (or preclude) one outcome x, it can also secure (or preclude) any other outcome y; only the status quo or "do nothing" out-

[5]) Some of the alleged "paradoxes of power" (e.g., "the paradox of quarreling members") based on power indices really result from inappropriate use of them [cf. *Barry*, 1980, 192–194]. As conceived here, the power of members of a voting body cannot increase (or, for that matter, decrease) as a result of their "quarreling" (i.e., always having opposite preferences), and the power of the non-quarreling third member is likewise unaffected. The non-quarreling third member will be highly successful, however, benefiting from preference-based advantage (iv) above.

come may be allowed a distinguished position. Thus, in simple games, every coalition belongs to one of just three categories: winning, losing, and blocking. A winning coalition is all-powerful; it can secure outcome x and also outcomes y, z, etc. A coalition that can secure (or preclude) outcomes x and y, but not outcomes z and w, takes us beyond the scope of simple games and "voting-like" situations and accordingly beyond the scope of the power indexes. But in general, we must take account of such more complex situations and be prepared to deal with them theoretically.

It might seem that we need only move from simple games to games in general. But games in general effectively incorporate preference information in a way unsuitable for our purposes. Thus the rules of the parlor games that provided the original models for game theory determine, in effect, the preferences of the players (e.g., simply by defining what constitutes "winning"). Likewise, the "rules" of the "economic games" for which game theory was originally developed [*von Neumann/Morgenstern*] substantially determine players' preferences by imposing on them such constraints as egoism and individualism (more for me is better than less for me; otherwise I am indifferent). In conventional mathematical game theory, and especially cooperative theory, games are, for the most part, played for money (strictly, for something called "transferable utility"), thus also determining players preferences. For this reason, while the Shapley-Shubik index is a special case of the *Shapley* [1953] "value" applied to simple games, and while the Shapley value itself is defined for all games, the "value" index does not provide an appropriate measure of power in general – it presumes in effect that all collective decision making is a battle over fully divisible spoils and that all actors prefer more of the spoils to less. But much (or most) collective decision making concerns fixing public policies, which are "public goods" (at least partial and/or local public goods) in that they bear on all actors, but at the same time are differently evaluated by different actors [cf. *Barry*, 1980, 189–191]. Thus, political rules and institutions do not determine or particularly constrain the preferences of those participating under the rules. Suppose, for example, that a given set of political rules gives some actor a "veto"; nothing in the nature of the rules themselves suggests how valuable this "power" may be to that actor. Nor in general can we specify the "value" of political coalitions; it all depends on the preferences of the participants, which likely vary from case to case.

For these reasons, "game forms" [the term is due to *Gibbard*], rather than games as such, provide the appropriate framework for our analysis. A *game form* is, in effect, a game minus any specification of the preferences (interests, utilities, payoffs, etc.) that motivate the players in any particular instance. It should be clear that a constitution, electoral system, voting procedure, or any other strategic environment for political action is formally described, not by a game, but by a game form.

The analysis of power that follows is based on game forms. Power in game forms is defined in what I believe to be a plausible and natural manner. I distinguish between two "faces" of power and identify general properties that characterize all power relations (and all game forms). I identify also certain special properties that may characterize some power relations (and some game forms). I define "effective" preference in a manner similar to "domination" in the sense of cooperative game theory. And finally I ask this question: what conditions on power relations will assure that, even as preferences may change, effective preference has "nice" properties such that society can make collective decisions easily.

The answer to the question is this: if there are three or more possible outcomes, and if no one actor has all the power, it is impossible to structure power in such a way that effective preference has "nice" properties. This conclusion clearly is a variant of *Arrow's* [1963] General Impossibility Theorem. As an analysis of power, however, what follows is most closely related to work by *March* [1957], *Rae* [1971, 1975], and perhaps *Goldman* [1972].

3. Game Forms

A game form is, in effect, a game without payoff functions. To quote *Gibbard* [1973, p. 589; notation has been modified]:

> Formally, then, a *game form* is a function g with a domain of the following sort. To each player 1 to n is assigned a non-empty set, $S_1, \ldots, S_n$ respectively, of *strategies* ... The domain of the function g consists of all n-tuples $(s_1, \ldots, s_n)$, where $s_1 \in S_1, \ldots, s_n \in S_n$. The values of the function g are called *outcomes.*

Following *Farquharson* [1969, p. 21], I call strategy n-tuples *situations*. A game form, then, maps situations into outcomes, in a deterministic fashion.

A two-player game form may be represented by a matrix, one row of which corresponds to each strategy in S_1 and one column of which corresponds to each strategy in S_2. Each cell then corresponds to a situation and the entry in the cell (say, x) indicates the outcome to which the situation belongs. (In a two-player game – as opposed to game form – in normal form, the cell entries would be numbers indicating utility payoffs to the players.)

An n-player game form may be likewise represented by an n-dimensional matrix. But from the point of view of any focal player i, the game form may be "contracted" into a two-dimensional matrix, a row of which corresponds to each strategy in S_i and a column of which corresponds to each possible *contingency* for i (again I follow the usage of *Farquharson* [1969, p. 28]), i.e., each $(n-1)$-tuple of strategies, one for each player other than i. Likewise, from the point of view of any focal coalition (subset) T of players, the game form may be "contracted" into a two-dimensional matrix, the rows of which correspond to all possible combinations of strategies, one for each player in T, and the columns of which correspond to all possible combinations of strategies, one for each player not in T.

The general result on game forms due to *Gibbard* [1973] says this: only under very limited conditions can a game form be "straightforward" – that is, offer each player i, regardless of his preferences, a *dominant* strategy, i.e., a clearly best strategy that, in every contingency, gives an outcome that is at least as good (according to i's preferences) as the outcome given by any other of i's strategies. In particular, a game form can be straightforward only if it has fewer than three outcomes or if it makes one player all-powerful. Gibbard's perspective is non-cooperative and individualistic: each player in isolation asks, "Do I have a clearly best strategy, or do I have to try to anticipate what other players will do?" The perspective here, on the other hand, is cooperative: each possible coalition asks, "What can we accomplish on our own, what outcomes can we impose or preclude – generally, what constraints can we impose on the realization of outcomes – regardless of what the other players do?" And roughly, we say the more numerous and diversified these possible constraints, the more powerful the coalition.

4. The Power of Players and Coalitions

We begin by considering the "potency" of a single strategy of a single player i. Let V designate the set of all outcomes in the game form. Then let $V_i' \subseteq V$ be the set of outcomes that can possibly be realized (which one depending on the strategy selections of the other players) given that player i selects his strategy $s_i' \in S_i$. In the contracted (from i's point of view) game form matrix, V_i' is simply the union of all outcomes in the row corresponding to s_i'. The complement $V - V_i'$ is, of course, the set of the set of outcomes that certainly cannot be realized (regardless of the strategy selections of the other players) given that player i selects s_i'. In other words, by selecting strategy s_i', player i can preclude any outcome in $V - V_i'$, so if this set is non-empty, he has some power.

Clearly $\emptyset \subset V_i' \subseteq V$.[6]) The inclusiveness of V_i' is a (negative) measure of the constraint that selection of s_i' imposes on the realization of outcomes; and thus it is a (negative) measure of the "potency" of the strategy s_i' [cf. *March*, 1957, p. 210]. If $V_i' = V$, s_i' is *impotent*; if $V_i' \subset V$, s_i' is (more or less) *potent* for all outcomes x in V_i'; and if $V_i' = \{x\}$ (i.e., if V_i' is a one-element set – in other words if x belongs to every cell in the row corresponding to s_i'), s_i' is maximally potent or, as we shall say, *decisive* for x.

We now consider the power of an individual player i. He has the strategy set S_i; corresponding to each strategy $s_i' \in S_i$ is the set of outcomes V_i' discussed just above. γ_i designates this family of sets of outcomes, one set for each of i's strategies. Some elements of γ_i may intersect; some may be identical; in the extreme, all elements of γ_i may be identical, in which case necessarily $V_i = V$ for all $s_i \in S_i$. If this extreme possibility holds, i.e., if $\cap V_i = V$ (where $\cap V_i$ designates the intersection of all elements of γ_i), every one of i's strategies is impotent and player i is *powerless*. Otherwise, i.e., if $(\cap V_i) \subset V$, i has at least one potent strategy and player i is (more or less) *powerful*. And if at least one element of γ_i is a one-element set, e.g., $V_i' = \{x\}$, i has at least one strategy that is decisive for x, and we say likewise that player i is *decisive* for x. A player who has at least one strategy decisive for each outcome $x \in V$ is all-powerful or a *dictator*.

A coalition T is simply a set of players. The *joint strategy set* S_T of coalition T is the set of all possible combinations of (individual) strategies, one for each player in T. Corresponding to each strategy combination s_T' is a set of outcomes V_T' that can possibly be realized given that the players in T select the strategies that define s_T'; in the contracted (from the point of view of the coalition T) game form, V_T' is the union of all the outcomes in the row corresponding to s_T'. Thus joint strategies may be characterized as impotent, (more or less) potent, and decisive (for a specified outcome) in just the same manner as individual strategies. And thus also coalitions may be characterized as powerless, (more

---

[6]) "$A \subset B$" means A is a *proper* subset of B, i.e., everything in A is also in B and something in B is not in A. "$A \subseteq B$" allows for improper set inclusion, i.e., A and B may be equal.

or less) powerful, and decisive (for specified outcomes) in just the same manner as individual players.

From now on, I shall speak generally of the power of a coalition, it being understood that an individual player can be regarded as a one-player coalition.

5. Affirmative and Preclusive Power

The power of a coalition T is fully specified by the family of sets of outcomes γ_T, one set for each of T's joint strategies. This specification may be complex, reflecting the possible complexity of power relations. Sometimes, therefore, it is convenient to look only at certain summary aspects of coalition power. And sometimes it is not necessary to look beyond these aspects – that is, sometimes power relations are not so complex.

Of particular interest as a summary aspect of a coalition T's power is the union of one element sets in γ_T; let $D(T)$ designate this set of outcomes. $D(T)$ specifies the outcomes for which T is decisive; T can impose any outcome in $D(T)$ as the realized outcome, i.e., if $x \in D(T)$, T has a joint strategy that, if used, assures that x is the realized outcome, regardless of the strategy selections of players not in T. Thus $D(T)$ specifies the *affirmative power*, or "power to impose," of the coalition T, which derives from decisive joint strategies.

An *all-powerful* coalition T has maximum (affirmative) power, i.e., $D(T) = V$ – in words, an all-powerful coalition can impose any outcome. The coalition of the whole is always all-powerful, i.e., always $D(N) = V$. In a majoritarian voting body, any majority coalition is all-powerful. A *minimal* all-powerful coalition is an all-powerful coalition that contains no proper subcoalition (subset) that is itself all-powerful. A dictator, of course, is a one-element all-powerful coalition, necessarily minimal.

Not all power is affirmative power; power has a "second face." For if a coalition T has any "power to impose," i.e., $D(T) \neq \emptyset$, it also has some "power to preclude." That is, to say that T can impose x as the realized outcome is also to say that that T can preclude any $y \in V - \{x\}$ as the realized outcome. But not all *preclusive power* is such a "complement" of affirmative power, since any potent strategy combination gives a coalition some preclusive power; i.e., given any s'_T such that $V'_T \subset V$, T can preclude any outcome in $V - V'_T \neq \emptyset$. In general, let $F(T)$ designate the set of outcomes any one of which T can preclude, i.e., $F(T) = [V - \cap V_T]$. Note that if $x, y \in D(T)$ and $x \neq y$, i.e., if T is decisive for at least two distinct outcomes, then $F(T) = (V - \{x\}) \cup (V - \{y\}) = V$.

Several points should be emphasized. First, T can preclude *any one* of the outcomes in $F(T)$, not (necessarily) *any several* simultaneously. T can preclude x and y simultaneously only if there is some particular joint strategy s'_T such that $x, y \notin V'_T$ (which implies, but is not implied by, $x, y \in F(T)$).

Second, and related to the previous point, preclusive power is not equivalent to "veto power" as the term is ordinarily used (e.g., in connection with the U.N. Security Council). To say an actor has "veto power" ordinarily means that the actor can *simultaneously* preclude every outcome but one (usually the status quo or "doing nothing"). But this is only a slightly roundabout way of saying that the actor is decisive for that one outcome. Thus "veto power" in the ordinary sense actually entails some affirmative power. And henceforth we shall say formally that a coalition that is decisive for a single outcome has *veto power*.

Finally, it bears repeating that in general the power of a coalition T is fully specified by the family of sets γ_T. $D(T)$ and $F(T)$ can always be inferred from γ_T but not vice versa.

6. General Properties of Power Relations

Thus far, we have considered the power of particular coalitions. We now turn to consider the general properties of power relations among coalitions.

A coalition T is *at least as powerful* as coalition S *with respect to outcome* x if, for every element V'_S of γ_S such that $x \in V'_S$, there is some element V'_T of γ_T such that $x \in V'_T \subseteq V'_S$. In words, for every joint strategy S has that precludes some outcome other than x, T has a joint strategy that precludes at least the same outcomes and perhaps others (but not x). T and S are *equally powerful with respect to* x if T is at least as powerful as S with respect to x and also vice versa. T is *more powerful* than S *with respect to* x if T is at least as powerful as S with respect to x but not vice versa.

More generally, T is *at least as powerful* as S if T is at least as powerful as S with respect to every outcome in V. And following the same pattern of definition as just above, we may say that T and S are *equally powerful*[7]) or that T is *more powerful* than S.

In many cases, of course, the power of coalitions cannot be compared, because comparisons are based on the incomplete relation of set inclusion.

However, the power of two coalitions can always be compared when one is a subset of the other. Consider a coalition T, any outcome x, and any joint strategy s'_T such that $x \in V'_T$. Now consider any coalition S of which T is a subset. Let $Q = S - T$, i.e., Q is the coalition made up of the players in S but not in T. Now consider any strategy s'_Q such that $x \in V'_Q$. Thus $x \in V'_T \cap V'_Q$, and the coalition $S = T \cup Q$ has a joint strategy (the combination of s'_T and s'_Q – call it s'_S) that is at least as potent for x as s'_T (or s'_Q). (Necessarily $V'_S \subseteq (V'_T \cap V'_Q)$, so $V'_S \subseteq V'_T$.) Since the same argument can be made for any outcome, the coalition S is at least as powerful as T (or Q). Thus in general:

Theorem 1. (Inclusiveness) If $T \subset S$, S is at least as powerful as T.

We now consider the relationship between the power of two *disjoint* coalitions T and S. Clearly this relationship must exhibit some kind of consistency – that is, the power of one coalition must be limited *at least* by the power of all disjoint coalitions (or, equivalently by virtue of Inclusiveness, by the power of its complement). Most clearly, the affirmative (preclusive) power of one coalition must be limited at least by the preclusive (affirmative) power of all disjoint coalitions.

T and S being two disjoint coalitions, consider, for any s'_T and s'_S, the intersection $V'_T \cap V'_S$. Since T and S are disjoint, all such strategy selections can happen simultaneously, and this intersection cannot be empty; in the limit, if T and S are complements

[7]) It follows – as we should hope it follows – that, if T and S are equally powerful, $D(T) = D(S)$ and $F(T) = F(S)$. This has been formally demonstrated by Harmut Kliemt (1980, unpublished). The reverse, of course, is not true.

$(T = -S)$, s'_T and s'_S together define a unique situation, which belongs to a given outcome, say x. Thus in any case we have $x \in V'_T \cap V'_S$. Formally:

Theorem 2. (*Consistency*) For every pair of disjoint coalitions T and S and for every pair of joint strategies s'_T and s'_S, $V'_T \cap V'_S \neq \emptyset$.

Once stated, this point is no doubt obvious and may not deserve to be labelled a "theorem." But it has some corollaries that are important and less obvious.

Suppose $V'_T = \{x\}$, i.e., $x \in D(T)$; then by the theorem x belongs to every element of γ_S; i.e., $x \in \cap V_S$. Generalizing:

Corollary 2.1. For every pair of disjoint coalitions T and S, $D(T) \subseteq (\cap V_S)$.

Recall that $F(S) = V - \cap V_S$. Substituting, we have $D(T) \subseteq V - F(S)$; and thus:

Corollary 2.1′. For every pair of disjoint coalitions T and S, $D(T) \cap F(S) = \emptyset$.

This is surely reasonable; indeed it is a formal statement of our initial observation regarding the requirements of Consistency. In words, what one coalition can impose a disjoint coalition cannot preclude and vice versa. In particular, if $D(T) = V$, then $\cap V_{-T} = V$ and $F(-T) = \emptyset$; in words, the complement of an all-powerful coalition is powerless (obviously).

Suppose $D(T)$ contains two or more outcomes. Then by the first corollary, $\cap V_S$ – and likewise every element of γ_S taken alone – contains the same two or more outcomes. Thus:

Corollary 2.2. For every pair of disjoint coalitions T and S, if $D(T)$ contains at least two outcomes, then $D(S) = \emptyset$.

In words, if one coalition is decisive for as many as two outcomes, no disjoint coalition can be decisive for anything (no disjoint coalition can have any affirmative power).

Suppose $D(T) \neq \emptyset$ and also $D(S) \neq \emptyset$. Then there is (at least) one element of γ_T and also one element of γ_S containing a single outcome. By the theorem, these one-element sets intersect; thus they must contain the same single outcome. Summarizing:

Corollary 2.3. For every pair of disjoint coalitions T and S, if $D(T) \neq \emptyset$ and $D(S) \neq \emptyset$, T and S are decisive for the same single outcome, e.g., $D(T) = D(S) = \{x\}$.

In words, if two disjoint coalitions both have some affirmative power, they are both decisive for the same single outcome (they both have veto power).

7. Power in the General Sense

The *power in the general sense* of a player (*not* a coalition) refers not only to what power a player has alone (he may be powerless) but also to what he can add by way of power to every coalition that he might possibly join. That is, player i has power in the general sense to the extent that there are coalitions $S \subseteq N - \{i\}$ such that $S \cup \{i\}$ is more powerful than S. Otherwise, i.e., if i is powerless and S and $S \cup \{i\}$ are equally powerful for all S, player i is *powerless in the general sense* (or a *dummy*).

Note that the various power indices discussed in this book are, in these terms, not measures of power but rather measures of power in the general sense. Thus such indices are typically used to evaluate the distribution of power among members of voting bodies, though (under almost all voting procedures) individual voters are powerless and have power only in combination with others.

8. Special Properties of Power Relations

The foregoing discussion has suggested that in general power relations may be highly complex. We now consider certain special conditions that make power relations less complex.

In introducing the notion of Consistency, we observed that the affirmative power of a coalition must be limited *at least* by the preclusive power of its complement and vice versa. We are now interested in the case in which the affirmative power of a coalition is limited *only* by the preclusive power of its complement and vice versa. Formally:

Definition 1. The power relationship between two complementary coalitions T and $-T$ is *determinate* if $D(T) \cup F(-T) = D(-T) \cup F(T) = V$.

Recall from Corollary 2.1 that Consistency requires that $D(T) \subseteq (\cap V_{-T})$. Put otherwise, Determinacy then means that $D(T) = \cap V_{-T}$ and $D(-T) = \cap V_T$. In words, the outcomes that T can impose are precisely those that $-T$ cannot preclude, and the outcomes that $-T$ can impose are precisely those that T cannot preclude.

Power relations are *determinate* if power relationships between all pairs of complementary coalitions are determinate – that is, if all affirmative power is limited only by preclusive power and vice versa.[8])

We are also interested in the following special property:

Definition 2. The power of a coalition T is *decisive* if $V'_T \subseteq D(T)$ for all $V'_T \subset V$.

This means that each element V'_T of γ_T meets one of these conditions: (i) it contains all outcomes (s'_T is impotent), (ii) it contains precisely one outcome, say x (s'_T is decisive for x), or (iii) it is "redundant" in the sense that each of its elements also belongs to some one-element set in γ_T (while s'_T is potent for x, there is some other s''_T that is decisive for x).

Put more intuitively, the power of a coalition T is decisive if whatever power it has derives from decisive joint strategies and thus its power is identical to its affirmative power and is therefore fully specified by $D(T)$. Note that by this definition the power of a powerless coalition T is decisive, for every s'_T meets condition (i) above. This terminology may seem odd, but it is convenient for stating the following definition.

---

[8]) *Rae* [1975] introduces the still stronger condition of *Robustness* on power relations (or "control structures"): if $D(T) = \emptyset$, then there is some S such that (i) $S \cap T = \emptyset$, and (ii) $D(S) \neq \emptyset$ (given Inclusiveness, we can say simply: if $D(T) = \emptyset$, then $D(-T) \neq \emptyset$). In words, the affirmative power of a coalition is limited only by the affirmative power of its complement.

If power relations are determinate, and if all power is affirmative power (i.e., if power relations are also "decisive" and thus "simple" in the senses defined below), Robustness must hold (indeed, Robustness, Determinacy, and Consistency collapse into the same condition); but otherwise it need not. Thus *Rae* [1975, p. 1280] is mistaken when he says that "we do not choose robustness; necessity chooses it for us." Rae overlooks the "second face" of power – "power to preclude" independent of "power to impose" – as well as the possibility of indeterminacy in power relations.

Power relations are *decisive* if the power of every coalition is decisive. It will also be convenient to introduce this definition: power relations are *almost decisive* if, for every coalition T, either the power of T is decisive or the power of $-T$ is decisive (or both).

We are particularly interested in those power relations that are both determinate and decisive. We call such power relations *simple*.

Consider any complementary pair of coalitions T and $-T$. If power relations are simple, there are only three possible power relationships between them.

1. Suppose $D(T) = \emptyset$; then by Decisiveness $F(T) = \emptyset$; and then by Determinacy $D(-T) = V$. So one possible relationship is $D(T) = \emptyset$ and $D(-T) = V$.
2. Suppose $D(T) = \{x\}$; then by Decisiveness $F(T) = V - \{x\}$; and then by Determinacy $D(-T) = \{x\}$. So a second possible relationship is $D(T) = D(-T) = \{x\}$.
3. Suppose $x, y \in D(T)$ (i.e., suppose T is decisive for more than one outcome); then by Corollary 2.2 $D(-T) = \emptyset$; then by Decisiveness $F(-T) = \emptyset$; and then by Determinacy $D(T) = V$. So a third possible relationship is $D(T) = V$ and $D(-T) = \emptyset$.

By Decisiveness, $D(T)$ fully specifies the power of T and $D(-T)$ the power of $-T$, so these are the only possibilities. And apart from the labelling of the coalitions, the first and the third are identical, so in fact we have only two basic possibilities. That is, given simple power relations and two complementary coalitions, either one is all-powerful and the other is powerless, or both are decisive for the same single outcome. Accordingly, if power relations are simple, every coalition is all-powerful, or has veto power only, or is powerless, and power relations can be fully specified by partitioning the set of all coalitions into these three classes.

And it follows further from the general properties of Inclusiveness and Consistency that simple power relations can be specified fully merely by indicating which coalitions are minimal all-powerful: all supersets of these are all-powerful, all complements of the all-powerful coalitions are powerless, and all other coalitions have veto power only.[9])

Power relations in general (and the game forms underlying them) may be arrayed on a rough spectrum from "weak" to "strong," Power relations are *maximally weak* if all coalitions, other than the coalition of the whole, are powerless; they are *maximally strong* if every coalition, or its complement, is all-powerful. Roughly, as power relations range from "weak" to "strong," two things happen. On one hand, some coalitions become more powerful – but not at the expense of others, i.e., power relations become more determinate. On the other hand, some coalitions become more powerful at the expense of disjoint coalitions, i.e., power relations become more decisive.

At the two extremes of maximally strong and maximally weak power relations, individual players are powerless; at some intermediate points, individual players have some power. If all players have some affirmative power, a "universal veto system" exists (cf. Corollary 2.3). To the extent that individual players have considerable preclusive power, but no affirmative power, power might be characterized as "dispersed."[10])

---

[9]) What we have, of course, is the basic structure of proper simple games, where all-powerful coalitions are "winning," powerless coalitions are "losing," and coalitions with veto power only are "blocking." Cf. *Shapley* [1962].

[10]) Such "dispersion" of power may constitute the most appropriate game-theoretical translation of *Sen's* [1970] "liberalism" condition in abstract social choice theory; cf. *Miller* [1977, esp. p. 25].

It is worth noting that as we range over the four possible types of power relations discussed just above – maximally weak, maximally strong, "universal veto system," and "dispersed" – a player's Shapley-Shubik, Banzhaf, etc., power index values may remain constant – for example $1/n$.[11]) This highlights the point made in the introduction that these are only summary indices that focus on the *distribution* of power in the general sense and take no account of very significant variations in the *structure* of power relations.

9. Effective Preference

When we move from game forms to games by adding preferences, we shall say that outcome x is "effectively preferred" to outcome y if "society" as a whole prefers x to y in some meaningful sense. Clearly, we may expect unanimous preferences to be effective in this sense. But we also expect that some less than unanimous preferences may also be effective; i.e., in any particular case the preferences of some proper subset of actors may be effective, and the possibly conflicting preferences of other actors may be simply overridden. The way in which effective preferences are "filled out" beyond unanimity obviously depends on the nature of power relations among these actors. Thus formal consideration of effective preference involves a meshing together of preferences with the power relations we have already looked at.

I here assume that all players have (complete, transitive) preference orderings over outcomes. If player i prefers outcome x to outcome y, we write $x\,P_i\,y$. $P_i\,(y)$ designates the set of all outcomes that i prefers to y.

Our initial notion of the sense in which outcome x may be effectively preferred to outcome y is that there is a set of players who jointly prefer x to y and who in coalition have power sufficient to make x the realized outcome. Thus formally, x is effectively preferred to y if there is some coalition T such that:

$$x \in D\,(T); \tag{1}$$

and

$$x\,P_i\,y \quad \text{for all } i \in T. \tag{2}$$

These two conditions suffice to meet our notion of effective preference but in general they are not necessary, since they take account only of the affirmative power of coalitions. For example, suppose that coalition T, while not decisive for x, can preclude y in such a way that any outcome (x among others) that may then be realized is preferred to y by all members of T; i.e., suppose that there is some s'_T such that $x \in V'_T$ and $y \notin V'_T$ and $V'_T \subseteq P_i\,(y)$ for all $i \in T$. It seems reasonable in this case to say at least that y is "effectively dispreferred" (to all outcomes in V'_T). We will, in fact, simply generalize our notion of effective preference and say that each outcome in V'_T is effectively preferred to y.

Definition 3. Outcome x is *effectively preferred* to outcome y if and only if there is some

[11]) Strictly speaking, though, no such indices would be defined in the fourth possible type since it does not correspond to a simple game.

coalition T with some s'_T such that:

$$x \in V'_T \quad \text{and} \quad y \notin V'_T; \tag{3}$$

and

$$V'_T \subseteq P_i(y) \quad \text{for all } i \in T. \tag{4}$$

T is the *effective coalition* for this effective preference relationship. Other coalitions may be effective for the same relationship. In general, of course, some subsets of T fail to be effective because they have insufficient power (though they have the requisite preference consensus); some supersets of T fail to be effective because they do not have the requisite preference consensus (though, by Inclusiveness, they have sufficient power).

If x is effectively preferred to y, we represent this relationship diagrammatically thus: $x \to y$. We also say x *dominates* y. If there is an effective preference path $x \to z \to \ldots \to y$, we say x *reaches* y.

We may make these observations concerning the effective preference relation. First, even when all individual preferences are strict, the effective preference relation is not in general complete (i.e., we may have neither $x \to y$ nor $y \to x$). Second, even when all individual preferences are strict, the effective preference relation is not in general asymmetric (i.e., we may have both $x \to y$ and $y \to x$; we write this $x \leftrightarrow y$[12])). Third, the effective preference relation is not in general transitive (i.e., we may have $x \to y$ and $y \to z$ but *not* $x \to z$) and it may in fact be cyclical (e.g., we may have $x \to y$ and $y \to z$ and yet $z \to x$). Clearly, unanimous preferences are always effective, since always $D(N) = V$.

10. The Significance of a Unique Undominated Outcome

If a system of effective preference is a strict ordering and accordingly replicates the properties of individual preference, we should expect collective decision making to proceed in a particularly satisfactory manner. One outcome would sit at the top of the ordering and would be realized, since every other outcome is dominated – that is, for every other outcome, there is some coalition that wants to and is able to bring about a change.

On the other hand, it does not seem to be necessary for effective preference to be an ordering, in order that collective decision making proceed satisfactorily. An individual, after all, can choose properly once he has established which outcome he most prefers; it is not necessary for him to establish a full ordering. In like manner, collective decision making can proceed satisfactorily if there is one "top" outcome in the system of effective preference, even if effective preference does not generate a full ordering.

We can identify a succession of increasingly weak requirements that we might demand of effective preference.

1. Effective preference is a strict ordering.
2. In the system of effective preference, there is a single undominated outcome that dominates every other outcome.
3. In the system of effective preference, there is a single undominated outcome that reaches every other outcome.

[12]) But such mutual domination can occur only when effective preference works through preclusive, not affirmative, power; and see Lemma 3 below.

4. In the system of effective preference, there is a single undominated outcome.

In each case, the *core*, i.e., the set of undominated outcomes, includes precisely one outcome. It is not at all clear that 4. is sufficient for satisfactory collective decision making, since 4. in the absence of any of the stronger requirements, implies that the system of effective preference is "disconnected," so the undominated outcome might never be realized.

Effective preference can fail to meet requirement 4. (or any stronger requirement) in either of two distinct ways. On the one hand, the core may be empty; pretty obviously this can occur only if the system of effective preference includes at least one cycle or symmetric relationship. On the other hand, the core may be large – i.e., include two or more outcomes; quite obviously this can occur only if the system of effective preference is incomplete, for there can be no effective preference relationship between two undominated outcomes.

An empty core implies what may be characterized as "social instability" – it is impossible for "society" to settle on an outcome that satisfies everyone (i.e., every coalition) who needs to be satisfied. For every outcome, there is some coalition with both the power and the desire to upset it. Such a society might be in constant flux, subject to an unending sequence of "realignments," "coups," "upheavals," etc., whatever term might be appropriate.

Though theorists have generally worried about empty cores more than large cores, the social consequences of the latter may be more devastating. A large core implies what may be characterized as "social bargaining" – undominated outcomes exist, but precisely because there are several, there is conflict over which *one* is to be realized. Since no coalition has power sufficient to resolve this matter in its favor, each has a strong incentive to resort to coercive influence based on threats and other bargaining tactics (such as those discussed in *Schelling* [1960]) in order to resolve the matter in the most favorable way. The result may be deadlock, conflict, and the realization of inefficient outcomes.

Unanimity as a decision rule (i.e., each player has veto power only) implies a non-empty core. It is often remarked that a unanimity requirement is likely to lead to social deadlock. But this is true in two distinct senses. First, it becomes very difficult to upset the status quo (or whatever is the outcome for which each player is decisive) x, since we must have $\bigcap_i P_i(x) \neq \emptyset$ – a quite restrictive condition. In this respect, unanimity rule may be unduly conservative, but it otherwise presents no problem. The second sense in which unanimity rule can imply deadlock is that several outcomes may be unanimously preferred to x, i.e., $\bigcap_i P_i(x)$ may include several outcomes, and among these unanimously preferred (to x) outcomes preferences are likely to conflict, in which case there is no effective preference among them.

11. The Possibility of a Unique Undominated Outcome

In this final section, we address the question of what conditions, if any, on power relations assure – at least if individual preferences are strict – the existence of precisely one undominated outcome – a condition necessary to avoid simultaneously the "social instability" and the "social bargaining" problems.

There can be no more than one undominated outcome – and thus the "social bargaining" problem is avoided – if effective preference is complete. What circumstances assure completeness of effective preference? One answer is the existence of an all-powerful coalition all the members of which have identical strict preferences. But this is a condition on preferences, as well as on power relations. We are looking for a condition on power relations alone that will assure completeness regardless of the nature of players' preferences, at least provided they are strict. (Clearly individual indifference can lead to incomplete effective preference, regardless of the nature of power relations.) One answer is fairly obvious.

Lemma 1. Given strict individual preferences, effective preference is complete if power relations are maximally strong.

Consider two outcomes x and y. If all preferences are strict, the set of all players can be partitioned into two subsets according to their preferences between x and y: $T = \{i \mid x\, P_i\, y\}$ and $-T = \{j \mid y\, P_j\, x\}$. Given maximally strong power relations, by definition either T or $-T$ is all-powerful and accordingly we have either $x \rightarrow y$ or $y \rightarrow x$.

What is less obvious and more important is that, if there are three or more outcomes, *only* maximally strong power relations assure completeness for all strict preferences.

Lemma 2. Given three or more outcomes, effective preference is complete for all strict preferences only if power relations are maximally strong.

Suppose that power relations are not maximally strong. This implies that there is some T such that $D(T) \subset V$ and $D(-T) \subset V$. Thus, provided that there are three or more outcomes, we can find a pair of outcomes x and y such that $x \notin D(T)$ and $y \notin D(-T)$ or vice versa. (This must be possible unless (i) either $D(T) = V$ or $D(-T) = V$, which is precluded by supposition, or (ii) both $V - D(T)$ and $V - D(-T)$ contain the same single outcome, which by Consistency is possible only if there are no more than two outcomes.)

Now suppose that the members of T are precisely those players who prefer x to y, and suppose further that all members of T also prefer y to each other outcome in $V - \{x, y\}$. Likewise suppose that the members of $-T$ are precisely those players who prefer y to x, and suppose further that all members of $-T$ also prefer x to each other outcome in $V - \{x, y\}$.

It now follows that there can be no effective preference relationship between x and y. T is not decisive for x; thus every element of γ_T that contains x but not y contains some other outcome as well. But all members of T prefer y to such a third outcome. Thus neither T, nor any subset of T, can be effective for $x \rightarrow y$, and all players not in T prefer y to x; accordingly x is not effectively preferred to y. We can make an identical argument for $-T$; accordingly y is not effectively preferred to x. Thus effective preference is incomplete.

The preceding argument in fact supports a somewhat stronger conclusion than Lemma 2.

Lemma 2'. Given three or more outcomes, there is no more than one undominated outcome for all strict preferences only if power relations are maximally strong.

In sum, we can be sure of avoiding the "social bargaining" problem only if we require maximally strong power relations.

We now turn to consider conditions necessary and/or sufficient to avoid the other problem, i.e., an empty core and resulting "social instability." Clearly every outcome can be dominated only if there is a cycle in effective preference or if there is a symmetric effective preference relationship. But it turns out that symmetric effective preference cannot itself result in an empty core since, if each of two outcomes dominates the other, there is a third outcome that dominates both.

Lemma 3. If $x \leftrightarrow y$, there is some z that dominates both x and y.

Let $T = \{i \mid x P_i y\}$ and let $S = \{j \mid y P_j x\} \subseteq -T$. By Inclusiveness and the definition of effective preference, there is some s'_T such that $x \in V'_T$, $y \notin V'_T$, and $V'_T \subseteq P_i(y)$ for all $i \in T$; likewise, there is some s'_S such that $y \in V'_S$, $x \notin V'_S$, and $V'_S \subseteq P_j(x)$ for all $j \in S$. By Consistency, there is some $z \in V'_T \cap V'_S$. Thus we have $z \rightarrow x$ and $z \rightarrow y$ (T being effective for the first relationship and S for the second).

Furthermore, it turns out that the condition of maximally strong power relations necessary to avoid "social bargaining" is more than sufficient to avoid mutual domination.

Lemma 4. If power relations are almost decisive, effective preference is asymmetric.

Consider two outcomes x and y, and let $T = \{i \mid x P_i y\}$ and $S = \{j \mid y P_j x\} \subseteq -T$. Since power relations are almost decisive, either the power of T is decisive or the power of $-T$ is decisive. Suppose the power of T is decisive. Then we have $x \rightarrow y$ if and only if $x \in D(T)$; but then we also have $x \in D(T) \subseteq (\cap V_S)$ (by Corollary 2.1), so we cannot have $y \rightarrow x$ (by Inclusiveness and the definition of effective preference). Suppose the power of $-T$ is decisive. Then, in like manner, we have $y \rightarrow x$ only if $y \in D(-T)$; but then we also have $y \in D(-T) \subseteq (\cap V_T)$, so we cannot have $x \rightarrow y$. Thus in either case effective preference between x and y cannot be symmetric, and the argument can be repeated for any other pair of outcomes.

The maximally strong power relations required to avoid "social bargaining" are of course also decisive, thus are also almost decisive, and thus preclude symmetric effective preference. Accordingly, "social instability" can result only from cyclical effective preference.

What conditions, then, will avoid cyclical effective preference? One sufficient condition is that the intersection of all effective coalitions (cf. Definition 3) be non-empty; this assures that effective preference is a subrelation of the preference ordering of each player in the intersection, and as such it must be acyclic. However, this is a condition on preferences, as well as power.

Given the previous lemmas, the following is a more significant proposition:

Lemma 5. Given three or more outcomes and maximally strong power relations, acyclic effective preference cannot be assured if there are two or more distinct minimal all-powerful coalitions.

Given maximally strong power relations, only all-powerful coalitions can be effective, and at least one minimal all-powerful coalition is effective for each effective preference relationship.

Consider three outcomes x, y, and z. Let us suppose that $x \rightarrow y$ and that T is a minimal all-powerful coalition effective for this relationship. And let us suppose that $y \rightarrow z$ and that S is a minimal decisive coalition effective for this relationship.

Given the transitivity of individual preference and the fact that no pair of all-powerful coalitions can be disjoint (by Consistency), at least those players in the non-empty intersection $T \cap S$ prefer x to z. However, given only that $x \rightarrow y \rightarrow z$ and in the absence of any restrictions on individual preferences, these are also the only players who *must* prefer x to z.

Therefore, we can be certain to preclude $z \rightarrow x$ only if $T \cap S$ is itself all-powerful (which assures $x \rightarrow z$). But this requires that $T = S = T \cap S$, for otherwise neither T nor S would be minimal all-powerful. And if every other outcome is dominated (for example, if each of x, y, and z is unanimously preferred to every $v \in V - \{x, y, z\}$), it follows that no outcome is undominated. Thus, we can strengthen Lemma 5 as follows:

Lemma 5'. Given three or more outcomes and maximally strong power relations, the existence of an undominated outcome cannot be assured for all preferences if there are two or more distinct minimal all-powerful coalitions.

Finally, we state the following:

Lemma 6. If power relations are maximally strong, either (i) there are at least three distinct minimal all-powerful coalitions or (ii) there is a dictator.

Let power relations be maximally strong and suppose that there is exactly one minimal all-powerful coalition T. Then for any $i \in T$, $D(N - \{i\}) = \emptyset$, for otherwise $N - \{i\}$ would be all-powerful and some subset of $N - \{i\}$, necessarily distinct from T, would be minimal all-powerful. But then $D(\{i\}) = V$, and i is a dictator (and $T = \{i\}$).

Now suppose that there are exactly two distinct minimal all-powerful coalitions T and S. Since both are minimal, neither is a subset of the other. Then for any i in T but not in S and any j in S but not in T, we have $D(N - \{i, j\}) = \emptyset$, for otherwise $N - \{i, j\}$ would be all-powerful and some subset of $N - \{i, j\}$, necessarily distinct from both T and S, would be minimal all-powerful. But then $\{i, j\}$ is all-powerful; and either $\{i, j\}$, distinct from both T and S, is a third minimal all-powerful coalition or one of i and j is a dictator.

In sum, maximally strong power relations are required to assure that there is no more than one undominated outcome, i.e., to avoid "social bargaining." But the same maximally strong power relations always entail the possibility that there is no undominated outcome, i.e., permit "social instability," if there are two or more distinct minimal all-powerful coalitions. And in fact maximally strong power relations always entail three or more minimal all-powerful coalitions, unless they are dictatorial. Thus:

Theorem 3. No non-dictatorial power relations can assure for all strict individual preferences the existence of a unique undominated outcome.

Put otherwise, it is impossible to devise a game form, and by extension a set of political institutions, that simultaneously avoids "social instability" and "social bargaining" for all preferences.

Clearly this theorem is closely related to *Arrow's* [1963] General Impossibility Theorem, and especially its reformulation due to *Wilson* [1971, 1972]. (Wilson shows that a consistent subset of Arrow's condition implies a strong simple game, i.e., maximally strong power relations, from which it readily follows that the core may be empty.) And, in a sense, it is the cooperative counterpart of Gibbard's theorem on straightforward game forms: every game form involving three or more outcomes that offers every player, regardless of his preferences, a dominant strategy is dictatorial. In parallel form, the present theorem says: every game form involving three or more outcomes that assures for all strict preferences the existence of a unique undominated outcome is dictatorial.

References

Arrow, K.J.: Social Choice and Individual Values. 2nd ed. New York 1963.

Banzhaf, J.F. III.: Weighted Voting Doesn't Work: A Mathematical Analysis. Rutgers Law Review **19**, 1965, 317–343.

Barry, B.: The Economic Approach to the Analysis of Power and Conflict. Government and Opposition **9**, 1974, 189–223.

– : Power: An Economic Analysis. Power and Political Theory. Ed. by B. Barry. London 1976, 67–101.

– : Is It Better to be Powerful or Lucky? Political Studies **28**, 1980, 183–194, and 338–352.

Brams, S.J., and *M. Lake*: Power and Satisfaction in a Representative Democracy. Game Theory and Political Science. Ed. by P.C. Ordeshook. New York 1978, 529–562.

Coleman, J.S.: Control of Collectivities and the Power of a Collectivity to Act. Social Choice. Ed. by B. Lieberman. New York 1971, 269–300.

Deegan, J. Jr., and *E.W. Packel*: A New Index of Power for Simple *n*-Person Games. International Journal of Game Theory **7**, 1979, 113–123.

Farquharson, R.: Theory of Voting. New Haven 1969.

Gibbard, A.: Manipulation of Voting Schemes: A General Result. Econometrica **41**, 1973, 587–601.

Goldman, A.I.: Toward a Theory of Social Power. Philosophical Studies **23**, 1972, 221–268.

March, J.G.: Measurement Concepts and the Theory of Influence. Journal of Politics **19**, 1957, 202–226.

– : The Power of Power. Varieties of Political Theory. Ed. by D. Easton. Englewood Cliffs, N.J., 1966, 39–70.

Miller, N.R.: 'Social Preference' and Game Theory: A Comment on 'The Dilemma of a Paretian Liberal'. Public Choice **30**, 1977, 23–28.

Rae, D.W.: Political Democracy as a Property of Political Institutions. American Political Science Review **65**, 1971, 111–119.

– : The Limits of Consensual Decision. American Political Science Review **69**, 1975, 1270–1297.

Schelling, T.C.: The Strategy of Conflict. Cambridge 1960.

Sen, A.K.: The Impossibility of a Paretian Liberal. Journal of Political Economy **78**, 1970, 152–157.

Shapley, L.S.: A Value for *n*-Person Games. Contributions to the Theory of Games, Vol. **II**. Ed. by H.W. Kuhn and A.W. Tucker. Princeton 1953, 307–317.

– : Simple Games: An Outline of the Descriptive Theory. Behavioral Science **7**, 1962, 59–66.

Shapley, L.S., and *M. Shubik*: A Method for Evaluating the Distribution of Power in a Committee System. American Political Science Review **48**, 1954, 787–792.

Straffin, P.D. Jr.: Power Indices in Politics. Modules in Applied Mathematics. Cornell University, 1976.

Tawney, R.H.: Equality. 4th ed., New York 1952.

Von Neumann, J., and *O. Morgenstern*: Theory of Games and Economic Behavior. 3rd ed., Princeton 1953.

Wilson, R.B.: A Revision of Arrow's General Possibility Theorem. Working Paper No. 181. Stanford Business School, February 1971.

– : The Game-Theoretic Structure of Arrow's General Possibility Theorem. Journal of Economic Theory **5**, 1972, 14–20.

Holler, M.J. (Ed.): Power, Voting, and Voting Power

A Philosophical View of Power

H. Kliemt, Mainz[1])

1. Introduction

There is a long philosophical tradition relating the concept of "power" to that of "causation". Especially before David Hume gave his celebrated analysis of causation philosophers often thought that the concept of power – then used in a specific non-social sense – was fundamental for the understanding of causation, and through common sense there still is to be found some of that anthropomorphic view.

When we watch two billard-balls clashing together, we intuitively believe that they "force" one another to alter their movement. Here we not only think of regular courses of events, but of "powers" bringing about a change, as we ourselves bring about changes in our surrounding. The common sense notion of this is based on the experience of an intentional use of one's "bodily powers", and this also holds for our notion of a "cause". We can make things happen by doing something; and, using the concept of the all-mighty God, some people even tend to identify every cause with an act of that actor who has the "power" to bring about anything he wants.

To modern scientists it seems to be the other way around, namely, that the understanding of causation is fundamental to the understanding of power. From this viewpoint "power" – in its social sense – is a kind of ability to exert purposefully a causal influence on social results or on other people. In short, "power" is the ability to influence social outcomes of any kind according to one's wants. At least this seems to be the minimal content of the concept of power, contained in all of the diverse usages of the term.

In this minimal concept of power, stress is laid on an ability to get what one "wants". Besides being "causal" and "purposeful", or to be more precise, "according to one's preferences" nothing is implied about the kind of influence that may be exerted. However, an exception is that the perspective is restricted to social outcomes. The latter term is used in a broad sense here to include the state of the world as well as the mind-state of other people, insofar as the preferences of those individuals who are able to exert influence on social outcomes are concerned.

The ability to overcome some resistance of other people is not excluded but it does not belong to the minimal content of "power" [in contrast to *Weber*, § 16]. Such a strong

[1]) I would like to express my gratitude to Mary Lise Rheault-Scherer for improving my English style and to Manfred J. Holler for many valuable suggestions.

concept of power would dangerously narrow our perspective of the diverse phenomena associated with our ability to influence social outcomes according to our preferences. Thinking of power as something intrinsically coercive leads either to an overly broad usage of "coercion", sometimes subsuming even propaganda and advertising under this term, or some techniques of influencing social outcomes, which in some contexts may be equivalent to coercive techniques of influence, are excluded from the outset. A further drawback of a narrow concept of power is, that it is not neutral with respect to some normative problems concerning "influence on social outcomes". But since the minimal concept of power will not exclude anything of importance, we can start with it regardless and return to the problem of coercion at a later point.

The ability to influence social outcomes has many "aspects" and can make use of different "techniques". From a purely theoretical point of view it is worthwhile to develop a conceptual framework of the minimal concept of power that does not exclude any of these aspects and techniques. In short, we attempt to develop an "all-including" concept of power. This, like a rough map, may bring some structure to a very complex field of varying questions, results, and opinions that center around the problem of power. Obviously such an all-including concept cannot comprise all information that we have thus far gained about power. At best it can be a scheme that indicates the appropriate place for each piece of information. However as a theoretical framework it may function as a map for purposes of theoretical orientation, showing how unique "partial" approaches are connected both to each other and to the problem of a valid measurement of power in general.

2. A Social Choice Framework of Power

Let $I := \mathbf{N}_n$ denote the $n > 1$ members of a collectivy or society and let $\mathcal{P}_i$, $i \in I$, denote the sets of all preference orderings of the individuals $i \in I$. As usual an n-tupel $(P_1, P_2, \ldots, P_i, \ldots, P_n) = P \in \mathcal{P} := \bigtimes_{i=1}^{n} \mathcal{P}_i$ is called a "(preference-)profile" [*Luce/Raiffa*, p. 332]. Now assume that there is a set of social outcomes $\mathcal{S}$ and a mapping F relating $\mathcal{P}$, the set of all profiles, and $\mathcal{S}$, the set of all outcomes, with $F(P) = S$, $P \in \mathcal{P}$, $S \in \mathcal{S}$. Finally let us define P^i as the complementary profile that is given by deleting P_i from a complete profile P and $\mathcal{P}^i$ as the set of all such profiles P^i which are, in this specific sense, "complementary" to P_i. If either P_i or P^i is held constant as a "parameter" this will be indicated by (P_i/P^i), where $(P_i/P^i) = P \in \mathcal{P}$ holds.

To state more precisely what it means to have influence on social outcomes according to one's preferences, we should look for a measure of similarity between preferences and social outcomes. Such a measure should indicate degrees of similarity between the individual preferences $P_i \in \mathcal{P}_i$ $(i \in I)$ and the social outcomes $S \in \mathcal{S}$ in a way that comes close to our intuitions about similarity between individual desires and overall social outcomes. In a way then individual satisfaction with social outcomes is also measured. This, as Straffin et al. point out in a contribution to this volume, has to be discerned from the measurement of power itself. On the other hand, measuring power seems to presuppose some assessment of *how* close social outcomes are to individual wants, and this, in turn, seems to demand for a measure of similarity between individual preferences and social outcomes. Without such a similarity measure we could only state that some influence has been exerted on social outcomes and we could not discriminate between different "intensities" of influence.

Avoiding similarity measures we could try to base the ascription of different amounts of power on the (incomplete) relation of set-inclusion between sets of social outcomes, as is done by Miller in another contribution to this volume. Indeed Miller's recourse on what he calls "game forms" [cf. also *Gibbard*, p. 587] serves the purposes of his analysis very well, namely proving a very interesting possibility result on "voting procedures" in the most general sense of the term. But within a truely general analysis of power it would be a bit dogmatic to eliminate individual preferences from the outset. This, however, is done by game forms, which take into account only the strategies that might be chosen by an individual according to his preferences. Because then, without the information contained in individual preference orders, the formation of equivalence classes in the process of measurement has to be based on the relation of set-inclusion between sets of social outcomes. But this makes the conditions for equivalence extremely severe and much more restrictive than need be from the point of view of common sense notions of "same power". We usually compare the power of individuals on a much wider basis than allowed for by the relation of set-inclusion among sets of social outcomes which are influenced by those individuals. Consequently, I think that in the most general framework of power measurement, individual preferences must play a role as well as the measures of similarity between individual preference orders and social outcomes.

But to say that preference orders and similarity measures have to be included into our *most general framework* does not imply that we can, in practice, solve the extremely difficult problems associated especially with the construction of valid similarity measures. To add them to our general map of the phenomenon of power serves merely the purpose of making entirely clear the character of simplifications that have to be made in any practical approach to the measurement of power.

For our present purposes it therefore suffices to make some heroic assumptions about individual preferences and similarity measures of preferences and social outcomes. First, it will be assumed subsequently that all individuals have preferences, which are orders (complete, transitive, and reflexive relations) of the same set of social outcomes $\mathcal{S}$. Especially therefore all P_i of all individuals are subrelations of $\mathcal{S} \times \mathcal{S}$, and the sets of all preference orders of every individual become identical, that is $\mathcal{P}_i = \mathcal{P}_j$ for all $i, j \in I$.

Second, it will be assumed that there are functions d_i: $\mathcal{S} \times \mathcal{P}_i \rightarrow \mathbf{R}_+$ with $d_i(S, P_i) = r \in \mathbf{R}_+$ which are sufficiently close approximations to the intuitive concept of "similarity between outcomes and wants" for each individual $i \in I$. It seems appropriate further on, that these measures of similarity are monotonic increasing with decreasing similarity – that is: increasing with increasing "distance".

We can now define for all $i \in I$

$$p(i, P^i) := \sum_{P_i \in \mathcal{P}_i} d_i (F(P_i/P^i), P_i)$$

$$:= \sum_{P_i \in \mathcal{P}_i} d_i (F(\bar{P}_1, \bar{P}_2, \ldots, P_i, \ldots, \bar{P}_n), P_i).$$

Assuming that all d-measures and F are known, we could actually compute the values of this sum or scheme of power measurement and thus have a "measure" or "index" for the influence of individual i on social results "at" P^i, the complementary profile which is held constant. This sum may be called a "local" measure of power because P^i is held constant, while the distances $d_i(F(P_i/P^i), P_i)$ between all possible preferences P_i of individual i and the collective or social outcomes $F(P_i/P^i) \in \mathcal{S}$ are totaled. Holding constant the complementary preferences of all other individuals, we try to find out what *would* happen if individual i had preferences P_i or P_i' or $P_i'' \in \mathcal{P}_i$ and so on. Via d_i and F the similarity between $P_i, P_i', P_i'' \in \mathcal{P}_i$ and social outcomes $S, S', S'' \in \mathcal{S}$ is measured and summed up at P^i. This states within the nomenclature of social choice theory that actual influence on social outcomes *may* depend crucially on the preferences of other people (the complementary profile P^i). The natural and social laws, as well as man-made rules all of which are comprised in F, operate differently on individual preferences P_i according to different complementary preferences from $\mathcal{P}^i$. This may clearly be the case even if there is no "feeling" of conflict or cooperation in the normal, social sense.

But we could also take a further step towards a "global" measure of power. We simply have to define $p(i) := \sum_{P^i \in \mathcal{P}^i} p(i, P^i)$. This can be interpreted as a measure of i's ability to influence social outcomes according to his preferences. This measure is "standardized" insofar as it is defined for all individuals on identical sets of preference orders. The standardization has been brought about by one of the "heroic" assumptions from above. But considering the dispositional character of power as an *ability* to exert some influence, it may be regarded as much less demanding than at first sight.

Though the assumption "$\mathcal{P}_i = \mathcal{P}_j$ for all $i, j \in I$" will rarely hold in reality, it may be useful or even necessary within a valid analysis of power. Such an analysis must take care of all ways an individual might try to influence social outcomes. Presumably no such way will be left out of account, if we fictitiously *ascribe* all preference orders to every individual and look how F operates on the different preference profiles. (No severe restriction of the set of possibilities is created when we consider only consistent preferences with the rational structure of an order.)

Counterfactual considerations of this type seem to be indispensable in any approach to power, in that power is an *ability* (or *potential*). For this reason values of the similarity measure which arise over counterfactual, entirely hypothetical preference profiles were included into the above summation. The concept of a counterfactual proposition seems to be necessary to an understanding of power. This seems to be quite clear because a person influences something causally only if without the person it did not happen. However counterfactual conditionals enter the stage in a different sense. Power as an *ability* depends on "what would happen if . . .", and thus has to be measured over a whole set of possibilities, most of which never will become reality. The problems associated with this cannot be avoided as long as power is taken to be what it really is – an ability, potential, or disposition. Dispositional concepts like "power" necessarily involve considerations of merely possible events, considerations about "what would happen if . . .". Any explication of everyday dispositional concepts must take care of this, as must any explication of power.

At this point our power concept seems to be adequate. On the other hand, however, including all preferences diminishes the value of a measurement of power for prognostical or explanatory purposes. If we attempt to explain or foresee the course of social affairs referring to different amounts of power held by participants of social interaction, we must face the problem that any global measure of power includes all possible profiles and thus (in a sense) all relevant circumstances.

Because of the dispositional character that we usually ascribe to power we cannot expect to get both an adequate explication of power and a high explanatory value of power (as a variable ranging over different values). This holds true at least for the explanation or forecast of specific social outcomes not depending on structural features of a whole situation. In measuring power we must already know, "what would happen if . . .", and therefore we cannot foresee or explain specific social outcomes on basis of a power measure.

Needed for purposes of forecast and explanation, is knowledge about the mapping F. If we know this mapping sufficiently well, we know what will happen under certain "circumstances" or why something actually happened. We cannot make use of power measures here because the measures of power themselves depend on F and not vice versa. A valid measure of power requires all the nomological knowledge that can be used for the purposes of forecasting and explaining. It cannot be part of this knowledge. Above all, "power" should not be regarded as a "cause" in the ordinary sense of that concept. A cause is one thing and an *ability* to exert a causal influence on social outcomes is quite another.

Paying attention to the dispositional character of power we should not be surprised or frustrated by the sometimes regretted fact that "power" has no "explanatory power" as far as specific outcomes are concerned. Nevertheless it may be of some value in explaining or foreseeing whole patterns of social processes. If for example $p(i) = 0$ would indicate that the individual i is a dictator, we should expect that his most preferred alternatives from $\mathcal{S}$ throughout time will be identical with the social outcomes. But we still do not know which kind of preferences the individual i will have, and consequently do not know the social outcomes that will have been determined by him.

3. The Problem of Adequacy

Power has been previously introduced as an ability or potential to get what one wants. This seems to be the basic and most central meaning in which the concept of power is used in everyday life. A sum of terms ranging over individual preferences has been introduced as an explicatory frame for this concept of power. (We are not interested in an "explanation of an event" but in the "explication of a concept".) Our purely conceptual analysis is intended to substitute a very vague concept with a more precise one. That is why we will speak of "explicandum" (the intuitive notion) and "explicatum" (the theoretical substitute) in the context of our explication. These terms are used in the specific sense appropriate to a *conceptual* analysis, which (regardless of similarity) should not be confused with an explanation [cf. *Alchourrón/Bulygin*, 7–9].

We may now ask whether or not our explication roughly fulfills the standard requirements of an adequate explication of a concept. There are four such requirements: precision of the explicatum, its simplicity, the similarity of explicandum and explicatum, and finally the fruitfulness of the result of the explication.

There is no doubt that a mathematical sum meets any reasonable standards of precision in social sciences. We could hardly do better in this realm. At least at first sight our sum seems to be "simple" too. But this is only so because of the "heroic assumptions" that have been made about measurability and nomological knowledge. Inevitably simplicity would get lost if we would go into the details of the d-measures and the mapping F, and summing over "all" conceivable preference orders becomes complicated because of the extremely large number of terms involved. So we might ask whether some assumptions may be weakened or avoided. But this in turn leads back to the question of similarity between explicandum and explicatum. Any gain in simplicity may involve some loss in similarity and vice versa.

It would be most desirable to find ways of simplification, which simultaneously involve gains in similarity, or at least minimize any losses in similarity, of explicandum and explicatum. Fortunately, some problems about the d-measures lead to such simplifications. Above all we would not accept a measurement of power in which individual differences in the *perception* of similarity between preferences and social outcomes would induce different values of the power measure. An individual $i \in I$ with a high "sensibility", who perceives more differences between his preferences and social outcomes or perceives them more strongly, should not be regarded as less powerful. This suggests that the d-measures, which already are all defined on the same set of ordered pairs, should also fulfill $d_i = d_j$ for all $i, j \in I$. The task of determining the d-measures then might be delegated to a detached, neutral observer who can ascribe values of similarity to all pairs from $S \times P_i$ for some $i \in I$ and thus construct a d-measure for all $i \in I$, or even a member $i \in I$ may accomplish this task if he considers the probability of being in any of the n individual positions in society as being equal. What emerges is a considerable simplification of our explicatum without loss and even some gain in similarity with the explicandum.

The last remarks strongly resemble some ideas of *Harsanyi* [1977, part 1] about the construction of intersubjectively meaningful utility measures. Generally, however, we should expect that the problem of commensurability is not so severe in the field of power measurement as it is when trying to compare utilities. Power is a much more „objective" quality then utility. Indeed we do *not* use the d-measures for assessing individual utility or satisfaction. They serve quite a different purpose, namely that of measuring how close social outcomes are to individual preferences "objectively", regardless of the individuals' perceptions of similarity and their feelings of satisfaction or dissatisfaction.

One could now ask, why, at all, indexed symbols for preference orders and d-measures have been introduced into our analysis if (as has been argued) the assumption of identity can be made throughout for all entities of both kinds within an adequate measurement of power. The answer is simply that for knowing the limits of a concept and for pointing out its specific character the ancient method of deriving it from a more general concept can be most appropriate. And this analogously holds for our general framework for the measurement of power. Presumably the best method of getting acquainted with it is its incorporation into even more general considerations. Fortunately these considerations bring about some gains of simplicity and similarity in the relation of explicandum and explicatum. But still our general framework is not a simple one and its fruitfulness has thus far not been shown. We now attempt to further simplify and also give some hints about the fruitfulness of the general framework of power measurement for purposes of theoretical orientation.

4. Adequate Simplifications

Our general framework for the measurement of power can be termed all-including because F is supposed to contain nomological information about any of the ways of influencing social outcomes that are open to members of the collectivity concerned. F is such an extremely complex mapping that it is impossible to specify it well enough for practical purposes. We always will have to restrict our analysis to certain aspects and techniques of the exertion of power, and consequently obtain only a partial specification of F.

Let us regard any ability of individual $i \in I$ to influence social outcomes through participation in specific institutional or organizational settings as an *aspect* of the power of i. These aspects arise within "families", "markets", "firms", "government institutions", "parliaments", "clubs" etc.

All of these aspects of power depend on socially accepted rules because the institutions or organizations (to which the aspects of power are restricted) are themselves defined by sets of socially accepted rules. These rules determine to what extent an individual may be able to influence social results according to a certain aspect of individual power, and which kinds of techniques the individual can use to that purpose.

Techniques of exerting influence on social results are well known too. Examples of such techniques are "fighting", "exchange", "arguing", "indoctrination", "propaganda", "proliferation of new ideas", "promising", "voting", "threatening", "announcing sanctions", "entering contracts" etc. Some of these techniques are closely related to specific aspects of power. But most of them are of importance to many different aspects of power and usually there will be an opportunity to make simultaneous use of some or many of them.

In most discussions about power we are only interested in a certain aspect of power under a certain technique, e.g., a committee and its voting procedure or a market and market exchange. Narrowing one's perspective in this way is a sound strategy when faced with so complex a phenomenon as power. Sometimes F even will be sufficiently specified by some *official* rules of interaction. This, for instance, may hold for the voting procedure of a certain voting body. For a partial analysis of power such a restriction on a certain aspect – the voting body – under a certain technique – the voting procedure – can be useful.

But still the counterfactual considerations necessary for a valid assessment of power would require very extensive summations over all preference orders. This calls for further simplification. It may be helpful here to review the aforementioned suggestion of Miller, who in his contribution to this book proposes to base the analysis of power on so-called "game forms". These game forms, for which he uses the symbol "f", are closely related to what has been denoted by "F" in the present article. But game forms are not mappings of preference profiles into social outcomes. Instead, they directly map strategies into sets of social outcomes. Preferences seem not to be taken into account.

But for many practical purposes the analysis of all strategies and their effect on social outcomes on basis of game forms, will be tantamount to explicitly analyzing all preference orders for all individuals. The set of all individual strategies comprises all individual chances, opportunities, abilities, or prerequesites for influencing social outcomes according to the aspect and technique of power exertion under consideration. Regardless of his preference order an individual $i \in I$ has to choose his (overt) acts from his set of strategies. Therefore this elegant elimination of preferences by simple neglect and the direct start with individual strategies may roughly fulfill the same functions as the hypothetical ascription of all preference orders over an identical set of alternatives to every individual. This in turn sheds a new light on some customary indices of power, in that now they may be regarded as implicitly taking care of all individual preferences.

The statement that customary indices (like that of Shapley and Shubik presented later in this volume) are of minor value in forecasting and explaining events seems to be true. But it presents no serious drawback. As far as customary indices measure what they purport to measure, they simply are not designed to fulfill the tasks of forecasting and explaining singular events. This reflects the dispositional character of power as an ability to influence social outcomes. It also shows how customary indices of power may fit into our general framework for the measurement of power.

We may now say that all of the combinatorics, upon which indices are usually based, aim at the characterization of necessary conditions for exerting a causal influence. Put very simply, such an index is a quotient between the number of "cases" an individual is in the position to exert influence – that someone is a "pivoter" for example – and the number of all "cases". This falls short of a measure for an aspect of power under a certain technique in the above-proposed sense. It is not concerned with preferences of individuals and the ability to influence social outcomes according to the preferences, but rather with necessary prerequesites of exerting such an influence. Nevertheless it seems to be quite plausible that a measure for the "amount" of such prerequesites is, or at least may be, rather closely related to a power measure based on a direct comparison of similarities between preferences and social outcomes.

At least the *chances* to exert a causal influence on social outcomes are "counted", and though we do not know the "weight" of such opportunities in terms of similarity and dissimilarity to individual preferences, we should expect that such a counting might be a rather accurate approximation to a "weighted" power measure, at least in some situations. Even the distinctions of global and local measures seem to apply to customary indices analogously – imagine for instance an ideologically restricted set of complementary profiles $\mathfrak{p}^i$ that an individual $i \in I$ has to take into account.

The practical advantage of further restricting the measurement of power to a measurement of prerequesites or strategies for the exertion of power which arise from *official rules* determining a certain aspect and technique of exerting power, stems from the entirely aprioristic character of the analysis possible at that time. Often a scrutiny of the official rules of an institution will be so simple that it allows for the actual computation of numerical values of a power measure. Such numerical values will induce an order between individuals or coalitions of individuals with respect to their "official" power, and this in turn might become especially useful in the context of some important questions of social ethics. In my opinion power indices may have fruitful applications in this field, and using our general framework for measuring power new light is shed on some central questions of normative ethics.

5. Power and Normative Ethics

People do not strive for utility or satisfaction directly but for certain activities that are useful or gratifying. This has been pointed out as a criticism of some hedonistic versions of utilitarianism. One objection is that identifying "utility" with "pleasure" inevitably leads to the conclusion that the goal of maximizing utility would be served best if we could implant an electrode into our heads giving us all the pleasure we could bear [cf., *Smart/Williams*, 18–21]. Even in the crude form, as presented here, the argument strongly suggests that we desire for certain activities – bringing about "utility" – and do not strive for utility or satisfaction directly.

Related considerations seem to apply to the whole process of social interaction. Within this process, above all, we want to have clearance for certain activities of our own choice. In other words, we want to have control over at least a certain "part" of the social outcome. Therefore the ability to influence social outcomes according to one's preferences becomes a primary good for everyone. Using our all-including concept which comprises "any ability to influence social outcomes according to one's preferences", power may even be regarded as the most fundamental resource that individuals, or coalitions of individuals, can possess. Measures of all-including power therefore, could be extremely helpful in the discussion of fundamental normative problems.

For reasons of complexity we do not have such measures, but merely approximations to measures of specific aspects under specific techniques. The usefulness of such approximations must be assessed case by case and will sometimes be quite apparent. Presumably this will hold if the aspect under consideration is central to individual need-satisfaction. Consequently an approximate index of an aspect of power under a certain technique may be important to the ethical evaluation of a society or its institutions. Whether a society, from a moral point of view, may be called a "good society" depends on the distribution of power among its members. If power is used in the sense as proposed here, it should be clear that "the" fundamental problems of distributional justice are problems of the just distribution of power over social outcomes. Also it should be clear that approaches to measure, at least approximately the different quantities of that "good", which are attached to different social positions, may be of some value to the normative assessment of any society, even if the analysis has to be partial or restricted.

Our concept of power may be of some theoretical value insofar as it affords a synthesis between two traditional views of freedom: one that looks at freedom as consisting of abstract rights to act in certain ways, and one that lays stress on the positive ability of doing that which one is allowed. If we think of power and different amounts of power as proposed here, both kinds of freedom are part of the ability to influence social outcomes. Their relative weight is "measured" on the same "scale" on the basis of similarity estimates (or their approximations) between individual wants and social outcomes under various hypothetical circumstances. Clearly, this has advantages. It can make common ethical approaches to a free *and* just society more homogeneous.

Take, for example, the most prominent modern theory of just distribution, John Rawls' *Theory of Justice*. We could interpret it now as a theory of just distribution of power. Power over social outcomes then becomes the sole object of the theory. The equal rights to basic (abstract) freedoms stated in the first of Rawls' two fundamental principles of justice [cf. *Rawls*, § 11] are granting an equal amount of "power", but this principle is now superceded by the second principle of justice requiring that differences in power are justified if and only if they are in favour of the least powerful. Rawls' theory would be compressed to his second principle of justice, if interpreted in terms of power over social outcomes. Whether this principle of a just distribution of power can be justified in itself is an additional question. Above all the meta-ethical problem of justifying the methods of deducing ethical judgements arises. Clearly such an intricate problem shall not be discussed here. But it might be of interest to observe that Rawls' own method of justification, which is based on a veil of ignorance behind which individuals, without knowing their "later" positions in society and their specific preferences, have to decide over the fundamental institutions of society comes very close to our counterfactual considerations within the realm of "power". In a sense, all possible preferences are included in both approaches.

That our general framework of power measurement, as well as its restrictions to customary indices, might prove fruitful for the discussion of central ethical questions becomes even more apparent if we turn to the theories of more sceptical ethical thinkers than Rawls, particularly the recent relativistic theory of rational compromise between partly conflicting individual interests proposed by the Oxford Philosopher *Mackie* [1977, 1978] forms a case in point. His hero David Hume, and Thomas Hobbes, also should not be omitted (an extremely helpful selection of their ideas on moral philosophy is contained in *Raphael* [1969]).

Mackie [1977, part I] offers some strong arguments against any ethical theory which is non-relativistic and based on objective normative standards to be discovered by reason and not to be invented by prudence. He argues that ethics is primarily concerned with prudential rules which can be shown to further the interests of everybody. The task of demonstrating this property of rules strongly resembles the task of finding out pareto-superior solutions in welfare economics. However, in the case of ethics we must think of more fundamental rules. Prohibitions of killing are typical examples of such rules, in that it seems to be in everybody's interest to accept and obey a norm, demanding not to kill other individuals, provided that other people do likewise. (This holds true if we ignore the prisoner's dilemma or assume that the dilemma is avoided because the situation has the character of a "supergame" of the kind that *Taylor* [1976, ch. 3] discusses.)

This kind of justification is almost identical with the legitimation Thomas Hobbes gave to, what he calls a "law of nature", which "is a precept, or general rule, found out by reason" [*Raphael*, 1969, I, p. 39]. Such precepts or rules are of a purely prudential character. They guide rational individuals as to how they should act to further their own good, or less egiosticly, how they can reach their goals. But from the point of view of Hobbes' theory, furthering one's own good is almost tantamount to a "struggle for power". His entire analysis is based on a very broad concept of power: "The powers of a man, (to take it universally,) is his present means, to obtain some future apparent good" [*Raphael*, 1969, I, p. 28], or according to our present terminology which Hobbes could easily have accepted, it "is his present means" or ability to influence some (future) social outcome according to his preferences. Hobbes thinks of any such ability in terms of power and consequently he regards the "appropriation" of power to be the central object of human interests [cf. *Raphael*, 1977, ch. IV]. So Hobbes puts "for a general inclination of all mankind, a perpetual and restless desire of power after power that ceaseth only in death" [*Raphael*, 1969, 32–33]. This inclination is the yardstick by which we must measure any norms or rules. Only those rules which further the "power" of everyone can be in the interest of everyone. Accidently this shows that power, according to Hobbes, cannot be "zero-sum".

Turning back to the modern theory of Mackie we can bring the Hobbesian tradition in social philosophy even one step closer to our general framework for power measurement. In a recent article *Mackie* [1978] asks whether there can be a "right-based moral theory", and subsequently answers this question affirmatively. He contends that besides goal-based moral theories like utilitarianism – based on the goal of reaching the "greatest happiness of the greatest number" – and duty-based moral codes – starting from e.g. the ten commandments – there could also be a right-based moral theory. He even goes a step further to claim that "there cannot be an acceptable moral theory that is not right-based" [*Mackie*, 1978, p. 355]. If this is correct and if, with *Mackie* [1978, p. 355], "we assume, that, . . . , what matters in human life is activity, but diverse activities determined by successive choices, we shall, . . . , take as central the right of persons progressively to choose how they shall live". With this assumption our all-including concept of power is easily adapted to the normative questions raised by a right-based moral theory: we can consider one side of the coin as the possession of power over social outcomes with the other side showing rights. In progressively choosing how we shall live, the ability of influencing social outcomes via certain activities is what we are interested in. Accordingly we demand from a "good" moral and legal order that it ascribes rights to us in a manner that allows for the greatest possible clearence and thus for the greatest individual ability to exert influence on social outcomes.

These suggestions are quite rough. They leave open such crucial questions as those concerning the distribution of rights and the concrete form of compromise between conflicting rights. But it becomes apparent that it is the power they confer on individuals that makes rights attractive and that we therefore could also speak of a power-based ethical theory (as far as influence on social outcomes arises from social norms) when we speak of a right-based one.

The considerations about the possibility of a right-based or power-based moral theory and the mutual relation of both approaches are of the meta-ethical variety. But as far as normative ethics itself is concerned power may also play a role which has not yet been mentioned. Namely, the analysis of the factual distribution of power may yield information about the feasibility of social institutions according to the meta-norm of "ought implies can". (An argument of this kind has even been used to give a "Hobbesian interpretation of the Rawlsian difference principle" [cf. *Buchanan*].

Yet there is something of central importance to some normative problems that seems to get entirely lost in our view of power. To have power according to a common opinion includes the ability to overcome some resistance on the side of other people. Nothing has been said about this though there are many discussions of power that center around this topic (especially approaches inspired by Max Weber). The normatively relevant "conflict" between "power" and "free choice" has been neglected. But quite often we think that power has been "applied" to overcome some resistance on the side of other people and we are accustomed to thinking of this as something illegitimate in many situations.

Undoubtedly there are important problems about kinds of influence on social outcomes that are somehow coercive. However, it seems inadequate to regard power as something intrinsically coercive. The everyday nomenclature of "power" is not restricted to certain coercive techniques. We "feel" for example, that in a process of free exchange there are different degrees of control over the process, though all contracts in the process are entered completely freely. According to different degrees of control over the process and different amounts of resources that are controlled by the participants in the exchange, we tend to ascribe different amounts of power to different participants. Nevertheless it would seem inappropriate to say that the exchange process itself is coercive under these conditions. Power over social outcomes *may* include techniques of exerting "power over someone" or coercion. But if we ascribe a coercive character to power itself and restrict "power" to "power over someone" we seem to regard power to be in itself a technique. We can certainly use the concept of power this way, but looking at the diverse forms of influencing other people more or less strongly it would seem a bit arbitrary to think of a subclass of them as being an exertion of power, while the others are not, and regard the whole subclass as one specific technique. Another, perhaps more serious objection against a power concept of this kind, is that it would not be faithful to the common conviction that power is an ability. Still we could say that it is only that part of the ability to influence social results according to one's preferences, that is based on techniques which can be coercive to other people. But this again would seem arbitrary, because the central feature of power is, that it includes an ability to get what one wants regardless of the specific techniques that can be applied to that purpose. In my opinion, the most "natural" approach therefore would be, to exclude no aspect or technique from the analysis and look at power from an all-including point of view.

6. Conclusion

I do not claim that the explication of "power" proposed here is a faithful reconstruction of all facets of that concept. But I believe that it might come close to some essential features of power and show how they can be "brought on the same map". On this map we have power, aspects of power, and techniques of the exertion of power; or in other words, the ability to influence social outcomes according to one's preferences, the institutions in which the influence can be exerted, and the different forms of influence. To put contourlines on the map we must remember the importance of counterfactual considerations to any measurement of power. Most of the time we will have only the rough methods of customary indices of power as tools applicable in practice. However these rough methods may be good approximations to a measurement of certain aspects of power in certain contexts. Though such an analysis from the point of view of an "all-including" concept of power (which even as a general frame is far from being all-including in leaving out of account the more dynamic aspects of power) could be regarded as rather partial and restricted, it may prove useful in specific circumstances and discussions including those of the normative variety.

References

Alchourrón, C.E., and *E. Bulygin*: Normative Systems. Wien–New York 1971.
Buchanan, J.M.: A Hobbesian Interpretation of the Rawlsian Difference Principle. Kyklos, 1976, p. 5ff.
Gibbard, A.: Manipulation of Voting Schemes: A General Result. Econometrica, 1973, p. 587ff.
Harsanyi, J.C.: Rational Behaviour and Bargaining Equilibrium in Games and Social Situations. Cambridge, Mass., 1977.
Luce, R.D., and *H. Raiffa*: Games and Decisions. New York 1957.
Mackie, J.L.: Ethics. Harmondsworth 1977.
– : Can There be a Right-Based Moral Theory? Midwest Studies in Philosophy, 1978, p. 350ff.
Raphael, D.D. (ed.): British Moralists 1650–1800 (I, II). Oxford 1969.
– : Hobbes. Morals and Politics. London 1977.
Rawls, J.: A Theory of Justice. Cambridge, Mass., 1971.
Smart, J.J.C., and *B. Williams*: Utilitarianism. For and Against. Cambridge, Mass., 1973.
Taylor, M.: Anarchy and Cooperation. New York 1976.
Weber, M.: Wirtschaft und Gesellschaft. 5th Edition. Tübingen 1972.

Holler, M.J. (Ed.): Power, Voting, and Voting Power ©Physica-Verlag, Würzburg (Germany) 1981

Power and Profit in Hierarchical Organizations[1])

D.C. Mueller, College Park

1. Introduction

The development of economics as a social science has rested on two postulates concerning human behavior: individuals act out of self interest, and are rational. Thus consumers are assumed to maximize their utility; entrepreneurs maximize profit. The economy is driven by self interest, the corporation by the profit motive.

Recently the postulates of rationality and self interest have been extended to the study of political science through the development of the public choice area. In one of the pioneering works in this area *Downs* [1957] postulated that candidates pursued their self-interest by trying to maximize the number of votes they obtained. Although vote maximization has proved to be a plausible and useful assumption to explain candidate behavior, it clearly cannot explain all political behavior, since many politicans are not elected and/or cannot be reelected. In particular, this postulate cannot explain bureaucratic behavior.

The classic analysis of bureaucracy is, of course, *Weber's* [1947], and the natural objective for the bureaucrat, following Weber, would be power. The large corporation is run by managers seeking profit; the public bureaucracies by individuals hunting for power. Economic man pursues profit; political man power.

In the pages which follow I attempt to develop an analogy between power and profit, and use it to analyse the objectives and conflicts that arise in hierarchical organizations. Since the literatures on both of these subjects are long and tortuous, I make only selective reference to each. Let us begin with power.

2. The Concept of Power

At the most intuitive level the world "power" connotes the ability or capacity to do something [*Wagner*, 3–4]. But "something" can stand for a variety of objects, each of which leads to a different conception of power. Physical power is the ability to apply force. Economic power the capacity to purchase goods, and so on. Political power must

---

[1]) Published in *Statsvetenskaplig Tidskrift*, No. 5, The Arne Ryde Symposium on Economic Theories of Institutions, Lars Jonung and Ingemar Stahl (eds.), 1981.

be defined as the ability to achieve certain ends through a political process. In this essay we shall take a rather broad view of the latter considering virtually any collective decision making body or organization from a committee to a bureaucracy as being governed by some form of political process. To observe the exertion of political power it is necessary that at least some participants in the political process have conflicting goals. If all members of a committee favor the same alternative as A, and this alternative is chosen we cannot say that A has exercised power. If only A favors an alternative and it is chosen, A has political power.

Political power can arise directly from the rules by which the political process operates. These rules might simply grant A a dictatorial right. Under most rules, the committee chairman has more capacity to influence the outcome than other members, yet he need not be the most powerful member of the committee. What interests us here is not the direct capacity to influence an outcome granted by the rules, but the differing capacities individuals have to influence a collective decision, independent of the set of rules.

Russell [1938] listed three ways in which an individual can exert influence in a political context (1) by direct physical power, e.g., imprisonment or death, (2) by offering rewards and punishments, and (3) by exerting influence on opinion through the use of education and propaganda. The first two are obviously closely related to procedural power. The dictator may have authority to imprison or execute subordinates, they most certainly will not have similar legal authority over him. As *Cartwright* has observed, "Of the many possible means of influence, persuasion is commonly advocated as most suited to a democratic, or rational, social system" [1965, p. 139]. Thus, the third of Russell's sources of influence is of most interest to us here. On the surface, it also seems to come closest to our description of power. For education, propaganda, and persuasion are all forms of information. As we shall attempt to demonstrate, political power, other than of a procedural kind, is possessed by those who have information. Uncertainty creates the potential to exercise power, information provides the capacity to do so.

Although information will provide the most power in a political process governed by persuasion, it is not limited to these most democratic forms of political interaction. To illustrate the generality of the uncertainty-information-power nexus we first examine a situation that seems to come closest to Russell's first source of influence, pure physical power. Consider the classic power struggle encapsulated by the demand "your money or your life." G has a loaded gun which he aims at W and demands that W give his loaded wallet over to G. Here we have what appears to be the simplest case of power by force with information playing no visible role. Let us examine it more closely. W must choose whether to hand over his wallet or not. He must, therefore, predict what G will do should he not hand it over and if he does. Suppose W *knows* that G will not shoot in either event, G is then without any power. W keeps his wallet and G does not shoot. Suppose W knows G will shoot in either event. Again G is without power, i.e., the ability to command, since W knows the wallet now belongs to G, and it is simply up to W to decide whether he wants to give it to G and then be shot, or let him take it after W is dead. The same holds true for the case when G will shoot if he does not get the wallet, but will not shoot if he gets it. If W knows this with certainty, suppose G is a programmed robot, G is without any real power to command. The choice is W's, whether to live without his wallet or die with it, and G merely carries out his programmed action following the real decision by *W*. The only situation in which *G* can actually command *W* to do something against his will, is when *W* does not know what *G* will do following *W*'s action. *W* might then give *G* the wallet when *G* would not have shot him anyway. It is in this situation, and really only in this situation, that *G* can be said to be exercising political power over *W*, as political power is typically defined [e.g., *Dahl*, p. 80; *Simon*, 1953]. If *G* would not shoot *W* if *W* failed to give him the wallet, and yet he can get *W* to give him the wallet, he has succeeded to get *W* to do something he would not otherwise have done. *G* has done so, however, not solely because he has a gun, but because *W* is uncertain about what *G* will do with the gun. It is not the presence of the gun per se, but the uncertainty that accompanies it that gives *G* power. In the absence of the gun, *G* does not have power over *W* because *W* is not worried that *G* will kill him. If *G* gets a gun, he will have power over *W*, because, or more precisely if and only if, *W* is uncertain about what *G* will do with it. *G* has power because he has the information about what he will do and *W* does not.

In this example, the gun plays the role of procedural power and clearly it places *G* in a better position to achieve his goals than *W*. But it alone does not determine the outcome so long as there is uncertainty on the part of the individuals to the other's reactions. It is this uncertainty that gives *G* power over *W*, and can give *W* some power over *G*.

The importance of uncertainty and information can be further demonstrated by slightly changing the example. Suppose that *W* has buried the wallet someplace in his yard and only he knows the location. Now there is considerable uncertainty on both sides: *W* not knowing whether he will get shot, *G* not knowing the location of the wallet. Given the increase in uncertainty and relevant information in the hands of *W* his power should be enhanced. He can now quite possibly force *G* to unload or throw away his gun in exchange for information on the wallet's location. Indeed, he might get off with both his life and his wallet. Even though the advantage of force still lies on the side of *G*, the increase in *W*'s possession of relevant information gives him the potential for exercising considerably more power over *G*.

As a final extreme example, assume *G* and *W* both have wallets and known programmed response patterns in the event that one has a gun. A gun is given to one on a flip of a coin. Given the programmed reactions of each, no real power is meted out via the coin flip, although the flip will affect the lives and/or wealth of *W* and *G*. What power that exists in the situation is with the coin flipper, or a fate which knows the outcome of the flip.

Returning to Russell's list of sources of power, we can see that it is the uncertainty that surrounds a dictator's use of physical power, or a supervisor's issuance of rewards and punishments that allows them to control their subordinates. If *B* knows with certainty that *A* will give him a reward if *B* does *X*, the rules require it, then *B* in carrying out *X* exercises as much power over *A* as *A* does over *B*. In a bureaucracy in which no uncertainty existed, lines of authority might exist, but no real power would accompany authority. All employees would know all of the possible events that might occur and all could predict the eventual outcomes or decisions that would follow each. Employee grievance procedures would be completely codified and both the supervisor's and the employee's reaction to any situation would be perfectly predictable. In a world of complete certainty, all individuals are essentially acting out a part, "going by the rules", and those at the top of the bureaucracies are as devoid of discretionary power as those at the bottom. All power is purely procedural [*Simon*, 1953, p. 72].

This type of situation comes close to the conditions existing in the French Monopoly *Michel Crozier* described in *The Bureaucratic Phenomenon* [1964]. As Crozier depicts it the monopoly does operate in a world of certainty – with one exception – the machines sometimes break down. This places the women operating the machines completely under the power of the mechanics responsible for repairing them, since the women have a quota of output for each day and must work harder to make up for any down time. More interestingly, the supervisors who nominally have more authority also have less power than the mechanics. Since the mechanics know how to repair the machines, and the supervisors do not, the supervisors are unable to exert any real control over the mechanics [*Crozier*, 98–111].

It is instructive to note the tactics used by the mechanics to preserve their power. The operators were severely scolded for "tinkering" with their machines in an effort to keep them going or repair them. Only, the mechanics knew how to repair the machines; each machine was different and just how it needed to be fixed was known only to the mechanics; repairing them was an art not a science. When clashes arose between the mechanics and the supervisors it was over whether the latter could, on occasion, work at repairing the machines. The supervisors were further hampered in this endeavor by the continual "mysterious" disappearance of machine blue prints from the factory. The mechanics always worked without the aid of blue prints.

It is easy to extend Crozier's description of the tactics employed by the mechanics to maintain their control of information and power to other groups of experts. One of the first things any group does to protect its position is to develop a set of terms of jargon that makes much of what it does inaccessible to outsiders. This can be further butressed by perfecting techniques of analysis so complicated that outsiders cannot follow them. This done it becomes extremely difficult for those outside the group to take away or evaluate the information possessed by the expert. Examples of this behavior are obvious. Scientists and engineers perhaps come first to mind. In these professions the nonspecialist is clearly at a loss to understand and exercise effective control over the professions. Even within the disciplines the tendency is for information boundaries to arise giving groups power vis-à-vis their colleagues. Thus, the inability of one branch of physics to evaluate the work of another strengthens the position of the inaccessible branch in gathering R&D funds, grants, department positions, or what have you on the basis of its own criteria. The "pecking order" both across and within disciplines tends to be from "hard" to "soft" science on the grounds that the more theoretical or mathematically oriented hard scientists can or could always understand and evaluate the "soft stuff", while the reverse is not necessarily true. The counter argument by the more applied is a rather weak claim of expertise because the theorists are not really familiar with the data or the institutions.

Other professions attempt to create and maintain power in the same way. Consider law. Here is a profession whose language could be, and once was, accessible to the average citizen. Over time, however, the profession has so complicated the language and procedures used in the judicial system that it is nearly impossible for an outsider to participate without hiring a lawyer. The medical profession follows a similar strategy, with the practice of writing prescriptions in Latin being an interesting illustration.

Lacking Latin or mathematics to conceal information and preserve their power, individuals typically resort to the more blatant device of secrecy. Examples ranging from the fraternal "secret handshake" to the classification procedures of the Pentagon and CIA come easily to mind. In each case the purpose is the same, to protect the insider's position by keeping relevant information from the outsider. Although the purported purpose for classifying many documents is to preserve national security by keeping them out of the hands of the nation's enemies, the true, intended "outsiders" often appear to be our own citizens, and the "insiders" whose security is being protected, government bureaucrats.[2])

Crozier further butresses the hypothesis that uncertainty is the source of power by examining the seemingly anomalous preference for technological change by the directors of the Industrial Monopoly and the resistence to this change by the technical engineers. On the basis of social background and status the technical engineers should be more liberal and promote technological change, while the more conservative backgrounds of the directors should lead them to resist it. Decisions to institute changes in technique are made by the directors, however. In the absence of these changes, decisions are sufficiently routine that effective control lies with the engineers. Thus, the only time that the directors can effectively demonstrate their authority is when they initiate changes in plant technique. Uncertainty is then introduced, with the top directors in possession of the relevant information on the new technique. Following the change, uncertainty gradually diminishes, routine returns, and power passes down to the lower levels, until the directors are forced to introduce another change in technique [*Crozier*, 155–156].

Again, one can easily think of additional illustrations of the importance of information in establishing a group's power. Perhaps, the best one is that of the military. Here one has a situation in which uncertainty, over a weapon's effectiveness, levels of preparation, offensive and defensive strategies, etc. is endemic to the activity. This gives the military a strong advantage over other federal bureaucracies in obtaining funds from both Congress and the Executive Branch. The development of an impenetrateable jargon, classification of data and so forth, all serve to maintain this uncertainty and strengthen the power of the leadership of the military hierarchy who have or claim to have the relevant information. The otherwise surprising preference of one of the oldest and most conservative bureaucracies, the military, for new and more sophisticated weapons systems, becomes understandable by analogy with the case studied by Crozier.[3])

These examples hopefully illustrate the role uncertainty and information play in creating and distributing power in a bureaucracy. We shall return to an examination of bureaucratic power, after investigating the role information and uncertainty play in generating economic profit.

---

[2]) The importance of secrecy to creating and preserving political power has been emphasized by *Rourke* [1961, 1969]. [See, also *Mills; Weber*].

[3]) See *Amacher/Tollison/Willett* [1976], and *Rourke* [1969, 55–58]. The military are one of the three major groups making up *Mills'* [1956] power elite. Mills also lays great emphasis on the importance of secrecy in maintaining power.

3. Profit

Consider a world of perfect certainty. All tastes and technologies are known. Labor, land and capital are combined to produce goods and services. Competition ensures that the prices on all goods and services are driven to the point where they just cover factor input costs. There is no residual left for the entrepreneur (other than a normal compensation for whatever labor services he provided), since there is nothing that requires entrepreneurial skill in a world of perfect certainty.

When uncertainty exists revenues and costs are not always equal. Unexpected changes in tastes, weather, competing technologies and so on produce changes in demand and cost schedules that leave positive or negative "residuals" between total revenues and costs. These revenues accrue to those who assume the responsibility for organizing the company, the entrepreneurs, and are defined as the profits of the firm.[4])

With uncertainty present, the possibility of "making" profits by correctly anticipating or inducing changes in tastes and technologies arises. The entrepreneur who knows what style of shoes will sell next spring, who knows that a certain technology will reduce costs, and so on, earns profits. Those who do not know these things or make mistakes earn losses. Entrepreneurial activity thus consists of gathering and evaluating information on what will sell, and what will reduce costs. As long as one entrepreneur has information on what will sell, and others do not (are uncertain) he can earn a profit. Information on consumer tastes and innovations thus provides a firm with the ability to earn more than other firms in the market – with power over the market. This power dissipates as others acquire information about consumer tastes, and imitate the innovations. As uncertainty vanishes so do profits. The "perennial gale of destruction" described by Joseph Schumpeter thus consists of a process of gathering or creating new information which produces surpluses for those who have it, but soon is obtained by all eliminating profits and setting the stage for a new finding, a new wave of profits and imitation, and so on.[5])

While Knight, Schumpeter, and Coase stressed the importance of information not held by "outsiders" to the firm in generating profit residuals, more recently *Alchian/Demsetz* [1972], and *Williamson* [1975] have emphasized the importance of the distribution of information inside the firm to the generation and sharing of the residual. Alchian/Demsetz emphasize the team aspects of production within a firm. These can perhaps be best illustrated by considering production a positive sum game of a prisoner's dilemma variety. The cooperative strategy can be interpreted as carrying out some previously agreed to set of tasks at a given level of care and effort. The noncooperative strategy is "shirking" on some of these tasks. All members of a team are better off if all adopt the cooperative strate-

[4]) The most extensive development of the uncertainty based theory of profit is by *Knight* [1921].

[5]) Schumpeter did not speak of information but of innovations. They amount to the same thing, however. For an innovation is nothing more than an idea that a new product (invention), or process, or organizational structure will produce a profit. And it is successful only to the extent that the idea (information) is a good one. *Schumpeter's* theory is best developed in *A Theory of Economic Development* [1934].

Other important theories of the firm and of profit can also be related to information of a specific kind. Thus, *Coase* stresses information about what kinds of activities are more efficiently handled within the firm than in the market [1937]. For further discussion see *Mueller* [1976].

gy than if all do not, but some may still be tempted into shirking if they think they can do so without affecting the choice of strategy by other members of the team. In a small, productive team each member may be able to observe and monitor the behavior of the other members. In a large team this will be inefficient, however. A specialist at monitoring must be chosen. To ensure that this monitor does not in turn shirk he must be given the claim to the residual profit of the firm. Thus, in the Alchian-Demsetz theory, profit is also information-uncertainty related. The potential for profit exists in the behavorial uncertainties surrounding the prisoner's dilemma-teamwork production relationship. The profits accrue to the manager-monitors who gather information on other members of the team and ensure that they do not engage in shirking.

4. Power, Profit, and the Goals of the Organization

Uncertainty creates the potential for gains and losses, for correct decisions and mistakes. He who has the knowledge or information or intuition to make the correct decisions obtains power. This is true both within and outside of organizations. The individual who chooses the 'right' career, buys the 'right' piece of property, backs the 'right' candidate, plants at the 'right' time of year, and so on is ahead of those making the wrong choices. The general principle, then, is that uncertainty creates power for those having the information to make correct decisions in the face of the uncertainty. In the corporation, where the pursuit of profit is an accepted goal, this power is frequently monetarized in the form of high salaries, stock options, insider trading gains by the managers and so on.[6]) In the nonprofit organization or the public bureaucracy power must more often be used to obtain nonpecuniary goals: security, leisure, status, and prestige [see, e.g., *Downs* 1967]. The contrast should not be overdrawn, however. Corporate managers are interested in prestige, security and other nonpecuniary goals. And a number of writers have argued that the corporate manager's objectives are a package of pecuniary and nonpecuniary goals rather than the maximization of profits [see, e.g., *Baumol; Marris; Williamson,* 1964; *Galbraith*]. Indeed, since reported profits are by custom and to some extent law the property of the stockholders, managers must exercise their claim on the firm's residual in such a way so that it appears as a legitimate operating cost. Their options for doing so in a way that produces direct pecuniary benefits are limited, so that managers are almost forced to accept part of their share of profits in a nonpecuniary form. On the other side, there are a variety of possibilities by which public officials can gain financially from their position including the use of insider information, the receipt of gifts, bribes, kickbacks, etc.

The analogous role information and uncertainty play in the profit-oriented corporation and the nonprofit bureaucracy suggests that the behavior of individuals in these organizations, managers and bureaucrats, should in many ways be similar.[7]) Both will seek

[6]) On the link between managerial salaries and profits see *Lewellen/Huntsman* [1970] and *Masson* [1971]. On insider trading see *Manne* [1966].

[7]) Several writers have sought an analogue for power in the economic sphere. *Blau* [1964] compares the Knightian entrepreneur's receipt of profit to the political leader's receipt of power as a reward for making risky decisions, but does not develop the analogy. *Parsons* [1963] compares power to money.

to acquire information – power. Where they will differ, if at all, will be in how they utilize whatever power they possess to achieve their own personal pecuniary and nonpecuniary goals. We can thus expect managers and workers in industrial enterprises to adopt strategems similar to those Crozier describes in the two French bureaucracies of creating self-serving uncertainty, maintaining secrecy regarding information in one's possession, and so on.

The monitoring function managers serve in a teamwork organization suggests another strategy they might employ to increase their power. Recall that the need for monitor-specialists arises essentially because of the free-rider problem created by the prisoner's dilemma nature of teamwork production. The free-rider problem is worse, the larger the team. Thus, the need for monitor-managers and the importance of the information they possess will increase the larger the size of their organization.

Several writers have posited size or growth in size as goals of corporate managers [*Baumol; Marris*]. The reasons given are typically the correlation between organizational size and managerial salaries, and the nonpecuniary rewards from managing a large, growing company. Our analysis suggests an additional reason why managers pursue size and growth. Growth can be expected to create uncertainty about the size of the residual profit and thus increase the value of the information managers gather. Increasing size worsens the free-rider problem again increasing the value of the monitor-managers' information. In short, the power of managers within the corporation should increase with size and growth. Managers should favor size and growth as corporate objectives, since they increase their power to achieve any other more direct personal goal the managers have.

The major constraint on management's claims on the profit-residual is the threat of outside takeover [*Marris; Manne; Alchian/Demsetz*]. The free-rider problem keeps the average stockholder from carefully monitoring managers, but the voting rights which accompany common shares provide incentives for outside entrepreneurs to buy out large blocks of shares and takeover the company transferring the incumbent management's share of profits to itself. To do so, however, the potential takeover-raider needs to have information on the profit he can earn from a successful takeover. This is information that is possessed and for obvious reasons guarded by the incumbent managers. Here again size and more specifically diversification can increase the power of managers vis-à-vis potential takeover raiders by increasing the volume and complexity of the information required to evaluate the potential gains from a takeover raid. *Singh* [1971] has presented empirical evidence that the probability of a company's being taken over, given its profitability, does decrease significantly with its size.[8]) Now size should not be an impediment to a takeover in a perfect capital market. But the capital market cannot operate perfectly if these are asymmetries in the distribution of the relevant information [*Stigler*]. Such asymmetries are precisely what we can expect managers to seek and create to protect their positions, and these would appear to correlate positively with size and growth.

---

[8]) *Kuehn* [1975] and *Smiley* [1976] present additional evidence regarding the slack in the takeover mechanism. Smiley's results are particularly interesting. He found that a successfully takenover firm had fallen to 50 percent of its potential value by the time of its takeover, but that only 30 percent of this loss appeared to be recoverable following the takeover. Thus, as one might expect, the managers exercised their claim on the company's profits in such a way as to limit the gains from successful takeover to a fraction of their potential magnitude.

Jensen/Meckling [1976] have developed a model of the managerial firm in which managers do have some discretion to pursue their own goals, but are induced to reveal information about their company's performance to raise capital. The predictions of their model would thus seem to be at odds with ours, and also, fortunately, with reality. The Securities and Exchange Commission was founded following the Great Crash of 1929, which revealed that many corporate managers had concealed information from investors, which furthered managerial interests at the expense of bond and stockholders. Since its inception the SEC has fought an on-and-off battle with corporations to induce their managers to reveal more information to which they are privy. The most recent round of this battle has been over the reporting of sales, profit and similar operating data by corporate division by large diversified corporations. This is precisely the kind of information one would not expect managers to reveal if they feared a takeover attempt, of course. Indeed, the reason why the company has diversified may be to conceal it. The situation in Europe is, if anything, worse.

The reason why corporations do not have to reveal information of this type to raise capital, as Jensen/Meckling predict, is that most corporations are not heavily dependent on the external capital market for investment funds. This is particularly true of large, mature companies. Thus, reliance on internal fund flows as a source of investment capital is complementary to a management's goals of preserving its power vis-à-vis the other factor owners.[9])

Once again, analogous arguments can be extended to regulated firms, nonprofit organizations, and government bureaucracies. *Niskanen* [1971] develops his model of bureaucracy on the assumption that bureaucrats are self-interested individuals, who maximize the size of their budget. Niskanen gives little justification for the latter behavioral assumption. The theory presented here helps to explain why this is a plausible goal and in so doing links Niskanen's theory to the traditional literature on bureaucracy extending back to Weber. Increasing the size and complexity of a bureaucracy should increase the insider-bureaucrat's control over information relative to that of its monitors, thus increasing the bureaucrat's power to achieve his personal goals, whatever they might be.

5. Hierarchy, Power, and the Distribution of Profits[10])

The traditional way of dealing with situations of uncertainty, in which one party may be able to take advantage of another, is for the parties to form a contract specifying the rights and obligations of each under the various contingencies that may arise as time enfolds and the uncertainties disappear. Should conflict at some point arise, the parties to the contract can then appeal to an impartial third party to arbitrate their claims as established and guaranteed under the contract. Given the uncertainties and potential for conflict over the distribution of residual share that exist in the firm, one would naturally expect the members of this team to resort to the use of contract to protect their claims to

---

9) For further discussion of the relation between the managerial theory of the firm and internal investment theories see *Grabowski/Mueller* [1972]. On the importance of firm maturity to the stockholder/manager conflict see *Mueller* [1972] and *Grabowski/Mueller* [1975].

10) This section draws in part on *FitzRoy/Mueller* [1978/79].

the residual share. The major factor owners of the firm are, of course, joined in a form of contractual relationship. Let us see therefore how information and uncertainty are handled under these contracts.

The contract between the common shareholders and the corporation is decidedly open-ended. Although the profits of the company figuratively belong to the stockholders, the determination of what gets reported as profits is made by the management, and the determination of what fraction of those profits that are reported gets paid as dividends is made by the board of directors. In principle, this latter body is supposed to serve as an impartial third party between management and stockholders to ensure that management does not abuse its insider's position at the expense of the stockholders. In practice it is typically under management control with management occupying several positions on the board, and undoubtedly wielding more power than its numbers suggest due to the greater amount of information its representatives possess about company operations. Indeed, since the board is heavily dependent on the management for information it must be largely under management's control. This fact is revealed in the following quote from the Board of Directors of the Pennsylvania Railroad made more than 100 years ago, and some 50 years before *Berle/Means* [1932]. "The present form or organization (part-time directors and full-time officers) makes practical ciphers of the Directors, and this is from no deliberate intention, but from the very necessities of the case." After presenting this quote *Chandler* went on to observe that, "Once a large business had reached a size that required the services of several full-time administrators, the board and the stockholders had only a negative or *veto* power on the government of their enterprise and on the allocation of its resources. They could say no, but they had neither the information nor the awareness of the company's situation to propose realistic alternative courses of action," [1962, p. 313].

Thus, the stockholder's contract with corporate management does not offer much protection against the management's power to claim a larger fraction of profits than was understood at the time both became parties to the contract. The stockholder's major means of controlling management remains his right to sell his shares, or refuse to buy. We are thus back to the threat of takeover, and the discipline of the capital market. It should be stressed that either of these would suffice if the management could not withhold information from the market. *Solow* [1971] has shown that the capital market can discipline a growth-maximizing management to maximize stockholder welfare by withholding capital from the company at the time of its inception. To do this, however, the market must know at the time the company is born what its growth and investment pattern will be throughout its entire life. Armed with this amount of information the capital market has full control (power) over management. But obviously the uncertainties which surround a company's future at its birth allow no such discipline. As time passes, and the future becomes the present, information as to how the various uncertainties facing the company are being resolved accrues asymmetrically to management and the stockholders. This unbalanced accumulation of information shifts the balance of power in favor of management and allows it to interpret the terms of the stockholder-management contract in a way which is most favorable to the latter.

As *Commons* once observed the wage contract typically "is not a contract, it is a continuing implied *renewal* of contracts at every minute and hour based on the continuance of . . . satisfactory service . . . and compensation" [1924, p. 285]. The chief and often only explicit stipulation of the contract is that the employee agrees to accept authority within some limits for a certain wage [*Simon*, 1957]. Thus, the labor contract is open-ended with respect to both time and duties. Given that labor and management participate in a teamwork activity, the fruits of their participation will appear as a joint product the division of which is in part arbitrary. The potential thus exists for conflict between worker and management over how the jointly produced residual is divided (wages), and how the vague limits to managerial authority are determined in practice.

The nature and complexity of the employment relationship requires that the bulk of the terms of this contract remain vague and implicit. Indeed, as *Williamson* [1975] has emphasized, implicit contracts are the distinguishing feature of hierarchial organizations. But with the bulk of the terms of the contract implicit, they cannot be arbitrated by impartial third parties. Instead, one of the parties to the contract itself must arbitrate the contract, and this task naturally falls to management given its role of information gatherer and monitor. But, this also gives management great latitude to interpret (arbitrate) the contract in ways most advantageous to itself.

The worker's ability to ensure his share of the company's joint product comes not from his ability to enforce the terms of contract on an ongoing basis, but, in much the same way as with stockholders, in his right to quit or not join the company. Economists often assume this right suffices. *Alchian/Demsetz* [1972, p. 777], for example, compare the worker-manager relationship to the customer-grocer relationship. But labor is seldom as mobile as this analogy suggests. Softness in the labor market, the accumulation of industry or firm specific skills, or merely the inertia residence in a given community builds up over time, produce rents that can be appropriated by management. The only way for labor to protect itself from this form of exploitation is to demand more explicit contracts amenable to third party arbitration.

It is interesting to note in this regard that employment contracts in the public sector have typically been much more specific and protective of employee rights than they have been in the private sector. Why this should be so is not clear. Public sector employees would not appear to be inherently less mobile, as a group, than private sector employees, although in some areas the government is in a monopsonist position, and conceivably could exploit employees with "firm" specific human capital. Whatever the explanation, it is interesting to observe the extension of civil service-type rules from the public to the private sector, a trend more pronounced in Europe than America but nevertheless observable there also. The growth of labor unions and the strengthening of the labor contract is also in part a method for increasing the worker's capacity to monitor managers, in part a formalization of the worker-management contract to allow third party arbitration. Finally, experiments in worker participation are efforts to involve workers directly in information gathering and the mutual monitoring of managers. Not surprisingly these have met with the greatest resistence from management.

6. Conclusions

Since the end of World War II both governments and businesses have grown tremendously in size. What is more, in most countries this appears to be a continuation of a secular process rather than the outgrowth of a cycle. In the United States at least, the growth of the former has recently been treated with some alarm. Social scientists from a variety of disciplines and ideological persuasions, even, have begun to explore models of budget maximizing bureaucrats and vote-maximizing legislators. Somewhat surprisingly the growth in business size has not met with a similar reaction. Economists, in particular, to the extent that they notice it at all, appear to treat it as the natural consequence of the Darwinian forces of the market seeking out more efficient organizational forms.

The arguments of this paper suggest that the two phenomena may be more closely related than generally believed. The differences between profit and nonprofit institutions may be far less than seems to be implied by the economics literature, at least. All organizations must deal with uncertainty, all must gather and process information to do so. In the process, certain individuals within the organization will be vested with the power to advance their own goals to the disadvantage of other members of the organization, and can be expected to exercise that power. These characteristics all organizations have in common, and they can be expected to produce important similarities in their performances. Rather than continually stressing the difference between profit-oriented and nonprofit-oriented bureaucracies, we might begin now to explore some of their similarities.

References

Alchian, A.A., and *H. Demsetz*: Production, Information Costs, and Economic Organization. American Economic Review **62**, 1972, 777–795.

Amacher, R.C., R.D. Tollison, and *T.D. Willett*: Risk Avoidance and Political Advertising. The Economic Approach to Public Policy. Ithaca 1976, 405–433.

Baumol, W.T.: Business Behavior, Value and Growth. Rev. ed. New York 1967.

Bell, R., D.V. Edwards, and *R.H. Wagner* (eds.): Political Power. New York 1969.

Berle, A.A., and *G.C. Means*: The Modern Corporation and Private Property. New York 1932.

Blau, P.M.: Exchange and Power in Social Life. New York 1964.

Cartwright, D.: Influence, Leadership and Control. Handbook of Organizations. Ed. by J. March. Chicago 1965.

Chandler, A.D.: Strategy and Structure. Cambridge, Mass., 1962.

Coase, R.H.: The Nature of the Firm. Economica **4**, 1937, 386–405.

Commons, J.R.: Legal Foundations of Capitalism. New York 1924.

Crozier, M.: The Bureaucratic Phenomenon. Chicago 1964.

Dahl, R.A.: The Concept of Power. Behavioral Science **2**, 1957, 201–215, reprinted in *Bell/Edwards/Wagner* [1969, 79–93].

Downs, A.: An Economic Theory of Democracy. New York 1957.

– : Inside Bureaucracy. Boston 1967.

FitzRoy, F.R., and *D.C. Mueller*: Contract and the Economics of Organization. Siena Series Number 8, Acton Society, 1978/79.

Galbraith, J.K.: The New Industrial State. Boston 1967.

Grabowski, H.G., and *D.C. Mueller*: Managerial and Stockholder Welfare Models of Firm Expenditures. Review of Economics and Statistics **54**, 1972, 9–24.

– : Life-Cycle Effects on Corporate Returns on Retentions. Review of Economics and Statistics **57**, 1975, 400–409.

Jensen, M.C., and *W. Meckling*: Theory of the Firm: Managerial Behavior, Agency Costs and Ownership Structure. Journal of Financial Economics 3, 1976, 305–360.

Knight, F.H.: Risk, Uncertainty, and Profit. New York 1965 (1st ed. 1921).
Kuehn, D.: Takeovers and the Theory of the Firm. London 1975.
Lewellen, W.G., and *B. Huntsman*: Managerial Pay and Corporate Performance. American Economic Review **60**, 1970, 710–720.
Manne, H.G.: Insider Trading and the Stock Market. New York 1966.
Marris, R.: The Economic Theory of Managerial Capitalism. New York 1964.
Masson, R.L.: Executive Motivations, Earnings, and Consequent Equity Performance. Journal of Political Economy **79**, 1971, 1278–1292.
Mills, C.W.: The Power Elite. New York 1956.
Mueller, D.C.: A Life Cycle Theory of the Firm. Journal of Industrial Economics **20**, 1972, 199–219.
– : Information, Mobility, and Profit. Kyklos **29** (3), 1976, 419–448.
Niskanen, W.A., Jr.: Bureaucracy and Representative Government. Chicago 1971.
Parsons, T.: On the Concept of Political Power. American Philosophical Society **107**, 1963, 232–262, reprinted in *Bell/Edwards/Wagner* [1969, 251–284].
Rourke, F.E.: Secrecy and Publicity. Baltimore 1961.
– : Bureaucracy, Politics and Public Policy. Boston 1969.
Russel, B.: Power. New York 1938.
Schumpeter, J.A.: A Theory of Economic Development. Cambridge, Mass., 1934.
Simon, H.A.: Notes on the Observation and Measurement of Power. Journal of Politics **15**, 1953, 500–516, reprinted in *Bell/Edwards/Wagner* [1969, 69–78].
– : Models of Man. New York 1957.
Singh, A.: Take-Overs. Cambridge, Mass., 1971.
Smiley, R.: Tender Offers, Transactions Costs and the Theory of the Firm. Review of Economics and Statistics **58**, 1976, 22–32.
Solow, R.M.: Some Implications of Alternative Criteria for the Firm. The Corporate Economy. Ed. by R. Marris and A. Wood. Cambridge, Mass., 1971, 318–343.
Stigler, G.J.: Imperfections in the Capital Market. Journal of Political Economy **75**, 1967, 287–292.
Wagner, R.H.: The Concept of Power and the Study of Politics. Political Power. Ed. by R. Bell, D.V. Edwards and R.H. Wagner. New York 1969, 3–12.
Weber, M.: The Theory of Social and Economic Organization. Ed. by T. Parsons. New York 1947.
Williamson, O.E.: The Economics of Discretionary Behavior. Englewood Cliffs, New Jersey, 1964.
– : Markets and Hierarchies. New York 1975.

Holler, M.J. (Ed.): Power, Voting, and Voting Power ©Physica-Verlag, Würzburg (Germany) 1981

Equivalent Concepts of Power in Voting Games

D. Wittman, Santa Cruz

There is little agreement regarding the appropriate definition of power. Consequently, there is always the underlying suspicion that research on power is critically dependent upon the particular concept of power being employed, and there is a great temptation to dismiss most of the literature as being idiosyncratic without general applicability. In this paper, I demonstrate that many of the approaches to power create identical results. Thus, the generality of the results in the literature are much greater than heretofore believed.

In order to make the analysis less abstract, power will be considered within the context of passing a bill.[1]) Each player has two strategies: to be for or against. The probability of a bill passing is a function of both players strategies and can be put into a two by two matrix (see Table 1). We now consider various definitions of power.

		Player *B* for	Player *B* against
Player *A*	for	*P*11	*P*12
	against	*P*21	*P*22

Tab. 1: Probability of a Bill Passing

1) Player Reversal: *A* (row) is more powerful than *B* (column) if $P12 > P21$.
   Under this definition of power one compares the probability of a bill passing when *A* is for and *B* is against to the probability of a bill passing when *B* is for and *A* is against. If the former is larger than the latter, then *A* is more powerful.[2]) This is similar to the testing of which football team is better. If team *A* can score more when *A* is the offense and *B* is the defense than team *B* can score when *B* is the offense and *A* is the defense, then *A* is a better team and wins the game.
2) Ability to restrict outcomes: *A* is more powerful than *B* if $P11 - P12 < P11 - P21$ and $P21 - P22 < P12 - P22$. A powerful actor will be able to restrict the deviations of outcomes from his preferred outcome more effectively than a weak actor, whatever his

[1]) The analysis is restricted to situations where the only outcomes are wins and losses (we ignore the possibility of ties). This reduces the need to make questionable quantitative assumptions and simplifies the problem of calculating a measure of power. For a discussion of power equivalences in non-zero sum games see *Wittman* [1975]. For a discussion of how different coalition formulae result in equivalent power rankings see *Wittman* [1978].

[2]) *Dahl/March/Nasatir* [1956] used this definition.

preferences may be. There are two conditions that must be satisfied in order for A to be more powerful than B. When A is for, he must be able to restrict outcomes more than B can when B is for; when A is against he must be able to restrict outcomes more than when B is against.[3])

Marginal change (multiple regression coefficient): A is more powerful than B if $B1 > B2$ in the following equation: $Pij = B0 + B1X1 + B2X2 + B3X1X2$, where Xk is a dummy variable ($X1 = 1$ if A is for; $X1 = 0$ if A is against; $X2 = 1$ if B is for; $X2 = 0$ if B is against). A multiple regression is run in order to determine the marginal contribution of A ($B1$) and of B ($B2$).[4])

Substituting the values of Xk gives the following equations:

$P11 = B0 + B1 + B2 + B3.$
$P12 = B0 + B1.$
$P21 = B0 + B2.$
$P22 = B0.$

The solutions are:

$B0 = P22.$
$B1 = P12 - P22.$
$B2 = P21 - P22.$
$B3 = P11 - P12 - P21 + P22.$

Marginal contribution can be restated in terms of the Pij.

3) Marginal change (multiple regression coefficient): A is more powerful than B if $B1 = P12 - P22 > P21 - P22 = B2$.

It can readily be shown that all of these definitions create identical power rankings. $P12 > P21$ implies that $P12 - P21 > 0$ and $P21 - P12 < 0$. It immediately follows that $P12 - P21 > P21 - P12$. Therefore player reversal and ability to restrict are equivalent. $P12 > P21$ also implies that $P12 - P22 > P21 - P22$. Thus all three definitions are equivalent.

References

Dahl, R.: The Concept of Power. Behavioral Science **2**, 1957, 201–215.

Dahl, R., J. March and *D. Nasatir*: Influence Ranking in the United States Senate. Paper delivered at the annual meeting of the American Political Science Association, 1956.

March, J.: Measurement Concepts in the Theory of Influence. Journal of Politics **19**, 1957, 202–226.

– : The Power of Power. Varieties of Political Theory. Ed. by D. Easton. Englewood Cliffs, N.J., 1966, 39–70.

Miller, N.: This volume, 1981.

Nagel, J.: The Descriptive Analysis of Power. New Haven 1975.

Thibaut, J.W., and *H.H. Kelley*: The Social Psychology of Groups. New York 1959.

Wittman, D.: Various Concepts of Power. British Journal of Political Science **6**, 1975, 449–462.

– : Power in Electoral Games. Foundations and Applications of Decision Theory. Ed. by Hooker, Leach, and McClennen. Dordrecht 1978, 185–206.

---

[3]) This approach has been used by *March* [1957], *Thibaut/Kelley* [1959] and *Miller* [1981].

[4]) This approach was taken by *Nagel* [1975].

Holler, M.J. (Ed.): Power, Voting, and Voting Power ©Physica-Verlag, Würzburg (Germany) 1981

Attribution and Social Power

H.-D. Schneider, Zürich

1. On Describing Power Relations

Social power is often defined as the ability to influence cognitive and behavioral aspects of other persons. Power relations then embrace almost the whole sphere of social behavior because in every interaction we are attempting to influence the other in his thinking, willing and acting, or the other way about, we succumb to the influence of the other.

Persons or groups are considered as possessing power on account of their *resources*. Such a statement is valid as much for the power relations in the family [*Blood/Wolfe*] as for the power play in international politics [e.g., *Dahl*]. Even though psychology has for a long time differentiated between objective and perceived qualities [e.g., *Köhler*], yet only recently did discussion center on the fact that with regard to power relations only *those resources as perceived by the other partner* can act as decisive variables. Not the really objective resources, but on the contrary only those resources as perceived by the actors are determinative in the establishment of power relations. These means can be real or imaginary. Only as long as the cognitive elements remain unchanged, will the existing power relation be respected. A change in the material support of power (bodily strength, military power, capacity to reward, external appearance, etc.) can only then affect the power relation, when first the attributions have changed.

This insight is not new, if one thinks of sky-jacking with toy pistols, of psychological warfare which should change the self-attributions of the enemy population or when one calls to mind the powerlessness of modern weapons in the face of invulnerable ideological or religious forces. Until now learning theories, exchange theories or decision making theories were resorted to in order to explain the power relations and in doing so the objective resources of the partner received an exaggerated share of importance [*Schneider*, 1977]; and we are still at the outset of an inquiry which aims at presenting the process of attribution in the other as the decisive factor in the establishment of power relations.

Indeed, for some time voices of protest have been raised against the suggestion to judge the power of a person from the resources he possesses. So, for example, *Olsen* [1970] and *Wrong* [1968] point out that power must be considered as a process, others [e.g., *Dahlströhm; Etzioni; Gamson*, 1968; *Krüger*] differentiate between potential and actual power and again others [*French/Raven*] include in the set of resources the psychical processes, like reference relations, or considerations of legitimacy. If we want to take into account the distinction between objective and phenomenal qualities, then we will come across those aspects to which the *theories of attribution* lay special claim.

Attributions are interpretations of the relations between cause and effect. So, for example, a pupil can attribute the good marks for his performance (the *effect*) to his own abilities, to his efforts, to the easiness of the task or simply to chance (the possible *causes*, *Weiner* et al. [1972]). In the next examination the pupil will conduct himself in a specific manner according to the explanation he had selected for himself. His attribution of cause has determined his action. But the teacher will also assign his pupil's good mark to one of these same causes. Hence his own behavior toward the pupil will also be governed by his attributions.

Our reactions toward tasks and toward other people are determined by attribution processes which we continually apply, most of the time, perhaps, unaware of doing so. Conversely our attributions are controlled by the environmental stimuli. So a teacher will attribute as a rule a higher ability to that pupil who at the beginning of the school year had shown excellent results, but who later towards the end had slackened, than to another pupil who obtained the same average results as the first, though at the commencement of the school year he had obtained poor results and towards the end had improved his scores. The pupils themselves will as a rule think differently. They will judge their ability as higher, if they improved, and as lower, if they went backward [*Jones/Nisbett*]. The same conditions can therefore lead to different attributions in the actor and the observer.

For any power relationship the deliberations of attribution theory will be of considerable importance since a person *A* can only then exercise influence over his partners when these partners attribute to him the corresponding resources. Other people will yield to his attempts to influence them then and then only when they can verify in him the means which appear as the cause of the influence and thus they can convince themselves and others of his power over them.

2. Fundamental Models of Power Attribution

Let us start from a given relationship between *A* and *B*. Each one of them possesses certain resources (e.g. potential for rewarding or punishing, expert knowledge, public legitimation), which can play an important role in their power relation. Whether in fact they become relevant or not depends on at least two attribution processes.

The way the person *A* infers the other's resources will be determined first by his *self-attributions* (Fig. 1), that is by the way these resources are perceived and evaluated as the possible cause which has influenced the person *B*. Accordingly this person will make his resources more or less effective. Besides one must take into account the *hetero-attributions* by which *B* on the basis of the known resources ascribes power to *A*. Conversely the auto- and hetero-attributions control also *B*'s conduct. So, for example, a boy, who has won several tough fights, will tend to overestimate his bodily strength and skill and will consequently be eager to get into fights with boys bigger than himself. But if his rival appraises the pugnacity of the first as the expression of a deep-rooted self-insecurity then he will fear much less the physical force of his pugnatious partner.

Whether *A* claims for himself superiority in the power relationship depends on what power he discerns in *B*. If the self-attributed power of *A* exceeds the power imputed to *B*,

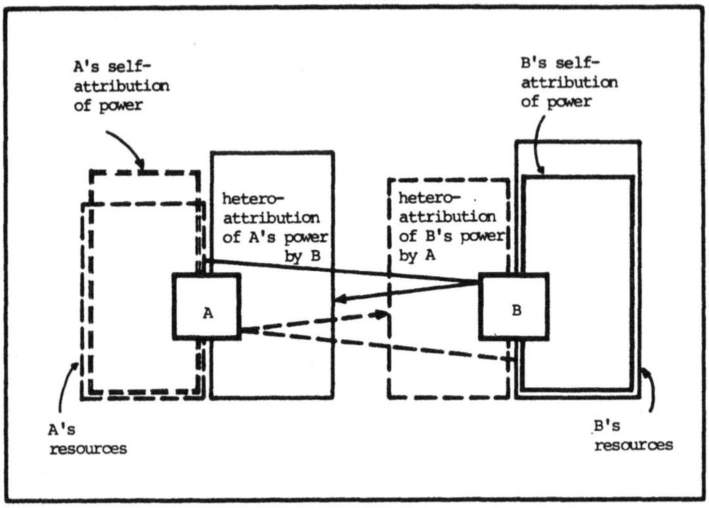

Fig. 1: Attributions of Power in a Two-Way Relationship

then *A* will consider himself superior and will act according to this conviction; balance of power and inferiority are other possible inferences. In the example in Figure 1, *B* possesses little power despite his superiority in resources, because *A* and *B* underestimate *B*'s resources and overestimate *A*'s capabilities.

Another question would comprise a third person *C* as an observer (Fig. 2). This observer can infer a specific behavior of *A* as the effect of *B*'s power. So he will clearly acquit *A* of responsibility for his action. In the future the observer can support or resist *A* so that he may influence the resources in one or both partners. Let us think of a mother who realizes that her child lies. Should she be under the impression (that is, should she attri-

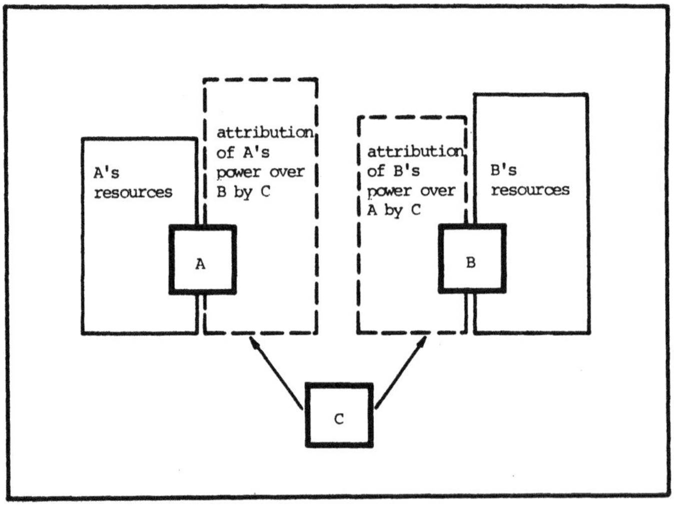

Fig. 2: An Observer's Attributions of Power

bute), that her child stays under the influence of a friend, she would react differently than if she suspects, that her child has taken up to telling lies on his own initiative. Similarly the government of a country will treat another country differently if it understands, that this country was forced by a big power to follow a specified course of action than if it does not observe this influence of a third party.

Both models must be considered important for the behavior of the actors *A, B,* and *C* in day-to-day situations and in extraordinary circumstances. Both models have theoretically and empirically been elucidated by several authors as we shall see now.

2.1 Power Attribution by an Observer

Schopler/Layton [1974] belong to the few social psychologists who extensively dealt with the conditions of power attribution by an observer. Their starting point is the definition that power is the induction of changes in another person. This definition is not fully satisfactory, because invariability in experience or conduct can also be the results of power relations. Their following considerations permit the application of this extended concept however.

An observer watching two partners may suppose that *A* has used his power over *B*, if *A* behaves in a certain way in the presence of *B*, who after that undertakes something which is derived not from the situation prevailing before *A*'s intervention, which nevertheless could have followed from *A*'s behavior. The spectator deduces from *B*'s behavior at that point in time t_1 the *subjective probabilities* for the kinds of behavior at the time t_2. The less the probability for the registered behavior to occur at the point in time t_2, all the more probability exists for the influence of other factors – such as *A*'s intervention.

A second relation of probabilities concerns *A*'s behavior at the point in time t_1 and *B*'s behavior in time t_2. The greater the probability, that *B*'s action at t_2 follows from *A*'s action at t_1, the greater is the probability that in this circumstance power must be imputed to *A*.

Now many other factors can be regarded as the cause of *B*'s conduct at that point t_2: actions of other persons, physical influences etc. The unmistakability of power attribution diminishes therefore, in proportion to the distinctness of alternative explanations with high probability.

Schopler/Layton arrived at a formula with which they attempted to illustrate the conditions of power attribution. The power imputed to *A* according to this formula is shown to lie in the difference between the probability that *B*'s conduct follows from the actions of *A* (ν_2) and the probability, that *B*'s conduct springs from his previous condition (ν_1):

$$\text{power}_A = \nu_2 - \nu_1 .$$

The greater the probability ν_2, and the smaller the probability ν_1, so much the greater will be the power assigned to *A* by the observer. The value can fluctuate between +1 and -1, whereby a negative value represents a smaller attribution of power and not something like "negative power" in the sense of boomerang effects. In an experiment *Schopler/Layton* [1972] could demonstrate, that one tends to attribute greater power to *A*, if the conduct of *B* changed than if it remained constant. The new unexpected action calls for an explanation which is deduced from *A*'s intervention.

This context receives a great practical importance because an actor's prestige increases with the amount of power imputed to him. When a person wants to attain a level whereby the social environment will attribute to him power over his partner, then he will try to make more conspicuous his attempts at exercising influence over the conduct of *B* and to reduce the weight of the other plausible causes. On the other hand if his first interest lies in influencing the conduct of his partner, then he will lessen the perceptibility of his intervention, so that the partner can save his face. It is in this context that ν_2 must be strengthened.

Setting aside the probability relationships, *Kaplowitz* [1978] brought forward a series of hypotheses as to which of two actors an observer would assign greater power. From the abundance of hypotheses neatly derived from axioms only a few examples can be cited here.

After the interaction according to Kaplowitz one would attribute so much more power to one person, the more important the result was to him, the oftener he attained an important goal, the greater the utility that acrued to him from it, the greater the harm the rival suffered on account of it, the deeper the interest conflict is between *A* and *B*, and *A* comes out victorious from it, the less the realized goals are supported by social norms, etc. *Before the interaction* so much more power will be imputed to a person the greater the power he has exercised in the past, the less important the outcome is for him, the more numerous the resources he had passed on to the partner, etc. [see *Kaplowitz*, pp. 142f.].

Although Kaplowitz had deduced all his theses from premises and supported them with logical cross connections, nevertheless they remain above all as hypotheses which stick at best in those frames of interpretation which he had constructed with the help of published empirical data.

2.2 Mutual Power Attributions by Interaction Partners

Michener/Lawler/Bachrach [1973] refer to Field Marshal Rommel, the German commander-in-chief of the African corps, who attempted to frighten the enemy through dummy tanks.[1]) He assumed, the greater the amount of – at least apparent – resources he could demonstrate, the greater would be the amount of power assigned to him. Further considerations or additional empirical researches on attributions of power by the interaction partners seem not to exist.

Another question to be posed concerns the effects of power attribution by interaction partners on their own behavior under competitive conditions. This theme too is not yet found in literature.

Let us start from the point that both *A* and *B* have at their disposal a certain amount of resource potential. If *A* desires to induce his partner *B* to behave in a certain way, then *B*'s reactions will depend upon how great the (means of) power he will attribute to his partner compared to himself. Should *B* suspect that *A* dominates him, i.e., *A* has at his

---

[1]) Independently of the considerations of attribution, Rommel could have speculated, that the probability of being hit by the enemy guns would be reduced if the guns have to aim at many more targets.

disposal more resources than he himself, B might be a great deal prepared to renounce the use of the means of power to defend his own sphere of influence. He will yield to the demands of A, because he knows, that a very potent adversary can easily overwhelm his opponent's feeble attempts at independence. Should B on the contrary speculate that A is weaker than himself, then he will respond to A's attempts at dominion with a demonstration of his own means of power, in order in the first place to exhibit his own possibilities and to ward off this and similar attempts in future (Fig. 3).

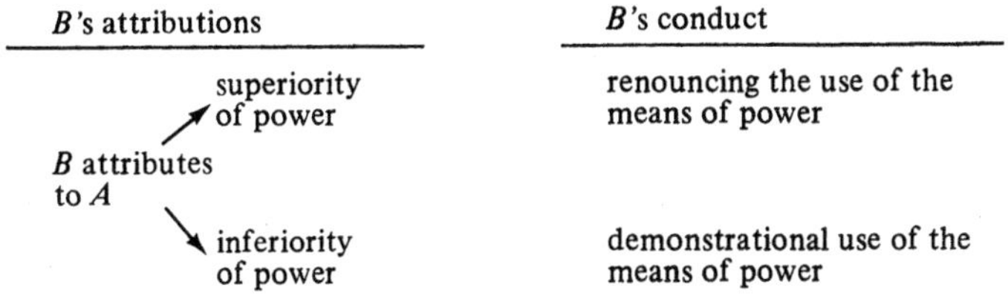

Fig. 3: B's Conduct in a Power Relationship Depending on B's Attribution of Power to A

That is the situation of a jeweller, who is threatened by a robber with a revolver. Should the jeweller believe, the revolver is loaded, he will submit to the robber's orders. On the contrary if he guesses, the weapon is a bluff or if he is confident of his bodily strength, then he will put up resistence.

With the intent of subjecting this hypothesis to a preliminary test, the students of the author's lecture course were asked to place themselves in a situation, where the student and his partner were aspiring for a goal that only one of them could obtain. Every one undergoing the test knew his own resources and knew from the instructions what he could guess about his partner's means. Would he employ his means of power to reach his goal or would he renounce the use of them? The different conditions of superiority and inferiority were allotted to the students in chance order. They could record their reaction on an eight point scale, whereby the opposite poles were characterized as using and correspondingly, not using the means of power.

	The person uses his means of power		
	in full	partly	N
The person feels himself superior	21	8	29
The person feels himself inferior	16	16	32
$Chi^2 = 3{,}18; p < .10$			

Tab. 1: Use of the Own Means of Power Depending on the Power Attributed to the Partner

The result (Table 1) indicates the predicted direction: if one attributes more power to one's partner than what one believes to possess, then one will make less use of one's means of power than if one should consider himself superior.

But what course of action would A take, if in addition he knows or believes to know the power attributions of B? Should B assign his partner A a superiority in power and comply with his expectations, without exercising his means of power, in that case A will presumably not undertake anything, because his position is secure – independently of his self-attribution. If on the other hand *B* judges his partner *A* as inferior and begins, therefore to make use of his means of power, and on the other hand *A* considers himself the stronger, then *A* will mobilise his own means of power in order to procure the general recognition of his self-attribution (Fig. 4). These are the jewellery robbers, who shoot, if resisted, even though they had planned a bloodless hold-up.

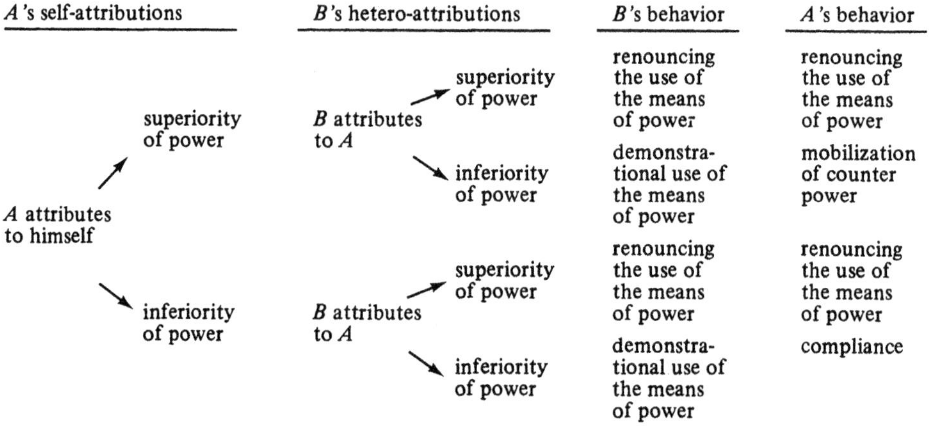

Fig. 4: *A*'s Conduct in a Power Relationship Depending on *A*'s Self-Attributions and on *B*'s Hetero-Attributions of Power

In case *B* suspects *A*'s superiority over him, and *A* on his part thinks himself to be the weaker, then neither *B* nor *A* will make a move in the sense of asserting their power. There will happen nothing, as in the case of the would-be-jewellery robber, who abstains from robbing due to the dangers of safety devices.

Finally *B* can believe, *A* is inferior to him and this opinion coincides with *A*'s self-attribution. Here *A* will not resist *B*'s employment of his means of power, but would submit

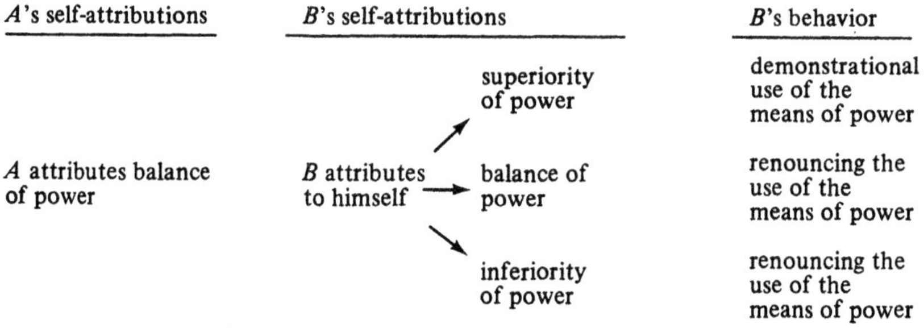

Fig. 5: *B*'s Conduct when *A* is Attributing Balance of Power Depending on *B*'s Self-Attributions

to *B*'s demands. Here we come across a jeweller who because of the self-assured entrance of the robber, saw it opportune to hand over his precious goods and only later realized that the robber was unarmed.

Besides calculating the superior and inferior positions, attribution of *balance of power* is also conceivable (Fig. 5).

If both sides are convinced of the equality of power, then immobility will occur together with the efforts at rearmament in order to achieve superiority at a favorable time. The armed jewellery robber might be confronted with a likewise armed policeman and try by means of cover or by taking hostages to gain some advantage, while the policeman may be hoping for reinforcement from his colleagues. In international politics we can notice the race for rearmament by the big powers on the basis of perceived balance of power.

As long as only *A* perceives an equality, but *B* starts from his superior power, *B* will then presumably make use of his means of power to bring into effect his self-attribution. It is the moment of tense watching on the part of both jewellery robber and policeman. This situation will reach a climax through the use of arms by that person who believes to have spotted an advantage for himself.

If *A* attributes balance of power and *B* his own inferiority, there will be no attempts to influence the other.

According to the above considerations two persons will make their behavior depend, under competitive conditions, not only on the actions of the partner but also on their own attributions of power and on the partner's attributions concerning the power relations, whereby each person's attribution would be affected by the conspicuousness of the resources. If we set out from the position of *A*, we shall arrive at a tree of conditions ever increasing in complexity as is illustrated in Figure 6.

By the operationalization of this tree into 18 different situations, in which the students placed themselves it could be shown, that those who attributed power superiority to themselves (fields 1–6) looked for more controversy than in the case of inferiority of power (fields 13–18; $Chi^2 = 4{,}95$; $df = 1$; $p = .05$). Should *B* impute superiority of power to his partner *A*, the subjects in the role of *A* reacted more restrained than when *B*

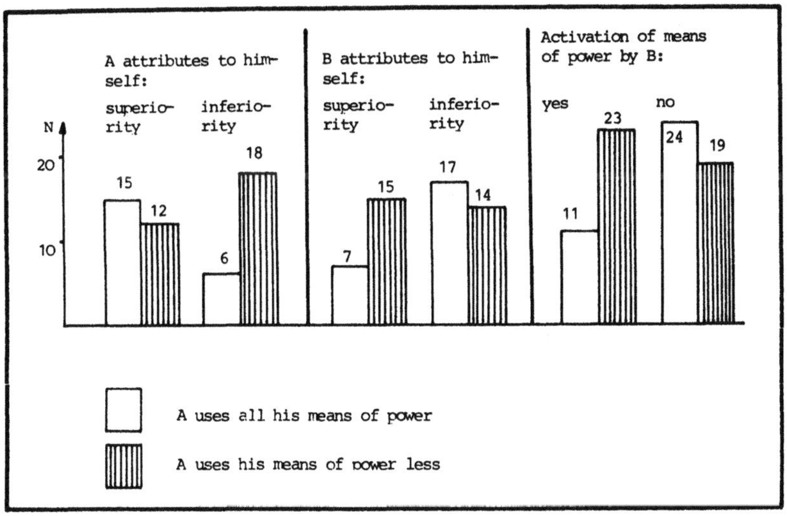

Fig. 7: The Influences of Self-Attribution, Hetero-Attribution, and Partner's Behavior on the Conduct of *A*

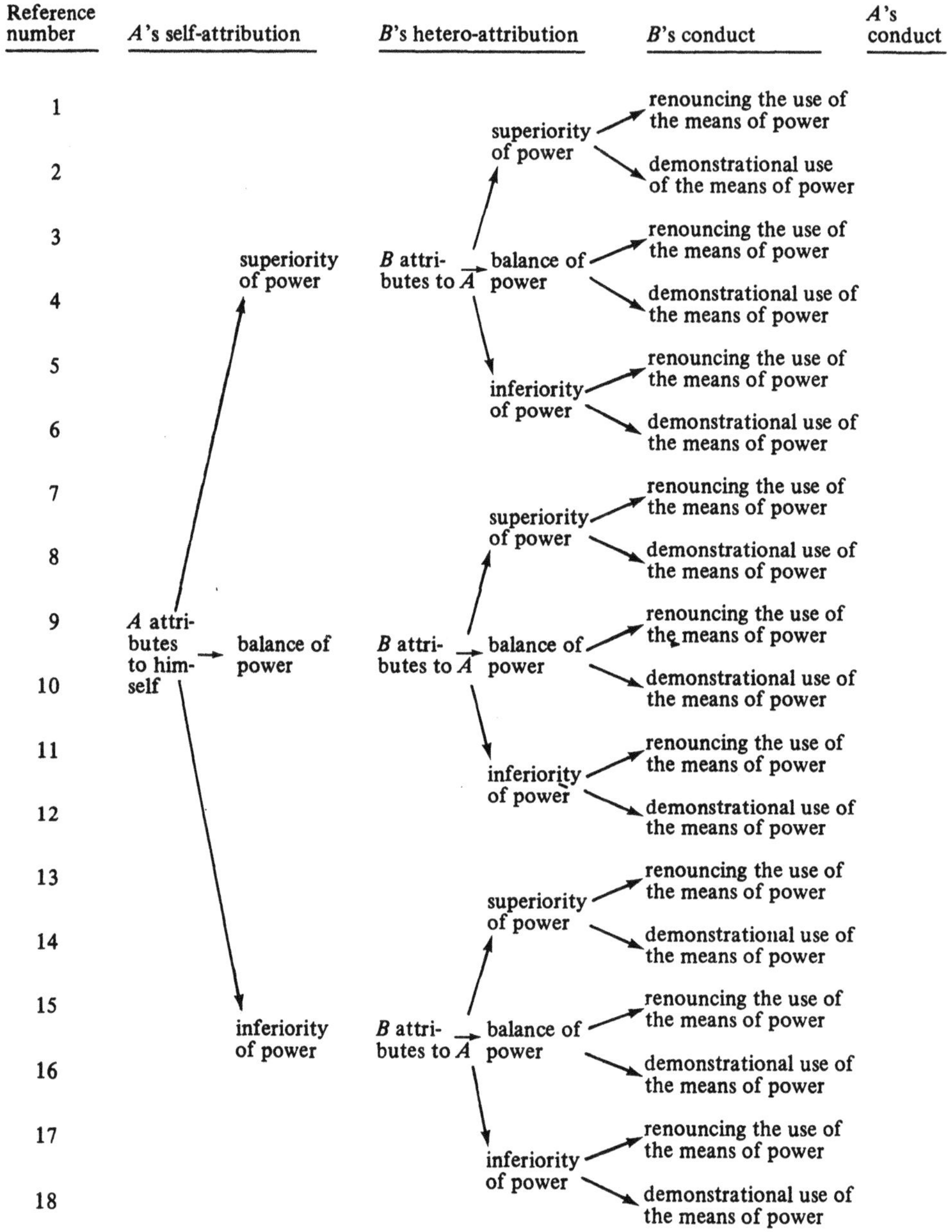

Fig. 6: *A*'s Conduct Depending on *A*'s and *B*'s Self- and Hetero-Attributions and on the Partner's Behavior

appeared to sense his own inferiority (fields 1, 2, 7, 8, 13, 14 against 5, 6, 11, 12, 17, 18; $Chi^2 = 2{,}67$; $df = 1$; $p = .10$). If *B* employed his means of power demonstratively, *A* showed more reserve, than if *B* renounced the use of his means of power (contrast uneven fields with even ones; $Chi^2 = 4{,}30$; $df = 1$; $p = .05$ – Fig. 7). Attribution of balance of power on the part of both *A* and *B* leads to an intermediary conduct.

Since the total number of subjects in this pilot study comprised only 77 persons, a differentiated evaluation of the individual fields is not possible. The present findings indicate, however, that the self- and hetero-attributions influence behavior, so that it seems meaningful to continue with further researches.

3. Power Attribution in Voting Assemblies

If a faction of a voting body has not the majority at its disposal it is forced in voting assemblies to find partners who are willing to vote for the same things as it intends to. Such *coalitions* are formed according to different principles, such as minimum resources, maximum resources, similarities etc. [cf. *Schneider*, 1978]. Each of these theories of coalition formation can be verified under certain assumptions.

So the *minimum resource theory* [*Gamson*, 1961; *Riker*, p. 32: "minimum winning coalition"] is valid under stable circumstances, provided that the rewards are distributed in proportion to the resources and that the attitudes of the coalition partners are irrelevant. This theory predicts the choice of that partner whose resources together with one's own means can help in bringing about just the majority because with him one's own portion of the rewards will be maximized. An actor must therefore signal or strengthen the attributions desired in him by the partner, so that the presence of these attributions can lead to a coalition with minimum majority. Precisely the additional precondition of complete information as stated by *Riker* [1962] must not be given; it is much more necessary for the actors only to believe that they are informed correctly and comprehensively.

Let us consider, for example, an assembly of three parties with the following allottment of seats: *A* = 45 %; *B* = 15 %; *C* = 40 %. Accoriling to the above mentioned requisites *B* and *C* will join together. If *A* wishes to prevail upon *B* to form a coalition, *A* must then evoke those attributions in *B*, such as, that the coalition *BC* has not or soon will not have the majority at their disposal, e.g., because certain deputies would probably abandon the party. On the other hand, the possibility that the coalition *AB* may in reality not be stronger than the coalition *BC*, which is objectively inferior in number, will bring *A* closer to its purpose of forming the coalition *AB*.

The *maximum resource theory* [*Cole*], can be verified under unstable conditions if a weak majority underlies the danger of losing their commanding position through marginal changes. In this case the actor must evoke in his desired partner the attribution of strong means of power.

Thus in our example party *A*, who desires to work together with *C*, will support the attributions about the instability of the power basis of *B* and of *C*. Hints regarding the crisis of the political system, the importance of the imminent enactments, which should be presented to the people with the support of a strong majority, could make the threat quite obvious to the faltering majority.

The theory on the *coalition between similar partners* [*Schneider*, 1978] examines the exceeding importance of the partner's attitudes. When attitudes or ideologies play a role for the coalition members, they are then a power factor for a party, if the party can present itself to the desired partner as the spokesman of similar ideas. Should the party want to form a coalition, it must foster within its partner the attribution that their attitudes conform to a large extent.

The parties considered would then refer less to seat ratios, but rather emphasize common convictions. If, e.g., *A* who is known to be a concervative party wants to form a coalition with *B* who inclines toward progressive opinions, *A* must evoke attributions in *B* that they have much in common. At the same time, *A* will stress the differences between *B* and *C*, so that *B* meets corresponding attributions, the coalition *BC* thereby becoming improbable. It is the art of steering useful attributions that help to overcome the disadvantages that other resources imply.

With this background in view one would expect, according to the nature of the desired coalition partner and according to the external circumstances, a differentiated self-representation of the actors geared at evoking a favourable hetero-attribution, with regard to power and/or attitudes, in the future partner.

In addition to this the presumed hetero-attribution of the desired coalition partner acts as a moderating influence, in as much as self-representation would manifest itself in one form when hetero-attribution is positive and quite differently if hetero-attribution were negative. It is here too that future research is still required.

4. Conclusions

The summarized theoretical constellations and the first empirical data on the subject show how the subjective speculation over one's own and the other's power can regulate behavior. When we see due to the use of the means of power, the military and economic strifes in the international sphere with their disasterous consequences for the nations concerned, and when we see in the sphere of human relations the kinds of behavior which lead to bodily or psychical injuries and to delusions, then arises the moral obligation to create such situations as promote the renouncement of the use of the means of power. Up to now only postulates are found for the above mentioned constellations and the validity of these postulates must still be tested extensively.

It is not a false perspective if until now the objective resources have occupied the central position in the discussions concerning the bases of power. These resources explain in the end the prerequisites for their intrusion into the living space. The perception of one's own power and that of the other, and the assumptions made about them might more strongly perhaps influence the conduct of the interaction partner, than their objective existence. These attributions of power determine the actions of the actors.

While the objective foundations of power are comparable to the physical waves of light, the attributions of power are similar to the color and form that are perceived by the eyes. It is high time to investigate the gorgeously coloured world of power relations in its entirety, making sure to include both the components.

References

Blood, R.O., and *D.M. Wolfe*: Husbands and wives. Glencoe, Ill., 1960.

Cole, S.G.: An examination of the power-inversion effect in three-person mixed-motive games. Journal of Personality and Social Psychology **11**, 1969, 50–58.

Dahl, R.A.: The concept of power. Behavioral Science **2**, 1957, 202–215.

Dahlström, E.: Exchange, influence and power. Acta Sociologica **9**, 1966, 237–284.

Etzioni, A.: The active society. London–New York 1968.

French, J.R.P., and *B. Raven*: The bases of social power. Studies in social power. Ed. by D. Cartwright. Ann Arbor 1959, 150–167.

Gamson, W.A.: A theory of coalition formation. American Sociological Review **26**, 1961, 373–382.

– : Power and discontent. Homewood, Ill., 1968.

Harvey, J.H., W.J. Ickes, and *R.F. Kidd* (Eds.): New directions in attribution research. Hillsdale, N.J., 1976.

Jones, E.E., and *K.E. Davis*: From acts to dispositions. The attribution process in person perception. Advances in experimental social psychology. Volume 2. Ed. by L. Berkowitz. New York 1965, 219–266.

Jones, E.E., and *R.E. Nisbett*: The actor and the observer: divergent perceptions of the causes of behavior. Attribution: perceiving the causes of behavior. Ed. by E.E. Jones et al. Morristown, N.J., 1972, 79–94.

Kaplowitz, S.A.: Toward a systematic theory of power attribution. Social Psychology **41**, 1978, 131–148.

Köhler, W.: Gestalt psychology. New York 1959.

Krüger, W.: Macht in der Unternehmung. Stuttgart 1976.

Michener, H.A., E.J. Lawler, and *S. Bacharach*: Perceptions of power in conflict situations. Journal of Personality and Social Psychology **28**, 1973, 155–162.

Olsen, M.E. (Ed.): Power in societies. London 1970.

Riker, W.H.: The theory of political coalitions. New Haven 1962.

Schneider, H.-D.: Sozialpsychologie der Machtbeziehungen. Stuttgart 1977.

– : Was determiniert Koalitionstendenzen in der Kleingruppe: Ressourcen oder Ähnlichkeit? Zeitschrift für experimentelle und angewandte Psychologie **25**, 1978, 153–168.

Schopler, J., and *B. Layton*: Determinants of the self-attribution of having influenced another person. Journal of Personality and Social Psychology **22**, 1972, 326–332.

– : Attributions of interpersonal power. Perspectives on social power. Ed. by J.T. Tedeschi. Chicago 1974, 34–60.

Weiner, B. et al.: Perceiving the causes of success and failure. Attribution: perceiving the causes of behavior. Ed. by E.E. Jones et al. Morristown, N.J., 1972, 95–120.

Wrong, D.H.: Some problems in defining social power. American Journal of Sociology 73, 1968, 673–681.

Holler, M.J. (Ed.): Power, Voting, and Voting Power ©Physica-Verlag, Würzburg (Germany) 1981

Power: An Amorphous Term – Diverse Conceptual Approaches

H. Behrens, Munich

A thing to which people attach many labels with subtly or grossly different meanings in many different cultures and times is probably not a thing at all, but many things.
Robert A. Dahl (The Concept of Power)

1. Power Concept and Analysis of Politics

Political scientists involved in research, teaching or writing can not avoid having to analyze, or at least describe the phenomena of political power. When trying to define the phenomena of politics, various aspects of power must be taken into consideration. This applies diversely to the *normative-ontological* concept of politics which emphasizes a "good" political structure, the political *realism* of authors like Hobbes and Machiavelli, the *marxist* concept which equates the relations of production and the material forces of production, as well as to the methodological concepts and its 'diluted' *cybernetic* analysis of power [*Noack/Stammen*, p. 235f.].

A universally valid definition of politics does not seem possible within the present realm of knowledge: one of its fundamental elements, the power concept, remains disputed. The only consensus is that the power concept plays as essential a role in the analysis of politics as the utilitarian concept does in the analysis of economics.[1])

Although economists can not unconditionally define satisfaction, pleasure or need-fulfillment, all derivable from the consumption of goods, because of their psychological components, the utilitarian concept can nevertheless be derived from the consumption of goods. In "Introduction to Political Theory: Power Theory," *Niemann* [1978, p. 290f.] indicates that a comparable scientific consensus of power, its conditions, causes and effects does not exist among power analysts. There is no one focal point, as is the case with the utilitarian concept; therefore, as will be demonstrated, a succession of particular factors can be detected which, although interdependent, are still analytically more or less unrelated. Thus power and the analysis thereof remains a point of contention in the realm

---

[1]) The utility concept is also used in political theory; see *Behrens* [1980, pp. 75ff.].

of political research. The plethora of theories analyzing and describing power indicates the diversity of this concept, contrasted to various other basic sociological concepts. The fact that the myriad facets have not yet been integrated indicates the amorphousness of the concept.

A condensed set of questions concerning the analysis of power will be implemented to deal with the diversity of this concept. These questions indicate that the varied political dimensions of power analysis can be pinpointed most comprehensively within one branch of politics – international relations, which is not the substance of this book but merely instrumental in generating some fundamental questions concerning power analysis in general. Several theoretical power concepts will be expounded upon to illustrate the common possibilities and difficulties exposed within the conflicting power analyses. An analogy of these diverse power concepts will be presented in the synopsis. The concluding statement will reflect upon the present function and the future role of power analyses.

2. Questions Concerning Power Analysis

In *The Analysis of International Relations* Deutsch stresses the importance of power analysis in his ten fundamental questions [*Deutsch*, p. 8ff.].

The basic observation is that political actors (generally speaking, not valid for nation states) are either *strong or weak*. In world politics, the strong political actors are the superpowers and, with qualifications, the middle powers; the weak actors are the third and fourth worlds. Peripheral states, such as Brazil in its present state of development, are given middle positions on the strong-weak scale. Specific case studies can be used to examine the conditions and causes of strong and weak states and, subsequently, their political power. Take the case of the Federal Republic of Germany: there was a change in the *governmental structure* with the transition from a large to small coalition, which enabled a possible reorientation of foreign policy and a restructuring of the atrophied relations to the Eastern European states. The American military withdrawal from Vietnam was largely provoked by growing public criticism; another example that *domestic political changes* and changes in public response can influence foreign policy and its power relations.

Case studies reveal the salient factors critical to the analyses of decision making in nation states; however, the conditions and causes of political power can be treated on a more comprehensive level. Which *power elements* do political actors have at their disposal? In the field of international relations: the geography and topography of the nation state, the existence and character of natural boundaries. A central element of political power is the extent and development of the economy: the availability of raw materials, scientific and technological progress, the development of 'human capital', as well as the industrial capacity. Considering the priority given to national security, the respective military potential is as important as the economic aspect of power. Further elements include the demography, national identity and ethnic homogeneity, the degree of social integration and the political structure or stability of the nation state. Its strength or weakness depends largely on the influence of these power resources which determine whether a state belongs to the group of superpowers, middle or small powers, peripheral or third and fourth world etc. If the resources available to a state (military and economic potential) as well as the environment (geography) are relatively easy to *quantitatively* understand, there are nevertheless certain unresolved problems on the level of collective behavior (social structure, integration, political order, or stability) when trying to analyze that numerically [*Aron*, p. 68ff.; *Fucks*].

If it seems feasible to classify a nation state according to the character of its fundamental power resources within the aforementioned hierarchy, an evaluation of the *actual power* must include additional influences from such heterogeneous areas as historical experience, alignment, or the special relation between two states within a divided nation. Three essential factors which denote salient traits of the Federal Republic of Germany's foreign policy provide excellent case study material; namely the historical burden of the Third Reich, inter-german relations with the GDR, and its integration in NATO. Only an analysis which includes these factors allows the potentials and limitations of power to be recognized under real conditions.

The transition from cold war to Détente, the new power constellations within the international state system since the intervention in Afghanistan, to which none of the analyses apply per se, raises the question of the *transformation of power*. It apparently does not suffice to define power solely as "power politics": in other words as an implementation of force. On the contrary, the implementation of power presupposes the development, transformation and application of political authority. The following is Max Weber's concept of power: "Power is the probability that one actor within a social relationship, will be in a position to carry out his own will, despite resistance, regardless of the basis on which this probability rests" [*Weber*, 1957, p. 152]. In international politics, the structure of the *political will* is commonly associated with the concept of national interests. Morgenthau defines the concept of foreign policy interests as the essence of possible actions whose historical realization maximally conforms with the essential interests of the state (security, power, welfare) [*Morgenthau*, 3–38]. The structure of political will, as well as coinciding interests are the factors examined in decision making and conflict theories, whose numerous hypotheses and case studies have made a large contribution to political power analysis [*Snyder/Diesing*].

Most of the dichotomous typologies of political power are common sense and need no further explanation like defensive and offensive power, internal and external power, power in peace and war [*Aron*, p. 182]. It is the frequent distinction between *potential and actual power* which needs elaboration. The questions raised regarding the forms of power will be used as guidelines to demonstrate the amorphousness of the political phenomena of power.

3. A Comparative Selection of Power Concepts

It was noted in the introduction that the power concept is central to the analysis of politics. The plethora of literature dealing, directly or indirectly, with the analysis of power is not coincidental. It should be noted there is as yet no consensus as to how power should be scientifically analyzed. Instead of introducing independent power definitions and hypotheses and drawing analogies, a limited set of questions as to the causes, elements, and limitations of power surprisingly reveals innumerable concrete political dimensions of the forms and transformations of political power.

The following points should be clear by now: (a) power implementation occurs only when stronger and weaker actors interact politically; power is *relative*, (b) power analysis applies to the relations between diverse *analytical units*: nation states, international organizations, groups, bureaucrats, individuals etc., (c) power has varied *sources* (environment, resources, collective behavior) [*Aron*, p. 71], (d) with the appropriate methodology certain resources can be *quantitatively*, objectively compared. Other resources, relevant to power analysis, are *difficult* or impossible *to evaluate*, (e) the last point refers specifically to the *limitations* of power which initially seem to be derived from economic potential and military strength; before historical dimensions, supportive and non-supportive (enemy) structures, personal characteristics of the decision makers, which can lead to difficult moments of decision-making that places high demands on a crisis management, are taken into account, (f) the interest or goal orientation of the *political will* could alter power relationships and (g) power has many guises and *diverse forms*.

Power relations, analytical units, power resources, methodology, power limitations and transformations, as well as the various forms of power will be analyzed from diverse points of view. Several fundamental studies have been chosen which explicitly deal with power analysis and raise questions dealing with conflicting theories, concepts and methodologies, to a certain extent.

The power concepts of following authors will be outlined: Robert A. Dahl's behavioristic theory; Max Weber's classical sociological power analysis which is considered the fundament for a modern sociological analysis of power [*Niemann*, p. 292]; Adolf A. Berle, economist and political advisor to Presidents Roosevelt and Kennedy – his most encompassing definition of power as the moving force behind history; the societal and political steering concept of Amitai Etzioni, a modern sociologist; and the anthropologically oriented theory of Carl Friedrich von Weizsäcker, the scientist and peace researcher, who deals with political systems and peace initiatives. Secondly, salient findings will be compared in a synopsis. The limitations of this paper necessitate restricting the study to several prominent authors with varied backgrounds, representing diverse approaches to power analysis. Analogies will be particularly instrumental here, as not only similar but diverse and opposite findings can be ascertained.

1) *Robert A. Dahl's Power Analysis*

Robert Dahl has made a substantial contribution to power analysis. As early as 1957, he published an article in 'Behavioral Science' titled 'The Concept of Power.' In the 1960's his book "Who Governs? Democracy and Power in an American City, New Haven" was a valuable contribution to community power research, analysing power and decision making. He also authored the chapter on power in the International Encyclopedia of the Social Sciences, dealing with the origins, elements of power analysis and the problems of research. The following refers primarily to the third chapter 'Political Systems; Similarities' in "Modern Political Analysis," published in 1963.[2])

Dahl assumes that in order to recognize complex relations when describing and explaining political phenomena, political scientists need to work with comprehensive con-

[2]) Author has used the following editions: *Dahl* [1963, 1976; and 1973].

cepts. As a behaviorist, it is his job to describe and explain the apparent behavior of individual actors by outlining operational terminology which tries to measure human behavior. In order to analyze power behavioristically, he introduces the concept or concepts of influence. In his opinion, it is impossible to analyze political life without comparing the influences implemented by varied actors.

Dahl defines influence and power as follows: "influence is a *relation among actors* in which one actor induces other actors to act in some way they would not otherwise act" [*Dahl*, 1963, p. 40]. On the other hand, "influence . . . , when compliance is attained by creating the prospect of severe sanctions for noncompliance, is often called power [*Dahl*, 1976, p. 47]. Per definition, power and influence are relative categories for Dahl.

Whether one, several or many actors implement political influence is, as Dahl recalls, one of the Aristotelian criterion for classifying political systems. This extensive level of influence corresponds to the analytical units of state, organizations, associations and groups. Dahl emphasizes that their research in Atlanta of salient factors instrumental in communal decision-making processes, is a sociological study which should be extended over several generations. It is but a fragment of his actual research – the analogy of individual influences.

Inspired by Galilean methodology, Dahl created a five-fold methodology, similar to mechanics. Its fundamental criterion for comparing influence are (1) *the amount of change in the position of the actor influenced.* When the relationship extends from two to three actors, the influence of two actors is measured by the level of change each affects in the third actor. The limitations are hard to establish as the initial strategy and interaction are equally difficult to fixate. (2) *The subjective psychological costs of compliance. A*'s strength is determined by losses (repurcussions) involved for *B* when *B* submits to *A*. A differential gap can be determined when *B*'s submission towards two different actors involves varied losses. Methodological difficulties arise when the established quantitative level of the losses is related to the psychological components. (3) *The amount of difference in the probability of compliance.* The extent of positional changes of the influenced actor and the respective losses are not taken into account; solely the attempt to influence, whether or not it involves regular or irregular behavior patterns. The difficulty involved in power analysis is apparent; lacking statistical analogies in the field of political decision making, there is no adequate theory of probability. (4) *Differences in the scope of the responses*: this is more of an hypothesis than methodology; it indicates the importance of differentiating various political levels (foreign, domestic, economic) when measuring influence, in order to maintain a basis for comparing influence relations. (5) *The number of persons who respond.* A direct, manifest measurement of influence, whereby it is necessary to record in which field (communal, countries, organisations etc.) reactions are noted.[3])

According to Dahl, these measurements reveal the many guises of power and the "thousands of diverse influence typologies." Within the framework of his influence analysis, Dahl differentiates between potential and actual power; one of the introductory

---

[3]) *Dahl* [1963, pp. 42ff.]; compare the formal elaboration in *Dahl* [1957]. A discussion of negatives and positives of the formalization of the amount of power is to be found in *Ziegler* [1976, pp. 94ff.].

points. An actor has potential influence when he has access to political power and other actors perceive this power as imminently implementable. A differentiation of the power concept more relevant to forecoming analogies is illustrated in the following graphic. A short explanation is necessary.

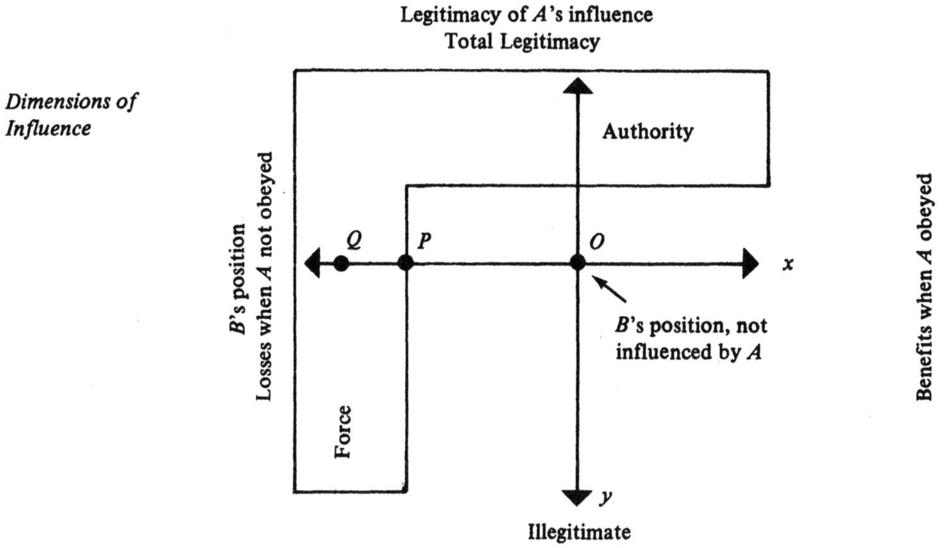

Source: *Dahl* [1963, p. 65]

The *x*-ordinate shows diverse values for factors important to *B* which will be seriously influenced should he move towards *Q*, which *A* can affect through implementation of power. The *y*-ordinate is another continuum: demands and order are placed at the apex which *B* considers legitimate and justified: the *SW* quadrant is unjustified power. Both dimensions combine influence and legitimacy. Considering the problem of clearly defining the limitations of concepts within this diagram, the previously defined concepts of power and influence can nevertheless be used to deduce related concepts: force as power implementation with illegitimate disadvantages, and authority as legitimate power.

Dahl not only contributed to the operationalism of terms and the elaboration of mathematical equations but also to the classification of power terminology.

2) *Max Weber's Power Analysis*

Niemann appropriately stresses Max Weber's successful combination of various elements of power analysis: behavioral emphasis, will, cause, external behavioral characteristics, and implementation, that are found in the works of earlier scholars.[4]) As mentioned before Weber defined: "power is the probability that one actor within a social relationship will be in a position to carry out his own will despite resistance, regardless of the basis on which this probability rests" [*Weber*, 1957, p. 152]. 'Social relationship' and

[4]) *Niemann* [1978, p. 292]; the same reference is made to the meaning of 'social action' as well as to 'probability'.

'probability' can be first understood in this context when Weber's concept of social behavior is used as a basis. The term social behavior will be reserved for activities whose intent is related by the individuals involved to the conduct of others and is oriented accordingly [*Weber*, 1972, p. 1]. Consequently, the probability of implementing one's interest within societal relationships depends in part upon knowledge of the norms of cultural units, experience, and anticipation of the other partner's goals [*Niemann*, p. 293]. This explains the popularity of Weber's power definition. On the one hand, it applies to elements of power definitions as depicted in political realism, when referring to the importance of strength (to carry out one's will) and conflict (resistance). The probability of this occuring within the scope of diverse cultures, normative structures, behavioral experience and goal structures is an indication that Weber's definition allows for new concepts and analyses of power. This explains why his power concept has been revived by contemporary authors [*White*, p. 8].

Based on the above, it could be assumed that Weber and Dahl establish an analysis of power relations on the societal behavior of the individual. However, this is looking at only one side of the coin. Weber's primary interest was an analysis of authority implementation within social relationships. In conjunction with this, he examined the most rational form of authority for an authority figure – bureaucracy. As *Niemann* [1978, p. 293] pointed out, for Weber, the power concept was nothing other than a logically necessary link between the concept "social relationship" and "authority". Simplified, authority can be understood as constant, institutionalized and rationally verifiable power implementation, which was the essential point for Weber as an active politician [*Niemann*].

Authority, as a sub-classification of power, is the "probability of a definite command being obeyed by certain persons" [*Weber*, 1972, p. 28]. Weber differentiated between three forms of authority, based on levels of legitimacy: charismatic authority, distinguished by the unusual character of a personality; traditional authority, based upon the sanctity of sovereign authority and traditional systems; and legitimate authority, characterized by an established structure and sub-classification of authority under established rules. A discussion of these forms of authority, as well as the ideal forms and their counterparts, elements of abstraction and utopia, will not be discussed based on the assumption that they are well known. One point should however be emphasized which *Bendix* [1979, p. 18], among others, has stressed. The elements of uncertainty within these ideal forms of authority – the rare occurence of the masses recognizing and agreeing with the moral duty of the prophet, the tension between traditional, legal rules and the arbitrary power of an individual ruler, the ideal form of bureaucracy as 'eisernes Gebäude' and the transforming specialization of the bureaucrat – should prevent these ideal forms from being "discarded as simple etiquettes." Each of these ideal forms represents an extensive research project where power and authority can be empirically analyzed within the scope of state organizations, i.e., bureaucracies.

3) *Adolf A. Berle's Power Analysis*

Adolf Berle differs from Dahl and Weber in that he tries to discuss the power concept and its innumerable manifestations without the restriction of a stringently behavioristic or sociological-behavioral concept. His book is the most extensive analysis of power: the origins of power, the intrinsic laws of power, economic power, international power, the demise of power [*Berle*]. For the sake of brevity, the historical analysis which begins with antiquity and the analysis of power's demise (based on the historical analysis) will be disregarded, as well as his analysis of economic power. Berle's definition of power is more pragmatically applicable and, as is also the case with Weizsäcker, anthropological. "Power is an attribute of man. It does not exist without a holder. Impulse to have it is included in the kit of instincts, emotions, and qualities of every normal person; and every normal person has had and exercised a measure of power" [*Berle*, p. 60]. According to Berle, power does not belong to classes, groups or elites: these are simply a part of the process which transforms individuals into power figures.

This is more of an hypothesis than a definition. It is based on his own political experience as a member of the Versaille Peace Delegation, as American Ambassador to Brazil and advisor to several American presidents. According to Berle a power vacuum is unavoidably filled in every human society. Rationally implemented power, such as Dahl's authority or Weber's legitimate power are accepted because they eliminate chaos and anarchy. The basis for implementation of political power is found in the inherently human instincts (egotism, ambition, altruism); the fundamental human need for law and order allows the implementation of rational power: order is preferred to chaos and anarchy.

After analyzing the personal and systematic aspects of power, Berle exposes in his third hypothesis the importance of ideal, normative, ideological-philosophical systems for power analysis. "Without an idea system, institutions cannot be constructed and certainly cannot endure." "I am convinced that a philosophy or idea structure is a precondition of formation of any organization – that is, it precedes the coming into existence of power in any form or at any level" [*Berle*, p. 84]. Berle cites the Mayflower Treaty, which the pilgrims signed at the founding of the colonies in New England, as an historical example for an inchoate power structure built upon an existent philosophy. In an established political system, Berle maintains there are "fundamental ideological limitations" which must be respected by authority figures, should the fundaments of their political structures be upheld and remain intact. Only few historical situations allow political leaders ideological "opportunism" [*Berle*, p. 88] – as was the case with Stalin's capricious behavior towards Hitler's Germany – without suffering a loss of power within their own internal political system.

The fourth hypothesis observes that rulers depend upon an institutional structure to implement their power. Normally, institutions elect political figures and thus transfer power. "Institutions perform a double function: they confer power and they are the instruments by which it is used" [*Berle*, p. 100]. Their existence limits and controls the implementation of authority and institutions can also retract power.

Berle's fifth hypothesis is closely linked to the limitations and control of power through institutions: power is invariably confronted with responsibility. Although its position varies greatly in diverse systems, responsibility is gaining importance in the Soviet's political system, indicated by the role played by the Central Committee in the overthrow of Chruschev [*Berle*, p. 119].

4) *Amitai Etzioni's Power Analysis*

The focus of Etzioni's "Active Society" is the transformation and steering of societies. "What is the place of power in an active society? Can a society bring about its transformation and the realization of its values without undermining the basis of authentic commitment, participation and legitimation?" [*Etzioni*, p. 350]. He does not analyze the power of individuals, or small groups, rather the macro-scopic aspect of total societal power. The initial premise is that necessary changes must be taken into account if society is going to be guided towards essential, desired macro-societal goals.

Etzioni presents an exhaustive three-fold classification of resources and the conversion of power from these assets as a means to overcome resistance. Coercive power is mobilized through force or violent measures carried out by the military or police etc., the coercive assets of most societies. Utilitarian assests, such as economic possessions, technical and administrative capabilities, manpower etc., facilitate through trade relations and economic sanctions the influencing of other actors' behavior. Besides coercion and utilitarian power, Etzioni classifies a third form of power implementation: persuasive power. "Persuasive power is structured and organized, allocated and applied in much the same way as other kinds of power." It is "exercised through the manipulation of symbols, such as appeals to the values and sentiments of the citizens in order to mobilize support and penalize those who deviate" [*Etzioni*, p. 358]. This refers to normative assets such as feelings, values and symbols. In the implementation of power, which is the capacity to overcome part or all of the resistance against the introduction of changes, coercion has the strongest, utilitarian a moderate and persuasive power the least alienating effects. Coercion transforms the situation for the person in question by introducing a situation where no true options are available. On the other end of the scale of alienation, persuasive power – which affects a change of will – is similar to influence. Etzioni describes main compliance structures which are "based on force and high alienation (coercive compliance), remuneration and comparatively lower alienation (utilitarian compliance) and normative control and commitment or low alienation (normative compliance)" [*Etzioni*, p. 364].

The lowest level of alienation is the normative compliance structure because this implementation of influence does not suppress the actor's will or preferences, rather tries to influence these preferences. Ideally, the power wielder's preferred course of action should coincide with the needs, interests and values of its subjects. Derived from this definition of influence, legitimate power is defined as the power which coincides with the values of those affected by its implementation.

In comparison, it is evident that Dahl's 'influence' is a general terminology which encompasses forms of influence and specifies power solely as a sub-classification thereof. For Etzioni, influence is a special form of power implementation, a positive form, namely, the possibility for legitimate transformation of an actor's preferences, whereby the actor is conscious of the change.

Similar to Weber, "The Active Society's" analysis works with ideal forms and introduces new research possibilities: i.e., exposing the actual combination of these ideal forms in concrete political systems. The postulate of the least possible alienation and the highest or most frequent implementation of normative resources initiates a praxeology for steering political systems and the application of political power.

5) *Carl Friedrich von Weizsäcker's Power Analysis*

It is not surprising that Carl Friedrich von Weizsäcker, the scientist and peace researcher, conceptually unites fundamental biological concepts such as aggression and evolution and the theoretical political concept of power balance within international state systems with the power concept. Weizsäcker takes an historical-dialectical approach based upon the antithesis "freedom and authority." Economic freedom in the form of free trade, free and productive private enterprise or union coalition were the prerequisites for the evolution of the present state of economics and technology in the industrialized countries. However, the freedom during the period of Manchester Liberalism proves that unlimited freedom – and not just in the case of economic freedom – contains serious conflicts and dangers. Freedom must be checked by elements of a legitimately controllable power (authority) [*Weizsäcker*, p. 141].

Similar to Etzioni, who uses aspects of political power implementation to facilitate political transformation and societal steering, Weizsäcker explicitly refers to the "constructive role" of power: without the appropriate power resources the development of civilized cultures and their influences would have been unthinkable. His "anthropology of power" touches upon irrational forces which endanger evolution, is the domain of evil conceptualized in the philosophy of Jaspers.

In constrast to Weber, for whom authority is a sub-classification of power, Weizsäcker views authority as a comprehensive "complex phenomena" with elements of hierarchy, functions and power. The animal kingdom exemplifies the discussion of hierarchy: the 'pecking order' amongst chickens, the leader of a herd or pack, the flying formations of birds. Apparently there are certain advantages to this hierarchical structure which more than counterbalance classification or subordination; however the hierarchies within the animal world are not a problem of choice, rather innate (see Lorenz for Studies regarding the instinctual behavior of new-born ducks). There are also hierarchies within human life structures: in the family, at work, in political groups; however in different areas the roles can vary greatly, dependent upon the accepted or acquired role of each individual.

It does not suffice to characterize human co-existence within a simple model of classification and subordination. Role distribution is a highly qualified division of labour which demands human insight into goals and assumes the recognition of necessary distinctions between implemented functions. This division of functions seems to be reasonable; it takes diverse human tendencies into account and contributes significantly to the survival of the species through division of labor, i.e., higher economic productivity.

Along with hierarchy and function, both components of peaceful human co-existence, Weizsäcker introduces a third element of authority which is the source for the severity and the forces leading to conflict [*Weizsäcker*, p. 144]. Despite a simplified application of Freudian terms, fear and aggression have been justifiably included in this power concept. Within the proper social classification, fear – fear for survival, self-preservation and defense, as well as aggression – with rationalized aspects of preferential selection and self-preservation (hierarchical stability, being saved from hopeless, dangerous situations) can not simply be viewed as the cause of conflicts which threaten peace [*Weizsäcker*, p. 146f.]; this is pragmatically confirmed by longer periods of peace in the history of mankind. Power as "Humanum" leans towards limitlessness when perceiving and reacting to danger. Instability and danger within international state systems have increased since the classical

Synopsis: Power Concepts

A comparative study of behavioristic, sociological-behavioral, encyclopedic, cybernetic and anthropological-evolutionary concepts: (Dahl, Weber, Berle, Etzioni, Weizsäcker)

Power concepts	Questions and hypotheses	Analytical units	Power definitions	Methodology	Classification of power terminology	Effects of power
1) Behavioristic (Dahl)	A political analysis necessitates comparing influences.	*Individuals*, small groups.	Influence is a relation between actors. Power is defined as a subdivision of influence which can cause heavy losses when it is not obeyed.	Formalization; operationalism of terms and elaboration of mathematical equations.	Influence-power, power-authority, force (legitimacy, losses)	Behavior of third actor altered
2) Sociological-behavioral (Weber)	Power is the link between societal relationships and authority.	Individuals, groups, *bureaucracies*, states.	Power is the probability that an actor within a social relationship will be in a position to carry out his own will despite resistance, regardless of the basis on which this probability rests.	Definitions open to further concepts, uncertain ideal types: future research.	Societal action; societal relationship, power, authority; forms of authority (charismatic, traditional, legal, i.e., rational)	Behavior of others determined within institutional, bureaucratic framework
3) Encyclopedic (Berle)	How can the diverse manifestations of power be defined?	*Individuals* with power instincts, struggling for order within institutions using ideologies.	Power is undeniably personal. Power is part of the web of instincts, emotions, psyche and drive which constitute man's personality.	Description based on personal experience: five theories (i.e., power laws).	Power, individual, chaos, order, ideologies, institutions, responsibility	Power as the progressive force between chaos and order
4) Cybernetic (Etzioni)	The function of power is to overcome social resistance to an 'active society.'	*Society* and its steering mechanism.	The place of power in an active society is to bring about its transformation and realization of its values with as little as possible undermining the basis of authentic commitment, participation and legitimation.	Construction of ideal types.	Power resources, coercion, utilitaristic and persuasive power.	Societal changes and varying levels of alienation
5) Anthropological-evolutionary (Weizsäcker)	Power has a constructive and a destructive role.	*Evolution* of civilized cultures, states, the international state system.	Power is the source for the severity of strife and leads to conflict.	Inductive-reflective, by means of economic, biological and psychological analogies.	Freedom, authority (functions, hierarchy, power)	Constructive and destructive evolutionary effects, war or peace

'Balance of Power' politics to the present 'Balance of Terror'. As a peace researcher, Weizsäcker recalls that since the beginning of political theories in Greece, politics has largely been a theory of reasonable limitations of power. Today, more than ever, reason must preside over power.

4. Synopsis

Power as a relative and relational category with conceivable analytical units on varied levels, power based on diverse resources which can be partly quantitatively analyzed, power limitations, power transformation, forms of power: these are concrete political dimensions unveiled by the original set of questions (Part 2). They can be found in the synopsis, either on a general (analytical units) or individual (power resource) level. The systematic comparison of varied power concepts clearly illustrates, through the sharp contrasts, why the power concept is correctly defined as an amorphous concept.

There are varied analytical unit levels: individuals, groups, bureaucracies, societies, nation states, international state systems, which are conceivable references for other political science concepts such as decision making, system, conflict etc. It is also obvious that diverse theories and hypotheses lead to varied results in the five categories. The contextual deviations of the power definitions and, more clearly, the diverse terminology applied to each power concept demonstrate the leeway available when integrating concepts and conceptually structuring political power relations. This range is not available among other fundamental political concepts.

5. Desiderata

Even with this limited approach to the analysis of power, it has been made evident that certain concepts are assigned contrasting definitions. Etzioni classifies influence within power, whereas influence is the comprehensive terminology for Dahl. The same problem arises with the concepts power and authority when comparing Weber and Etzioni. There are also examples where overlapping concepts will be referred to, or defined with diverse terminologies [*White*, p. 16]. This calls for further contextual, terminological clarifications and integration.

The second problem derived from an analogy of concepts touches on the aspect of power measurement – a central topic of this book. Formalization or the operationalism of concepts, as well as the use of mathematical analyses (methodological stringency) to determine power relations is, in comparison to other power concepts, only achieved when serious limitations are taken into account. It could be a challenge to formalize certain power aspects on the levels covered in the concepts listed in 2) – 5). At the same time, there remains a constant challenge to integrate the formalized aspects and the more general classification of power terminology (i.e., Dahl's influence terminology, power, authority, force) such that there would be mutual benefit.

In conclusion, these diverse attempts to analyze power have unveiled descriptive, empirical-analytical and normative elements which can be found in the questions and hypotheses listed in the synopsis. A future analysis of power must cover all three levels. The elaboration and sophistication of the analytical methods, the importance of analyzing problems from a normative point of view – i.e., the transformation and steering of societies as well as the maintenance of peace – are motivations for destroying artificial barriers and attempting to integrate empirical and normative power analyses.

References

Aron, R.: Frieden und Krieg, Eine Theorie der Staatenwelt. Frankfurt 1963.

Behrens, H.: Politische Entscheidungsprozesse, Konturen einer politischen Entscheidungstheorie. Wiesbaden 1980.

Bendix, R.: Westeuropa als Gegenstand und Quelle sozialwissenschaftlicher Forschung. Sozialer Wandel in Westeuropa, Verhandlungen des 19. Deutschen Soziologentages. Ed. by J. Matthes. Frankfurt 1979.

Berle, A.A.: Power. New York 1969.

Dahl, R.: Modern Political Analysis. Englewood Cliffs 1963, 3rd ed. 1976.

– : Die politische Analyse. München 1973.

– : The Concept of Power. Behavioral Science 2, 1957, 201–215.

Deutsch, K.W.: The Analysis of International Relations. Englewood Cliffs 1968.

Etzioni, A.: The Active Society, A Theory of Societal and Political Processes. New York 1968.

Fucks, W.: Mächte von Morgen, Kraftfelder, Tendenzen, Konsequenzen. Stuttgart 1978.

Morgenthau, H.J.: Politics among Nations. New York 1960.

Niemann, B.: Machttheorie. Grundkurs Politische Theorie. Ed. by O.W. Gabriel. Köln 1978.

Noack, P., and *T. Stammen* (eds.): Grundbegriffe der politikwissenschaftlichen Fachsprache. München 1960.

Snyder, H.G., and *P. Diesing*: Conflict among Nations, Bargaining, Decision Making and System Structure in International Crises. Princeton 1977.

Weber, M.: The Theory of Social and Economic Organization. Glencoe, Ill. 1957.

– : Wirtschaft und Gesellschaft, Grundriss der verstehenden Soziologie. Tübingen 1972.

Weizsäcker, C.F.v.: Wege in der Gefahr, Eine Studie über Wirtschaft, Gesellschaft und Kriegsverhütung. München 1976.

White, D.M.: The Concept of Power: Semantic Chaos or underlying Consensus. IPSA Paper, Moskau 1979.

Ziegler, J.: Konzepte zur Messung der Macht. Berlin 1976.

3. Formal Analysis of Representation and Voting Procedures

Holler, M.J. (Ed.): Power, Voting, and Voting Power ©Physica-Verlag, Würzburg (Germany) 1981

Proportional Representation and Effective Number of Parties in Finland

M. Laakso, Helsinki and *R. Taagepera*, Irvine[1])

1. Introduction

Representative democracy ideally requires that the strength of every opinion in the representative assembly should be proportional to its share of popular support. Various electoral procedures have been devised to achieve near-proportionality between popular votes and the number of assembly seats of political parties. The most widely used method methods are d'Hondt, the Sainte Laguë and quota (the largest remainder) procedures. For a description of calculations involved see, e.g., *Rae* [1971].

But representative assemblies must also maintain a fair level of efficiency in their decision-making. Such efficiency may be impaired when there are too many parties represented in the assembly. An increase in the number of splinter parties lengthens and complicates the legislative process. It is more difficult to form government coalitions, and these last for a shorter time. The need to restrict the mushrooming of political parties has been widely recognized by statesment and scholars alike, although the connection between the number of parties and political stability is by no means clear and simple [*Lijphart; Nilson*].

The number of parties in a representative assembly can be controlled by denying representation to small parties whose popular vote falls below a certain threshold. Such thresholds are superimposed to an otherwise near-proportional procedure, e.g., in West Germany and Sweden. A similar effect is achieved, without an explicit threshold, by using simple majority (plurality) rule with single-seat districts as practiced by most Anglo-Saxon countries. Control of number of parties through electoral law always seems to conflict with the proportionality principle. A threshold denies the small party voters their due share of representation. The plurality procedure results in disproportionality even for major parties, as expressed by the well-known and much-disputed "cube law of elections" [see, e.g., *Taagepera*]. It ought to be mentioned, however, that the cube law does not affect local parties whose support is geographically concentrated.

Thus there is an inherent conflict between two goals. The ideals of democracy and equality require as proportional a representation as possible while efficient government often requires less proportional representation [cf. *Rae*, 1967, p. 144].

---

[1]) The authors wish to thank Professors Arend Lijphart and Pertti Pesonen for very helpful criticism.

Finland has been one of the relatively few countries where a nearproportional d'Hondt highest average formula has been applied since 1906 without any threshold to the elections for the single-chamber 200-member Finnish Parliament, *Eduskunta*. (For an overview of the Finnish party system see, e.g., *Pesonen* [1972]; *Nousiainen* [1971]; or *Laakso* [1975a]). But lately the number of parties has increased, and consequently debate has arisen regarding the possible introduction of a votes threshold. Thus Finland may be entering a period of electoral reform that is of twofold interest to political science worldwide:

1) This is a place and time where an input of scholarly wisdom gained elsewhere may have an effect on the outcome of a political reform. It would be a pity, if changes in the Finnish electoral system were carried out solely on the basis of statesmen's intuition (important though it is) without making use of the results of modern electoral studies.
2) The intensified study of electoral data in Finland during the reform debate may produce results that could be applied or should be rechecked elsewhere.

This paper reports the main results of a study pertaining to the second category. Our results involve measurement of effective number of parties, and of random and systematic deviation from proportionality.

Since the reform debate was triggered by an increase in the number of parties, and the goal is to reduce this number, an operational definition for the number of parties is needed in order to measure accurately the past trends and the potential impact of proposed changes. Such a definition will be given, and will obviously be useful for country studies elsewhere as well as for cross-national comparisons.

Since any attempt to reduce the number of parties through changes in electoral law is likely to reduce proportionality, one should define and measure the degree of disproportionality involved in the present system and in the potential alternative system. This is an old problem, and definitions abound [see, e.g., *Brams*, 1976, p. 151]. What this paper adds is a distinction between random and systematic deviation from proportionality.

Once the systematic deviation from proportionality and the effective number of parties are both measured for various possible electoral systems, their interrelations can be investigated. In the Finnish context, it is a question of identifying the system which, for a given degree of systematic disproportionality, yields the smallest effective number of parties, or vice versa. In the worldwide context it would be a matter of testing whether the correlations evolving from Finnish data analysis are confirmed elsewhere; but this aspect is outside the scope of this paper, apart from a brief comparison with *Rokkan/Hjellum* [1966] analysis of Norwegian data.

2. Effect of Different Electoral Laws on Seats Distribution

Jaakkola [1975] has applied various electoral rules to the actual votes distribution in nine Finnish parliamentary elections (1945–1972), and has calculated the seat distribution among parties that would have resulted. This is an approach *Rokkan/Hjellum* [1966] have used for Norway, and *Wildenmann* et al. [1968] and *Conradt* [1970] for West Germany. The rules Jaakkola used were the d'Hondt rule with electoral alliances among parties allowed (which Finland actually uses), d'Hondt with electoral alliances prohibited, Sainte Laguë with initial coefficient 1, modified Sainte Laguë (with initial coefficient 1.4), and the Droop quota used in conjunction with the largest remainder. In a quota system, parties get one seat with a fixed number of votes which for the Droop quota for a constituency of any size is defined as

$$\text{Droop quota} = \frac{\text{Total votes}}{\text{Total seats} + 1} + 1.$$

Jaakkola found that d'Hondt (especially without alliances) led to more deviation from proportionality than did the other rules. The deviation criterion used was

$$D_1 = \frac{1}{2} \sum_{i=1}^{n} \left| s_i - v_i \right| \tag{1}$$

where v_i is the fractional share of votes and s_i is the fractional share of seats for the i-th party (out of a total n parties involved). When all seat shares are equal to the respective vote shares, then D_1 takes its minimum possible value of zero. When a party with zero votes gets all the seats, then D_1 would reach its maximum possible value of 1. The D_1 values in Table 1 show that in Finnish postwar elections, the deviation from proportionality ranged from 2.3 % of the maximum possible deviation up to 6.8 %. Table 2 shows that the d'Hondt-with-alliances system used by Finland leads to an average deviation (4.4 %) intermediate between those that would have resulted, if Ste. Laguë or quota rules had been applied (2.5 to 2.9 % average deviations) or if the d'Hondt rule had been used with alliances prohibited (6.0 %). Such analysis assumes that change in electoral rules would not alter the voting habits of the electorate. In view of the relatively small changes in seats distribution this assumption is reasonable. Outcomes for individual elections that would result from alternative rules are tabulated by *Laakso* [1977]. No trends in time can be seen for D_1.

	Deviation from proportionality				Effective number of parties		Fractionalization of seats
Year	Total (D_1)	Random (D_{min})	Systematic (D_{syst})	a_{opt}	Votes (N_v)	Seats (N_s)	(F_s)
1945	.042	.028	.014	1.15	5.1	4.8	.79
1948	.045	.032	.013	1.11	4.9	4.5	.78
1951	.023	.022	.001	1.03	5.0	4.8	.79
1954	.032	.019	.013	1.10	5.0	4.7	.79
1958	.038	.023	.015	1.14	5.2	4.9	.79
1962	.068	.056	.012	1.19	5.8	5.1	.80
1966	.045	.044	.001	1.02	5.2	5.0	.80
1970	.056	.028	.028	1.24	6.1	5.6	.82
1972	.043	.027	.016	1.12	5.9	5.5	.82

Based on election data from Finland (1946–1973).

Tab. 1: Deviation from Proportionality and Effective Number of Parties in Finnish Parliamentary Elections, 1945 to 1972 (d'Hondt Rule with Electoral Alliances Permitted):

Electoral Rule	Deviation from proportionality: Total (D_1)	Random (D_{min})	Systematic (D_{syst})	a_{opt}	Effective number of parties: Seats (N_s)	Shapley power simple major.	2/3 major.
Perfect proportionality	.000	.000	.000	1	5.36	–	–
St. Laguë (1.0) with alliances	.025	.021	.004	1.05	5.22	5.09	4.99
St. Laguë (1.4) with alliances	.026	.020	.006	1.07	5.18	5.10	5.00
Quota (Droop) with alliances	.029	.022	.007	1.08	5.15	5.03	4.98
d'Hondt with alliances	.044	.031	.013	1.12	4.98	4.76	4.89
d'Hondt no alliances	.060	.032	.028	1.25	4.79	4.27	4.79

Based on seat distributions in *Jaakkola* [1975]. For individual elections results (except for Shapley power indices) are tabulated in *Laakso* [1977]. Rae/Taylor F can be calculated from N using $F = 1 - 1/N$.

Tab. 2: Average Effect of Different Electoral Rules on Seats and Power Distribution in Finnish Parliament (*Eduskunta*), Based on Actual Votes Distribution (1945 to 1972):

It would seem that, if the aim of the Finnish electoral rule were to ensure proportionality, a non-optimal procedure was picked, since both Droop quota and Ste. Laguë rules would have led to appreciably smaller disproportionality than the d'Hondt rule. But if the aim were to ensure near-proportionality for large parties while imposing a covert penalty on the very small ones, then the issue is not clear. We would have to distinguish between systematic deviation in favor of the larger parties and the "random" deviation that may hurt or help parties regardless of their size. (The random deviation in this context also may include cases where a party, large or small, regularly profits from its favorable geographic distribution among electoral districts.) For this purpose Jaakkola's data are reanalyzed in the first part of this paper.

3. Systematic and Random Deviation from Proportionality

Starting from fairly general preassumptions, *Theil* [1969] has shown that a systematic distribution of seats according to votes has to be of the form

$$\frac{s_i}{s_j} = \left(\frac{v_i}{v_j}\right)^a \tag{2}$$

for the sake of self-consistency. As before, s_i and v_i stand for the seat and vote shares, respectively, of the i-th party, and j designates any other of the parties. This expression can be transformed into

$$s_i = \frac{v_i^a}{\sum\limits_{j=1}^{n} v_j^a}\,. \tag{3}$$

The parameter a can in principle take any positive values. With $a = 1$ perfect proportionality is obtained. With $a = 3$ we obtain the "cube law" of simple majority systems which discriminate heavily against small parties. In general, the larger the a value, the more the large parties are favored. For a less than one, on the contrary, small parties would be favored. For $a = 0$, all n parties would receive equal shares of seats, regardless of vote shares. Equation (3) thus expresses a systematic rule of deviation from proportionality. Random deviations from such systematic rule can be expressed by

$$D_a = \frac{1}{2} \sum_{i=1}^{n} \left| s_i - \frac{v_i^a}{\sum_{j=1}^{n} v_j^a} \right| \tag{4}$$

which is analogous to Eq. (1). In fact, Eq. (4) yields Eq. (1) when $a = 1$. Note that D_a can vary from 0 to 1, like D_1.

For a given set of votes data (v_i) and the seat distribution (s_i) resulting from a given electoral rule, D_a can be calculated for any value of a. An example is given in Figure 1 where the 1972 votes and seats data (using the actual seat distribution) are applied to obtain a curve of D_a versus a. What we are looking for is the "optimal" value a_{opt} that minimizes the value of D_a. This residual deviation (designated as $D_{\min}$) represents the *random* deviation from proportionality in the sense that it profits neither small nor large parties on account of their sheer size, according to the Theil formula. (In other words, $D_{\min}$ can be understood as a residue which our exponential model does not explain.) This does not exclude the possibility that a party, large or small, may be hurt or helped by its geographic distribution among electoral districts or by a residual systematicity not expressed by Eq. (2). The degree of systematically size-dependent deviation could be expressed by the

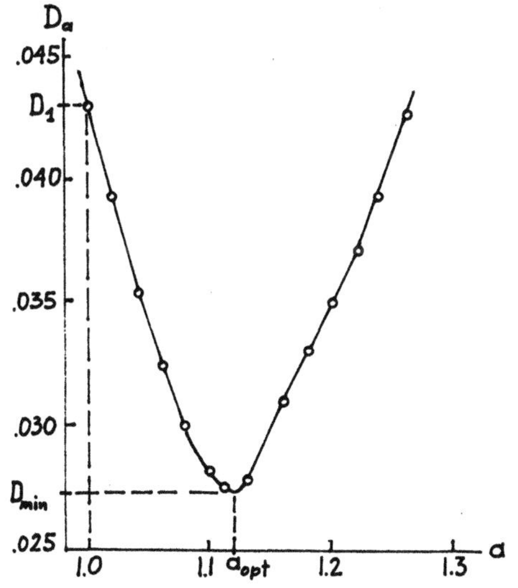

Fig. 1: Deviation from proportionality (D_a) vs. systematic disproportionality exponent (a), for Finnish 1972 elections (d'Hondt rule, electoral alliances allowed).
Data from *Jaakkola* [1975], calculations using Eq. (4).

difference between the total deviation (D_1) and the random deviation (D_{min}):

$$D_{syst} = D_1 - D_{min}. \tag{5}$$

If Eq. (3) applies exactly for each party when $a = a_{opt}$ then $D_{min} = 0$ and $D_{syst} = D_1$. In all other circumstances, $D_{min} > 0$ and $D_{syst} < D_1$. However, D_{syst} does not tell us whether the large or small parties are favored. Therefore, a_{opt} might be a better measure of systematic disproportionality. For a_{opt} larger than 1, we know that large parties are favored. It can be shown that, for a given constellation of votes, the ratio of D_{syst} and of $|a - 1|$ is approximately constant as long as a is not much different from 1; the proof is available from authors on request.

In Figure 1, $a_{opt} = 1.12$ which shows a small but clear systematic deviation in favor of large parties. With $D_1 = .043$ and $D_{min} = .027$, the extent of systematic deviation is $D_{syst} = .016$. In other words, the total deviation from proportionality is 4.3 % of the possible maximum, out of which 1.6 % is systematic (in favor of large parties) while 2.7 % is random profiting neither large or small parties). The random component is larger; this is the case for nearly all elections and rules investigated.

No straightforward calculus method has been found for determining a_{opt} because the summation of *absolute* values in Eq. (4) complicates the problem. Thus a_{opt} has to be determined from plots such as Figure 1, although experience enables one to guess the approximate location of the minimum.

The values of D_1, D_{min}, D_{opt} and a_{opt} for nine elections are given in Table 1. No trends in time can be seen. The corresponding average values for alternative election rules are shown in Table 2. All electoral systems tend to favor the larger parties. But for Droop quota and Ste. Laguë, this systematic bias is overshadowed by a much larger random deviation. In comparison, d'Hondt without alliances has almost equal systematic and random components although the latter also increases. Thus d'Hondt not only discriminates more but seems to be more erratic than the other systems. Tayloring electoral districts to suit the advantage of certain parties may be one possible reason for large D_{min} in the case of d'Hondt with alliances (which is actually used in Finland) but not in the case of the purely hypothetical d'Hondt rule without alliances allowed. Note that for all systems considered, $D_{syst} / |a - 1| = .10 \pm .02$ is nearly constant as stated before on the basis of theoretical calculations.

Individual election outcomes for alternative rules are available in *Laakso* [1977]. In a few elections (1951 and 1966) the Ste. Laguë and/or Droop quota rules would have yielded a_{opt} values slightly smaller than one (down to 0.98), thus effectively favoring small parties to a minute degree.

4. Effective Number of Parties on Votes, Seats and Power Share Level

Studies of the effect of electoral laws on fragmentation of party systems have often made use of the *Rae/Taylor* [1970] fractionalization indices. Fragmentation of an assembly into party shares s_i can be expressed by

$$F_s = 1 - \sum_{i=1}^{n} s_i^2 \tag{6}$$

provided that the number of seats is much larger than one. The same format applies to the vote fragmentation index F_V which is defined as $F_V = 1 - \sum_{i=1}^{n} v_i^2$. Both can in principle vary from 0 (when there is only one party) to nearly one (when every seat or vote goes to a different party). The Rae/Taylor fragmentation index is closely related to Herfindahl-Hirschman concentration index

$$\mathrm{HH} = \sum_{i=1}^{n} s_i^2 \tag{7}$$

and to a number of other apparently unrelated indices, as pointed out in *Taagepera/Ray* [1977].

It can be shown that the inverse of HH tells us how many parties effectively share the seats (or votes). Suppose first that all n parties have equal shares. Then each party has a share $1/n$ of the seats so that

$$\mathrm{HH} = \sum_{i=1}^{n} (1/n)^2 = n\,(1/n)^2 = 1/n. \tag{8}$$

When the shares are not equal, we can still define an "effective number" (N_s) of parties such that, by definition, we again have HH $= 1/N_s$. Then

$$N_s = 1/\mathrm{HH} = [\sum_{i=1}^{n} s_i^2]^{-1} = 1/(1 - F_s). \tag{9}$$

We are using the adjective "effective" here in the sense in which it is widely used in physical sciences [see, e.g., *Richards* et al., p. 594]: if a constant value of some quantity has an effect equivalent to that of a non-constant set of values, it is called an "effective value" of that quantity. While the effective number N_S carries the same information content as the fragmentation index F_S from which it can easily be calculated, N_S is intuitively more informative than F_S because it can be interpreted in terms of such a non-abstract entity as the number of parties. A more detailed discussion of the relations between N_S, F_S and the *Wildgen* [1971] hyperfractionalization index is given in a separate paper [*Laakso/Taagepera*].

The effective number of parties (as well as fractionalization) can be determined at several levels. *Rae* [1967] considered fractionalization at the votes and at the seats level, and concluded that, with very few exceptions, "electoral systems defractionalize parliamentary party systems," i.e., $F_S < F_V$. Because of the relationship $N = 1/(1 - F)$, Rae's conclusion also implies that $N_S < N_V$. As seen in Table 1, Finland has continued to obey this rule. In contrast to deviation indices which have remained in the same range, the effective number of parties shows a clear change in time, both on vote and seat level. After remaining stable at 4.8 ± 0.3, from 1945 to 1966, N_S has jumped to 5.5 since then. This is of course why talk about a vote threshold has started – a still manageable 4-plus-some party system has turned into a noticeably less manageable 5-plus-some party system. In terms of fractionalization, the corresponding shift of F_S (also shown in Table 1) from 0.79 to 0.82 would seem to be a minor one. In this particular case, the effective number of parties reflects the political situation better than does the fractionalization index.

But there is a further level at which N or F should be calculated – the level of potential power to affect decision-making. In an assembly where the seat shares are 51 % and 49 %, we have N_s very close to 2, reflecting the almost even distribution of seats. Yet on the level of being able to carry a vote, the 51 % party has absolute power, assuming strong party discipline and decisions by simple majority. But if decisions are made by 2/3 majority, then parties with 65 % and 35 % of seats, respectively, would have equal power, since any decision would require both party's support, although $N_s = 1.8$, reflecting the numerical predominance of one party.

One way to calculate potential power is that devised by *Shapley/Shubik* [1954]. For alternative possibilities, see *Brams* [1975, 157–198]. The simplest form of Shapley power share P_i for the i-th party is

$$P_i = p_i / n! \tag{10}$$

where p_i is the number of permutations in which the i-th party is pivotal in changing a minority into a majority, and $n!$ is the number of all possible permutations of n parties. These power shares (which add up to unity) can be used in Eq. (9) to calculate the effective number of parties (or the fractionalization index). The effective number of parties on simple majority basis (N_{majority}) is calculated from formula

$$N_{\text{majority}} = 1 - \sum_{i=1}^{n} P_i^{\text{maj}}$$

where P_i^{max} is the power share for i-th party using simple majority decision rule.

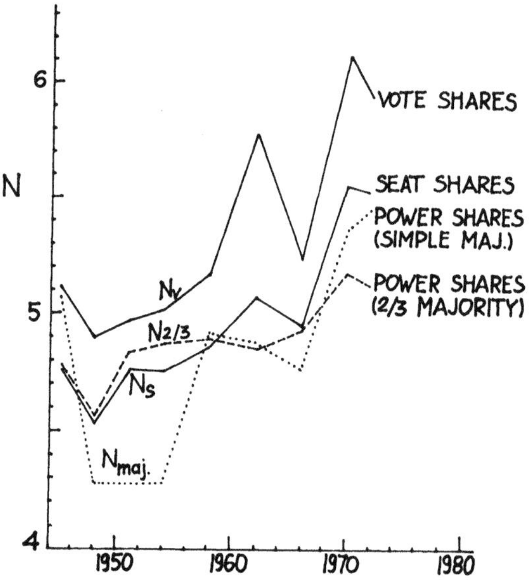

Fig. 2: Effective number of parties in Finland in years 1945–1972 (d'Hondt rule, electoral alliances allowed).
Based on election data in *Finland* (1946–1973) and calculations using Eq. (9) and (10).

Figure 2 shows the effective number of parties in Finland in nine elections on four different levels: seats and votes (as tabulated in Table 1), and also assembly voting power on simple and 2/3 majority basis (for which numerical data are not tabulated). It is seen that, at least in Finland, the Parliament power structure tends to defractionalize the party system even further compared to votes and seats, especially on the simple majority decision basis. The effective number of parties rises again on the 2/3 majority basis which is used in Finland for some basic decisions. The implication of this result is that the 2/3 majority rule in the Finnish parliament is in some sense more "democratic" than the simple majority rule, since the effective number of parties is larger. It is worthwhile to note, that the Shapley values with 2/3 majority also correspond more accurately than those with simple majority rule to parties' vote and seat shares in Finnish Parliament elections [see *Laakso*, 1975b].

The markedly wider fluctuations of N_{majority} compared to N_s or N_v reflect the discontinuous nature of political power when shares vary only slightly. For seat distribution 49-49-2, $N_{\text{majority}} = 3$ reflects adequately the key position of the third party for coalition formation, while $N_s = 2.1$ does not. Assume a slight shift of seats "in favor" of the third party but also of one of the major parties, during the next election, yielding the seat distribution 51-45-4. We still have $N_s = 2.1$ but now $N_{\text{majority}} = 1$, accurately reflecting the monopoly position of the largest party. While doubling its seat share, the third party suffers a total loss of power!

The effect of different electoral systems on the effective number of parties is shown in Table 2 on seat and decision levels. (On the vote level, of course, all systems are perfectly proportional by definition.) It is seen that the d'Hondt rule with alliances has on the average reduced the effective number of parties from 5.36 on the votes level to 4.98 on the seat level – a net decrease of about 0.4 party units. The more proportional quota and Ste. Laguë rules would have reduced N by only 0.2 units, while d'Hondt without alliances would have achieved a 0.6 unit reduction. On fractionalization scale (results not shown but easily calculable from $F = 1 - 1/N$) the reduction $F_v - F_s$ would be 0.01 to 0.02 for d'Hondt and 0.00 for the other rules. On the power share level, the system is defractionalized, compared to seat level, irrespective of electoral system for distributing seats. This further defractionalization does not depend on the electoral rule but only on the seat configuration, however it be obtained from a combination of votes and rules. For the rather stable votes distribution among parties that Finland has inherited from its history, it would seem from Table 2 that Ste. Laguë and quota rules would lead not only to more fractionalized seat distribution but also to more fractionalized power distribution than does the present d'Hondt rule.

5. Number of Parties vs. Disproportionality

Figure 3 shows the effective number of parties on seat level (N_s) plotted versus the systematic disproportionality indicator (a_{opt}), for perfect proportionality and for various electoral rules. There is a clear tradeoff between the two, and the relation is almost linear for the 1945–1972 averages shown. The linear correlation coefficient is very high ($r^2 = .96$). The regression line equation with respect to Finland is

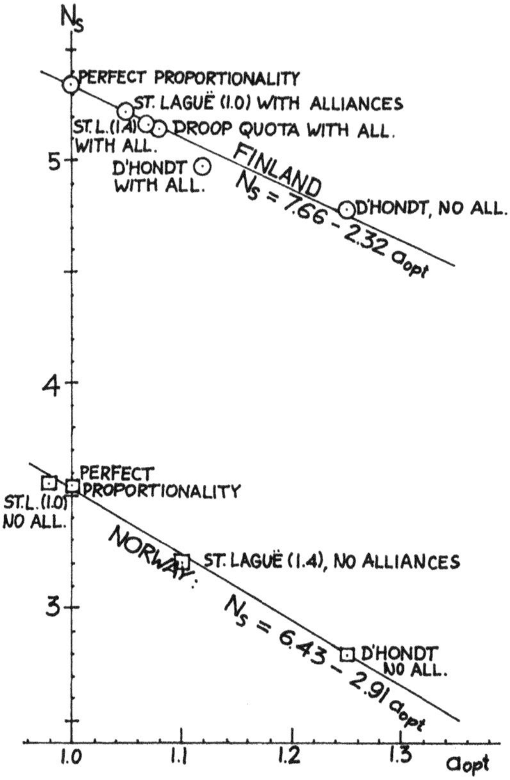

Fig. 3: Effective number of parties sharing assembly seats (N_S) vs. systematic disproportionality exponent, for Finnish and Norwegian data and for different electoral rules. Data from Tables 2 and 3.

$$N_s = 7.66 - 2.32\, a_{\text{opt}}. \tag{11}$$

The intersect coefficient 7.66 reflects the actual number of parties participating in the elections. For elections in which more parties participated, the individual election data yields points above the average regression line and the reverse is true for elections with few parties. The slope coefficient 2.32 may reflect a more basic relationship between N_S and a_{opt}, since it seems to maintain itself in all election years, although data scatter for individual elections is expectedly larger than is the case for the average of nine elections.

As a quick test of this possibility, we analyzed the Norwegian national assembly seat distributions according to different electoral rules, as calculated by *Rokkan/Hjellum* [1966]. Results are shown in Table 3 and also in Figure 3. The relation between N_S and a_{opt} is again linear ($r^2 = .98$) with regression equation

$$N_s = 6.43 - 2.91\, a_{\text{opt}}. \tag{12}$$

The slope is somewhat higher than Finland's. Combining the results for Finland and Norway, we may wonder whether the slope equation

$$dN_s / da_{opt} = 2.6 \pm 0.3 \qquad (13)$$

may not have more general validity. The systematic deviation index a_{opt} has the value 1.25 for d'Hondt rule (without alliances) for both countries. The values for Ste. Laguë differ markedly. Partly this result may be due to the limited number (4) of Norwegian elections analyzed. With unmodified Ste. Laguë rule, the Norwegian party system seems to lead to a small but fairly regular bonus for smaller parties, since a is less than unity.

	Deviation from proportionality				Effective number of parties
	Total	Random	Systematic		
Electoral Rule	(D_1)	(D_{min})	(D_{syst})	a_{opt}	(N_s)
Perfect proportionality	.000	.000	.000	1	3.55
St. Laguë (1.0), no alliances	.043	.037	.006	0.98	3.56
St. Laguë (1.4), no alliances	.054	.042	.012	1.14	3.20
d'Hondt, no alliances	.091	.036	.055	1.25	2.80

Based on seats distribution in *Rokkan/Hjellum* [1966].

Tab. 3: Average Effect of Different Electoral Rules on Seats Distribution in Norwegian National Assembly, Based on Actual Votes Distribution (1953 to 1965):

On the theoretical side it should be noted that, according to the basic Eq. (2), $a = 0$ would give equal shares of seats to all parties who receive votes, so that $N = n$. At the other extreme, when a tends toward infinity, only one party would receive seats so that $N = 1$. These conceptual "boundary conditions" suggest an exponential relationship between $(N - 1)$ and a_{opt} which can be approximated by a straight line (such as Eq. (11) and (13)) over a narrow range of a_{opt}.

Figure 3 presents in a nutshell the dilemma of efficiency versus proportionality: how much disproportionality would a polity be willing to tolerate in order to reduce the number of parties to a manageable level? It is largely a matter of philosophy. Only the $N - a_{opt}$ combinations near the regression line seem to be available for a given historically evolved system, unless one can find a device for lowering the very line. In this respect the d'Hondt rule with alliances stands out by being noticeably below the regression line, i.e., it produces a relatively large reduction in party number combined with a relatively moderate increase in disproportionality. If this observation should be confirmed by other country data, that would be a point in favor of the d'Hondt rule as used by Finland. *Rokkan/Hjellum* [1966] did not deal with this alternative in their Norwegian study.

6. Implications for Finland

A study of the effect of election rules on the fortunes of individual Finnish parties [*Laakso*, 1977] suggests that the d'Hondt rule with alliances allowed tends to give a bonus to parties with more than 17 % of votes, and to penalize the parties with less than that.

Until 1966 the Conservative Party (*Kokoomus*) remained slightly under this critical level, but since 1970 it has surpassed it. From the viewpoint of the electoral functioning, the formerly "small" *Kokoomus* has become one of the "large" parties. The significance of the critical level is reinforced by a coincidence: 17 % (actually 1/6) of *Eduskunta* seats enable a party to block constitutional legislation, a passive power that the *Kokoomus* has already had occasion to wield.

At the same time that *Kokoomus* grew, the Center Party (*Keskustapuolue*) and the Communist-dominated SKDL have seen their votes decline from around 20 % to around 17 %. A further loss in popular votes would result in an even larger loss of seats. If that should make them fall below 1/6 of the *Eduskunta* seats, the psychological effect may be appreciable, since recent political events have brought the 1/6 level to the attention of the electorate. The same applies to reverses that *Kokoomus* may suffer. With only the Social Democrats (25 % of votes) safely above the "large" party threshold, Finnish party politics may enter a period of increased fluctuations.

A vote threshold would introduce a much stronger penalty on small parties than does the present d'Hondt system alone. Parties which on proportional basis would earn two seats in the 200-seat *Eduskunta* would as a rule maintain at least one seat even if the systematic disproportionality index (a) were 1.25 (as it is for d'Hondt rule with alliances prohibited). A 4 % threshold which is presently discussed in Finland would block parties that even a value $a = 2$ could not eliminate completely. On the other hand, parties ever so slightly over the threshold may only profit from it while it has been seen that even the present modest value of $a = 1.12$ has affected negatively all party sizes up to 17 % of votes.

Because it would leave the small parties above 4 % level unaffected, a vote threshold would only marginally alter the effective number of parties. Recalculations for 1945–1972 votes data show that, for $a = 1.25$, a 4 % threshold would have reduced the effective number of parties in the *Eduskunta* only by 0.1 party units [see *Laakso*, 1977, for details]. Such calculations pre-assume of course that voting patterns would not have been altered by introducing the threshold, an inevitable but questionable assumption since the elimination of small-party representation would be a highly visible measure. In contrast, the electorate does not seem to be aware of the disproportionality involved in the present d'Hondt procedure.

If the goal of electoral reform were an effective 4-party system (Social Democrats, Communists, Center, and Conservatives), then even the d'Hondt rule with a 4 % threshold would be insufficient – the effective number of parties would remain around 5. In order to reach $N_S = 4$, a systematic disproportionality corresponding to $a = 2$ would be needed, i.e., parties should obtain seats in proportion to the *square* of their popular votes. At such attrition rate the effect of a threshold around 4 % would become negligible. But none of the near-proportional election rules considered here comes even close to the disproportionality needed. On the other hand, simple majority rule with single-seat districts with its "cube law" ($a = 3$) is likely to reduce N much below 4, thus eliminating some of the present 4 major parties. The present d'Hondt rule in conjunction with small electoral districts (4–5 seats per district instead of the present average of 14) may result in a 4-party system.

7. Implications Beyond Finland

This paper has presented a method to measure the degree of systematic disproportionality involved in near-proportional (and any other) electoral rules. While the existence of some bias against very small parties is a well-known and not altogether undesirable fact, the ability to measure it separately from random deviation seems to be new. It may be of special interest that the d'Hondt rule involves definitely more systematic disproportionality than do the Ste. Laguë or quota rules. The Finnish electoral politics may have adjusted itself to its d'Hondt rule, but the result is confirmed by data from Norway which uses the Ste. Laguë rule.

The notion of effective number of parties offers an easily computable and readily interpretable way to describe the evolution of party system fractionalization, and the reduction of number of parties from vote to seat level through the action of electoral rules. It is more sensitive than the Rae/Taylor F to small changes, and this has been seen to be an advantage in some contexts.

Since the number of seats does not always reflect a party's coalition formation power, the effective number of parties (or fractionalization index) based on Shapley power shares should also be kept in mind. N (power) tends to be smaller than N_s (seats) but is also more unstable.

Finally, the tradeoff between the effective number of parties and the deviation from proportionality, as effected by various electoral rules, may be subject to approximately the same rate of change (Eq. (13)) everywhere. This hypothesis is well worth testing with data of various countries.

References

Brams, S.J.: Game Theory and Politics. New York 1975.

– : Paradoxes in Politics. New York 1976.

Conradt, D.P.: Electoral Law Politics in West Germany. Political Studies **18**, 1970, 341–356.

Finland. Suomen Virallinen tilasto/Official Statistics of Finland. Series **XXIX A**, Nos. 20–32, 1946–1973.

Jaakkola, A.: The Proportionality of Finnish Parliamentary Elections, 1945 to 1972 (in Finnish). University of Jyväskylä. Institute of Social Science. Publ. No. 24, 1975.

Laakso, M.: Cooperativeness in a Multi-Party System: A Measure and an Application. European Journal of Political Research **3**, 1975a, 181–197.

– : The Proportional Methods of Representation and the Finnish Parliamentary Decision-Making System (in Finnish). Research Reports, Institute of Political Science, University of Helsinki. No. 35, 1975.

– : The Proportional Methods of Representation and Fragmentation of the Finnish Party System (in Finnish). Politiikka **3**, 1977, 202–225.

Laakso, M., and *R. Taagepera*: "Effective" Number of Parties: A Measure with Application to West Europe. Comparative Political Studies **12**, 1979, 3–27.

Lijphart, A.: Typologies of Democratic Systems. Comparative Political Studies **1**, 1968, 3–44.

Nilson, S.S.: The Consequences of Electoral Laws. European Journal of Political Research **2**, 1974, 283–290.

Nousiainen, J.: The Finnish Political System. Cambridge 1971.

Pesonen, P.: Political Parties in the Finnish Eduskunta. Comparative Legislative Behavior. Ed. by S.C. Patterson, and J.C. Wahlke. New York 1972.

Rae, D.W.: The Political Consequences of Electoral Laws. New Haven–London 1967.

– : The Political Consequences of Electoral Laws. 2nd ed. New Haven–London 1971.

Rae, D.W., and *M. Taylor*: The Analysis of Political Cleavages. New Haven–London 1970.

Richards, J.A., et al.: Modern University Physics. Reading, Mass., 1960.

Rokkan, S., and *T. Hjellum*: Norway: The Storting Election of September 1965. Scandinavian Political Studies **1**, 1966, 237–246.

Shapley, L.S., and *M. Shubik*: A Method for Evaluating the Distribution of Power in a Committee System. American Political Science Review **48**, 1954, 787–792.

Taagepera, R.: Seats and Votes: A Generalization of the Cube Law of Elections. Social Science Research **2**, 1973, 257–275.

Taagepera, R., and *J.L. Ray*: A Generalized Index of Concentration. Sociological Methods and Research **5**, 1977, 367–384.

Theil, H.: The Desired Political Entropy. American Political Science Review **63**, 1969, 521–525.

Wildenmann, R., *W. Kaltefleiter*, and *U. Schleth*: Auswirkungen von Wahlsystemen auf das Parteien- und Regierungssystem der Bundesrepublik. Zur Soziologie der Wahl. Ed. by E.K. Scheuch, and R. Wildenmann. Köln 1968.

Wildgen, J.K.: The Measurement of Hyperfractionalization: Comparative Political Studies **4**, July, 1971, 233–243.

Holler, M.J. (Ed.): Power, Voting, and Voting Power ©Physica-Verlag, Würzburg (Germany) 1981

The Relationship Between Voting and Party Strength in an Electoral System

N. Schofield, Colchester[1])

1. Introduction

There has recently been some discussion and interest expressed in Europe on the question of the appropriate criteria by which to judge electoral systems. The discussion has to some extent been stimulated by the attempt by the European Community to reach agreement on the allocation of seats in the European Parliament to the various members of the Community, and to decide on the adoption of a uniform electoral procedure throughout the Community as required by the Treaty of Rome.

A Commission on Electoral Reform has just made its report [The Report of the Hansard Society Commission on Electoral Reform] to the Hansard Society for Parliamentary Government. This Report presents a number of criticisms of the present electoral system in Great Britain and suggests various improvements.

The electoral system in Great Britain is a plurality, or winner takes all, system consisting of constituencies of about 65000 electors returning a single member of parliament. This system exhibits a distortion between the share of the total vote and the share of the seats obtained by the various parties. The distortion is generally to the advantage of the larger parties, and to the disadvantage of the smaller parties. For example in the election of February 1974, the Labour party with about 37 % of the vote, obtained 301 seats, or 47.4 %, and was able to form a government. The Liberal party with 19.3 % of the vote obtained 14 seats, or 2.2 %. This medium sized party with widely dispersed support is particularly disadvantaged. The smaller, regional, parties are not so severely disadvantaged. For example the Scottish Nationalists with 2 % of the vote, obtained 7 seats (1.1 %). Aside from these large scale distortions, there are distortions introduced by variation in constitutency size. Scotland is advantaged, with one member of Parliament representing, on average, about 52000 electors, whereas in Northern Ireland one member represents about 86000 electors.

It may well be the case that an electoral system which faithfully represents electoral choice could give rise to many small parties. In such a situation single party government

[1]) This material is based upon work supported by a British Academy Wolfson Fellowship at the Institute of Management Science, Berlin, 1976. I am grateful to John Yeabsley, previously of the Economics Department, Essex University, and now in the Department of Trade and Industry, New Zealand, and to Andrew Duffy of the Hansard Society, London.

could well be impossible, and certain instabilities, resulting from the necessity of coalition government, could arise. The report accepts that this is a possibility, and argues that some bias in the electoral system towards single party government may be acceptable. However such a bias should not be so extreme as to permit a single party, with considerably less than 50 % of the votes, to form a majority government. The bias in the electoral system may have been perfectly acceptable in 1955, say, when the Labour and Conservative parties obtained 96.8 % of the vote, and 98.56 % of the seats. In 1974 however they obtained 75 % of the vote and 94.17 % of the seats. These changes certainly indicate a decline in support for the major parties that should be reflected, in some fashion, in their political strength.

A modified, less biased, electoral system need not give rise to governmental instability as assumed by the conventional wisdom. *Dodd* [1974] has indicated, by an analysis of coalition government in Western Europe, that coalitions may be very stable indeed in terms of duration at least. What is relevant is the degree of polarisation between the parties. The Hansard report mentions that there appears to have been a process of increasing polarisation between the two major parties. This process may well be linked to the decline of support. Since the electoral system magnifies the changes in representation associated with changes in support. it may give rise to rapid changes of government. As a consequence there may be too rapid changes in policy, as each party, when in office, attempts to undo the previous government's policies.

Electoral bias may not therefore be necessarily associated with greater governmental stability. However the representation of very small parties may introduce some complexities into the electoral situation. The Hansard report argues that there should be some threshold which excludes such parties, except where these parties have fairly well defined natural constituencies.

Lack of bias may be regarded as an ethical criterion, since its ultimate justification may be through welfare considerations. Stability on the other hand, is an efficiency criterion, since its justification is in terms of the consequences of its occurrence. As is common in welfare economics, these two criteria cannot be simultaneously satisfied. Any argument about the optimal balance between the two criteria is necessarily subjective. However some measure of both bias and stability will give precision to the relationship between the two, and define a particular trade off between them.

The purpose of the present paper is to present a class of such measures. Some of these will give greater priority to stability, and some will emphasise the lack of bias. The bias component of the measure will be simply a measure of distortion between the expressions of preference by voters, and their eventual representation. Stability will be defined in terms of the concentration or fragmentation of the final pattern of representation. The next section of the paper introduces a general class of concentration measures, adopted from economic usage, and illustrates how they can be used to obtain measures of cross cutting between different patterns. The paper finally shows how information flow measures can be adapted for our purpose. This measure can then be used to compare different electoral systems, and can also indicate the effects of different constituency patterns.

2. Measures of Fragmentation and Cross Cutting

Rae [1967] and *Rae/Taylor* [1970] have defined and made use of a measure of diversity which can be used to describe political systems. In a specific application *Rae* [1967, p. 5] called this measure *fractionalisation*, and based it on

> "the probability that any two randomly selected voters will have chosen different parties in any given election. It is, in effect, an indicator of the frequency with which pairs of voters would disagree if an entire electorate interacted randomly."

More generally, suppose that a society is divided into a number of disjoint groups, labelled $y_1, \ldots, y_n$ say, such that the number of individuals in group y_i is $f(y_i)$, and the number of individuals in the society is N. The probability that a randomly selected individual belongs to group y_i is $p(y_i) = (f(y_i))/N$. This division of society into n groups can be called a cleavage, and can be regarded as a random variable denoted Y.

The Rae-Taylor measure of *fragmentation*, denoted $F(Y)$ for the moment, is defined as the probability that a randomly selected pair of individuals from the population belong to different groups in Y. In this case then, the fragmentation is given by

$$F(Y) = \sum_{i \neq j} f(y_i) \,/\, \binom{N}{2}$$

where $\binom{N}{2}$ is the total number of pairs in the society.

Let $\bar{F}(Y)$ be the probability that a randomly selected pair of individuals belong to the same group. Then

$$\bar{F}(Y) = \frac{1}{2} \sum_{i=1}^{n} f(y_i)\,(f(y_i) - 1) \,/\, \binom{N}{2}$$

and

$$F(Y) = 1 - \bar{F}(Y).$$

If N is large, then an approximation to $\bar{F}(Y)$ is given by

$$\bar{F}(Y) = \sum_{i=1}^{n} \frac{f(y_i)^2}{N^2} = \sum_{i=1}^{n} p(y_i)^2$$

and similarly

$$F(Y) = 1 - \sum_{i=1}^{n} p(y_i)^2.$$

In a number of the applications of this measure, the fragmentation along a particular cleavage is implicitly regarded as a measure in some sense of a social bad. For example *Rae/Taylor* [1970, p. 41] find a high negative correlation between fragmentation among political parties and the existence of party majorities, as might be expected. Herman and Taylor define governmental stability in terms of the life span of a government, and show that there is a significant negative correlation between fragmentation among political parties and governmental stability [*Herman/Taylor*, p. 31, hypothesis 5].

One justification for the hypothesis that fragmentation along a cleavage is a 'bad' may be that social groups generate collective goods for themselves that exhibit positive returns to scale [see *Schofield*]. The adoption of a quadratic concentration measure depends then on the suggestion that collective goods exhibit quadratic returns to scale.

Of course there exist various concentration, or fragmentation, measures and these have been used to study industrial concentration, or the distribution of income. Any fragmentation measure has the property that it will increase as small groups gain from larger groups. We can see this more formally by referring to the famous theorem by *Hardy/Littlewood/Polya* [1934], in the version due to *Dasgupta/Sen/Starrett* [1973]. Suppose

$$Y_1 = (y_{11}, \ldots, y_{1n})$$

and

$$Y_2 = (y_{21}, \ldots, y_{2n})$$

are two divisions along the same cleavage, ordered such that

$$p(y_{ir}) \leqslant p(y_{is}) \qquad \text{for } r < s.$$

Here $p(y_{ir})$ is the proportion of the population belonging to the r-th group on division Y_i. Write

$$p(Y_i) = (p(y_{i1}), \ldots, p(y_{in})).$$

Lemma. The following conditions are equivalent.

a) $$\sum_{j=1}^{k} p(y_{2j}) \geqslant \sum_{j=1}^{k} p(y_{1j})$$

for all $k \leqslant n$, with strict inequality for some k.

b) $p(Y_1)$ may be transformed into $p(Y_2)$ by a series of operations of the form

$$p(y_{1r})' = p(y_{1r}) + e$$
$$p(y_{1s})' = p(y_{1s}) - e$$

for $r < s$, and $e > 0$, with $p(y_{ij})' = p(y_{ij})$ if $j \neq r$ or s.

c) $p(Y_2)$ is not a permutation of $p(Y_1)$ but there is a bistochastic matrix Q such that

$$p(Y_2) = Qp(Y_1).$$

d) $R(Y_2) > R(Y_1)$ for any strictly S-concave real valued function R on $p(Y)$, or $\bar{R}(Y_1) > \bar{R}(Y_2)$ for any strictly S-convex real valued function $\bar{R}$ on $p(Y)$.

Condition a) of the lemma implies that the concentration curve of Y_1 lies above Y_2, and the lemma itself implies that the measure $\bar{R}$ will give the same ranking as the concentration curve if and only if $\bar{R}$ is strictly S-convex.

One may consider, for the measure R, the class of symmetric and strictly concave functions on $p(Y)$. More restricted still is the class of additively separable and iso-elastic functions.

The theorem has been used among others by *Sen* [1973] and *Atkinson* [1970] in studying inequality in income distribution. In this context one regards R as a social welfare function defined by

$$R(Y) = \sum_{j=1}^{n} U_j(p(y_j))$$

where $p(y_j)$ is the proportion of the total income obtained by individual j, and U_j is a strictly concave utility function defined on income for individual j.

For our purposes we may consider the class of additively separable and strictly convex functions given by

$$\bar{R}_\alpha(Y) = \sum_{j=1}^{n} p(y_j)^\alpha.$$

By the lemma this is a concentration measure for $\alpha > 1$, since it increases as larger groups gain from smaller groups.

The Rae-Taylor measure of concentration $\bar{F}$ is simply the Herfindahl index, and is defined essentially by considering dyadic relations between members of the society. This measure will be written $\bar{R}_2$ from henceforth.

If we define

$$R_\alpha(Y) = 1 - \bar{R}_\alpha(Y),$$

then for $\alpha > 1$, this is a strictly concave function of the division, and by the lemma, is a measure of fragmentation.

We can interpret this function analogously, for large n and integer α, as the probability that a randomly selected subgroup of size α from the society do not all belong to the same group on the division Y.

We may proceed as above and say that a division Y_1 is Rae preferred, with respect to α, to Y_2 when

$$\bar{R}_\alpha(Y_1) > \bar{R}_\alpha(Y_2),$$

and write $Y_1 \, \bar{R}_\alpha \, Y_2$.

We have restricted α to the range $(1, \infty)$. However *Hannah/Kay* [1974] have shown that, as $\alpha \to 1$ from above, the ranking $\bar{R}_\alpha$ approaches the ranking obtained from the entropy measure

$$\bar{H}(Y) = \sum_{j=1}^{n} p(y_j) \log_e p(y_j).$$

We may therefore take $\bar{R}_1$ to be this entropy measure; it will of course be a concentration measure.

The information measure

$$H(Y) = -\bar{H}(Y)$$

called the uncertainty in Y, is a fragmentation measure, so we may define $R_1(Y)$ to be $H(Y)$.

We may define $\bar{R}_\alpha$ for α in the range $(-\infty, 1)$. In this range $\bar{R}_\alpha$ will be a fragmentation measure, and $R_\alpha = 1 - \bar{R}_\alpha$ will be a concentration measure. As $\alpha \to -\infty$, $\bar{R}_\alpha$ corresponds to the maxmin criterion of justice of *Rawls* [1971]. Conversely as $\alpha \to +\infty$, $\bar{R}_\alpha$ ranks the divisions by the size of the largest groups.

Suppose now that the society is divided into groups along two different cleavages X

and Y. Let $p(x_i, y_j)$ be the probability that a randomly selected individual belongs to group x_i on the cleavage X, and to group y_j on the cleavage Y.

Rae/Taylor defined a measure of cross cutting $C(X, Y)$ between the cleavages as the probability that a randomly selected pair of individuals, who belong to one group on one cleavage, belong to different groups on the other.

Let us extend this definition by considering the probability $C_\alpha(X, Y)$ that a randomly selected subgroup of α individuals who belong to the same group on one cleavage do not all belong to the same group on the other. Thus

$$C_\alpha(X, Y) = \sum_{i,j} p(x_i, y_j)\,[p(x_i)^{\alpha-1} - p(x_i, y_j)^{\alpha-1}]$$

$$+ \sum_{i,j} p(x_i, y_j)\,[p(y_j)^{\alpha-1} - p(x_i, y_j)^{\alpha-1}]$$

$$= \sum_i p(x_i)^\alpha + \sum_j p(y_j)^\alpha - 2 \sum_{i,j} p(x_i, y_j)^\alpha.$$

Let us define

$$\bar{R}_\alpha(X, Y) = \sum_{i,j} p(x_i, y_j)^\alpha = 1 - R_\alpha(X, Y).$$

Then we may see that

$$C_\alpha(X, Y) = \bar{R}_\alpha(X) + \bar{R}_\alpha(Y) - 2\bar{R}_\alpha(X, Y)$$

$$= 2R_\alpha(X, Y) - R_\alpha(X) - R_\alpha(Y).$$

The Rae-Taylor cross cutting measure is given by

$$C_2(X, Y) = 2F(X, Y) - F(X) - F(Y).$$

Since C_α may be defined for all $\alpha > 1$, we have obtained a more generalised cross cutting measure based on α-ary relations rather than dyadic relations in the society. Further C_α has the same properties as C_2.

If the two cleavages X and Y are dependent then

$$p(x_i, y_j) = \delta_{ij}\, p(x_i) = \delta_{ij}\, p(y_j)$$

where

$$\delta_{ij} = 1 \quad \text{if } i = j, \text{ and } 0 \text{ otherwise.}$$

In this case

$$\bar{R}_\alpha(X, Y) = \bar{R}_\alpha(X) = \bar{R}_\alpha(Y),$$

so

$$C_\alpha(X, Y) = 0.$$

On the other hand if the cleavages are independent then

$$p(x_i, y_j) = p(x_i)\, p(y_j)$$

so that

$$\bar{R}_\alpha(X, Y) = \bar{R}_\alpha(X)\,\bar{R}_\alpha(Y)$$

and

$$C_\alpha(X, Y) = \bar{R}_\alpha(X) + \bar{R}_\alpha(Y) - 2\bar{R}_\alpha(X)\bar{R}_\alpha(Y)$$
$$= R_\alpha(X) + R_\alpha(Y) - 2R_\alpha(X)R_\alpha(Y).$$

We can define a cross cutting measure in the 'information' case, given by $\alpha = 1$, as follows.

The information uncertainty in Y given X is defined to be

$$H(Y/X) = -\sum_{i,j} p(x_i, y_j) \log_e p(y_j / x_i)$$

where

$$p(y_j / x_i) = \frac{p(x_i, y_j)}{p(x_i)}$$

is the conditional probability of y_j given x_i.

The joint uncertainty in X and Y is given by

$$H(X, Y) = -\sum_{i,j} p(x_i, y_j) \log_e p(x_i, y_j).$$

This may easily be shown to be $H(X) + H(Y/X)$; the uncertainty in X and Y together is equal to the uncertainty in X alone plus the uncertainty in Y given X.

Let us write

$$C_1(X, Y) = 2H(X, Y) - H(X) - H(Y).$$

Then

$$C_1(X, Y) = H(X, Y) - H(X) + H(X, Y) - H(Y)$$
$$= H(Y/X) + H(X/Y).$$

If X and Y are dependent, then obviously

$$H(X, Y) = H(X) = H(Y).$$

Thus

$$H(Y/X) = H(X/Y) = 0,$$

so

$$C_1(X, Y) = 0.$$

On the other hand if X and Y are independent, then knowing X, say, gives no information about Y. Thus

$$H(Y/X) = H(Y)$$

and

$$H(X/Y) = H(X).$$

Hence

$$C_1(X, Y) = H(Y) + H(X).$$

This definition of C_1 suggests that for general α we can define

$$R_\alpha(X/Y) = R_\alpha(X, Y) - R_\alpha(Y)$$

and regard $R_\alpha(X/Y)$ as a generalized uncertainty in X given Y. We may thus regard

$$C_\alpha(X, Y) = R_\alpha(X/Y) + R_\alpha(Y/X)$$

as the symmetric uncertainty between X and Y.

The relative uncertainty $H(Y/X)$ is a measure of the distortion in transmission between X, regarded as an input variable, and Y, regarded as an output variable. More generally then $C_\alpha(X, Y)$ may be regarded as a symmetric measure of distortion in the relationship between the two cleavages X and Y. Since an electoral system is essentially a method of transmitting information, from the structure of party support in cleavage X, to the structure of party strength in cleavage Y, we may define a measure of the distortion of this transmission.

3. On Distortion in Electoral Systems

Let X be the division of party support in the electorate, so that $p(x_i)$ is the proportion of the electoral voting for or preferring party i. Similarly Y is the division of party strength in the house of representatives. We define $p(y_i)$ to be the proportion of the electorate represented by the i-th party, and $p(x_i, y_j)$ to be the probability that an individual who votes for party i is represented by party j. We might suppose that in a perfect electoral system everyone is represented either by himself, or by the party of his choice. Such a system is essentially a direct democracy, satisfying the properties of symmetry and anonymity. However in any representational electoral system this cannot occur. Thus X and Y will not be completely dependent, and there will be some distortion. In a proportional representation system there will be some distortion due to the indivisibility of seats. As *Rae/Loosemore* [1971] have shown there will be a threshold of representation or share of the popular vote which a party must obtain to obtain any seats at all, and a higher threshold of exclusion or vote share which a party must obtain to be sure of obtaining some seats.

Since $C_\alpha(X, Y)$ is zero for the case of perfect representation, and increases as X and Y become randomly related, we may regard this measure as a measure of distortion in the process of translation of electoral support into representation. This measure of distortion is very much dependent on the nature of the constituency structure. In a single member constituency each voter is assumed to be represented by the party to which the representative belongs. Thus $p(y_i)$ is obtained by summing the number of voters belonging to constituencies which have a representative of party i. In a system with many constituencies the joint probabilities may be quite complex to calculate.

To show how the distortion measure behaves let us consider the two examples of Figure 1.

			Y: party strengths		
			A	B	total
Case I	electoral support X	A	.4	.2	.6
		B	.1	.3	.4
		total	.5	.5	

$R_2(X, Y) = .7$, $R_2(X) = .48$, $R_2(Y) = .5$, $C_2(X, Y) = .42$, $R'_2(X, Y) = .74$, $C'_2(X, Y) = .5$

Fig. 1

Suppose there are two constituencies. In the first constituency 80 % of the electorate vote for A, and under majority rule are represented by party A. In the second 60 % vote for B, and the constituency is represented by party B. When the two constituencies are the same size then the fragmentation measures on X and Y are R_2 $(X) = .48, R_2 (Y) = .5$ and the distortion index is C_2 $(X, Y) = .42$. If the two constituencies are combined and represented by one seat for party A then in this case R_2 $(Y) = 0$, and the distortion index increases to C_2 $(X, Y) = .48$. On the other hand if that constituency has two seats allocated to it, and under some proportional representation system both party A and party B receive one seat, then the distortion index becomes C_2' $(X, Y) = .5$. To see why, of the forty percent of the electorate who voted for party A in the first old constituency, 50 % are represented by party A and 50 % by party B. In other words the two cleavages are now *independent*. Only 50 % of this constituency is represented by the "correct" party and the cross fragmentation R_2' (X, Y) increases to .74.

If the constituency boundaries are redrawn so that 60 % of the electorate are represented by six seats of party A, and 40 % by four seats for party B, then in general the distortion will drop. In a sense a proportional representation system with a number of seats allocated to a single constituency will tend to increase distortion since an individual cannot say unequivocally whether representation is by one party or another. In general the finer the constituency system the lower the level of distortion.

As we have pointed out however if the support for a small party is widely dispersed throughout a number of constituencies then its electoral representation under a "first past the post" system is likely to be much lower than in a proportional representation system with large constituencies. The trade offs that are implicit in these features of both the electoral system and the constituency structure can be captured by our notion of distortion.

A somewhat crude measure of distortion in an electoral system can be obtained by ignoring the constituency structure. If we assume that the cleavages X, Y are independent, then this means we assume that when proportion $p(x_i)$ of the electorate in the country vote for party i, and the party has a proportion $p(y_i)$ of the seats, then a proportion $p(x_i, y_i) = p(x_i)\, p(y_i)$ of party i supporters are correctly represented. On this basis we obtain an upper bound for the distortion of the electoral system of the country. We call this the gross distortion.

In Britain for example after the 1970 election the R_2 concentration indices for electoral support and party representation were 0.4069 and 0.484 respectively. The gross measure C_2 of distortion was 0.497. In Germany after the 1972 election these indices were 0.418, 0.428 and 0.488 respectively (see Figures 2 and 3).[2]) This certainly suggests that the German proportional representation system has a tendency to less distortion. Figure 4 reports the result of the British election after October 1974, and illustrates some of the reasons for the concern expressed in the Hansard Report. Political support become much more fragmented with the small parties gaining 25 % of the vote (and 6 % of the seats) in 1974 as against 10 % and 2 % respectively in 1970.

The gross distortion measure (assuming independence) does not fully reflect the lack

---

[2]) The electoral results used here are taken from *Mackie/Rose* [1974a; 1974b and 1975].

Party	Vote	Seats	Proportion of seats
Labour	43.1	288	45.7
Liberals	7.5	6	1.0
Scottish Nationalists	1.1	1	0.15
Welsh Nationalists	0.6	0	0
Irish Representatives	0.7	3	0.5
Communists	0.1	0	0
Conservatives	46.4	330	52.4
Others	0.6	2	0.3
Number of Valid Votes 28 344 798			

Distortion Indices

α	$\bar{R}(X)$	$\bar{R}(Y)$	$C(X, Y)$	$T(X, Y)$
2	.4069	.484	.497	- 0.013

Fig. 2: Election results in the United Kingdom after the election of June 1970

Party	Vote	Seats	Proportion of seats
Christian Democratic Union	44.9	225	45.4
Social Democrats	45.8	230	46.4
Free Democrats	8.4	41	8.3
Communists	0.3	0	0
National Democratic Party	0.6	0	0
Others	0.1	0	0
Number of valid votes: 37 459 750			

Distortion Indices

α	$\bar{R}(X)$	$\bar{R}(Y)$	$C(X, Y)$	$T(X, Y)$
2	.418	.428	.488	- 0.06

Fig. 3: Election results in Germany after the election of November 1972

of responsiveness to electoral change in Britain between 1970 and 1974, and one should properly use the constituency data.

The theme of the Hansard Report was that some electoral distortion was acceptable if it could be interpreted as conducive to political stability. Assuming that stability and concentration in representation are positively related (though this is open to question) a welfare measure for the electoral system could be any function increasing in $\bar{R}(Y)$ and decreasing in $C(X, Y)$.

Party	Vote	Seats	Proportion of seats
Labour	39.3	319	50.2
Liberals	18.6	13	2.0
Scottish Nationalists	2.9	11	1.7
Welsh Nationalists	0.6	3	0.5
Irish Nationalists	0.2	1	0.2
Scottish Democratic Party	0.5	1	0.2
United Ulster Union	1.2	11	1.7
Communists	0.1	0	0
Conservatives	35.8	277	43.6
Number of Valid Votes:	28 900 292		

Distortion Indices

α	$\bar{R}(X)$	$\bar{R}(Y)$	$C(X, Y)$	$T(X, Y)$
2	.31822	.44307	.47931	-.02424

Fig. 4: Election results in the United Kingdom after the election of October 1974

For example

$$T_\alpha (X, Y) = \bar{R}_\alpha (Y) - C_\alpha (X, Y)$$

is such a welfare function: different values of α induce a different implicit trade off between stability and distortion.

As an example of the use of this welfare function, consider the European Parliament in 1974. Before direct elections there were 198 seats: representatives of a country's parties were sent to the European Parliament supposedly on the basis of electoral or domestic parliamentary strength. In the parliament the representatives belonged to one of seven groups or loose coalitions (Christian democrats, socialists, liberals, independents, progressive democrats, communists, conservatives). For example the French members of the Union des Democrates pour la Republique (UDR) essentially made up the Progressive Democrats. Figure 5 presents the structure of group membership by country at the beginning of 1975.[3]) Since the allegiance of parties to the groups is known one can *for each country* compute the electoral fragmentation and the representational fragmentation. Here for example a vote for the Labour party and representation 'in' the British subgroup of the Socialist group is a success (note that I assumed that the Labour party members actually took up their seats). Assuming each country is a single constituency (i.e., X and Y independent in the country) gives a gross distortion measure for the country. Britain not only had the highest measure ($\bar{R}_2$) of representation concentration, but the highest distortion index (C_2) and the highest stability index ($T_2 = -0.038$).

There was some variation between distortion in a country's parliament and in the European Parliament. For example the French Communist Party had 24.6 % of the vote and 15.5 % of the French parliamentary seats. However they only had four of the 36 French seats (about 11 %) in the European Parliament. As a result the gross distortion index in the French Parliament was .353 but .367 in the European Parliament.

Figure 6 aggregates electoral votes for the various "groups" in the European Parliament. Regarding the whole system as one constituency the distortion is .325, and this drops to .301 when the countries are regarded as separate constituencies. From this it would seem that there was some relationship between group strength and constituency structure (i.e., that different countries aggregated preferences rather differently for the European Parliament).

Let Z be the country cleavage (the division into nine country groups). If X and Z are independent then so will be Y and X. In this case the entropy index $H(Y/X)$ equals $H(Y)$. This will imply that the Ashby transmission index[4])

$$I(X:Y) = H(Y) - H(Y/X) \text{ will be zero.}$$

Figure 6 presents $H(Y/X) = H(XY) - H(X) = 1.43$. But $H(Y) = 1.63$ so $I(X:Y) = 0.2$ for the European electoral system. This seems to suggest that the overall dependence between X and Y is obtained from a relationship between voting strength and constituency structure: by this I mean that different countries use somewhat different "rules" in transmitting voting data to party strength in the European Parliament. However I have only

---

[3]) This data is taken from the Bulletin of the European Parliament, and *Fitzmaurice* [1975].

[4]) See *Ashby* [1965], and *Boyd* [1972] and *Conant* [1974] for the properties of the relative transmission indices.

Country	Christian Democrats	Socialist Group	Liberals & Allies	Independents	Progressive Democrats	Communist	Conservatives	Total
Belgium	6	4	2	2				14
Denmark		3	3		1	1	2	10
France	3	9	9		11	4		36
Germany	16	17	3					36
Ireland	3	2			5			10
Italy	16	6	2	3		9		36
Luxembourg	2	2	2					6
Netherlands	5	5	3			1		14
United Kingdom		15	1	1			19	36
Totals	51	63	25	6	17	15	21	198

Distortion Indices ($\alpha = 2$)	Country	$\bar{R}(X)$	$\bar{R}(Y)$	$C(X, Y)$	$T(X, Y)$
	Belgium	.218	.308	.392	−0.084
	Denmark	.189	.240	.338	−0.098
	France	.220	.237	.353	−0.1157
	Germany	.418	.426	.488	−0.0612
	Ireland	.358	.380	.465	−0.086
	Italy	.273	.297	.407	−0.110
	Luxembourg	.280	.332	.426	−0.093
	Netherlands	.247	.306	.402	−0.096
	United Kingdom	.407	.453	.491	−0.038

Fig. 5: Distribution of seats in the European Parliament in 1974, by Group and Country

presented this example to indicate the use of the indices. In some later work I hope to analyse the enlarged European Parliament after the election of June, 1979 to compare the gross differences, if any, between the representational system used by each country in determining party strength at the European constituency level.

Group	Vote	Seats	Proportion of seats
Christian Democrat	.253	51	.257
Socialist	.313	63	.318
Liberal	.106	25	.126
Independents	.052	6	.030
Progressive Democrats	.056	17	.085
Communists	.119	15	.075
Conservatives	.097	21	.106

Distortion indices ($\alpha = 2$)

$\bar{R}(X)$	$\bar{R}(Y)$	$C(X, Y)$	$T(X, Y)$
.201	.208	.325	−.1176

Separate Constituencies:

.201	.208	.301	−.093

Entropy measures for separate country constituencies:

$H(X, Y)$	$H(X)$	$H(Y)$	$H(X/Y)$	$H(Y/X)$	$I(X:Y)$
3.1	1.67	1.63	1.47	1.43	0.2

Fig. 6: Aggregate Distortion in the European Parliament in 1974

4. Conclusion

The various indices that have been introduced could be used to analyse various possible constituency structures for the European Parliament. While distortion, as we have defined it, may be reduced by dividing the country constituencies into smaller member constituencies, smaller political groupings with diverse support would be under represented. A proportional representation system for a whole country introduces distortion since there is no representation by a member of a single area. The suggestion by the Hansard Report of a mixed constituency and proportional representation system could give rise to a lower level of distortion. A choice of some parameter value α, and implicitly the acceptance of a certain trade off between stability and faithful representation, would theoretically permit the attainment of some 'optimal' electoral system, through the use of the indices introduced above.

References

Ashby, W.R.: Measuring the Internal Informational Exchange in a System. Cybernetica **VIII**, 1965, 5–22.

Atkinson, A.B.: On the measurement of inequality. Journal of Economic Theory **II**, 1970, 244–263. Reprinted in Atkinson, A.B. (ed.): Wealth, Income and Inequality. Harmondsworth, 46–68.

Boyd, J.P.: Information distances for discrete structures. Multidimensional Scaling, Vol. 1: Theory. Ed. by R.N. Shepard, A.K. Romney and S.B. Nerlove. New York 1972, 213–233.
Bulletin of the European Parliament (1975–1976).
Conant, R.C.: Information flows in hierarchical systems. General Systems **I**, 1974, 9–18.
Dasgupta, P., A. Sen, and *D. Starrett*: Notes on the measurement of inequality. Journal of Economic Theory **VI**, 1973, 180–187.
Dodd, L.: Party Coalitions in multi-party parliaments: a game theoretic analysis. American Political Science Review **LXVIII**, 1974, 1093–1117.
Fitzmaurice, J.: The Party groups in the European Parliament. Lexington, Mass., 1975.
Hannah, L., and *J.A. Kay*: Mergers and Concentration in the United Kingdom. Mimeo, Department of Economics, University of Essex, 1974.
Hardy, G., J. Littlewood, and *G. Polya*: Inequalities. London 1934.
Herman, V., and *M. Taylor*: Party systems and government stability. American Political Science Review **LXV**, 1971, 28–37.
Mackie, T., and *R. Rose*: The International Almanac of Electoral History. London 1974a.
– : General elections in western nations during 1973. European Journal of Political Research **2**, 1974b, 293–298.
– : General elections in western nations during 1974. European Journal of Political Research **3**, 1975, 319–328.
Rae, D.: The Political Consequences of Electoral Laws. New Haven 1967.
Rae, D., V. Hanby, and *J. Loosemore*: Thresholds of representation and thresholds of exclusion. Comparative Political Studies **III**, 1971, 479–488.
Rae, D., and *M. Taylor*: An analysis of cross cutting between political cleavages. Comparative Politics **I**, 1968, 534–547.
– : The Analysis of Political Cleavages. New Haven 1970.
Rawls, J.: A Theory of Justice. London 1971.
Schofield, N.: A Game Theoretic Analysis of Olson's Game of Collective Action. Journal of Conflict Resolution **19**, 1975, 441–461.
Sen, A.: On Economic Inequality. Oxford 1973.
The Report of the Hansard Society Commission on Electoral Reform (1976).

Holler, M.J. (Ed.): Power, Voting, and Voting Power ©Physica-Verlag, Würzburg (Germany) 1981

Manipulation of the Agenda by Strategic Voting: Separable and Nonseparable Preferences

E.M. Uslaner, College Park[1])

1. Introduction

The literature on vote trading and, more generally, strategic voting has largely been one of negative results. The most prominent is instability of voting or vote trading outcomes [*Gibbard; Satterthwaite; Riker/Brams; Oppenheimer*, 1973, 1975; *Uslaner/Davis; Koehler; Enelow/Koehler; Schwartz*]. There are, however, grounds for optimism about the prospect for finding some stability conditions [*Bernholz*, 1978; *Oppenheimer*, 1979]. In this paper, I shall examine some conditions for social choice in a democratic society which may lead to the adoption of the most preferred outcome (as determined by the Condorcet criterion, that outcome which is preferred to all others in pairwise comparisons). Specifically, I shall examine how strategic voting and vote trading might yield such outcomes under varying distributions of voter preferences across issues. The critical distinction here is between preferences which are independent across votes and those which are not.

The two main results which I shall establish are: (1) When preferences are not independent across issues, the outcomes from sincere and strategic voting will necessarily be distinct if a Condorcet winner exists (and if the voting is subject to strategic voting); and (2) when there is such a Condorcet winner, the outcome from strategic voting (or vote trading) cannot ultimately be upset by any coalition of voters with different preferences. The route to these results will lead us to a series of related questions, focusing on the different outcomes which might be selected (given a set of preferences) under varying voting

[1]) I am grateful to the General Research Board of the University of Maryland – College Park for a Faculty Research Award which provided the released time to work on this paper. I benefitted greatly from remarks by J.A. Oppenheimer, N.R. Miller, and M.J. Holler. P. Bernholz and his colleagues at the Institut für Sozialwissenschaften at the University of Basel, Switzerland, also provided many useful comments on an earlier draft I presented at the Institut in January, 1978. An earlier version of this paper was also presented at the 1978 Annual Meeting of the American Political Science Association, August 31 – September 3, 1978, New York, N.Y. J. Horney and T. Schwartz also gave me useful comments and ideas. This project began [see *Uslaner*, 1976] at the 1976 Mathematical Association of American College Faculty Workshop at Cornell University in the summer of 1976 and was funded by the National Science Foundation and The MAA. The comments of P. Straffin, Jr., P. Rice, and R.M. Thrall at the Workshop are also gratefully acknowledged. I bear sole responsibility for the interpretations therein.

procedures when preferences are not independent. We shall see that these voting procedures are not neutral and shall compare decision-making in legislative bodies, which generally vote upon proposals in sequence, with referenda, in which the mass public may be called upon to make a set of interrelated decisions at the same time.

This dual concern for sincere as opposed to strategic voting and for alternative voting procedures focuses our attention on a generic problem, that of manipulation. Strategic voting is one form of manipulation, manipulation of the outcome given a set of voting procedures through an assessment of which choice among a set of alternatives will yield the most utility for the voter. Agenda manipulation, on the other hand, is any structuring of the order of voting on propositions so that the order affects the outcome [cf. *Farquharson; Niemi* et al.; *Miller*, 1977b]. *Shepsle* [1978, 1979] has referred to outcomes which are not affected by agenda manipulation as "preference-induced," while those which are determined either by the order of voting or other factors of a legislative body as "structure-induced." As is shown in Shepsle's work, the question of agenda manipulation is particularly applicable to voting bodies such as the United States Congress where individual members can affect the agenda by proposing amendments to a pending bill; furthermore, the order of voting on proposed amendments is determined by long-standing rules in each house, so any legislator who proposes an amendment would be interested in obtaining the best possible strategic situation for it among the set of all amendments being offered. When we speak of the order of voting, we shall refer to agenda manipulation.

A voter is "sincere" if he (she) always votes according to his (her) preference ordering. Specifically, the voter always casts a ballot for his (her) most preferred outcome on an issue or set of issues. "Strategic" voting, on the other hand, includes all forms of manipulation of the outcome so that a voter may attempt to prevent a less desired alternative from being adopted – or attempt to get a more preferred alternative adopted – when the operative collective choice rule (given sincere voting) might select some alternative which the voter does not prefer. Vote trading is clearly a form of strategic voting. Whenever either the individual act of strategic voting or the coalitional act of vote trading has the potential to change the outcome from that determined by the voting procedure, the situation is said to be "manipulable."

Following *Dummett/Farquharson* [1961], I offer three further definitions which facilitate understanding the analysis below. (1) An *outcome* is the selection of some alternative by a collective choice rule – i.e., it is the final result of a voting procedure. (2) A *situation* is a strategy for a voter (or set of voters) over a given set of alternatives which yield an outcome. Finally, (3) a situation is *stable* only if there are no voters (or coalitions of voters) who can change the outcome associated with the situation by changing their voting strategies, so that the new outcome is preferred to the old for each member of the voting bloc. When a situation is stable, it is not subject to manipulation. Thus, the outcome must also be stable – and, hence, we have no manipulation of the outcome. But we must further answer the question as to whether a stable outcome also yields a stable situation. The literature on vote trading suggests that this may not be the case, but the conditions identified by Dummett/Farquharson suggest the contrary. Indeed, they sought to determine [1961, p. 35] that ". . . the existence of a stable outcome or of a stable situation, depends only on the preference scales of the voters and not at all on the actual voting procedure." We shall see in this paper how this result is established, although we caution the reader that: (1) The effects of the order of voting are hardly trivial; and (2) other institutional factors than the order of voting, such as the existence of a committee system for bill referral [*Shepsle*, 1978, 1979], may have a profound impact on the ultimate outcome selected which no strategy across voting outcomes might be able to reverse.

When a situation is not subject to possible manipulation of the outcome, the outcome selected, associated with that situation, must be stable. But the more prevalent – and interesting – cases studied involve unstable situations when an outcome might be upset by strategic behavior. Such behavior may be open to counter-manipulation so that the outcome is restored and cannot be overturned by any further strategy. In this case, both the outcome and its associated situation are stable at the final round of strategic behavior. *Farquharson* [1969, ch. 9] has called these stable situations "collective equilibria." We shall be concerned with the conditions under which such equilibria might exist. Clearly, any such analysis must also take into consideration manipulation of the agenda in order to demonstrate the Dummett/Farquharson claim that the structure of preferences also has an identifiable impact upon the outcomes of voting procedures.

We need one final set of definitions; unless specified, all definitions (implicit as well as explicit) follow those of *Schwartz* [1977]. I assume that each voter confronts a set of issues $[G_1, \ldots, G_n]$, each of which offers him (her) a binary choice; furthermore, these choices are made by voters with strict linear preference orders. Thus G_1, e.g., contains the set of alternative outcomes $[G_1^1, G_1^2]$ and each voter either prefers G_1^1 to G_1^2 or vice versa. A voter's preferences across the n-tuple G are said to be *separable* if the outcome G_1^1 (or G_1^2) does not affect the voter's preferences on the remaining issues $[G_2, \ldots, G_n]$. Separability and independence are the same thing. When preferences are separable, voting can proceed on an issue-by-issue basis without affecting the outcome over the n-tuple G; *Plott* [1971] has called this "path independence." When preferences are nonseparable, on the other hand, the order of voting is not independent of the outcome selected. Two voting methods that we shall consider here are: (1) *issue by issue voting*, in which motions (amendments) are considered serially according to some order of procedure; and (2) *simultaneous voting*, in which motions are all considered at the same time even when preferences are not independent. The initial results of this paper focus on both the order of voting and separability, while the final result is more general in that it does not depend upon the issue of separability. But this final result differs markedly from the others.

When preferences are nonseparable, the order of voting on issues is critical. If voters are sincere and if there is an undominated outcome (a Condorcet winner), nonseparable preferences may prevent this outcome from being selected. If the initial outcome from sincere voting is manipulable, sincere voting on each issue brought up for consideration simultaneously will never yield the Condorcet winner. We shall discuss this below. But note here that such simultaneous voting on issues is exactly what we find in initiatives and referenda. On the other hand, issue-by-issue voting (whether preferences are separable or not) typifies legislative decision-making. I shall examine the conditions for selecting the Condorcet winner when voters' preferences may either be separable or nonseparable and where the collective choice rule is either majority decisions through simultaneous voting or majority decisions with issue-by-issue voting. If voting is strategic, on the other hand, the undominated outcome (when one exists) will always be chosen. These results will be discussed in detail below.

The discussion will proceed largely through an example I have developed [cf. *Uslaner*]. It involves seven voters and three binary issues (eight possible outcomes). The preferences of the voters are nonseparable and there is a Condorcet winner. The example will be used to demonstrate how strategic voting can be used to ensure that the Condorcet winner is selected, how agenda manipulation can affect the outcomes chosen, and how an outcome and its associated situation can be stable. In the exposition of the more general theses about strategic voting, I shall limit the strategic possibilities to a somewhat restricted form of vote trading.

The restraints on the trading situation include: (1) Only feasible trades (in the sense that at least two voters must "exchange votes" on two or more motions) are allowed; (2) no voter will accept anything other than a "tit-for-tat" trade; i.e., no voter will agree to shift his (her) votes on two issues in return for another's exchange on a single issue; (3) the only trades considered will be those which alter the outcome of at least two elements of the n-tuple G; (4) only trades which are individually rational (which yield more utility, as ordinally measured, to each trader) will be considered; (5) voters prefer trades which yield more utility to those which yield less; (6) voters have perfect information regarding the preferences of all others; and (7) voters will be allowed to renege on trades made on the k-th round of trading on any future round.[2]) Minority-supported trades [cf. *Miller*, 1975, 1977a] will be permitted.

The results presented are rather general for strategic voting, assuming perfect information for the voters and that strategic voters (like vote traders) will employ strategies designed to yield as much (ordinal) utility as possible. The example serves to demonstrate the logic behind the arguments of the two theorems to be presented below. The first is a new result, the second a "rediscovered" one. We employ the vote trading example first to indicate how the separability of preferences affects the Condorcet winner when such an outcome exists; a theorem is then presented for all strategic voting situations. The example is employed again to demonstrate the stability of the strategic voting situation and a theorem is presented which indicates the conditions for the stability of such situations. Finally, a conjecture about the outcomes from alternative collective choice rules and their relationships to the feasible trading sets under agenda manipulation will be offered.

Vote trading is examined here for heuristic purposes. Any results which occur under such cooperative behavior also obtain under strategic voting without cooperation [cf. *Enelow/Koehler*]. Thus, the vote trading example is easily generalizable to discussions of strategic voting, although the converse is not necessarily the case. Furthermore, the new theorem offered here as well as the results incorporated later in the paper from other sources apply to strategic voting in general, not just to vote trading. The trading example serves expository purposes; it should also point to more optimism for the literature focusing on trading which, after all, is derived from that on strategic voting.

---

[2]) In permitting voters to renege on trades made on round k in previous rounds, I am not contradicting my assumption that voters have perfect information regarding each other's preferences. Instead, the situations in which a voter makes a trade and then reneges on it to form a coalition with another voter can be considered to be equivalent to the strategic calculations that such a rational voter might make in deciding whether to trade in the first place.

2. Nonseparable Preferences and Agenda Manipulation

Whether voters' preferences are separable or not, the undominated outcome (assuming that one exists) will always be chosen if voters cast ballots for elements of an entire n-tuple. The n-tuple $G = [G_1, G_2, \ldots, G_n]$ of binary issues will have 2^n possible outcomes if preferences are strict. If the voters are to select from among these n-tuples, they will select (by definition) the Concorcet winner when one exists in pairwise voting. However, voting situations generally do not involve choices over n-tuples. Legislative bodies consider each of the n issues serially; *Riker* [1958] and *Blydenburgh* [1971] have shown that in the American Congress, manipulation of the order of voting can induce a paradox of voting. But such a paradox is not the only instance in which the order of voting can affect the outcome. Legislatures make serial decisions on budgetary items, but any dollar spent on defense cannot be spent on welfare. We shall see that issue-by-issue voting in legislatures, when subject to manipulation, may not yield the undominated outcome, assuming one exists, when preferences among the issues voted upon are nonseparable. Furthermore, the order of voting will determine which outcome will be selected. But such manipulation will also be open to counterstrategies which can yield the Condorcet winner when one exists.

Issue-by-issue voting under nonseparable preferences may or may not select the Condorcet winner as the element in the choice set, $C(S)$, depending upon which of the n issues is voted upon first. However when preferences are nonseparable and voting occurs simultaneously, the Condorcet winner will not be chosen under sincere voting. Furthermore, if the initial outcome is manipulable, the undominated strategic outcome will differ from that selected by sincere voting when preferences are nonseparable. The best examples of actual voting procedures which may involve nonseparable preferences are initiatives and referenda in states and municipalities. What distinguishes such selection procedures is that they force voters to choose among a set of alternatives simultaneously rather than serially. When preferences are nonseparable across the range of issues, such a procedure will effectively ensure that an undominated outcome will not be selected. We shall discuss this in greater detail below.

Consider, first, the example in Table 1. There are seven voters, each of whom has strict linear order over three binary issues (eight possible outcomes). Furthermore, these preferences are nonseparable for all voters. In the table, the outcomes on each issue are denoted by a_1, a_2, b_1, b_2, c_1, and c_2. When necessary, I shall refer to motions by the letters a, b, and c (with their respective subscripts for the i-th voter); otherwise the order $a_1 b_2 c_1$ will be denoted by 121, etc. Table 2 shows the members preferring each outcome to every other. The entries above the main diagonal in cell (r, c) are those voters who prefer c to r, where r is the row outcome and c is the column outcome. From Table 2, it is clear that there is a Condorcet winner among the eight outcomes and that it is 122. Indeed, of the seven other outcomes, only four get as many as three votes against 122 in pairwise comparisons.

Given nonseparable preferences, how do we go about determining the majority winner? One could argue that 122 should be considered the majority winner, given that it defeats in pairwise comparisons every other alternative. However, neither legislative voting nor referenda employ such round-robin voting rules. In a referendum, in particular, voters must cast their ballots for several alternatives simultaneously to select a particular outcome over the issues. Hence, the method employed is that of issue-by-issue voting, which would be entirely appropriate and would select the Condorcet winner if preferences were separable [*Kadane*]. However, preferences are not separable in this example. If we were to employ simultaneous voting, the social choice would be 111. But 111 is the first choice of only voter 7.

Voter 1	Voter 2	Voter 3	Voter 4	Voter 5	Voter 6	Voter 7
$a_1b_2c_1$	$a_2b_1c_2$	$a_1b_1c_2$	$a_2b_2c_1$	$a_2b_1c_1$	$a_1b_2c_2$	$a_1b_1c_1$
$a_1b_1c_2$	$a_2b_2c_1$	$a_2b_1c_1$	$a_1b_2c_2$	$a_1b_2c_1$	$a_2b_1c_2$	$a_1b_2c_2$
$a_1b_2c_2$	$a_2b_2c_2$	$a_1b_1c_1$	$a_2b_2c_2$	$a_2b_2c_1$	$a_2b_2c_2$	$a_1b_2c_1$
$a_1b_1c_1$	$a_2b_1c_1$	$a_2b_1c_2$	$a_1b_2c_1$	$a_1b_1c_1$	$a_1b_1c_2$	$a_1b_1c_2$
$a_2b_1c_1$	$a_1b_2c_2$	$a_1b_2c_2$	$a_2b_1c_2$	$a_1b_1c_2$	$a_2b_2c_1$	$a_2b_2c_1$
$a_2b_2c_2$	$a_1b_1c_1$	$a_2b_2c_1$	$a_1b_1c_1$	$a_2b_2c_2$	$a_1b_1c_1$	$a_2b_1c_2$
$a_2b_2c_1$	$a_1b_1c_2$	$a_2b_2c_2$	$a_1b_1c_2$	$a_1b_2c_2$	$a_1b_2c_1$	$a_2b_1c_1$
$a_2b_1c_2$	$a_1b_2c_1$	$a_1b_2c_1$	$a_2b_1c_1$	$a_2b_1c_2$	$a_2b_1c_1$	$a_2b_2c_2$

Tab. 1: Preference Orderings for Seven Voters on Three Issues: Nonseparable Orderings with an Undominated Outcome

Row Outcome (r) \ Column Outcome (c)	122	111	112	121	221	212	211	222
122	X	1246	2467	23467	1367	14567	1467	13467
111	357	X	2457	2367	137	1357	1467	1357
112	135	136	X	236	1367	1357	13467	1357
121	15	145	1547	X	1567	1457	1467	157
221	245	2456	254	2346	X	1457	2467	23457
212	23	246	246	236	236	X	2467	2367
211	235	235	25	235	135	135	X	1357
222	25	246	246	234	16	145	246	X

Numbers above the main diagonal correspond to voters who prefer row outcome *r* to column outcome *c*; numbers below the main diagonal correspond to voters who prefer the column outcome *c* to the row outcome *r*.

Tab. 2: Voters' Preferences for Each Pair of Outcomes

Table 2 indicates that if the voters were casting ballots over the entire triple, they would select the Condorcet winner, 122. However, simultaneous sincere voting has yielded 111. Voters 1, 3, 6, and 7 constitute the "majority coalition" for a_1; 2, 3, 5, and 7 for b_1; and 1, 4, 5, and 7 for c_1. Of the coalition supporting b_1, voters 2 and 5 would have cast ballots for b_2 if they had prior knowledge that a_1 would be selected as the outcome on the first motion. It is thus far from clear what is a majority winner under nonseparable preferences. The collective choice rule of issue-by-issue voting yields (at least in this example) a different outcome from the Condorcet winner.

Let us consider another collective choice rule, issue-by-issue voting, and three alternative voting procedures under this rule. The first procedure involves voting on a first and then either *b* or *c*; the second involves voting on *b* first and then either *a* or *c*; finally, we vote upon *c* first and then either *a* or *b*. The choice of which alternative is voted upon second (or third) is of little consequence, since for three issues selection of the first issue determines the outcome over the entire triple. This is demonstrated in Tables 3, 4, and 5 below in which the numbers in parentheses identify the voters supporting each outcome and the bracketed outcomes are selected by the voting procedure. The issue-by-issue (serial) voting rule is as follows: an issue, say *a*, is selected to be voted upon first and members cast their ballots sincerely. As we see in Table 3, voters 1, 3, 6, and 7 choose a_1 while voters 2, 4, and 5 select a_2. For the second outcome, say *b*, voters continue to cast ballots sincerely but on the basis of their nonseparable preferences. Thus voters 2 and 5 now cast their ballots for b_2 instead of b_1 – although they would prefer, according to Table 1, that b_1 be selected. However, given that a_1 has been chosen by the voting body, voters 2 and 5 now prefer b_2 to b_1. Given the partial outcome $a_1 b_2$ after round two of the issue-by-issue voting, voters must choose between c_1 and c_2. While voter 4's preference in simultaneous voting was for c_1, given $a_1 b_2$ he (she) will vote for c_2 (second choice) over c_1 (fourth choice). Thus, we arrive at the Condorcet winner. However, we should not be overly optimistic about deriving a quick and easy method for selecting the Condorcet winner when one exists. The decision to vote on alternative a first was purely arbitrary. Had we relabelled issues *b* or *c* as *a*, we would not have arrived at 122. Note that 122 is chosen (see Table 3) regardless of which of the remaining alternatives is voted upon second.

Order of Voting:

		abc				*acb*	
[a_1]	(1, 3, 6, 7)	a_2	(2, 4, 5)	[a_1]	(1, 3, 6, 7)	a_2	(2, 4, 5)
b_1	(3, 7)	[b_2]	(1, 2, 4, 5, 6)	c_1	(1, 5, 7)	[c_2]	(2, 3, 4, 6)
c_1	(1, 5)	[c_2]	(2, 3, 4, 6, 7)	b_1	(1, 3, 5)	[b_2]	(2, 4, 6, 7)
	Outcome: $a_1 b_2 c_2$				Outcome: $a_1 b_2 c_2$		

Tab. 3: Outcomes from Serial Voting with Nonseparable Preferences: Issue *a* Voted Upon First

Order of Voting:

		bac				*bca*	
[b_1]	(2, 3, 5, 7)	b_2	(1, 4, 6)	[b_1]	(2, 3, 5, 7)	b_2	(1, 4, 6)
a_1	(1, 3, 7)	[a_2]	(2, 4, 5, 6)	c_1	(5, 7)	[c_2]	(1, 2, 3, 4, 6)
c_1	(1, 3, 5)	[c_2]	(2, 4, 6, 7)	a_1	(1, 3, 5)	[a_2]	(2, 4, 6, 7)
	Outcome: $a_2 b_1 c_2$				Outcome: $a_2 b_1 c_2$		

Tab. 4: Outcomes from Serial Voting with Nonseparable Preferences: Issue *b* Voted Upon First

Order of Voting:

cab				*bca*			
$[c_1]$	(1, 4, 5, 7)	c_2	(2, 3, 6)	$[c_1]$	(1, 4, 5, 7)	c_2	(2, 3, 6)
a_1	(1, 5, 7)	$[a_2]$	(2, 3, 4, 6)	b_1	(3, 5, 7)	$[b_2]$	(1, 2, 4, 6)
b_1	(1, 3, 5)	$[b_2]$	(2, 4, 5, 6)	a_1	(1, 5, 7)	$[a_2]$	(2, 3, 4, 6)
	Outcome: $a_2b_2c_1$				Outcome: $a_2b_2c_1$		

Tab. 5: Outcomes from Serial Voting with Nonseparable Preferences: Issue *c* Voted Upon First

When *b* is voted upon first, we arrive at the outcome 212. When *c* is the first alternative selected, 221 is the outcome. The issue chosen for first consideration will always have outcome 1 selected; this can easily be derived from the 111 outcome from issue-by-issue voting. The other two issues will have the 22 outcomes selected. It seems disturbing that any outcome other than 122 can be selected by a voting procedure. How can this occur?

We shall see that the outcomes 122, 212, and 221 constitute a trading set, *W*, containing outcomes which can be reached from other outcomes in the set by the conditions for vote trading described above. Note that 111 is not an element in *W*. Nor does the simultaneous voting method yield the same outcome as *any* serial voting rule. We denote the choice sets represented by each of these outcomes as C^1 $(S) = 111$ (simultaneous voting), C^2 $(S) = 122$, C^3 $(S) = 212$, and C^4 $(S) = 221$. The latter three outcomes are obtained from issue-by-issue voting using different issues to begin the voting procedure.

The critical distinction we wish to draw is first not between issue-by-issue and simultaneous voting procedures but rather between separable and nonseparable preferences when voting is simultaneous. If preferences across the set of alternatives are separable by issue, then it does not matter whether voting occurs serially or simultaneously; this follows directly from the definition of separability. Separability of preferences is the key issue. Specifically, if there is an undominated outcome which can be reached by vote trading or individual strategic voting, simultaneous voting will fail to yield that outcome when voters are sincere and at least some have nonseparable preferences. Forcing voters to cast their ballots simultaneously or to make binding commitments to support certain positions when preferences are nonseparable will prohibit voters from assessing the strategic situation at each round of voting so that they can adjust their strategies accordingly on the basis of results in the earlier rounds. Thus, in the example given above, simultaneous voting yields 111 whereas the Condorcet winner is 122. The latter outcome will be shown to be the strategic outcome below; furthermore, it will be seen to be stable so that at some point in vote trading no other outcome can be reached. There is, however, one restriction to this argument: There must be some voter(s) who can manipulate the outcome away from the initial result. This is hardly unreasonable. We thus propose the following theorem based upon the results presented above and previous work by *Kadane* [1972], *Kramer* [1972], and *Ferejohn* [1974]:

Theorem:

When an undominated strategic outcome exists, it will be distinct from simultaneous sincere voting if and only if there is a set of voters: (1) whose preferences are nonseparable and (2) who can manipulate the outcome of the voting game.

To prove sufficiency, we must demonstrate that the "if" statement holds; necessity requires that the "only if" condition holds, i.e., that nonseparability and manipulability imply that the undominated strategic outcome and that of simultaneous sincere voting will be distinct. The proof is based upon the assumptions that an undominated outcome exists, and that voters have perfect information about each others' preferences. The first assumption is contained in the theorem, the second is contained at least implicitly in similar results.

Ferejohn [1974], drawing upon results of *Kadane* [1972] and *Kramer* [1972], has proved that when there are separable preferences, the undominated strategic outcome will be the same as that for simultaneous sincere voting. He does not assume manipulability because when preferences are separable his theorem shows that there is no incentive for voters to try to manipulate the outcome from that obtained from simultaneous sincere voting. In Ferejohn's proof: (1) strict separable preferences are assumed; and (2) the undominated outcome is assumed to be unique and stable. If preferences are strict, the undominated outcome will be unique. We do not need these assumptions either for this theorem or for a result, to be presented below, which establishes the stability of the undominated outcome to attempts at manipulating the outcome. We turn now to the proof.

Proof:

Denote two possible outcomes over the n-tuple G as g and g'. Let g be the outcome from simultaneous sincere voting and g' be the undominated strategic outcome. Ferejohn's proof for necessity has shown that separable preferences imply that $g = g'$. We also know that nonmanipulability implies $g = g'$ or, alternatively, $g \neq g'$ implies preferences must be nonseparable or the outcome must be manipulable. To demonstrate sufficiency, we must show that $g \neq g'$ implies *both* nonseparability *and* manipulability.

Assume that $g \neq g'$. Define a set of voters on the n-tuple G as K, a subset of the entire electorate. If the situation is not manipulable, then $g = g'$ by definition (whether the preferences of voters in K are separable or not). Thus, the condition of manipulability must hold. Now assume that preferences are separable for voters in K and, without loss of generality, that the voters in K constitute a bloc which can manipulate the outcome. By the proof for necessity, however, separability of preferences implies that $g = g'$. Since voters outside of K cannot manipulate the outcome, $g = g'$ for them as well. Hence, for all voters, $g = g'$, establishing a contradiction. Thus, if $g \neq g'$, manipulability must hold and the preferences of at least the voters in K, those who can manipulate the outcome, must be nonseparable. This establishes sufficiency, i.e., that when the undominated strategic outcome differs from that of simultaneous sincere voting, there will be a set of voters whose preferences are nonseparable and who can manipulate the outcome. Q.E.D.

The preferences of only a minority need be nonseparable if that minority can manipulate the outcome, Clearly, if $g \neq g'$, the voters who favor g' can manipulate the outcome and, as we shall see, this result will be stable. While some set of voters K might be able to manipulate the outcome to some other alternative, say g^*, this potential for manipulability does not affect the above theorem. But g' dominates g^* by definition and we assume that g' exists. Thus, any minority-supported intermediate trades which might lead to g' eventually would be restored. Thus, within the context of undominated outcomes, the potential for voters to manipulate the outcome and the separability of preferences suffice to determine the conditions under which $g = g'$.

Schwartz [1977, p. 1005] has shown that if preferences are separable and the sincere and strategic outcomes are distinct under simultaneous voting, there will be no undominated outcome. However, we have assumed that an undominated outcome exists and thus either (or both) preferences for some voters must be nonseparable or the sincere and strategic outcomes are identical. Thus, when there is an undominated strategic outcome different from that of simultaneous sincere voting, preferences for at least some voters must be nonseparable – and also that the outcome must be manipulable (which is implicit in Schwartz' theorem). We note further that the set of voters who can manipulate the outcome and whose preferences are nonseparable need not be a majority of all voters.

We have seen that simultaneous sincere voting must lead to outcomes which are different from the undominated outcome if preferences are nonseparable and if the outcome is manipulable. To see that the manipulability condition is required, suppose that every member of an electorate has the nonseparable preference order on two issues of: a_1b_1, a_2b_2, a_1b_2, a_2b_1. Then regardless of the collective choice rule employed (and, thus, regardless of the order of voting), the Condorcet winner a_1b_1 will always be chosen. Indeed, we need not require that all voters have this preference order. A simple majority is sufficient to ensure that a_1b_1 will be invulnerable to manipulation by any other set of voters. However, if there is a heterogeneity of preferences across an electorate so that a situation is potentially manipulable, only a minority of voters need have nonseparable preferences to insure that the Condorcet winner is *not* chosen. If the remaining voters (whether their preferences are separable or not) could ensure the adaption of the Condorcet winner (and do not constitute a coalition of minorities themselves), the undominated outcome will always be selected by sincere voting. Thus, the set of voters K whose preferences are nonseparable may even be a singleton if one voter can change the outcome on any of the elements of the n-tuple G.

It is clear that manipulation of the agenda can produce suboptimal outcomes (compared to Condorcet winners). And the outcomes from the collective choice rule of issue-by-issue voting (without strategic voting) will produce distinct outcomes from the rule of simultaneous sincere voting. What I now seek to show is that: (1) strategic voting (specifically, vote trading) can ensure that the undominated outcome is reached; and (2) at some point the trading cycle is broken and the undominated outcome (and its associated situation) become(s) stable.

3. Issue-by-Issue Voting with Vote Trading

The literature on vote trading has highlighted the instability of strategic behavior, with the basic sources of argument being the sources of this instability (*Bernholz* [1973, 1974, 1975]; *Enelow* [1975]; *Ferejohn* [1974, 1975]; *Koehler* [1975]; *Miller* [1975, 1977a]; *Oppenheimer* [1973, 1975]; *Riker/Brams* [1973]; *Schwartz* [1975, 1977]; *Uslaner/Davis* [1975]; cf. *Enelow/Koehler* [1979]; *Bernholz* [1978]; *Oppenheimer* [1979]; and *Uslaner* [1976] for the beginnings of the search for stability conditions rather than "impossibility" results). Furthermore, as a type of strategic voting, vote trading includes all actions which could be obtained from such cooperative behavior. However, the general results which will be established cover all forms of strategic voting so that further examples may not be needed.

We now move to a consideration of whether the outcomes from simultaneous issue sincere voting *or* sincere issue-by-issue voting can be altered by strategic voting so that the undominated outcome can be reached if the operative decision rule did not initially select it or can be upset if it has been reached. I shall argue here that from either type of agenda manipulation which does not select the Condorcet winner, vote trading can be successfully employed: (1) to reach the Condorcet winner; and (2) to ensure that the undominated outcome is stable.

We first seek to determine whether the outcome 111 from simultaneous sincere voting for the preferences in Table 1 *can* yield 122 by vote trading. Let voters 2 and 4 trade on issues *b* and *c* (2 votes for b_2 while 4 votes for c_2). The outcome 122 is reached and the trade is obviously individually rational for both voters (cf. Table 2 above). Of the seven remaining outcomes, two cannot be reached by trades (121 and 112) since only one outcome would be changed. Outcome 222 cannot be reached through vote trading from 122 since only one issue (*a*) would be affected and, hence, cooperative trading is not possible. Note, however, that every other alternative is preferred by some majority to 222. Of the remaining alternatives, it is easily verified that (1) 211 would involve a three-member trade and cannot be achieved given the preferences in Table 1 and the trading conditions outlined above; and (2) only 212 can upset the strategic outcome 122. We get to 212 by a trade between 2 (who now votes for b_1, his original position before the first trade) and 3 (who votes now for a_2). But 122 can be restored since a majority (voters 1, 4, 5, 6, and 7) prefers this outcome to 212.[3]) Here 4 (to a_1) and 5 (to b_2) would exchange votes. At either situation (going directly or indirectly back to 122), we reach a stable situation so that *outcome 122 is invulnerable to any future trades.*

We state without demonstration that any trade from 111 to an alternative other than 122 will lead back to 122 and thus to a stable outcome. This result, while hardly intuitive, is consistent with the argument presented below and, as we shall see, follows directly from the work of *Enelow/Koehler* [1979]. We thus claim that we can get to the undominated strategic outcome through strategic voting (vote trading) even when simultaneous voting procedures are employed. We seek to show next that for serial voting procedures: (1) when the sincere and strategic outcomes do not differ, any attempts to manipulate the outcome to produce another result can be upset so that the undominated outcome will be stable; and (2) when these outcomes are distinct, strategic voting can be employed to yield the undominated outcome which will ultimately also be invulnerable to manipulation.

For sincere issue-by-issue voting, we can also derive trades such that: (1) in the case of C^2 $(S) = 122$ a trade might lead away from the undominated outcome but will not take place; and (2) for the cases of C^3 $(S) = 212$ and C^4 $(S) = 221$, there are trades which can bring us to 122. Any trades which can bring us to 122 either produce stable situations or chains of trading which can ultimately be broken (see the next section for a demonstration of this). In the case of C^3 (S) when the order of voting is *bac*, voters 5 and 7 can trade on issues *b* and *c* respectively and thereafter all voters cast their ballots according to

[3]) We can also get to 122 from 111 by a trade on *b* and *c* between voters 2 and 1 respectively. Furthermore, we can get from 122 to 212 by a trade on *a* and *c* between voters 6 and 4 respectively. However, these trades will form the same trading set as those presented in the text and will also yield 122 as the stable outcome.

their nonseparable preferences. The coalition supporting a_1 is now (1, 3, 4, 7); b_2 is (1, 4, 6, 7); and c_2: (1, 2, 3, 6). I shall not demonstrate the stability of these trading situations here. To do so would be too tedious. Instead, I shall examine the stability of C^2 (*S*) at both *abc* and *acb*.

Is 122 stable for C^2 (*S*)? We do not need to consider three-member trades on the triple since they are ineffective. The potential two-way trades from 122 involve the outcomes 212, 221, and 111. We shall consider each possibllity in turn. First denote C^2 (*S*) from *abc* as 122(1) and C^2 (*S*) from *acb* as 122(2).

First consider a trade to 212. At 122(1), there are already five votes for b_2 and only voters 2 and 3 prefer this trade to 122. Thus, no trade can be consummated which will yield 212. However, at 122(2), voters 2 and 3 can agree to trade on issues *a* and *b*, with 2 switching to b_1 and 3 to a_2. At this point, a three-way trade among voters 1, 4, and 5 to yield 121 *appears* possible, but it will not be consummated since 4 prefers 122 to 121 and a trade to 122 is possible. While either voter 1 or 5 is needed to consummate that trade and both prefer 121 to 122, they both prefer 122 to 212 (the last choice of each); and, in the absence of a trade with voter 4, 212 would remain the outcome. Thus, voter 4 can trade with either 1 or 5 (say, 1) so that voter 4 now votes for a_1 and voter 1 for b_2, yielding 122 again. One can show that only one further trade is possible from this situation, yielding 221 if 2 (switching to c_1) and 4 (switching to a_2) exchange votes. However, voters 1 (switching to c_2) and 3 (to a_1) can restore 122 and now it can be shown that this situation is invulnerable to any further manipulation.

Next, consider a direct trade to 221, which is preferred by voters 2, 4, and 5 to 122. For 122(2), 2 and 4 cannot trade since they are both at 222 and a reciprocal trade would yield 121 rather than 221; both voters prefer 122 to 121. For 122(1), the same situation holds for voters 2 and 4. In both cases, voter 5 is already at 221 and cannot trade. Finally, it is obvious that 111 cannot be reached from 122(2). At 122(1), *b* has five votes so no trade which could yield 111 is possible. The stability of 122 has been demonstrated. By the definition of a Condorcet winner, no majority-supported trade against 122 is possible and we have shown that no minority-supported trade can occur either. *The undominated outcome is invulnerable even to unrestricted vote trades.*

By similar arguments, we can show that once we have arrived at 122 from other outcomes, we can always get back to it and eventually be in a position from which we can never leave it through vote trading. Indeed, we shall do so below. However, we are forced to revise our argument that the issue-by-issue voting is "as arbitrary" as the simultaneous sincere voting function when preferences are nonseparable. First, at least one of the outcomes from the former procedure will yield the Condorcet winner, if one exists. Secondly, from any other outcome derived from this type of agenda manipulation, strategic voting (including vote trading) can ensure that the Condorcet winner will be selected. Now, this is also the case for simultaneous sincere voting. Yet, manipulation of the agenda by issue-by-issue voting is characteristic of legislative voting situations. Thus, it will always be *possible* (if not realizable in actual situations) for the undominated outcome to be obtained either by trading or by individual strategic voting.

Simultaneous sincere voting, however, is found most typically in referenda and the large, unorganized, and often uninformed electorate is quite unlikely to realize the strategic opportunities open to it. Transaction costs are immense; furthermore, there are more incentives for legislators who must interact with each other on a wide variety of issues to engage in such strategic behavior (even if subconsciously) than there are for citizens as electors to do so. Most citizens who are quite well informed and perhaps even willing to exchange votes simply do not have the opportunities to develop even partially cooperative strategies with others. Furthermore, the assumption of perfect information is considerably less plausible for such large and unorganized electorates. Thus, *the referendum is a particularly poor device for making social choices if preferences across the issues under consideration are not independent of each other. If such preferences are not independent the undominated outcome* (according to the theorem proved above) *will be beaten by some inferior alternative with certainty.* In contrast, legislative bodies will be considerably more likely to arrive at the Condorcet winner when one exists. Collective decision making by legislatures thus (according to the criteria advanced here) is preferable to that done by the larger electorate because the decisions of the latter are more subject to uncontrollable manipulation of the agenda. Lest legislative decision-making become dictatorial, however, there must be some mechanism for assuring the accountability of the elected representatives to the electorate, even if the larger body is not given the power to participate directly in policy formation [*Schattschneider*, ch. 8].[4])

Most discussion of constitution-making seems less concerned with faithful representation of the mass public by elites than with arriving at the undominated outcome for the preferences of whichever group is making the decisions. And there is ample evidence from referendum voting to indicate that there is cause for alarm that such elections may not yield the Condorcet winner if one exists. Voters may often be called upon to decide whether to raise or lower taxes (as occurred with property taxes in Ohio and California in June, 1978). In both cases, the referendum voters rejected higher taxes; indeed, the Jarvis-Gann initiative (Proposition 13) in California involved a state constitutional amendment which sharply reduced property taxes and also placed severe restrictions on increasing taxes in the future. While both the Ohio and California results could be viewed as indicating widespread voter rejection of high property taxes, we must note that in each case there were other issues which were not on the ballot. In each case, it is not clear whether the Condorcet winner was in fact chosen – or could have been. The issue in Ohio was not simply higher property taxes, but also whether schools would open in many municipalities in the fall.

In California, almost two-thirds of the voters supported Proposition 13, but 70 percent of the respondents to a Los Angeles Times-CBS News Poll indicated that they did not believe that services would have to be cut [*Kraft*]. Certainly, this case of not having to pay for services that one receives would be everyone's Condorcet winner; just as clearly (except, perhaps, to the supporters of Jarvis-Gann), there is no free lunch. Fewer than five

[4]) In examining the question of legislative decision-making relative to referenda or initiatives, one must also recognize that the legislators might have a different set of preferences than the voters who elected them. Thus, the comparisons between referenda and legislative decision-making must keep in mind the prospect that the suboptimal referendum outcome may nevertheless be preferred by a majority of the voters to a decision which might be reached by the legislature. The suboptimality of referendum decision-making when preferences are nonseparable and potentially manipulable remains a real concern – and it is most disturbing when one believes that the members of the legislature have preferences which are similar to those of the electorate.

percent of the sample indicated that they would be willing to exchange their tax dollars for reduced fire and police protection. The voters were not offered these choices at the polls, but this is precisely the point I want to stress: Referenda often artificially separate issues on which voters have nonseparable preferences. When such outcomes are manipulable (whenever there is no majority which is able to enforce its preference ordering, whether separable or nonseparable), issue-by-issue voting with nonseparable preferences will fail to yield the Condorcet winner. And this is particularly likely to occur among mass electorates, when compared to legislative settings in which members deal with each other over long periods of time and must develop a sense of mutual trust. The referendum electorate never meets collegially – and most voters do not know each other. Hence, they certainly cannot know others' preferences. Furthermore, a mass electorate is a much larger body than most legislatures, thus making communication among its members is – even when there is perfect information about preferences – virtually impossible. The sheer size of that body makes assimilation of all relevant information most difficult and thus inhibits successful strategic calculations.

Joining several issues when preferences are nonseparable may be the only way to reach a Condorcet winner when one exists, whether such joining occurs through individual strategic voting or vote trading. Yet there is widespread distrust of such arrangements. In December, 1978, a three-judge state appeals court in New Jersey invalidated a $100 million bond issue in New Jersey because it violated the provision in the state's constitution which stated that the legislature "shall not . . . create debt or debts . . . unless the same shall be authorized by a law for some single object or work distinctly specified" [*Waldron*]. A bond issue of such magnitude perforce contains appropriations for a variety of projects, thus ensuring that there will be at least some trade-offs and probably vote trades in the proposition as it appears on the ballot. Not only did the judges fail to realize that vote trading might produce a socially desirable result, but they also were implicitly insisting that all issues are separable with respect to the preferences of the electorate. Constitution makers may thus be as poorly informed on how to reach a Condorcet winner as popular writers who also denounce such strategic behavior by legislators.

4. Stability in Voting: A General Result

How general is the example in Table 1 and what are the broader implications for stability? It is my contention that the example is quite general. Let us note here that there are three trading sets: $W = (122, 212, 221)$; $Y = (111, 121, 211, 112)$; and $Z = (222)$. Outcome 222 is not preferred by a majority to any other alternative. Furthermore, there is a majority preference for W over Y and (as noted) Y over Z and this collective preference is transitive. Among the elements of W, 122 is the undominated outcome and will be reached at some point. We know that this is the case from a theorem of *Enelow/Koehler* [1979] which states that if a majority-supported vote trade is upset by strategic voting, that trade can be restored by further strategic voting even if there is no cooperation among the voters (i.e., there are individually rational incentives to restore this outcome). Thus, the elements of W do not cycle among themselves. However, those in Y do have the potential to form a cycle of trading outcomes. If trading is restricted to elements of Y, then outcome 111 is preferred to the other members of this trading set and outcome 211 is beaten in pairwise voting by all other members of *Y*. When trading is allowed with alternatives in both *W* and *Y* (*Z* is irrelevant here), cycles among the elements of *Y* can emerge because of the preference distributions for outcomes 212 and 221 in the set *W*. So far, we have established a set of results about the stability of outcomes under various voting orders and voting strategies; these are summarized in Table 6. The result to which I now turn involves the argument that at some point one can never leave the undominated outcome once it is reached through strategic voting (vote trading).

	Simultaneous Issue-by-Issue		Serial	
Preference Type	Outcome Manipulable	 Non-Manipulable	Outcome Manipulable	 Non-Manipulable
Separable	Sincere Outcome = Strategic Outcome = Condorcet Winner[1])	Sincere Outcome = Condorcet Winner[1]) Strategic Outcome Not Relevant	Sincere Outcome = Strategic Outcome = Condorcet Winner[1])	Sincere Outcome = Condorcet Winner[1]) Strategic Outcome Not Relevant
Nonseparable[2])	Sincere Outcome ≠ Strategic Outcome = Condorcet Winner[1])	Sincere Outcome ≠ Condorcet Winner[3]) Strategic Outcome Not Relevant	Sincere Outcome may = Strategic Outcome (Depends upon Order of Voting) Strategic Outcome = Condorcet Winner[1])	Sincere Outcome may = Condorcet Winner[1]) (Depends upon Order of Voting) Strategic Outcome Not Relevant

[1]) Actual result depends upon distribution of voters' preferences.

[2]) For at least those voters who can manipulate the outcome.

[3]) Regardless of preference distribution for voters.

Tab. 6: Order of Voting and Strategic Possibilities: Assuming Existence of Condorcet Winner

While this claim seems somewhat bold, particularly given the basically negative results of the vote trading literature of the recent past (and the force behind such arguments which the Gibbard-Satterthwaite impossibility results on manipulability have added), the conditions for stability are not as stringent as one might expect. Furthermore, they are not newly discovered – although they have been ignored. The reason for the state of blissful ignorance is that the source of most of the argument is a rarely cited and poorly organized article by *Dummett/Farquharson* [1961, p. 33] in which the basic conclusion is stated explicitly, albeit incomplete, only in one sentence of the abstract.

We state the following theorem and indicate how it has been proved:

Theorem:

An outcome (or set of outcomes that do not cycle) is stable, as is its associated situation, if it is undominated for majority voting games.

Dummett/Farquharson [1961, 36–40] present a rather detailed set of conditions relaxing the Black-Arrow concept of single peakedness to prove that for majority games, the set of outcomes (denoted as *"U"* in their article) has a top (one or more undominated outcomes that do not cycle). They also demonstrate, albeit in the midst of their more general argument, that if a set of outcomes has a top, the situation must be stable [1961, p. 36]. The question remains: Is the stable situation/outcome the same as the top? According to the Enelow/Koehler result (and the example presented above gives added force to this argument), it must be that the undominated outcome is the stable one. If this were not the case, then one could always upset by strategic behavior the "stable" outcome and restore the undominated outcome. But this argument is clearly contradictory. Hence, the undominated outcome is the only one which can be stable and also have an associated stable situation.

The rather complex conditions that *Dummett/Farquharson* [1961, p. 39] identify as being sufficient for the set of outcomes to be undominated need not be repeated here. *Sen* [1970, p. 184] has established a much weaker result:

*Theorem (Sen's 10*6)*:

The necessary and sufficient condition for a set of individual orderings over a finite set of alternatives to be in the domain of the majority-decision [social decision function] is that every triple of alternatives must satisfy at least one of the conditions [Value Restriction, Extremal Restriction, and Limited Agreement].

A social decision function is simply a function which selects the top element in an outcome set, rather than rank ordering all of the elements (which is accomplished by a social welfare function). We need not be concerned with Extremal Restriction or Limited Agreement since they are much stronger conditions than Value Restriction. Value Restriction [*Sen*, 1970, p. 174] is defined as a condition such that "[*i*]*n* a triple (x, y, z) there is some alternative, say x, such that all concerned individuals agree that it is not worst, or agree that it is not best, or agree that it is not medium." This condition is weaker than that of Black on single-peakedness or of the Dummett-Farquharson conditions.

Beginning with a rather simple example of agenda manipulation, we have worked our way through comparison of agenda manipulation devices for separable and nonseparable preferences, the differences in voting outcomes for separable and nonseparable preferences, the capacity for vote trading agreements to yield the Condorcet winner even when obstacles such as agenda manipulation are present, the difficulties in circumventing agenda manipulation in referenda (particularly in comparison with legislative decision-making), and the stability of undominated outcomes with respect to strategic manipulation under very general conditions. We have moved from a very specific case to an extremely general result, building upon previous steps along the way. We are not finished quite yet.

I offer a final conjecture: The outcomes in the trading set W for a set of binary decisions when voters have nonseparable preferences are equivalent to the elements in the set containing the outcomes of the possible orders of sincere issue-by-issue voting. Note that this is the case for the example in Table 1; the two sets contain only the elements (122, 212, 221). The trading set *W*, which dominated the other two elements in the set, was restricted to those alternatives which could defeat the Condorcet winner 122 by minority-supported trades. Hence, the elements of *W* can easily be shown to dominate the other alternatives. It is thus not surprising that the same outcomes should constitute the results of sincere issue-by-issue voting with nonseparable preferences when the agenda is manipulated to alter the order of voting. When all possible orders are considered, we have a set of alternatives which is in some sense "superior" to all others. This is the case even though stable traces can ensure the adoption of 122. Is this result unique to the example presented in this paper? Perhaps, but the linkage between agenda manipulation and strategic alternatives seems far from spurious. We have established some general conditions for stability through strategic voting. We now must examine the relationships among situations leading to stability so that we can better understand the processes of arriving at stable out outcomes.

References

Bernholz, P.: Logrolling, Arrow-Paradox, and Cyclical Majorities. Public Choice **15**, 1973, 87–102.

– : Logrolling, Arrow Paradox and Decision Rules: A Generalization. Kyklos **22** (1), 1974, 49–62.

– : Logrolling and the Paradox of Voting: Are They Really Logically Equivalent? A Comment. American Political Science Review **69**, 1975, 961–962.

– : On the Stability of Logrolling Outcomes in Stochastic Games. Public Choice **33** (3), 1978, 65–82.

Blydenburgh, J.C.: The Closed Rule and the Paradox of Voting. Journal of Politics **33**, 1971, 57–71.

Dummett, M., and *R. Farquharson*: Stability in Voting. Econometrica **29**, 1961, 33–43.

Enelow, J.M.: A Few Remarks on Vote Trading, Logrolling and the Voting Paradox. University of Rochester, mimeo, 1975.

Enelow, J.M., and *D.H. Koehler*: Vote Trading in a Legislative Context: An Analysis of Cooperative and Non-Cooperative Strategic Voting. Public Choice **34** (2), 1979, 157–176.

Farquharson, R.: Theory of Voting. New Haven 1969.

Ferejohn, J.A.: Sour Notes on the Theory of Vote Trading. California Institute of Technology Social Science Working Paper 41, 1974.

– : Sophisticated Vpting with Separable Preferences. California Institute of Technology Social Science Working Paper 77, 1975.

Gibbard, A.: Manipulation of Voting Schemes: A General Result. Econometrica **41**, 1973, 587–601.

Kadane, J.B.: On the Division of the Question. Public Choice **13**, 1972, 47–54.

Koehler, D.H.: Vote Trading and the Voting Paradox: A Proof of Logical Equivalence. American Political Science Review, 1975, 954–960.

Kraft, J.: Populist Hedonism . Washington Post (June 11), 1978, C7.

Kramer, G.H.: Sophisticated Voting Over Multidimensional Choice Spaces. Journal of Mathematical Sociology **2**, 1972, 165–180.

Miller, N.R.: Logrolling and the Arrow Paradox: A Note. Public Choice **21**, 1975, 107–110.

– : Graph-Theoretical Approaches to the Theory of Voting. American Journal of Political Science **21**, 1977b, 769–803.

– : Logrolling, Vote Trading, and the Paradox of Voting: A Game-Theoretical Overview. Public Choice **30**, 1977a.

Niemi, R.G., et al.: Strategic Voting: Some New Results and Some Old Questions. Presented to the Seminar on Mathematical Models of Congress, Aspen, Colorado, June, 1974.

Oppenheimer, J.A.: Relating Coalitions of Minorities to the Voters' Paradox, Or Putting the Fly in the Democratic Pie. University of Texas, mimeograph, 1973.

– : Some Political Implications of 'Vote Trading and the Voting Paradox: A Proof of Logical Equivalence': A Comment. American Political Science Review **69**, 1975, 963–966.

– : Outcomes of Logrolling in the Bargaining Set and Democratic Theory: Some Conjectures. Public Choice **34** (3–4), 1979, 419–434.

Plott, C.R.: Path Independence, Rationality, and Social Choice. Econometrica **41**, 1971, 1075–1091.

Riker, W.H.: The Paradox of Voting and Congressional Rules for Voting on Amendments. American Political Science Review **52**, 1958, 349–366.

Riker, W.H., and *S.J. Brams*: The Paradox of Vote Trading. American Political Science Review **67**, 1973, 1235–1247.

Satterthwaite, M.A.: Strategy-Proofness and Arrow's Conditions: Existence and Correspondence Theorems for Voting Procedures and Social Welfare Functions. Journal of Economic Theory **10**, 1975, 187–217.

Schattschneider, E.E.: The Semisovereign People. New York 1960.

Schwartz, T.: Vote Trading and Pareto Efficiency. Public Choice **14**, 1975, 101–109.

– : Collective Choice, Separation of Issues and Vote Trading. American Political Science Review **71**, 1977, 999–1010.

Sen, A.K.: Collective Choice and Social Welfare. San Francisco 1970.

– : Social Choice Theory: A Re-Examination. Econometrica **45**, 1977, 53–89.

Shepsle, K.A.: Institutional Structure and Policy Choice: Some Comparative Statistics on Amendment Control Procedures. Presented at the 1978 Annual Meeting of the American Political Science Association, New York 1978.

– : Institutional Arrangements and Equilibrium in Multidimensional Voting Models. American Journal of Political Science **23**, 1979, 27–60.

Uslaner, E.M.: Vote Trading in Legislative Bodies: Opportunities, Pitfalls, and Paradoxes. Mathematical Association of America College Faculty Workshop in Applied Mathematics Module. Department of Operations Research, Cornell University, mimeo, 1976.

Uslaner, E.M., and *J.R. Davis*: The Paradox of Vote Trading: Effects of Decision Rules and Voting Strategies on Externalities. American Political Science Review **69**, 1975, 929–942.

Waldron, M.: Court in Jersey Voids Bond Plan Passed by Voters. New York Times (December 2), 1978, p. 25.

Holler, M.J. (Ed.): Power, Voting, and Voting Power © Physica-Verlag, Würzburg (Germany) 1981

Order-of-Voting Effects

B.H. Bjurulf, Lund and *R.G.Niemi*, Rochester

1. Introduction

The order in which alternatives are voted on is one of a variety of techniques of agenda manipulation that affect the outcome of voting processes. Our purpose in this paper is to derive strategies for such manipulation under two widely used voting procedures and to analyze the effects of such manipulation on voting outcomes. Our work builds directly on the pioneering efforts of *Black* [1958] as extended and modified by *Farquharson* [1969] and *Miller* [1977]. For the procedures analyzed, it effectively completes this particular line of inquiry.

In 1958 *Black* concluded that under the amendment procedure "... the later any amendment enters the voting, the greater its chance of adoption" [1958, p. 40]. *Farquharson* [1969, Appendix 1], on the basis of a few examples, generalized this advice to the successive procedure. However, he also noted that this conclusion only applied if voting were sincere (i.e., in accord with voters' preferences). For sophisticated voters (i.e., those who vote strategically in a sense to be defined below), the exact opposite was true – "the earlier a proposal is voted on, the better its chance." From these observations, *Farquharson* made the general recommendation that "to favour a proposal put it last if the voters are sincere, but if they are sophisticated, put it first" [1969, p. 62].

Farquharson's advice is good, but it is not optimal. That is, by making the advice more specific, it can be improved upon. Numerous examples of this will be given below. Working independently from us, *Miller* [1977] derived propositions which further support, extend, or modify Black's and Farquharson's work. He established certain necessary conditions on the voting order for a proposal to be selected under a given voting procedure and assumption about how individuals vote. These results improve our understanding of the effects of voting order. Yet the problem remains that Miller's conditions are necessary but not sufficient. Hence they are not a complete guide to the selection of optimum strategies.

In addition to providing the best possible advice about voting strategies, complete specification of the results yields other important insights. These concern the effects of voting order under sincere vs. sophisticated voting and the relationship between the "strength" of an alternative (i.e., how many alternatives it is socially preferred to) and the voting outcome. The results also yield the probability that an alternative in a given position in the voting order will win, results that are likely to be generally useful in the study of agenda manipulation.[1])

In the first section of the paper we define the voting procedures to be considered and specify our assumptions about individual voting behavior (sincere and sophisticated voting). We also describe a classification of social preferences which will be of considerable use in the analysis. Then we analyze, in turn, sophisticated and sincere voting under the amendment procedure and sophisticated and sincere voting under the successive procedure. The final section shows the relationship between strength, position in the voting order, and the probability of winning, and yields strong support for the possible superiority of sophisticated over sincere voting.

2. Voting Procedures, Individual Voting Behavior, and Classification of Social Preferences

Amendment Procedure[2])

With the alternatives arranged in some predetermined order, the initial poll is taken between the first two alternatives. A second poll is taken between the winner of the first poll and the next alternative in the voting order. This process of pairing the winner of one poll against the next alternative in the voting order continues through the entire list of alternatives. An alternative cannot be reintroduced once it is defeated. In the end, one of the alternatives emerges as the social outcome.[3])

Successive Procedure[4])

The initial poll is taken for or against the first alternative in a previously determined voting order, such as $a_1, a_2, \ldots, a_n$. If a_1 is accepted, $a_2, \ldots, a_n$ are rejected. If a_1 is rejected, a second poll is taken for or against a_2, with similar consequences. Ultimately, if a_{n-1} is rejected, a_n is automatically accepted. In many parliaments, a_n is always the status quo.

Sincere Voting

If individuals vote sincerely, they vote strictly in accordance with their preferences. When only two alternatives are involved, this means voting for the alternative higher in the individual's preference order. In a binary vote between two *sets* of alternatives, an individual votes for the set containing the alternative he or she most prefers. If the most

---

[1]) These are the kinds of probabilities used by *Plott/Levine* [1978] (which they called the strength of an agenda), though they used a different voting procedure and different assumptions about individual voting behavior in their work.

[2]) The amendment procedure is used in Great Britain and in its previous colonies around the world, including the United States. It is also used, in a slightly modified form, in Sweden and Finland.

[3]) In some variants of this procedure, the set of alternatives is not defined when the first vote is taken – that is, amendments can be put forward during the voting process. We do not deal with that situation here.

[4]) The successive procedure is used in Denmark, Norway, France, Germany, and the European Council. The Nordic Council and the United Nations use a rather similar procedure.

preferred alternative can be reached by voting either way, the individual votes on the basis of second choices. If these can be obtained either way, third choices are used, and so on.

Sophisticated Voting

The method of sophisticated voting employed here was independently developed by the first author (for the amendment procedure) but is equivalent to the definition formalized by *McKelvey/Niemi* [1978] for all binary voting procedures. A simple example yields a general understanding of the definition.[5])

With three alternatives to be voted on by the amendment procedure, we can illustrate the voting process as follows:[6])

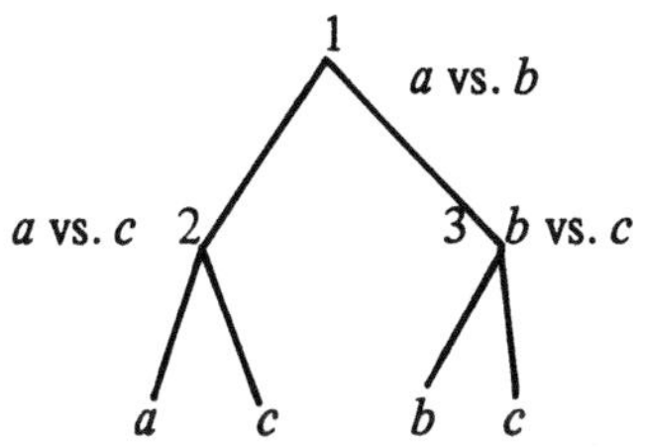

The first vote, represented by node 1, is between alternatives a and b. The winner of that vote then faces alternative c – at node 2 or 3. The winner of the second vote is the alternative selected.

Note that at the final vote (node 2 or 3), only two alternatives remain and no strategic voting is possible. Thus, if the social preference is acb (i.e., a is preferred socially to both c and b and c is preferred socially to b), a would be the winner at node 2 and c would be the winner at node 3. This simple observation implies that node 1 is in effect a choice between a and c: if the left-hand branch is chosen at node 1, a will be the winner; if the right-hand branch is chosen, c will be the winner.

Now consider the choice to be made by individual voters. All those who prefer a to c should vote for the left-hand branch at node 1 (i.e., vote for a over b even if they prefer b to a). Their ranking of b is irrelevant since b cannot be obtained. Similarly, all those who prefer c over a should vote for the right-hand branch (i.e., vote for b over a) regardless of their preferences between a and b. These sophisticated votes at node 1 are sincere votes between "what is really going to happen" if the left-hand branch is chosen versus what is really going to happen if the right-hand branch is chosen. McKelvey/Niemi refer to "what is really going to happen" as the sophisticated equivalent while *Miller* [1977] calls this the anticipated decision.

---

[5]) This method of sophisticated voting differs from Farquharson's reduction method in the strategies it yields for individual voters. However, it is likely that the outcomes arrived at are identical for both procedures. A formalization, additional examples, and arguments in support of the "multistage" method of sophisticated voting are contained in *McKelvey/Niemi* [1978].

[6]) Where there seems no possibility of confusion, we will use the notation $a, b, c, \ldots$ for alternatives in place of the more cumbersome $a_1, a_2, \ldots, a_n$.

From the perspective of the whole group, *b* cannot win since *c* is socially preferred to *b* and will thus defeat *b* if a vote is taken at node 3. Therefore the real choice at node 1 is between *a* and *c*, and all those who prefer *a* to *c* should vote for *a* (regardless of their preference between *a* and *b*). Since *a* is socially preferred to *b*, we know that if everyone votes sophisticatedly, *a* will win. In general, by beginning at the last stage of the voting process and working one's way to the beginning – calculating what will happen at each point if the voting reaches that point – it is possible to determine how each person should vote and what the outcome will be.

Classification of Social Preferences

Under the amendment procedure, two preliminary results greatly simplify the analysis. First, the outcome depends only on the social preference. This is so because the voting decision at each node depends only on the two alternatives that are being voted on at that node – the nominal alternatives if voting is sincere or the sophisticated equivalents if voting is sophisticated. This means that we do not need to know the preference ordering of each individual. Indeed, we need not even ascribe characteristics such as completeness and transitivity to individual preferences, though the *social* preference must be complete and contain no ties. All we need to know is, for each pair of alternatives, which one is preferred by society.[7]) The second simplifying result under the amendment procedure is that if there is an undominated alternative – an alternative that is preferred to all others in pairwise comparisons – it will win whether voting is sincere [*Black*, p. 43] or sophisticated [*McKelvey/Niemi*, 17–18].[8])

Together these results mean that we need only analyze the effect of the voting order when there is no undominated alternate and then only for all the distinguishable cases of social preferences (i.e., not separately for each combination of individual preferences). Fortunately, *Bjurulf* [1973] has classified sets of social preferences for three, four, and five alternatives. For three alternatives there is only one such set (without an undominated alternative), which can be conveniently illustrated as follows:

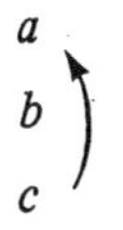

where each alternative is preferred by society to those listed below it except where an arrow indicates otherwise. That is, in the case illustrated, *a* is preferred to *b*, *b* is preferred to *c*, and *c* is preferred to *a*. Any other cyclical set simply involves a change of labeling. For example,

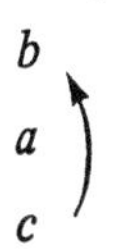

[7]) Note that we need not assume majority rule nor any other specific decision rule. All that we need to know is the order in which alternatives are socially preferred by whatever rule is in use.

[8]) These results also apply to sophisticated voting under the successive procedure but not to sincere voting under that procedure.

is still a set in which each alternative is preferred to exactly one other alternative which in turn is preferred to the remaining alternative.

It is also useful to characterize sets by the number of alternatives which each given alternative is ranked above in the social preference. This measure is one indicator of the "strength" of each alternative vis-à-vis the others and will be used later in analyzing the effects of the voting order.[9]) For three alternatives there is only one case with an undominated alternative and one case (illustrated above) with no undominated alternative:

Three Alternatives: Classification of Social Preferences

Case I		Case II	
Social Preference (SP)	Place Score (PS)	Social Preference (SP)	Place Score (PS)
a	2	*a*	1
b	1	*b*	1
c	0	*c*	1

* The number of alternatives to which a given alternative is socially preferred.

For four alternatives there are two cases with an undominated alternative and two without an undominated alternative:

Four Alternatives: Classification of Social Preferences

Case I		Case II		Case III		Case IV	
SP	PS	SP	PS	SP	PS	SP	PS
a	3	*a*	3	*a*	2	*a*	2
b	2	*b*	1	*b*	2	*b*	2
c	1	*c*	1	*c*	2	*c*	1
d	0	*d*	1	*d*	0	*d*	1

For five alternatives there are four cases with an undominated alternative and eight without an undominated alternative. Examples are shown as needed until Tables 7 and 8, where all 12 cases are displayed.

Since these sets are a mutually exclusive and exhaustive classification of social preferences, we need only determine the effects of voting order for these cases. As noted above, there is actually no need to analyze cases in which there is an undominated alternative. However, we include them in the tables that follow for the sake of completeness.

The effects of voting order can now be determined for each case of three or more alternatives. One way to do this is simply to write out all possible voting orders and to determine the winner under each order for each set of social preferences. Such an exhaustive listing is useful for some purposes, and we have in fact done this for three and four

[9]) This is an important measure not only because it allows us to classify social preferences, but because it is used in defining some decision rules, e.g., that proposed by Copeland.

alternatives. However, that approach offers little insight into the results and makes it difficult to translate the results into simple advice for the legislative or committee decision maker. Hence in the next two sections – first for the amendment procedure and then for the successive procedure – we shall state the logic for determining which alternative will win and then use that logic in developing advice for decision makers.

3. Amendment Procedure

Sophisticated Voting

For the amendment procedure it turns out that it is easier to formalize the logic behind sophisticated voting than sincere voting. Therefore we begin with that case. Assume the following:

1. There exists a finite set of alternatives, $a_1, \ldots, a_n$.
2. The social preference among $a_1, \ldots, a_n$ is known and is complete and strict (i.e., no ties).
3. Voting is by the amendment procedure among $a_1, \ldots, a_n$.
4. Voting is sophisticated.
5. The voting system is nonperverse. That is: (1) If the outcome of a binary vote is a_i when a given individual votes for a_j, then the outcome is also a_i when the individual votes for a_i and all others vote as before; (2) There are no dummies; i.e., for all individuals at all votes there exists a contingency (a way in which all other individuals will vote) in which the outcome of a binary vote is a_i when the given individual votes for a_i and is not a_i (either a_j wins or a_i and a_j are tied) when the given individual votes for a_j.

We can now derive the following propositions and theorems. Proofs are given in the Appendix.

Proposition 1. Those alternatives ranked lower in the social preference than the last alternative in the voting order cannot win.

Proposition 1 permits us to consider only the set of alternatives ranked higher in the social preference than a_t, the last alternative in the voting order. In Theorems 1–4 we consider which alternative will win when one, two, three and four alternatives, respectively, are ranked above a_t in the social preference.

Theorem 1. If only one alternative, a_k, is socially preferred to a_t, then a_k will be the winner.

Theorem 2. If exactly two alternatives, a_k and a_j, are socially preferred to a_t, then the winner will be

$$a_k \text{ if } a_k > a_j$$

$$a_j \text{ if } a_j > a_k,$$

where ">" means "is socially preferred to."

Theorem 3. Suppose exactly three alternatives, a_k, a_j, and a_m are socially preferred to a_t. Then either one of the three alternatives, say a_k, is socially preferred to the other two or there is a cycle among the three alternatives. If $a_k > a_m$, and $a_k > a_j$ then a_k is the sophisticated winner. If $a_k > a_j > a_m > a_k$ (a cycle), then the alternative in the cycle which is socially preferred to the alternative voted on last (among the three) is the sophisticated winner.

Before dealing with the situation in which four alternatives are socially preferred to the last alternative, it is useful to define a new concept and to state Theorem 4.

Definition. A completely dominated alternative is an alternative that is not socially preferred to any other alternative.

Theorem 4. If a completely dominated alternative, a_d, is in the last position in the voting order, it can be disregarded for purposes of applying Proposition 1 and Theorems 1–3 and the next-to-last alternative can be regarded as the last.

Now consider the case in which exactly four alternatives are socially preferred to the last alternative in the voting order. Either (a) the last alternative is socially preferred to some other alternative, or (b) the last alternative is not socially preferred to any other alternative. If (a), then there are at least six alternatives in the set to be voted on. We will not deal with this case here, although in principle it can be dealt with in a fashion similar to the cases already dealt with. If (b), then the last alternative, a_d is a completely dominated alternative and can be disregarded (Theorem 4) and the next-to-last alternative, a_t, can be regarded as the last. Theorems 1–3 are sufficient in dealing with this case since no more than three alternatives are socially preferred to a_t.

Proposition 1 and Theorems 1–4 give us a straightforward way of determining the winner for sets of three, four or five alternatives if we know the social preference and the voting order. We simply begin with the last alternative in the voting order (or the next-to-last alternative if the last one is a completely dominated alternative), determine which alternatives are ranked above that alternative in the social preference, and apply whichever of Theorems 1–4 is appropriate. This means that given a particular voting order, it is easy to determine the winner. The propositions and theorems do not, however, yield a ready answer to the "reverse" question: Given a particular alternative, under what voting order(s) will it win? Nor do they directly answer a second question: Given a particular voting order, what advice do we give to the decision maker who wants his or her alternative to win? We provide the answers to these questions in two forms. First we list all voting orders for three and four alternatives in Table 1. Using this table one can see at a glance the precise voting order(s) in which a particular alternative wins. (The table includes results for sincere voting, which we shall deal with shortly.)

					Voting Orders[1])		
				First	a	a	b
			Winner when		b	c	c
	SP[2])	PS	voting is	Last	c	b	a
I.	a	2	Sincere		a	a	a
	b	1					
	c	0	Soph		a	a	a
II.	a ↖	1	Sincere		c	b	a
	b ⎱	1					
	c ⎰	1	Soph		b	a	c

* * * * * * *

					Voting Orders (vertically, first to last)[1]											
				Winner when	*a*	*a*	*a*	*a*	*a*	*a*	*b*	*b*	*b*	*b*	*c*	*c*
					b	*b*	*c*	*c*	*d*	*d*	*c*	*c*	*d*	*d*	*d*	*d*
					c	*d*	*b*	*d*	*b*	*c*	*a*	*d*	*a*	*c*	*a*	*b*
SP	PS	SP	PS	voting is	*d*	*c*	*d*	*b*	*c*	*b*	*d*	*a*	*c*	*a*	*b*	*a*
I. *a* 3 *b* 2 *c* 1 *d* 0		II. *a* *b* ↖ *c* *d*	3 1 1 1	Sincere	*a*	*a*	*a*	*a*	*a*	*a*	*a*	*a*	*a*	*a*	*a*	*a*
				Soph	*a*	*a*	*a*	*a*	*a*	*a*	*a*	*a*	*a*	*a*	*a*	*a*
		III. *a* ↖ *b* *c* *d*	2 2 2 0	Sincere	*c*	*c*	*b*	*b*	*c*	*b*	*a*	*a*	*c*	*a*	*b*	*a*
				Soph	*b*	*b*	*a*	*a*	*b*	*a*	*c*	*c*	*b*	*c*	*a*	*c*
		IV. *a* *b* ↖ *c* *d*	2 2 1 1	Sincere	*d*	*c*	*d*	*b*	*b*	*b*	*d*	*a*	*a*	*a*	*a*	*a*
				Soph	*b*	*a*	*b*	*a*	*a*	*a*	*b*	*d*	*a*	*d*	*a*	*d*

[1]) Since the first two alternatives enter the voting process simultaneously, voting orders such as *bca* and *cba* are equivalent and the number of voting orders we need to deal with is only half the number of permutations of the alternatives. E.g., with 3 alternatives, any one of the 3 can be last, and for each of these there is only one remaining pair of alternatives. Therefore, 3 · 1 = 3 voting orders to be analyzed. For 4 alternatives, the appropriate calculation is 4 · 3 · 1 = 12 voting orders.

[2]) SP: Social Preference
PS: Place score

Tab. 1: Voting Orders and Outcomes under the Amendment Procedure (3 and 4 alternatives)

More useful than the listing – and more in the spirit of Black's and Farquharson's original observations – is the advice that can be generated for how to make a particular alternative win (Table 2). Since we have shown that the effects of voting order depend on the social preference, advice must be given for each distinct case of social preferences. No single statement such as "go last" or "go first" will suffice. Nevertheless, for any one case the advice is relatively simple. And contrary to Black's and Farquharson's rules, or to Miller's conditions, the advice is the best possible in the sense that it gives both necessary

Three Alternatives

	SP	
I.	*a* *b* *c*	*a* wins. Voting order is irrelevant [*McKelvey/Niemi*].
II.	*a* ↖ *b* *c*	Vote last on the alternative that your first choice is socially preferred to (Theorem 1).

Therefore:

For *a* to win, vote on *b* last
For *b* to win, vote on *c* last
For *c* to win, vote on *a* last

* * * * * * *

Four Alternatives

	SP		SP	
I.	*a*	II.	*a*	*a* wins. Voting order is irrelevant [*McKelvey/Niemi*].
	b		*b*	
	c		*c*	
	d		*d*	

III.	*a*	If *a* is last, *c* wins (Theorem 1)
	b	if *b* is last, *a* wins (Theorem 1)
	c	if *c* is last, *b* wins (Theorem 1)
	d	if *d* is last, it can be ignored (Theorem 4) and Theorem 1 re-applied with the next-to-last alternative considered last.

Therefore:

For *a* to win, vote on *b* last or vote on *d* last and *b* second last.
For *b* to win, vote on *c* last or vote on *d* last and *c* second last.
For *c* to win, vote on *a* last or vote on *d* last and *a* second last.
Alternative *d* cannot win.

IV.	*a*	If *a* is last, *d* wins (Theorem 1)
	b	If *b* is last, *a* wins (Theorem 1)
	c	If *c* is last, *a* wins (Theorem 2)
	d	If *d* is last, *b* wins (Theorem 2)

Therefore:

For *a* to win, vote on *b* or *c* last.
For *b* to win, vote on *d* last.
For *d* to win, vote on *a* last.
Alternative *c* cannot win.

Tab. 2: Advice on How to Win: Amendment Procedure, Sophisticated Voting (3 and 4 alternatives)

and sufficient conditions for a given alternative to win. With knowledge only of the social preference, one can select any and all voting orders which will lead to the selection of a given alternative. In this sense, for sophisticated voting under the amendment procedure, this completes the line of work on voting orders begun by Black and Farquharson.

Advice is given in Table 2 for all cases of three and four alternatives. For five alternatives we show two cases in the Appendix; advice for the other cases can be quite simply developed using the theorems in the manner illustrated. In all cases the advice is arrived at by considering each alternative in turn as the last alternative in the voting order and applying the theorems.

Sincere Voting

Surprisingly, analysis of sincere voting under the amendment procedure is more cumbersome than analysis of sophisticated voting, and the advice for how to make a given alternative win often proves to be more complicated. We begin with three simple propositions about sincere voting under the amendment procedure:

Proposition 2. If an alternative is undominated, it will be the outcome.

Proposition 3. A completely dominated alternative cannot win any vote.

Proposition 4. If there are only three alternatives to be voted on, or if there are only three that are not completely dominated, and if there is a cycle in the social preference among the three (not completely dominated) alternatives, the one (of the three) voted on last will win.

Propositions 2 and 3 follow obviously from the definitions of undominated and completely dominated alternatives and from the fact that voting is sincere. Proposition 4 follows obviously from Proposition 3 and from observing that in the first vote (among the three "relevant" alternatives) the alternative less preferred than the last alternative will defeat the remaining alternative.

These propositions suffice for the case of three alternatives and for some cases of four and five alternatives. However, they are not sufficient for all cases. When they are not, a simple but tedious procedure must be employed. This requires (a) looking at the first two alternatives in the voting order and eliminating the one which is less preferred in the social preference; (b) Repeating step (a), if necessary, with the next pair of alternatives (i.e., the winner of the preceding vote and the next alternative in the voting order) until only three alternatives are left; (c) Determining the social preference among the remaining three alternatives. At this point either Proposition 2 or 4 will suffice. This procedure allows one to determine the voting orders in which each alternative wins. One can then derive relatively simple statements about how to make a given alternative win.[10]

Table 3 displays advice on how to make a given alternative win (and the derivation of that advice) for all cases of three and four alternatives. Advice is also derived for a single case of five alternatives in the Appendix. In addition, Table 1, presented earlier, shows the winner for all voting orders for three and four alternatives for each distinguishable case of social preference.

Three Alternatives

	SP	
I.	*a*	*a* wins. Voting order is irrelevant.
	b	
	c	
II.	*a* ↖	Vote last on your first choice (Proposition 4). Therefore:
	b	For *a* to win, put it last.
	c ⤴	For *b* to win, put it last.
		For *c* to win, put it last.

* * * * * * *

Four Alternatives

	SP		SP	
I.	*a*	II.	*a*	*a* wins. Voting order is irrelevant.
	b		*b* ↖	
	c		*c*	
	d		*d* ⤴	

[10]) Given any particular voting order, one can determine the winner by simply following the voting order from the beginning to end, and, since by definition all vote according to their preferences, eliminate alternatives that are socially less preferred than the one preceding alternative that has not been eliminated. Thus, for example, if the social preference is *baced* (with an arrow from *c* back to *a*), and the voting order is *acbde*, one goes through the following steps: *a~~c~~bde*, *~~a~~~~c~~bde*, *~~a~~~~c~~b~~d~~e*, *~~a~~~~c~~~~b~~~~d~~e*. Thus *e* will be the winner.

III. *a*, *b*, *c*, *d*

Position of *d* is irrelevant (Proposition 3). Therefore:

For *a* to win, put it last among *abc* (Proposition 4).
For *b* to win, put it last among *abc* (Proposition 4).
For *c* to win, put it last among *abc* (Proposition 4).

IV. *a*, *b*, *c*, *d*

First pair	Social preference among alternatives remaining after first vote	Consequently (Propositions 3 and 5)	Voting orders in which each alternative wins.[1] *a*	*b*	*c*	*d*
ab	*acd*	If *c* last, it wins			(*ab*) *dc*	
		if *d* last, it wins				(*ab*) *cd*
ac	*abd*	if *b* last, it wins		(*ac*) *db*		
		if *d* last, it wins				(*ac*) *bd*
ad	*bcd*	*b* wins		(*ad*)(*bc*)		
bc	*abd*	If *a* last, it wins	(*bc*) *da*			
		if *d* last, it wins				(*bc*) *ad*
bd	*abc*	*a* wins	(*bd*)(*ac*)			
cd	*abc*	*a* wins	(*cd*)(*ab*)			

[1]) ( ) indicates that the alternatives enclosed may be permuted. Thus, for example, the first entry in the top row means that *c* will win with the voting order *abdc* or with the voting order *badc*.

Tab. 3: Advice on How to Win: Amendment Procedure, Sincere Voting (3 and 4 alternatives)

As noted above, this advice is often not as simple as that for sophisticated voting and is clearly more complex than advice such as "go last." Yet it also completes this particular line of inquiry (for sincere voting) in the sense that it yields both necessary and sufficient conditions for a given alternative to win. Knowing only the social preference, one can quickly find any and all voting orders that will lead to the selection of a given alternative.

4. The Successive Procedure

Sophisticated Voting

An insight by *Miller* [1977, 785–786] makes analysis of sophisticated voting for the successive procedure extremely simple. He observed that the results are simply the "reverse" of those for *sincere* voting under the *amendment* procedure. Thus, one can apply the exact same procedure we used in that case, but work through the voting order from last to first. One begins with the last pair of alternatives, moves to the third-from-last alternative, and so on, up to the first. This "reversal" phenomenon means that if we reverse the voting order the outcome of sophisticated voting under the successive procedure will be identical to the outcome of sincere voting under the amendment procedure.[11])

This observation means that we do not have to derive advice for sophisticated voting under the successive procedure. We can simply "reverse" the advice for sincere voting under the amendment procedure. For example, with three alternatives the advice for sincere voting under the amendment procedure was to put one's preferred alternative *last* (Table 3). For sophisticated voting under the successive procedure, the advice is therefore to put one's preferred alternative *first*.[12]) As an additional example, consider Case IV for four alternatives. The advice for making *a* win with sophisticated voting under the successive procedure is: have *a* precede *d* in the voting order, but *a, d* not last. As a convenience, we list the voting orders and outcomes for three and four alternatives in Table 4. In the same sense as before, then, we feel that our work completes this particular line of inquiry on voting orders.

				Voting Orders[1])		
			First	*a*	*b*	*c*
				b	*a*	*a*
	SP[2])	PS	Last	*c*	*c*	*b*
I.	*a*	2		*a*	*a*	*a*
	b	1				
	c	0				
II.	*a*	1		*a*	*b*	*c*
	b	1				
	c	1				

* * * * * * *

					Voting Orders (vertically, first to last)											
					a	*b*	*a*	*c*	*b*	*c*	*a*	*d*	*b*	*d*	*c*	*d*
					b	*a*	*c*	*a*	*c*	*b*	*d*	*a*	*d*	*b*	*d*	*c*
					c	*c*	*b*	*b*	*a*	*a*	*b*	*b*	*a*	*a*	*a*	*a*
					d	*d*	*d*	*d*	*d*	*d*	*c*	*c*	*c*	*c*	*b*	*b*
	SP	PS		SP	PS											
I.	*a*	3	II.	*a*	3	*a*	*a*	*a*	*a*	*a*	*a*	*a*	*a*	*a*	*a*	*a*	*a*
	b	2		*b*	1											
	c	1		*c*	1											
	d	0		*d*	1											

[11]) We can illustrate this point and at the same time show how one can quickly determine the outcome of sophisticated voting under the successive procedure for a given voting order. Consider the social preferences *baced* and the voting order that is the reverse of that in footnote 10, viz., *edbca*. In a manner analogous to that in footnote 10, but working from the last pair up to the first alternative, we successively cross out *c, a, d,* and *b*, leaving *e* as the sophisticated outcome.

[12]) Alternatively, one could use the advice for sincere voting, amendment procedure, and then take the reverse of the prescribed voting orders. E.g., sincere, amendment: "For *a* to win, put it last" implies voting orders (*bc*) *a*. Therefore, to make *a* win under sophisticated, successive voting, use the voting order *a* (*bc*).

III.	*a*	2	*a*	*b*	*a*	*c*	*b*	*c*	*a*	*a*	*b*	*b*	*c*	*c*
	b	2												
	c	2												
	d	0												
IV.	*a*	2	*a*	*a*	*a*	*a*	*b*	*b*	*a*	*d*	*b*	*d*	*c*	*d*
	b	2												
	c	1												
	d	1												

[1]) Under the successive procedure the last two alternatives effectively enter the voting process simultaneously. Hence voting orders such as *abcd* and *abdc* are equivalent and we need to analyze only half the number of permutations of the alternatives.

[2]) SP: Social Preference
PS: Place Score

Tab. 4: Voting Orders and Outcomes Under the Successive Procedure, Sophisticated Voting (3 and 4 alternatives)

Sincere Voting

Sincere voting under the successive procedure is complicated by the inapplicability of the two simplifications used up to this point. First, more than the social preference needs to be considered in determining the outcome of a particular voting order. A simple example shows this. Consider two sets of preference orderings: (1) *abc, bac, cab*; (2) *abc, bac, abc*; and assume that the social preference and voting decisions are determined by majority rule. Both sets of preference orderings yield the social preference *abc*. Yet suppose the voting order is *a, b, c*. If the preferences are those in (1), *b* wins; if the preferences are those in (2), *a* wins. This example also shows that an undominated alternative will not necessarily be selected as the outcome. With the preferences in (1), *a* is preferred to both *b* and *c*. Yet *b* wins under the voting order shown. Hence we cannot limit the analysis to cyclical sets.

For three alternatives the situation is reasonably manageable. Obviously if an alternative has a majority of first place preferences, it will win regardless of the voting order. If we know that there is no such alternative, we need only know (in addition) the social preferences in order to determine the outcome. The reason for this should be apparent. Since the first alternative in the voting order will be defeated, there are only two remaining alternatives and the one which is preferred by a majority to the other will win. Thus in Table 5 we show the winners under different voting orders where an undominated alternative exists (assuming no alternative has a majority of first place preferences) as well as for a cyclical set. Advice on how to make a given alternative win is also shown, though it is not as simple as for the other situations with only three alternatives.

For more than three alternatives even this degree of simplification is impossible. Suppose there are four alternatives. If one alternative has a majority of first place preferences, it will win under any voting order. But suppose there is no such alternative. Then the first alternative in the voting order will lose. This puts us in the three alternative situation discussed above. If, after deleting the first alternative in the voting order, there is an alternative with a majority of first place preference, it is selected under any voting order. If not, the social preference among the three alternatives suffices to determine which alternative will win under each voting order.

			Voting Orders		
		First	a	b	c
			b	a	a
	SP[2])	PS / Last	c	c	b
I.[3])	*a*	2	*b*	*a*	*a*
	b	1			
	c	0			
II.	*a*	1	*b*	*c*	*a*
	b	1			
	c	1			

Advice on How to Win

Most preferred alternative is:	Advice
Undominated alternative	Vote last or next-to-last on own first choice
Middle of noncyclical social result	Vote first on the alternative that "beats" own first choice
In cyclical social result	Vote first on the alternative that "beats" own first choice
Completely dominated alternative	Cannot win. Voting order is irrelevant

Tab. 5: Voting Orders and Outcomes Under the Successive Procedure, Sincere Voting[1])
(3 alternatives)
[1]) Majority rule assumed
[2]) SP: Social Preference
PS: Place Score
[3]) Results shown assume *a* does not have a majority of first-place preferences.

The difficulty is that to do the above often requires rather detailed knowledge of the preferences of the voters. Complete knowledge of all of the preference orderings is not necessarily required. In fact, under certain circumstances conclusions might be drawn despite quite a bit of uncertainty about individual preference orderings. Consider the set of preferences shown in Table 6. We can determine which alternative wins for each voting

		Voting Orders (vertically, first to last)											
		a	*a*	*a*	*b*	*b*	*b*	*c*	*c*	*c*	*d*	*d*	*d*
Individual Prefer-		*b*	*c*	*d*	*a*	*c*	*d*	*a*	*b*	*d*	*a*	*b*	*c*
ence Orderings[2])		*c*	*b*	*b*	*c*	*a*	*a*	*b*	*a*	*a*	*b*	*a*	*a*
		d	*d*	*c*	*d*	*d*	*c*	*d*	*d*	*b*	*c*	*c*	*b*
3[3])	*ab (cd)*	*b*	*b*	*b*	*a*	*a*	*a*	*b*	*a*	*a*	*a*	*a*	*a*
2	*ba (cd)*												
1	*b (acd)*												
3	*da (cb)*												
9													

Tab. 6: Voting Orders and Outcomes Under the Successive Procedure, Sincere Voting[1])
(4 alternatives)
[1]) Majority rule assumed.
[2]) ( ) indicates that the alternatives enclosed may be permuted. Thus, for example, *ab (cd)* means either preference ordering *abcd* or *abdc*.
[3]) Number of voters with the indicated preference ordering.

order in spite of incomplete knowledge about each of the preference orderings. In general, however, there does not seem to be any simple way of characterizing just what information is needed – other than to say that at each stage in the vote one needs to know if the alternative being voted on has a majority of first place preferences among the alternatives that have not been eliminated.

Two conclusions can be drawn about sincere voting under the successive procedure. One is that no simple advice is adequate for a large set of circumstances other than the obvious point that an alternative cannot be voted on first and win unless it has a majority of first-place preferences. The second conclusion is that for any set of individual preferences orderings – and in some cases partial orderings – it is a simple (though perhaps laborious) matter to determine the outcome under various voting orders. These conclusions are of necessity less satisfactory than those for the amendment procedure and for sophisticated voting under the successive procedure. Nonetheless, these, too, seem to complete this line of work on voting orders.

5. Strength, Position, and the Probability of Winning

Having determined the necessary and sufficient conditions for each alternative to win, we now need to take an overall look at the results in order to draw some general conclusions about the effects of voting order as well as some conclusions about sincere versus sophisticated voting. Since the results for sincere voting under the amendment procedure are so situation specific, comparisons of sincere and sophisticated voting are necessarily limited to the amendment procedure and comparisons between the two voting procedures are limited to sophisticated voting.

Tab. 7: Proportion of Times Each Alternative is the Winner with Three, Four or Five Alternatives

Three Alternatives	Social Preference (SP)/Place Scores (PS) I	II
a	2	1
b	1	1
c	0	1
Sincere (amendment) and Sophisticated (successive) voting Proportion of times that each alternative wins		
a	1.0	0.33
b	0	0.33
c	0	0.33
Sophisticated (amendment) voting Proportion of times that each alternative wins		
a	1.0	0.33
b	0	0.33
c	0	0.33
Number of voting orders	(6)	(6)

Tab. 7 (continued)

Four Alternatives

	Social Preference (SP)/Place Scores (PS)			
	I	II	III	IV
a	3	3	2	2
b	2	1	2	2
c	1	1	2	1
d	0	1	0	1
Sincere (amendment) and Sophisticated (successive) voting Proportion of times that each alternative wins				
a	1.0	1.0	0.33	0.42
b	0	0	0.33	0.25
c	0	0	0.33	0.08
d	0	0	0	0.25
Sophisticated (amendment) voting Proportion of times that each alternative wins				
a	1.0	1.0	0.33	0.5
b	0	0	0.33	0.25
c	0	0	0.33	0.0
d	0	0	0	0.25
Number of voting orders	(24)	(24)	(24)	(24)

Five Alternatives

	Social Preference (SP)/Place Score (PS)											
	I	II	III	IV	V	VI	VII	VIII	IX	X	XI	XII
a	4	4	4	4	3	3	3	3	3	3	3	2
b	3	3	2	2	3	3	3	3	2	2	2	2
c	2	1	2	2	3	2	2	2	2	2	2	2
d	1	1	2	1	1	2	1	1	2	2	2	2
e	0	1	0	1	0	0	1	1	1	1	1	2
Sincere (amendment) and Sophisticated (successive) voting Proportion of times that each alternative wins												
a	1.0	1.0	1.0	1.0	0.33	0.42	0.40	0.45	0.45	0.33	0.38	0.20
b	0	0	0	0	0.33	0.25	0.27	0.22	0.12	0.30	0.27	0.20
c	0	0	0	0	0.33	0.08	0.25	0.08	0.12	0.10	0.18	0.20
d	0	0	0	0	0.00	0.25	0.02	0.05	0.12	0.18	0.12	0.20
e	0	0	0	0	0.00	0.00	0.07	0.20	0.20	0.08	0.05	0.20
Sophisticated (amendment) voting Proportion of times that each alternative wins												
a	1.0	1.0	1.0	1.0	0.33	0.50	0.47	0.60	0.60	0.40	0.46	0.20
b	0	0	0	0	0.33	0.25	0.27	0.20	0.07	0.40	0.27	0.20
c	0	0	0	0	0.33	0.00	0.27	0.00	0.07	0.00	0.20	0.20
d	0	0	0	0	0.00	0.25	0.00	0.00	0.07	0.20	0.07	0.20
e	0	0	0	0	0.00	0.00	0.00	0.20	0.20	0.00	0.00	0.20
Number of voting orders	(120)	(120)	(120)	(120)	(120)	(120)	(120)	(120)	(120)	(120)	(120)	(120)

We turn first to the relationship between the "strength" of an alternative (its relative position in the social preference) and its likelihood of winning. This leads to an important contrast between sincere and sophisticated voting. In Table 7 we have tabulated for each social preference the proportion of times that each alternative is the winner. It is obvious, first of all, that there is considerable variation in the likelihood that any given alternative will win. With five alternatives, for example, an alternative may win in exactly two of the 120 voting orders (sincere voting, amendment procedure, Case VII, alternative *d*) or in as many as 72 (sophisticated voting, amendment procedure, Cases VIII and IX, alternative *a*).

In general (for the amendment procedure), there is greater variance in the proportion of times each alternative wins when voting is sophisticated. This means that less advantaged alternatives are especially disadvantaged under sophisticated voting and have a relatively better chance of winning when voting is sincere. Conversely, alternatives that are most likely to win anyway are especially advantaged by sophisticated voting. Consider what this means in a specific instance. Suppose that the social preference is as in Case IX (five alternatives). Suppose further that I most prefer the dominant alternative, *a*, and that I cannot control the voting order in order to assure that *a* will win. Still, I can give a relative advantage to my most preferred alternative by encouraging sophisticated voting. Assuming that I cannot predict which voting order will occur and therefore have to assume that each voting order is equally likely, the probability that *a* wins jumps from .45 to .60 as voting changes from sincere to sophisticated. Conversely, if I most prefer *b, c,* or *d*, I should support sincere voting. In that case my most preferred alternative has a greater, though still small, chance of winning.

Perhaps a better way of showing the relationship between the strength of an alternative and its likelihood of winning is to relate the probability of winning to the "place score" of the alternatives. This can be done in Table 7 with the aid of the place scores indicated at the top of each part of the table. For example, under Case VII with five alternatives, alternatives *a* and *b* are each ranked above three other alternatives in the social preference; the table shows that together these alternatives have .67 probability of winning under sincere voting and a .74 probability of winning under sophisticated voting. Alternative *c*, which is ranked above two other alternatives, is also slightly better off if voting is sophisticated. In contrast, alternatives *d* and *e*, which are each ranked above one other alternative, cannot win at all if voting is sophisticated, whereas they do have a small chance of winning if voting is sincere.

Looking at the results from this perspective yields an interesting interpretation of sophisticated voting. On the one hand, strategic voting of any kind is often thought of as manipulative and therefore bad. Outcomes are chosen because of misrepresentation of preferences and other "tricks." Yet most people would probably consider the outcome of a voting process as unfair if the winning alternative is ranked above few other alternatives and as more fair if the winner "beats" most other alternatives. The latter is exactly what sophisticated voting encourages. In general, alternatives with a place score of one are disadvantaged by sophisticated voting. With five alternatives, the same is typically true of alternatives with a place score of two. Almost invariably, however (except in cases such as V where there is no difference whatsoever between sincere and sophisticated voting), an alternative that is ranked above two other alternatives (out of four) or three other alternatives (out of five) has a *better* chance of winning under sophisticated than under sincere voting.

McKelvey/Niemi [1978, p. 7] earlier showed that given pairwise voting a "majority alternative" – one that is preferred by a majority to each of the other alternatives – would always win under sophisticated voting but might lose if voting were sincere. Now we have seen that in the absence of an undominated alternative, sophisticated voting tends to advantage the alternatives that come closest to being undominated. Thus, far from being altogether bad, it more and more appears as if sophisticated voting promotes outcomes that most would regard as fair.

As noted, this way of looking at the results assumes non-manipulation of the voting order. Does the type of voting make any difference if the voting order is manipulated? After all, whether voting is sincere or sophisticated it is often possible to make a given alternative win by selecting a particular voting order even though it would lose under some or even most other voting orders. We believe that our results also suggest sophisticated voting is perhaps to be preferred if voting orders are manipulated (and the amendment procedure is in use). This is because if voting is sincere, very "weak" alternatives – which are highly unlikely to win without such manipulation – can be made the group choice; in comparable situations with sophisticated voting, such alternatives cannot be made to win.

An example of this occurs with four alternatives (Table 7, Case IV). The social preference is such that, in the absence of manipulation, alternative *c* is very unlikely to win. However, if voting is sincere, control of the agenda would make it possible for *c* to win, while no amount of control over the voting order could make *c* win if voting were sophisticated. Numerous similar examples occur with five alternatives.[13]) In this sense, then, sophisticated voting under the amendment procedure would have to be judged less manipulable than sincere voting, and consequently might be preferred.

Utilizing precisely the same reasoning, one might also conclude from the results in Table 7 that the amendment procedure is preferable to the successive procedure.[14]) Perhaps in recognition of greater order-of-voting effects, the Danish and Norwegian parliaments, which use this system, appear in almost all cases to limit the number of alternatives under consideration to two [*Bjurulf/Niemi*, p. 19]. Manipulation, if it occurs, takes place prior to the roll call stage.

A final perspective on the overall results brings us back to the viewpoint taken by Black and Farquharson. Are alternatives greatly advantaged by the place they occupy in the voting order? In one sense we have already answered this question. It is not invariably true, as Black and Farquharson suggested, that the last (for sincere voting) or first (for sophisticated voting) alternative in the voting order wins. Nonetheless, it could still be the case that different positions in the voting order are greatly favored on average or are invariably the winner under certain conditions.

In the case of sincere voting (amendment procedure) it turns out that the last alterna-

[13]) There are a few situations (e.g., Table 7, case XI, alternative *d*) in which an alternative is especially unlikely to win under sophisticated voting and yet can be made to win since it has a non-zero probability. However, these instances are infrequent.

[14]) Additionally, the successive procedure is vulnerable to voting order effects even when voting is sincere and there is a majority alternative. Unless that alternative also has a majority of first place preferences, it can lose.

tive is indeed greatly advantaged whatever the social preference (except, of course, where there is an undominated alternative). Table 8 shows that the last alternative has at least a .60 chance of winning. Also, the first two alternatives voted on never win, and that voted on third has only a moderate (four alternatives) to minimal chance (five alternatives). The results for sophisticated voting offer a sharp contrast. Farquharson's advice to "go first" is really appropriate only in the sense that the very last alternative never wins (again excepting cases where there is a majority winner). The other four places make little difference on average no matter what the social preference is.[15])

For sophisticated voting under the successive procedure the results are just the "reverse" of sincere voting (amendment). The *first* alternative is greatly advantaged, having at least a .60 chance of winning (except where there is an undominated alternative). The *last* two alternatives can never win. In this case, in contrast to the amendment procedure, Farquharson's advice to "go first" under sophisticated voting is more reasonable, though it still is an incomplete guide to the selection of optimal voting orders.

Tab. 8: Proportion of Times That Place *k* in the Voting Order is the Winner

Three Alternatives

		Social Preference (SP)/Place Score (PS) I	II
	a	2	1
	b	1	1
	c	0	1
Sincere voting (amendment)	Sophisticated voting (successive)		
last	first	0.33	1.00
next-to-last	second	0.33	0.00
first	last	0.33	0.00
	Sophisticated voting (amendment)		
	last	0.33	0.00
	next-to-last	0.33	0.50
	first	0.33	0.50

Four Alternatives

	Social Preference/Place Score I	II	III	IV
a	3	3	2	2
b	2	1	2	2
c	1	1	2	1
d	0	1	0	1

[15]) As noted, the results in Table 8 are averages. While not shown, we have tabulated the results for each separate alternative for each social preference. Under sincere voting it is always true that one is better off having one's preferred alternative later in the voting order. For example, under Case VI (five alternatives) alternative *a* will win with probabilities 1.00, .75, and .33, respectively, if it is last, next-to-last, or third-from-last; alternative *b* will win with probabilities .67, .42, and .17 alternative *c* with probabilities 1.0, .25, 0, etc. With sophisticated voting, one is never better off by having one's preferred alternative later in the voting order, but often the position makes little or no difference. In Case IX (five alternatives), for example, alternative *d* has probabilities of winning of .125, .125, .08, and 0, respectively, if in first through fourth places. Alternative *a* has a probability of winning of .75 if in any of the first four places.

Tab. 8 (continued)

Sincere voting (amendment)	Sophisticated voting (successive)				
last	first	0.25	0.25	0.75	0.75
next-to-last	second	0.25	0.25	0.25	0.25
second	next-to-last	0.25	0.25	0.00	0.00
first	last	0.25	0.25	0.00	0.00
	Sophisticated voting (amendment)				
	last	0.25	0.25	0.00	0.00
	next-to-last	0.25	0.25	0.25	0.33
	second	0.25	0.25	0.38	0.33
	first	0.25	0.25	0.38	0.33

Five Alternatives

	Social Preference/Place Score												
		I	II	III	IV	V	VI	VII	VIII	IX	X	XI	XII
	a	4	4	4	4	3	3	3	3	3	3	3	2
	b	3	3	2	2	3	3	3	3	2	2	2	2
	c	2	1	2	2	3	2	2	2	2	2	2	2
	d	1	1	2	1	1	2	1	1	2	2	2	2
	e	0	1	0	1	0	0	1	1	1	1	1	2
Sincere voting (amendment)	**Sophisticated voting (successive)**												
last	first	0.20	0.20	0.20	0.20	0.60	0.60	0.63	0.63	0.70	0.63	0.67	0.67
next-to-last	second	0.20	0.20	0.20	0.20	0.30	0.30	0.27	0.23	0.20	0.30	0.27	0.33
third	third	0.20	0.20	0.20	0.20	0.10	0.10	0.16	0.13	0.10	0.06	0.07	0.00
second	next-to-last	0.20	0.20	0.20	0.20	0.00	0.00	0.00	0.00	0.00	0.00	0.00	0.00
first	last	0.20	0.20	0.20	0.20	0.00	0.00	0.00	0.00	0.00	0.00	0.00	0.00
	Sophisticated voting (amendment)												
	last	0.20	0.20	0.20	0.20	0.00	0.00	0.00	0.00	0.00	0.00	0.00	0.00
	next-to-last	0.20	0.20	0.20	0.20	0.15	0.20	0.20	0.25	0.20	0.25	0.20	0.25
	third	0.20	0.20	0.20	0.20	0.25	0.27	0.25	0.25	0.25	0.25	0.25	0.25
	second	0.20	0.20	0.20	0.20	0.30	0.27	0.28	0.25	0.28	0.25	0.28	0.25
	first	0.20	0.20	0.20	0.20	0.30	0.27	0.28	0.25	0.28	0.25	0.28	0.25

6. Conclusion

We began this paper as an attempt to complete the line of work on voting orders begun by Black and modified by Farquharson and Miller. By determining both necessary and sufficient conditions for a given alternative to win under the amendment procedure for both sincere and sophisticated voting and under the successive procedure for sophisticated voting (and showing that general conditions are virtually unachievable under sincere voting), we feel that we have effectively achieved that goal. The conditions are not as simple as Black's and Farquharson's original advice, but then a part of our accomplishment is to show that their advice was only rudimentary and that by being specific, much better advice can be given.

But we have accomplished a good deal more as well. We noted earlier that *McKelvey/ Niemi* [1978] proved that under any binary voting process an undominated alternative would be selected if voting were sophisticated but might not be selected if voting were sincere. While very worthwhile, their result does not tell us what happens in the absence of an undominated alternative. Here we have dealt primarily with that case and have shown that sophisticated voting favors "strong" alternatives (those most frequently preferred to the other alternatives in pairwise comparisons) while sincere voting favors weak alternatives. This suggests that in the absence of manipulation, the effects of voting order are such that sophisticated voting is actually to be preferred from a normative perspective because it results in "better" alternatives being selected.

We also suggested that sophisticated voting is perhaps preferable if voting orders are manipulated and the amendment procedure is in use. While manipulation of the voting order (and consequently of the outcome) is possible if voting is sincere or sophisticated, very weak alternatives can often be made to win under sincere voting but not under sophisticated voting.

Finally, assuming that it is just as easy to control the voting so as to arrive at the reverse of a given voting order as it is to arrive at the voting order itself, we have shown that order-of-voting effects are equivalent for sincere voting under the amendment procedure and sophisticated voting under the successive procedure. Given this equivalence and the possible manipulability of sincere voting under the successive procedure even in the presence of a majority alternative, one can conclude that the successive procedure is less subject to order-of-voting effects than is the amendment procedure.

Appendix

Proofs of Proposition and Theorems

Assumptions are given in the text.

Proposition 1. Those alternatives ranked lower in the social preference than the last alternative in the voting order cannot win.

Proof: Assume that a_t is the last alternative in the voting order. By the definition of sophisticated voting [*McKelvey/Niemi*], all individuals vote sincerely in the final vote. Since by assumption a_t is in the final vote, any alternative ranked lower in the social preference than a_t, if it is not defeated previously, will be defeated by a_t in the final vote.

Q.E.D.

Theorem 1. If only one alternative, a_k, is socially preferred to a_t, then a_k will be the winner.

Proof: Under the amendment procedure, a_k appears in the voting order at some stage. At that and all succeeding stages, all those who prefer a_k to a_t will vote for a_k. To show this, consider what happens if some other alternative, a_i, beats a_k at some stage in the voting process. By Proposition 1 and the assumption that only a_k is socially preferred to a_t, the only alternative that can beat a_t at the last stage is a_k. Since under the amendment procedure alternatives cannot be reintroduced once they are defeated, a_k will lose if it is defeated at any stage of the voting process. Thus, once a_k is introduced, each vote involving a_k in effect becomes a choice between a_t and a_k.

Now each voter who prefers a_k to a_t is at least as well off voting for a_k at each stage.

If the voter is decisive between a_k and the alternative it faces at a given stage, he is better off voting for a_k; if he is not decisive between a_k and the alternative it faces, he is no worse off voting for a_k. Since the voting rule is assumed to be nonperverse, for each voter there exists a contingency in which he is decisive between a_k and the alternative it faces at each stage. Therefore the sophisticated strategy for each voter who prefers a_k to a_t is to vote for a_k at each stage once it is introduced. Since by assumption there is a decisive set that prefers a_k to a_t, a_k will win at each stage once it is introduced, including the last stage when it is paired directly against a_t. Therefore, a_k will be the winner.

Q.E.D.

Theorem 2. If exactly two alternatives, a_k and a_j, are socially preferred to a_t, then the winner will be

$$a_k \text{ if } a_k > a_j$$

$$a_j \text{ if } a_j > a_k,$$

where ">" means "is socially preferred to".

Proof: Suppose that a_k is socially preferred to a_j. Alternative a_k must appear in the voting order at some stage. By Proposition 1 no alternative other than a_k or a_j can defeat a_t. Alternatives cannot be reintroduced once defeated. Thus once a_k is introduced each vote involving a_k is in effect a choice between either a_k and a_j or a_k and a_t.

To show this, suppose that a_j has not been defeated when a_k enters the voting process. Now suppose that a_k were defeated. Then only a_j could defeat a_t, and by the same reasoning as in Theorem 1, all voters who prefer a_j to a_t would vote for a_j at all subsequent stages (or at all stages after a_j was introduced if it had not already entered the voting when a_k was defeated). Thus a_j would be the winner. By exactly the same reasoning, if a_j were defeated, a_k would be the winner. Thus once a_k enters the voting, each vote involving a_k is in effect a choice between a_j and a_k until one of them is eliminated. All voters who prefer a_k to a_j are at least as well off voting for a_k (and are at least once better off). Since $a_k > a_j$, a_k will win each vote until a_j is eliminated.

Now if a_j has been eliminated, before or after a_k enters the voting process, only a_k can defeat a_t, which is last in the voting order. By Theorem 2, a_k will win.

By the same reasoning, if $a_j > a_k$, a_j will be the winner.

Q.E.D.

Theorem 3. Suppose exactly three alternatives, a_k, a_j, and a_m are socially preferred to a_t. Then either one of the three alternatives, say a_k, is socially preferred to the other two or there is a cycle among the three alternatives. If $a_k > a_m$, and $a_k > a_j$ then a_k is the winner. If $a_k > a_j > a_m > a_k$ (a cycle), then the alternative in the cycle which is socially preferred to the alternative voted on last (among the three) is the winner.

Proof: We start with the cyclical situation. Without loss of generality, assume that $a_k > a_j > a_m > a_k$ and, for convenience, that the voting order among these alternatives is $a_k, \ldots, a_j, \ldots, a_m$.[16]) By Proposition 1, no alternative other than a_k, a_j, or a_m can de-

[16]) There is no loss of generality in assuming that a_j (the alternative that a_k is preferred to) precedes a_m in the voting order. The proof in this and the next paragraph could be repeated for the voting order $a_k, \ldots, a_m, \ldots, a_j$; the only change necessary would be to substitute a_m for a_j and vice versa.

feat a_t. Consider what happens when a_j enters the voting process. If a_k is already defeated, it cannot win since alternatives cannot be reintroduced. If a_k has not been defeated previously, it will be paired in a vote against a_j. In either event (a_j vs. a_k or a_j vs. some other alternative a_i), this vote and all subsequent votes involving a_j are in effect between a_j and a_m until one of them is eliminated. This follows from a consideration of what will happen at succeeding stages: (1) If a_j is eliminated, we have a situation in which only a_m (of the remaining alternatives) is socially preferred to a_t or a situation in which only a_k and a_m (of the remaining alternatives) are socially preferred to a_t. In the former situation, a_m will win by Theorem 1. In the latter situation, a_m will win by Theorem 2. Thus, if a_j is defeated, a_m will win; (2) If a_j eliminates a_k or a_i, we have a situation in which only a_j and a_m (of the remaining alternatives) are socially preferred to a_t. By Theorem 2, a_j will win. We have thus shown that all votes in which a_j is involved after it enters the voting process are in effect a vote between a_j and a_m until one of them is eliminated. All voters who prefer a_j to a_m are at least as well off voting for a_j (and are at least once better off). Since $a_j > a_m$, a_j will win each vote until a_m is eliminated.

With a_m and a_k eliminated, only a_j can defeat a_t, which is last in the voting order. By Theorem 1, a_j will win. This completes the proof for the cyclical situation.

Next suppose that $a_k > a_m$ and $a_k > a_j$ and, without loss of generality, that $a_m > a_j$. By Proposition 1, no alternative other than a_k, a_m, or a_j can defeat a_t. Consider what happens when a_k enters the voting process. If a_m has already been defeated, it cannot win since alternatives cannot be reintroduced. If a_m has not been defeated previously, a_k will be paired against a_m or against some other alternative a_i. In either event, this vote and all subsequent votes involving a_k are in effect between a_k and a_m until one of them is eliminated. This follows from a consideration of what will happen at succeeding stages: (1) If a_k were eliminated, then of the remaining alternatives only a_m is socially preferred to a_t or only a_j and a_m are socially preferred to a_t. In the first case, a_m will win by Theorem 1. In the second case, a_m will win by Theorem 2; (2) If a_m were eliminated, then of the remaining alternatives only a_k is socially preferred to a_t or only a_k and a_j are socially preferred to a_t. In the first case, a_k will win by Theorem 1. In the second case, a_k will win by Theorem 2. We have thus shown that all votes in which a_k is involved after it enters the voting process are in effect between a_k and a_m until one of them is eliminated. All voters who prefer a_k to a_m are at least as well off voting for a_k (and are at least once better off). Since $a_k > a_m$, a_k will win each vote until a_m is eliminated.

If a_j has already been defeated when a_m is eliminated, it cannot win since alternatives cannot be reintroduced. By Theorem 1, a_k will win. If a_j has not been defeated, only a_k and a_j can defeat a_t by Proposition 1. By Theorem 2, a_k wins.

Q.E.D.

Theorem 4. If a completely dominated alternative, a_d, is in the last position in the voting order, it can be disregarded for purposes of applying Proposition 1 and Theorems 1–3 and the next-to-last alternative can be regarded as the last.

Proof: From the definition of sophisticated voting, the last vote is always sincere. Since by assumption the last alternative in the voting order, a_d, is not socially preferred to any other alternative, it will be defeated by whichever alternative is paired against it. This means that whichever alternative wins the next-to-last vote will be the ultimate winner.

This in turn means that all individuals will vote sincerely in the next-to-last vote. Since it is this feature of sophisticated voting that is used directly in Propositions 1 and indirectly in Theorems 1–3, the alternative in the next-to-last position can be regarded as being in the last position.[17]

Q.E.D.

Advice on How to Win: Five Alternatives (Illustrations)

Sophisticated Voting (Amendment Procedure)

VII.	*a*	3	If *a* is last, *c* wins (Theorem 1)
	b	3	if *b* is last, *a* wins (Theorem 1)
	c	2	if *c* is last, *b* wins (Theorem 2)
	d	1	if *d* is last, *a* wins if *b* is last among *a*, *b*, and *c* (Theorem 3)
	e	1	if *d* is last, *b* wins if *c* is last among *a*, *b*, and *c* (Theorem 3)
			if *d* is last, *c* wins if *a* is last among *a*, *b*, and *c* (Theorem 3)
			if *e* is last, *a* wins (Theorem 3).

Therefore:

For *a* to win, vote on *b* last or
vote on *d* last and vote on *b* last among *a*, *b*, and *c* or
vote on *e* last.

For *b* to win, vote on *c* last or
vote on *d* last and vote on *c* last among *a*, *b*, and *c*.

For *c* to win, vote on *a* last or
vote on *d* last and vote on *a* last among *a*, *b*, and *c*.

Alternatives *d* and *e* cannot win.

XI.	*a*	3	If *a* is last, *b* wins (Theorem 1)
	b	2	if *b* is last, *c* wins (Theorem 2)
	c	2	if *c* is last, *a* wins (Theorem 2)
	d	2	if *d* is last, *a* wins (Theorem 2)
	e	1	if *e* is last, *a* wins if *d* is last among *a*, *d*, *b* (Theorem 3)
			if *e* is last, *b* wins if *a* is last among *a*, *d*, *b* (Theorem 3)
			if *e* is last, *d* wins if *b* is last among *a*, *d*, *b* (Theorem 3)

Therefore:

For *a* to win vote on *c* last or
vote on *d* last or
vote on *e* last and *d* last of *a*, *d*, *b*.

For *b* to win vote on *a* last or
vote on *e* last and *a* last of *a*, *d*, *b*.

For *c* to win vote on *b* last.

For *d* to win vote on *e* last and *b* last of *a*, *d*, *b*.

Alternative *e* cannot win.

* * * * * * *

[17]) An alternative way of conceptualizing this result is to think of a parallel set of Proposition 1 and Theorems 1–3 in which "next-to-last" is substituted for "last" and the last alternative is assumed to be completely dominated.

Sincere Voting (Amendment Procedure)

VII. *a* 3
b 3
c 2
d 1
e 1

First pair	Third alternative in the voting order	Social preference among alternatives remaining after first two votes	Consequently (Propositions 3 and 5)
ab	*c*	$\overset{\frown}{cde}$	If *d* last, it wins if *e* last, it wins
	d	$\overset{\frown}{eca}$	if *e* last, it wins if *c* last, it wins
	e	*cad*	*c* wins
ac	*b*	*bde*	*b* wins
	d	*bec*	*b* wins
	e	*bde*	*b* wins
ad	*b*	$\overset{\frown}{eca}$	If *c* last, it wins if *e* last, it wins
	c	*bec*	*b* wins
	e	$\overset{\frown}{abc}$	If *b* last, it wins if *c* last, it wins
ae	*b*	*cad*	*c* wins
	c	*bcd*	*b* wins
	d	$\overset{\frown}{abc}$	If *b* last, it wins if *c* last, it wins
bc	*a*	*ade*	*a* wins
	d	*abe*	*a* wins
	e	*abd*	*a* wins
bd	*a*	$\overset{\frown}{eca}$	If *c* last, it wins if *e* last, it wins
	c	*abe*	*a* wins
	e	$\overset{\frown}{abc}$	If *a* last, it wins if *c* last, it wins
be	*a*	*cad*	*c* wins
	c	*abd*	*a* wins
	d	$\overset{\frown}{abc}$	If *a* last, it wins if *c* last, it wins
cd	*a*	*bec*	*b* wins
	b	*abe*	*a* wins
	e	*abe*	*a* wins
ce	*a*	*abd*	*a* wins
	b	*abd*	*a* wins
	d	*abd*	*a* wins
de	*a*	$\overset{\frown}{abc}$	If *b* last, it wins if *c* last, it wins
	b	$\overset{\frown}{abc}$	if *a* last, it wins if *c* last, it wins
	c	$\overset{\frown}{abc}$	if *a* last, it wins if *b* last, it wins

Therefore:

For *a* to win,	have *b* and *c* precede *a* or have (*ce*) first or have one of the voting orders (*cd*) *e* (*ab*).
For *b* to win,	have *a* and *c*, in that order (unless they are the first pair), precede *b* or have *c* and *a* precede *b* with *e* after *a* or before *c*, but (*ce*) not first.
For *c* to win,	have it last or have *d* last and *c* next-to-last.
For *d* to win,	have one of the voting orders (*ab*) *ced*.
For *e* to win,	have it last and *c* next-to-last or have one of the voting orders (*ab*) *cde*.

References

Bjurulf, B.H.: A simulation analysis of selected voting procedures. Scandinavian Political Studies 8, 1973, 37–68.

Bjurulf, B.H., and *R.G. Niemi*: Strategic voting in Scandinavian parliaments. Scandinavial Political Studies **1**, new series, 1978, 5–22.

Black, D.: The Theory of Committees and Elections. Cambridge 1958.

Farquharson, R.: Theory of voting. New Haven 1969.

McKelvey, R.D., and *R.G. Niemi*: A multistage game representation of sophisticated voting for binary procedures. Journal of Economic Theory **18**, 1978, 1–22.

Miller, N.R.: Graph-theoretical approaches to the theory of voting. American Journal of Political Science **21**, 1977, 769–803.

Plott, C.R., and *M.E. Levine*: A model of agenda influence on committee decisions. American Economic Review **68**, 1978, 146–160.

Holler, M.J. (Ed.): Power, Voting, and Voting Power © Physica-Verlag, Würzburg (Germany) 1981

Strategic Voting in Multicandidate Elections under Uncertainty and under Risk

S. Merrill, Wilkes-Barre

1. Introduction

A number of voting systems for multicandidate elections stipulate that the voter may, under certain constraints, cast $v_i \geqslant 0$ votes for the i-th candidate, $i = 1, \ldots, K$ (where K is the number of candidates), and that the candidate receiving the greatest total vote wins. We will refer to these methods as *numerical* voting systems. Each can be characterized by the constraints imposed: e.g., *simple plurality* voting permits one of the v_i to be 1 but the others must be 0; *approval voting* permits each of the v_i to be either 0 or 1; the *Borda* system requires that the set $\{v_i: i = 1, \ldots, K\}$ consist of the numbers $K-1, K-2, \ldots, 0$; *cardinal measure* voting requires that $0 \leqslant v_i \leqslant M$ for some fixed positive number M. For background on these and other multicandidate voting systems, see *Black* [1958], *Brams* [1978], *Merrill* [1980], and *Weber* [1978].

We will address the question: Given a particular voting system, how might the voter choose the v_i in order to maximize his influence or power on the outcome of the election? Our approach will fall under the heading of decision analysis; in particular we will investigate the optimal decision or strategy for the voter under *uncertainty* and under *risk*, i.e., under different assumptions concerning the voter's knowledge of the likely outcome of the election.

2. A Model for Decision Analysis

For simplicity of exposition, we begin with the approval voting system and then later modify the analysis to incorporate other numerical voting systems. Recall that under approval voting, a voter may vote for as many candidates as he wishes, but may cast no more than one vote per candidate. We fix a *focal* voter, assume there are K candidates, $c_1, \ldots, c_K$, and that:

The focal voter can associate numerical ratings f_i to the candidates c_i where the quantity $f_i - f_j$ is intended to represent the utility to that voter if candidate c_i is elected instead of candidate c_j. (1)

The voter exercises *power* only if his votes are decisive, i.e., for some pair of candidates he breaks a tie for first place which would have occurred had (2) he abstained, or produces such a tie for some pair of candidates (which is resolved, say, by lot).

If the voter is decisive by voting for c_i but not c_j, he receives a *payoff* of $(f_i - f_j)$. The contingencies for which the focal voter has a chance to be decisive will be specified by the notation (c_i, c_j). The number of voters is assumed large enough that the probability of a tie between three or more candidates is negligible, relative to that for a two-way tie.

Choice of a criterion for determining which candidates to vote for depends on the extent of the voter's knowledge of the likely success of the candidates. If we assume that the voter has no knowledge of the relative likelihood of the various contingencies (c_i, c_j), the voter is said to be making a decision under *uncertainty*. The *Savage regret* (minimax regret) and the *Laplace* (Bayes) methods may be appropriate.[1] [See *Luce/Raiffa*, pp. 280 and 298.]

If, on the other hand, the voter is capable of assigning subjective probabilities to the relative likelihood of the various contingencies (c_i, c_j), he is said to face a decision under *risk*. A decision based on *expected utility* may be appropriate.

It seems reasonable to believe that a voter's knowledge typically lies in between these two extremes representing no information and complete information. Hence, investigation of each type of decision rule may shed light on the voter's decision.

3. Decisions under Uncertainty and under Risk for Approval Voting

The Savage regret method chooses that decision which minimizes the maximum regret over all contingencies which might be suffered for a given decision. Regret is computed relative to the best payoff that could be achieved for a particular contingency. For the approval voting system, we will refer to a subset of candidates (for whom the voter might vote) as a *decision* or *strategy*.

For example, if there are three candidates A, B, C, rated in that order, it is easy to check that only strategies $\{A\}$ and $\{A, B\}$ are admissible, i.e., are undominated by any other strategy. (A strategy is said to dominate another if the payoff for the former is as good as or better than that for the latter for every contingency and strictly better for some contingency.) Since decisions do not depend on changes of scale or position of the set of ratings, we may assume, without loss of generality, that the ratings satisfy $1 = f_1 \geqslant f_2 \geqslant f_3 = 0$. For simplicity, we denote the contingency of a tie (had the focal voter abstained) between, say, candidates A and C by AC. We obtain the following payoff and regret matrices:

Strategy	Contingency: AB	AC	BC
{A}	$1-f_2$	1	0
{A, B}	0	1	f_2

Payoff Matrix

Strategy	Contingency: AB	AC	BC	Maximal Regret
{A}	0	0	f_2	f_2
{A, B}	$1-f_2$	0	0	$1-f_2$

Matrix of Regrets

[1]) Since the term Bayes rule is sometimes used to denote the method of expected utility as well as the Laplace method, we will use the latter term to avoid ambiguity.

It follows that the maximal regret is minimized by strategy $\{A\}$ if $f_2 < .5$ and by strategy $\{A, B\}$ if $f_2 > .5$. Thus under this criterion the voter should vote only for candidate A if $f_2 < .5$ and for A and B if $f_2 > .5$. (He should be indifferent between these two options if $f_2 = .5$.) That this result remains true for the general K-candidate race follows from the following proposition.

Proposition 1. In a K-candidate race under approval voting, the optimal strategy under the criterion of Savage regret is to vote for all candidates c_i for whom

$$f_i > (f_1 + f_K)/2, \tag{3}$$

where the candidates are ordered so that $f_1 \geqslant f_2 \geqslant \ldots \geqslant f_K$. This result will be proved in section 4.

The second method for decisions under uncertainty, the Laplace method, treats all contingencies as equally likely and determines the expected value of the payoffs (i.e., the average payoff over all contingencies) for each possible strategy. The criterion then chooses that strategy for which this expected value is largest.

For three candidates, we see from the payoff matrix above that the expected value for strategy $\{A\}$ is $(2 - f_2)/3$ and for strategy $\{A, B\}$ is $(1 + f_2)/3$. Thus strategy $\{A\}$ is chosen over $\{A, B\}$ when $(2 - f_2)/3 > (1 + f_2)/3$, i.e., when $f_2 < .5$, just as under the Savage regret method. However, for $K > 3$, the Laplace criterion is slightly different from the Savage criterion:

Proposition 2. In a K-candidate race under approval voting, the optimal strategy under the Laplace criterion is to vote for all candidates c_i for which

$$f_i > (1/K) \sum_{j=1}^{K} f_j. \tag{4}$$

Proof. See *Merrill* [1979, 1981] or *Weber* [1978].

Thus the Laplace criterion suggests that the voter compare his rating for each candidate with the average for all candidates; the Savage regret method, with the average for his most and least preferred candidates.

The method of expected utility is similar to the Laplace method, except that the expected value is computed using the voter's subjective probability for each contingency. We denote by p_{ij} the probability that in the voter's estimation there would be a tie for first place between c_i and c_j given that there is such a tie between some pair of candidates if the focal voter abstains. For convenience, we set $p_{ii} = 0$. Thus, e.g., if this probability is assumed to be the same for all pairs of candidates in a 4-candidate race, then $p_{ij} = 2/(4 \times 3) = 1/6$ for all $i \neq j$. More generally, large values of p_{ij} tend to correspond to pairs of strong candidates; small values are associated with weaker candidates. Methods for estimating the probabilities p_{ij} based on sample polls are discussed in *Hoffman* [1977].

Proposition 3. In a K-candidate race under approval voting, the optimal strategy under the criterion of expected utility (with subjective probabilities p_{ij}) is to vote for all candidates c_i for which

$$f_i > \sum_{j=1}^{K} (p_{ij}/p_i) f_j \tag{5}$$

where $p_i = \Sigma_{j=1}^{K} p_{ij}$.

Proof: See *Merrill* [1979, 1981], *Hoffman* [1977] or Proposition 5 in section 5 below.

Note that under the optimal strategy for expected utility, the voter compares his rating for each candidate with an average for the other candidates, weighted roughly in proportion to their strength.

4. Decisions under Uncertainty for Numerical Voting Systems

For general numerical voting systems, we replace assumption (2) in section 2 by a more general statement:

> The voter exercises power only if his vote $V = (v_1, \ldots, v_K)$ is decisive for some pair of candidates c_i and c_j in the sense that reversal of v_i and v_j would alter the winner. (2′)

It is assumed that a tie for first place after the focal voter has voted is resolved by, say, lot. The payoff when the focal voter casts vote $V = (v_1, \ldots, v_K)$ and encounters contingency (c_i, c_j) with $i < j$ is given by

$$P(V; c_i, c_j) = (v_i - v_j)(f_i - f_j).$$

Note that $(v_i - v_j)$ is proportional to the probability that the focal voter be decisive, while $(f_i - f_j)$ represents his payoff if he is decisive.[2])

We assume, without loss of generality, that

$$1 = f_1 \geqslant f_2 \geqslant \ldots \geqslant f_K = 0$$

and that $0 \leqslant v_i \leqslant M$, for a positive constant M determined by the voting system. Thus the best that the focal voter can attain for the above contingency is $M(f_i - f_j)$, so the regret for vote V is given by

$$R(V; c_i c_j) = [M - (v_i - v_j)](f_i - f_j).$$

Thus the maximal regret for vote V is given by

$$MR(V) = \max_{i<j} [M - (v_i - v_j)](f_i - f_j). \tag{6}$$

---

[2]) We have included the term $(v_i - v_j)$ because the potential for reversing the result is proportional to the quantity $(v_i - v_j)$ regardless of the relative strength of the candidates or the voter's knowledge of their strength. This follows since the number of voters is assumed to be large so that the probability that, say, c_j leads c_i by exactly m votes before the focal voter votes is approximately the same for each possible value of m, where m is small.

We derive the optimal regret strategy for each voting system separately. First we prove Proposition 1 concerning *approval voting*, which was stated in section 3.

Proof of Proposition 1. Without loss of generality, we may assume that $\nu_1 = 1$ and $\nu_K = 0$, since any vote V not satisfying these conditions is dominated by a vote for which they are true. We must show that the strategy represented by the vote $\bar{V} = (\bar{\nu}_1, \ldots, \bar{\nu}_K)$ defined by setting

$$\bar{\nu}_i = 1 \qquad \text{if } f_i > .5$$

and

$$\bar{\nu}_i = 0 \qquad \text{if } f_i \leqslant .5$$

is an optimal Savage regret strategy.

Since $\nu_i \leqslant 1$ for any approval voting strategy V, $M = 1$, and by (6)

$$MR\,(V) = \max_{i<j}\,[1 - (\nu_i - \nu_j)]\,(f_i - f_j).$$

It is not hard to check that

$$MR\,(\bar{V}) = \max_{\bar{\nu}_i = \bar{\nu}_j}\,(f_i - f_j) \leqslant .5.$$

If, on the other hand, $V \neq \bar{V}$, there exist k such that either ($\nu_k = 0$ and $f_k > .5$) or ($\nu_k = 1$ and $f_k \leqslant .5$). In the first case,

$$MR\,(V) \geqslant [1 - (\nu_k - \nu_K)]\,(f_k - f_K) = f_k > .5,$$

and in the second case,

$$MR\,(V) \geqslant [1 - (\nu_1 - \nu_k)]\,(f_1 - f_k) = 1 - f_k \geqslant .5.$$

It follows that $MR\,(\bar{V}) \leqslant .5 \leqslant MR\,(V)$, so that $\bar{V}$ is an optimal Savage regret strategy.

We now determine the optimal Savage regret strategy for the *Borda system.*

Proposition 4. Under the Borda system, the optimal Savage regret strategy is $\bar{V} = (K - 1, K - 2, \ldots, 1, 0)$.

Proof: Noting that here the constant M is $K - 1$, we have

$$\begin{aligned} MR\,(\bar{V}) &= \max_{i<j}\,[M - ((K - i) - (K - j))]\,(f_i - f_j) \\ &= \max_{i<j}\,[M - (j - i)]\,(f_i - f_j). \end{aligned}$$

Again it suffices to show that

$$[M - (j - i)]\,(f_i - f_j) \leqslant MR\,(V)$$

for all $i < j$ and for any vote V permissible under the Borda system. Let us fix i and j such that $i < j$.

First note that

$$(f_i - f_j) \leqslant (f_m - f_n) \tag{7}$$

for all $m = 1, \ldots, i$, and $n = j, \ldots, K$. In fact we will show that

$$[M - (j-i)]\,(f_i - f_j) \leqslant \max_{\substack{m \leqslant i \\ n \geqslant j}} [M - (v_m - v_n)]\,(f_m - f_n) \leqslant MR\,(V). \tag{8}$$

The second inequality follows from the definition (6) since the maximum in (8) is taken over a subset of the pairs (m, n) with $m < n$. If the first inequality in (8) is not the case, we see from (7) that for all $m \leqslant i$ and $n \geqslant j$, $M - (j - i) > M - (v_m - v_n)$, or more simply,

$$(j - i) < (v_m - v_n). \tag{9}$$

But since the v_m and v_n must take distinct values from the set $\{K-1, \ldots, 0\}$,

$$\min_{m \leqslant i} v_m \leqslant (K - i)$$

and

$$\max_{n \geqslant j} v_n \geqslant (K - j).$$

Hence

$$\min_{\substack{m \leqslant i \\ n \geqslant j}} (v_m - v_n) \leqslant (K - i) - (K - j) = (j - i).$$

But this contradicts (9), completing the proof of the proposition.

We now show that for *cardinal measure voting*, with *three* candidates, the optimal Savage regret strategy is $\bar{V} = (f_1, f_2, f_3) = (1, f_2, 0)$. Using $M = 1$ (and allowing fractional votes) for convenience, it is easy to see that we need only consider strategies $V = (v_1, v_2, v_3)$ such that $v_1 = 1$ and $v_3 = 0$. Using (6) we compute directly that

$$\begin{aligned} MR\,(\bar{V}) &= \max_{i<j} [1 - (f_i - f_j)]\,(f_i - f_j) = \max\{f_2\,(1 - f_2), 0, (1 - f_2) f_2\} \\ &= f_2\,(1 - f_2). \end{aligned}$$

To see that $MR\,(\bar{V}) \leqslant MR\,(V)$, we need to show that

$$f_2\,(1 - f_2) \leqslant \max\{v_2\,(1 - f_2), (1 - v_2) f_2\}.$$

Either $f_2 \leqslant v_2$ in which case the result follows, or $f_2 > v_2$ so $(1 - f_2) < (1 - v_2)$ and the result also follows.

Unfortunately, the corresponding result does not hold for four candidates. Suppose, for example, that the candidate ratings are $(1, .75, .25, 0)$ and $\bar{V}$ is the same vector. If $V^* = (1, .8, .2, 0)$, direct computation shows that $MR\,(V^*) = .2 < .25 = MR\,(\bar{V})$, and in fact V^* is the optimal Savage regret strategy for these ratings.

Since the Laplace criterion for decisions under uncertainty is mathematically a special case of the expected utility criterion, we delay a discussion of it until the next section.

5. Decisions under Risk for Numerical Voting Systems

For the class of numerical voting systems, the expected utility for a strategy $V = (v_1, \ldots, v_K)$ for the focal voter is:

$$U(V) = \sum_{v_i > v_j} (f_i - f_j)(v_i - v_j)\, p_{ij},$$

where the probabilities p_{ij} depend on the voting system in question.[3]) Note that $(v_i - v_j)\, p_{ij}$ is proportional to the probability that the focal voter be decisive, while $(f_i - f_j)$ represents his payoff if he is decisive.

For a particular voting system and focal voter, we define the *strategic value* $E(c_i)$ for candidate c_i by

$$E(c_i) = \sum_{j=1}^{K} (f_i - f_j)\, p_{ij}. \tag{10}$$

The strategic value $E(c_i)$ represents the expected payoff accruing to one incremental vote for candidate c_i. It is shown in *Merrill* [1981, section 2] that

$$U(V) = \sum_{i=1}^{K} E(c_i)\, v_i. \tag{11}$$

In light of this result, the following result is not hard to obtain.

Proposition 5. The optimal strategies for the criterion of expected utility are as given in the following table:

Voting System	Optimal Strategy
Simple Plurality	Vote for the candidate for which $E(c_i)$ is largest.
Approval voting	Vote for c_i if and only if $E(c_i) > 0$.
Borda system	Rank the candidates in order of the values of $E(c_i)$.
Cardinal measure	Give the highest permitted vote if $E(c_i) > 0$ and the lowest permitted vote if $E(c_i) < 0$.

Proof: For approval voting, for example, (11) shows that voting for c_i increases $U(V)$ if $E(c_i) > 0$, whereas it decreases $U(V)$ if $E(c_i) < 0$; if $E(c_i) = 0$, voting for c_i has no effect on $U(V)$. The other parts of the proposition follow similarly.

Under the Laplace criterion, all p_{ij} are assumed to be equal. Hence by (10) the strategic value is proportional to

$$E(c_i) = \sum_{j=1}^{K} (f_i - f_j) = K f_i - \sum_{j=1}^{K} f_j.$$

Hence $E(c_i) > 0$ if and only if

[3]) For a given voting system, p_{ij} denotes the relative probability that the vector $(0, \ldots, 1, \ldots, 0)$, with 1 in the i-th position, be decisive for the pair of candidates c_i and c_j. Furthermore, we set $p_{ii} = 0$.

$$f_i > (1/K) \sum_{j=1}^{K} f_j, \tag{12}$$

which is the condition given in (4). Thus by Proposition 5, the Laplace criterion for approval and cardinal measure voting are the same; the criterion for simple plurality is to vote for one's first choice and for Borda the criterion is to rank the candidates in order of the ratings.

6. Sincerity of Strategies

For a particular voting system, a strategy V is called *sincere* if it reflects the true rankings of the voter for the candidates, i.e., if $v_i \geqslant v_j$ whenever $f_i > f_j$. We have seen, in effect, that the optimal strategies for decisions under uncertainty (for either the Savage regret of Laplace criterion) are always sincere for simple plurality, Borda, and approval voting. This is also true for cardinal measure voting under the Laplace criterion and we conjecture that it is true for Savage regret, although the latter is left as an open question. On the other hand, with the exception of approval voting for three candidates, optimal strategies for decisions under risk in multicandidate elections are not necessarily sincere for any of the numerical voting systems studied.

7. Conclusion and Related Work

Recognizing that voters have incomplete knowledge of the contingencies in a multicandidate election, we have investigated power-optimizing strategies both as decisions under uncertainty and as decisions under risk. Assuming that voters use optimal strategies under risk, *Merrill* [1980] has analyzed the possible empirical impact of various numerical voting systems using thermometer ratings by voters obtained by the CPS 1972 American National Election Study.

For the model and voting systems considered in the present study, the optimal strategies under uncertainty are in most cases sincere reflections of the voter's rankings of the candidates. For decisions under risk, however, this need not be the case.

By exploiting this difference in optimal strategies for the two types of decision criteria, which is intuitively clear for simple plurality voting, *Black* [1978] and *Cain* [1978] have each presented guarded empirical support for the criterion of decision under risk and hence of the expected utility model. Their results are based on election data and surveys of voting intensity of preference in connection with Canadian and British elections, respectively.

Acknowledgments

The author would like to thank Steven Brams of New York University and Robert Freysinger of Wilkes College for helpful comments during the progress of this work.

References

Black, D.: The Theory of Committees and Elections. Cambridge 1958.

Black, J.: The Multicandidate Calculus of Voting: Application to Canadian Federal Elections. American Journal of Political Science **22**, 1978, 609–638.

Brams, S.: The Presidential Election Game. New Haven 1978.

Cain, B.: Strategic Voting in Britain. American Journal of Political Science **22**, 1978, 639–655.

Hoffman, D.: A Model for Sophisticated Voting. Mimeographed, 1977.

Luce, D., and *H. Raiffa*: Games and Decisions. New York 1957.

Merrill, S.: Approval Voting: A 'Best Buy' Method for Multicandidate Elections? Mathematics Magazine **52**, 1979, 98–102.

– : Strategic Decisions under One-stage Multicandidate Voting Systems. Public Choice **36**, 1981, 115–134.

Weber, R.: Comparison of Voting Systems. Cowles Foundation Discussion Paper # 498A, Yale University, 1978.

Holler, M.J. (Ed.): Power, Voting, and Voting Power ©Physica-Verlag, Würzburg (Germany) 1981

Electoral Rules and Rational Voting: The Effect of Candidate Viability Perceptions on Voting Decisions

R.F. Bensel, College Station and *M.E. Sanders*, Houston

Duverger's classic work on political parties [1963] established a theoretical link between electoral rules and the number of viable parties. Systematic empirical evidence for this linkage has been provided by *Rae* [1967]. The proposition that plurality rules produce two-party competition and majority rules, a multi-party system, has assumed the status of a sociological law.[1]) This tendency probably operates through the coercive effect of electoral rules on the candidate preferences of individuals.

In the United States, most elections for national office have one-step, plurality-determined outcomes in single-member districts. The one exception to this pattern is the two-tiered presidential election system. At the state level there are many winner-take-all, plurality-determined races. National victory, however, is not determined by a plurality of the electoral votes cast by the various states. Because the Electoral College is governed by a majority rule, the election of a president is not a single-stage plurality system. Thus, the plurality rule operating at the state level tends to produce a dichotomous choice set within each state. But this choice set need not be the same for any two states. Hence, in the nation as a whole, there may be two, three or even more strong candidates.

Third-party campaigns, given the rules governing presidential elections, can be viable at the national level providing they possess several characteristics. First, third-party candidates must be competitive alternatives in at least some states. In other words, the probable vote distribution must give them at least a second-place finish within these states. Second, their support must be relatively stable vis-a-vis changes in the distribution of candidate preferences in the nation as a whole. In the states where the third-party candidate is viable, his support must be relatively insensitive to the erosion of support in the remainder of the nation. In this paper, we will investigate third-party "vote-slippage": the drop off in the actual proportion of the final vote won by a third-party candidate compared to his percentage of pre-election preferences in national polls. This slippage will be analyzed with regard to the strategic position in which third-party supporters find them-

[1]) All single member plurality systems are one-step elections (i.e., the candidates do not enter a second election stage unless they tie). Single-member majority systems, of necessity, are at least two-step elections. Usually, the second step (e.g., run-off between the top two candidates) takes place only if no candidate receives a majority in the first election. For evidence that single-member majority systems tend toward multi-party competition see *Duverger* [1963, 239–245].

selves within their individual states. In addition, the argument will be extended to include a brief discussion of campaign techniques which are specifically intended to stabilize third-party preferences. These techniques will be connected to the structure of inherently stable preference orderings. Finally, we discuss what types of third-party campaigns are encouraged by the rules of the Electoral College and indicate a few of the implications this research might have for the comparative study of electoral systems.

A necessary assumption in this discussion of voting decisions is that the individual voter is instrumentally rational and casts his ballot for his most preferred viable candidate.[2]) Viability depends both on the electoral rules and the distribution of pre-election preferences. In single-stage elections in single-member districts, at least two candidates are always viable. Thus, if there were only two candidates in such a district, a voter would never have a strategic reason for voting for the favorite rather than his preferred candidate regardless of the certainty with which he perceives the outcome. However, if there are three candidates in a single-stage election, a voter may have a strategic reason for shifting his vote to his second choice if his most preferred candidate is very likely to trail the remaining candidates in the final tabulation.

In a two-candidate contest the decision of the individual voter requires no information regarding the viability of his preferred candidate. The rational voter casts a ballot for the candidate he prefers. However, the rational voter who has a strong-order preference ranking for all candidates in a three-candidate race faces a more complicated calculus.[3]) He must attempt to assess the preferences and predict the behavior of other voters because he has an option other than straightforward or sincere translation of his preference.[4]) In a plurality election with three candidates it may be to his advantage to shift his vote to his second preference if the expected outcome is victory for his least-preferred candidate. In a three candidate race, the rational strategy for partisans of the two front-running candidates is sincere voting. For voters with weak-order schedules involving indifference between two or more candidates, those with top-tied (henceforth labelled R_1) schedules should select the candidate in the strongest position to defeat their last preference. Those with bottom-tied (henceforth R_2) should vote straightforwardly, if they vote at all, since each of the other two candidates is equally distasteful. Holders of schedules tied on all three (R_3) should vote at random, if they vote. Assuming equal "citizen duty" utility and

---

[2]) A rational vote, as *Downs* [1957] has argued, is one which maximizes the predicted utility accruing to the voter as a result of the selection of one alternative government over another.

[3]) A strong-order preference schedule *"P"* is a complete, transitive ordering (A over B over C implies A over C, the corresponding *"P"* schedule is ABC). A weak ordering has one or more ties. For example, A is preferred to B and C but the voter is indifferent between B and C. In a three-candidate race a weak-order schedule may be top-tied, e.g., (AB)C or bottom tied A(BC). Throughout this paper we will label the former R_1 and the latter R_2 schedules. R_3 will designate three-way ties in which the subject is indifferent among all three candidates, i.e., (ABC).

[4]) The terms "straightforward" and "sincere" have been used for first-preference voting; "sophisticated," for a shift to a second preference in order to defeat one's last choice. While utilizing "sincere" and "straightforward," we have avoided employing the term "sophisticated" since it originated in a game-theoretic context. The notion of "shift-voting" employed here is more closely related to the utility-maximizing calculus described by *Riker/Ordeshook* [1968] and *McKelvey/Ordeshook* [1972]. We use the word "translation" to indicate the behavioral outcome resulting from the preference ordering – i.e., the voting choice.

costs, one would expect to find, among holders of complete preference schedules, the largest percentage of non-voters in the R_3 category.[5])

The 1968 election provided an opportunity to explore these propositions. The nationwide survey conducted by the Institute for Social Research asked respondents to place the three presidential candidates on a "feeling thermometer." They were cued that zero indicated very negative feelings; fifty, neutral, and so on up the scale. A "don't know" response was also permitted.[6]) Given this data base, twenty-six different preference orderings were theoretically possible. Those which actually occurred among survey respondents are listed in Table 1 with their respective frequencies. The letters N, H, and W stand for the three presidential candidates (Richard Nixon, Hubert Humphrey, and George Wallace respectively).

These are, of course, ordinal rankings and say nothing of the relative distances between candidates for each individual schedule. The feeling thermometer in effect forces the respondent to convert to a single currency, or collapse, salient dimensions of his preferences. Behind the score indicating his summated feelings toward the candidate may stand a host of weighted (in importance to him) judgments, as well as reactions to the personal attributes of the candidate. For our purposes, candidate location points may be in one or several dimensions [*Weisberg/Rusk*]. We are concerned only that the thermometer scores represent a summated ordering for each prospective voter.

Third-party candidate George Wallace was shown to be a strong national contender, drawing over twenty percent of the vote, by national opinion surveys in early September, 1968. As the campaign developed, however, the electorates in the northern states returned for the most part to the traditional dichotomous choice set. In the North, the major-party candidates argued that a Wallace vote would be "wasted" (cast for a candidate with no chance of winning). In the South, the campaign remained an unpredictable scramble until the day of election. Here, Wallace could counter that he might be able to deadlock the Electoral College by carrying enough electoral votes to deny anyone a majority in the nation as a whole. If he successfully deadlocked the Electoral College, he would be in a position to bargain with the major-party contenders for policies favored in the South. In both regions, Wallace minimized the differences between the two major-party candidates. By calling them "tweedle-dum and tweedle-dee" and claiming that there wasn't "a dime's worth of difference" between their policy stands, Wallace attempted to implant a strategic cue which would have stabilized the preferences of Wallace partisans. By tying his supporters' preferences for the major-party candidates, Wallace attempted to minimize vote-

[5]) The impact of the "citizen duty" factor on voting is analyzed by *Riker/Ordeshook* [1968]. An assumption we make in analyzing non-voting by schedule type is that the presidential race was the primary interest for prospective voters in the 1968 election. In order to simplify the analysis, we have interpreted the voting act as a product of preferences and probabilities and, thus, implicitly ignored both voting-costs and the "citizen-duty" factor. For evidence supporting the importance of both costs and duty in a two-candidate race, see *Sanders* [1980].

[6]) The feeling thermometer question was asked *after* the 1968 election. There is reason to doubt the accuracy of responses. Seventy-six percent of our sample claimed to have voted in the 1968 election – a figure which, even considering that our sample omits about 250 cases not coded on all relevant questions, seems inflated. A bias toward the winner in the thermometer scores, reported votes or both is likely. An extreme example is schedule 23 in which three respondents who answered "don't know" when asked to place each of the three candidates, claimed to have voted for Nixon.

Schedule #		Stfd.	Shift		Violation	Abstention
"P" Schedules[2])						
1. NHW	365	290	7		2	66
2. NWH	93	67	5		1	20
3. HNW	369	288	4		0	77
4. HWN	46	26	2		3	15
5. WNH	84	52	13		0	19
6. WHN	29	21	1		1	6
		Stfd. Vote for			Violation	Abstention
"R" Schedule		H	N	W		
7. (HW) N	3	3	0	0	0	0
8. (NH) W	101	40	26	–	1	34
9. (WN) H	12	0	4	5	0	3
10. H (NW)	43	30	0	0	0	13
11. W (HN)	35	–	–	17	2	16
12. N (HW)	64	0	46	0	0	18
13. (HNW)	24	4	3	2	0	15
		Stfd. Vote for			Violation	Abstention
Incomplete Schedules		N	N	W		
14. (HN)	5	1	2	0	0	2
15. H	1	0	–	0	1	0
16. W	1	0	0	0	0	1
17. N	1	0	1	0	0	0
18. HN	4	3	0	0	0	1
19. NH	2	0	1	0	0	1
20. WH	2	0	–	0	1	1
21. HW	2	1	0	0	0	1
22. NW	1	–	0	0	1	1
23. ?	11	0	–	0	3	8

Tab. 1: Schedule Frequencies and Voting Patterns[1])

[1]) The abbreviation "stfd." stands for "straight-forward" voting (for a first preference). A "shift" is a vote for one's second preference. A "violation" is a vote for a last preference or a candidate the respondent was not able to rank (choosing the "don't know" response). Incomplete schedules are those in which the respondent was unable to rank one, two or all three candidates (as in the last schedule, designated by a question mark).

[2]) *"P"* designates strong preferences, e.g., NHW expresses the ordering N over H over W which implies N over W.

slippage in all regions. His partisans would cast a straight-forward vote for Wallace because they would perceive neither of the two major party candidates as preferable to the other. Schedule eleven in Table 1 is the preference ordering produced where Wallace supporters internalized his cue.

One of the purposes of this paper is to describe, using the 1968 data, the effects of American laws governing presidential elections on the propensity of the rational voter to vote for the candidate he most prefers. Table 1 provides a cross-tabulation of each respondent's preference ordering in the 1968 campaign by his reported vote. Seventy-six percent of the respondents are found to have strong-order schedules ordering all three candidates. One and three are the modal patterns. Twenty-two percent have weak-order schedules and two percent possess incomplete schedules.

A shift is any vote for a second-order preference. No shift is logically excluded from the rational choice set. However, any third-order vote-translation constitutes a *"violation"* of the individual's preference schedule. Whereas a voter in some cases may decide to "shift" his vote to his second preference in order to defeat the least-preferred candidate, any voter who casts a ballot for his least-preferred candidate has no strategic reason for doing so. This conception of "rationality" then includes all possible translations except a third-order preference vote.[7])

The primary focus of this study is on the objective factors – originating in the electoral system – that determine second-order or "shift" votes.[8]) We are primarily interested in the rules governing presidential elections and voter perceptions of candidate viability in the two main environments about which voters receive strategically relevant information (the state and the nation). The first task at hand is to define the *primary electoral invironment* – the distribution of first-order candidate preferences in the prospective voter's state. The SRC survey cannot provide an accurate sample within each of the 36 states from which the respondents were drawn. For this reason, and since shifts and violations represented a fairly small percentage of all votes, we assumed that the actual 1968 election returns reflected the candidate preference distribution within each state. The use of election returns probably understates, in most cases, the individual voter's pre-election perceptions of the electoral strength of the last-place candidate. Further, we realize that this distortion was not similar in size, though probably similar in direction, for all states. For example, in border states where a viable three-way race was maintained until November, the last-place candidate would have been almost impossible to predict; thus, shifts by individuals from a last-place but most-preferred candidate would have been smaller as a percentage of all such first-order preferences compared to states where the last-place candidate was obvious.[9])

The reasoning behind "shift" voting is as follows: Defining "A" as the candidate with the largest number of first-order preferences in the state, "B" as the candidate with the second largest number, and "C" as the candidate with the least number, six strong-order individual preference schedules (in terms of candidate place) are possible. They are displayed in Table 2. The act of voting "translates" the preference-ordering into candidate selection. A "shift-indicated" schedule is one which rationally suggests voting for one's

[7]) This discussion assumes that the individual voter can either differentiate successfully between candidate electoral strength or does not differentiate at all. Even though we include under the definition of "rationality" voting shifts that are due to mistaken perceptions of candidate viability, the main patterns of vote-translation and perception upon which this theory is based presume accurate viability perceptions of the candidates within either the state or nation. Such questions have been explored in *Weisberg/Rusk* [1970].

[8]) Ferejohn/Fiorina have objected to the definition of rationality exclusively in terms of utility maximizing strategies. They suggest an alternative decision calculus – based on Savage's "minimax regret" criterion – by which voting for one's second choice is never an optimal strategy. To the extent that sophisticated voting occurs, the minimax regret criterion is disconfirmed. In other words, if a substantial percentage of individual voters in shift-indicated situations do, indeed, shift, a calculus that implies that no voter would ever shift is invalidated.

[9]) For example, in Tennessee the vote distribution for Nixon, Wallace and Humphrey was 38, 34 and 28 percent. Given imperfect information, the prospective voter would be unlikely to abandon his first preference in so close a race.

second-most preferred candidate because of the non-viability (given the statewide distribution of candidate preferences) of one's first choice. A preference schedule is "non-shift-indicated" if straightforward translation of the first preference is the only rational strategy, given correct information about the distribution of first-order preferences. Such would be the case if the first-preferred candidate were one of the two front-runners. Any vote for a third-order preference constitutes a "violation" of the individual's preference ordering.

The prospective voter whose preferences were ordered ABC as in schedule one of Table 2 obviously had no reason to shift. Individuals who held schedules three and four and

Non-shift-indicated Schedules	Shift-indicated Schedules
1. ABC	5. CAB
2. BAC	6. CBA
3. BCA	
4. ACB	

Tab. 2

who perceived correctly that C was a last-place candidate with little viability would not have shifted from one of the two front-runners. Schedule two requires some elaboration. Generally speaking, an individual would have shifted only to prevent his last-order preference from winning. Since C must have been a viable candidate in the voter's state in order to induce a shift, the individual perceptions of the preference distribution in the state electorate would have been of a three-way race with no clear front-runner. Thus, we rea-

Schedule[1])	# Cases	Stfd.	Vote Shift	Violation	Abstention
Non-shift indicated					
ABC	377	294 (78/95.4)	14 (3.7/4.5)	0 (0)	69 (18.3)
ACB	86	65 (75.6/94.2)	2 (2.3/2.9)	2 (2.3)	17 (19.8)
BCA	79	53 (67.1/93)	4 (5.4/7)	0 (0)	22 (27.8)
BAC	334	265 (79.3/98.5)	3 (.9/1.1)	1 (.3/.4)	65 (19.5)
Total	876	677 (77.3/96.3)	23 (2.6/3.3)	3 (.3/.4)	173 (19.7)
Shift-indicated					
CBA	55	31 (56.4/88.6)	3 (5.4/8.6)	1 (1.8/2.9)	20 (36.4)
CAB	54	36 (66.7/81.8)	7 (13/15.9)	1 (1.9/2.3)	10 (18.5)
Total	109	67 (61.5/84.8)	10 (9.2/12.7)	2 (1.8/2.5)	30 (27.5)
Grand Total	985	744 (77.5/95.1)	33 (3.4/4.2)	5 (.5/.6)	203 (20.6)

[1]) The letters indicate the candidate's final position in the election results of the respondent's state. Percentages in the second line are proportions of total holders of that schedule and proportions of total voters among holders of the schedule. (For abstainers it is percentage of total schedule-holders.)

Tab. 3: Summary of Voting Decisions by Holders of *"P"* Schedules

son, schedule-two individuals with relatively accurate information, would never entertain the idea of a shift in vote translation. The remaining individuals with schedules five and six, however, would have been tempted to shift in those states where C was obviously running a poor third. In sum, only individuals who perceived their first-order preference as a last-place candidate would have been expected to shift.

Table 3 provides a breakdown of voting decisions by the two types of strong-order schedules. The results support our expectations relating to the incidence of shift-voting. Among those voters holding what we described as shift-indicated schedules, the percentage of shifts was nearly four times as great as it was among non-shift indicated schedule holders (a difference significant at the .05 level).

In contrast to strong-order preference orderings, all R_2 schedules should have produced stable and straightforward vote translations. Because this schedule type is characterized by a second-order tie, no one least-preferred candidate is indicated. For that reason, no R_2 schedule holders should shift and all second-order vote translations are considered violations. Table 4 provides the actual voting decisions for this schedule type.

		Vote-Translation		
Schedules	Cases	First-Order	Violation	Abstention
A (BC)	48	34	0	14
C (AB)	26	11	1	14
B (AC)	68	48	1	19
Total	142	93 (65.5/97.9)	2 (1.4/2.1)	47 (33.1)

Tab. 4: Voting Decisions Among Holders of Weak-Order R_2 Schedules

Following the logic put forward for schedule 2 in Table 2, individuals with R_1 schedules in which the front-running candidates are preferred (AB) C should *not* be expected to vote disproportionately for candidate A. Where C is close to, and threatens to overtake A, the voter would be hard-pressed to identify the stronger of his tied first-order preferences since B, by definition, is even closer to A than C is. Therefore, as the "incentive" to choose the stronger of the candidate-pair increases, the likelihood of being able to do so successfully decreases. The other weak-order schedules suffer less from this dilemma but are few in number. In line with the foregoing argument, Table 5 reveals only a slight difference between the frequency with which R_1 schedule-holders chose the stronger over the weaker of their tied preferences.

		Vote-Translation			
Schedules[1])	Cases	Stronger	Weaker	Violation	Abstention
(AB) C	98	35	28	1	34
(AC) B	9	2	5	0	2
(BC) A	9	5	3	0	1
Total	116	42 (36.2/53.2)	36 (31.0/45.6)	1 (.9/1.3)	37 (31.9)

[1]) Schedules are coded by state election returns in tables four and five.

Tab. 5: Voting Decisions Among Holders of Weak-Order (R_1) Schedules

As expected, the percentage of non-voters was higher among weak-order than among strong-order schedule holders, and was greatest among those preferring the last-place candidate but indifferent between the two front-runners. In the R_1 schedules alone, the greatest incidence of non-voting was found among those tied on the two top candidates. The straightforward voting rate for all R_1 and R_2 individuals who voted is 98.3 percent. While this exceeds the 95.0 percent first-order translation rate for all strong-order individuals who voted, it should be noted that shift-voting is not possible given the structure of these preference schedules.

To engage in shift-voting, voters must have information about the probable outcome of the election, based on the distribution of preferences within the state electorate. In states where the outcome differed markedly from the national results, the information the prospective voter received from national and local sources was discordant. If we categorize our states into those where state election results agreed with the national outcome

A. State Election Results Agree with Nation on Last-place Candidate (Wallace)

Shift-indicated Schedules	Number of Cases	Stfd.	Shift	Violation	Abstention
CAB and CBA	73	43 (81.1 %)	9 (17.0 %)	1 (1.9 %)	20 (27.4 %)
Non-shift-indicated Schedules					
ABC, ACB, BAC, and BCA	784	612 (96.8 %)	17 (2.7 %)	3 (.5 %)	152 (19.4 %)

B. State and National Results Disagree on Last-place Candidate

Shift-indicated[2]) Schedules	Number of Cases	Stfd.	Shift	Violation	Abstention
	36	24 (92.3 %)	1 (3.8 %)	1 (3.8 %)	10 (27.8 %)
Non-shift-indicated Schedules					
	92	65 (91.5 %)	6 (8.5 %)	0	21 (22.8 %)
Nation indicates shift[3])		27 (84.4 %)	5 15.6 %)	0	6 (15.8 %)
Nation does not indicate shift		38 (97.4 %)	1 (2.6 %)	0	15 29.6 %)

Tab. 6: Sophisticated Voting and Congruence of Electoral Environments[1])

[1]) Letters in schedules indicate the candidates' ranks in state results. Percentages in parentheses are percentages of *voters* holding schedules, except in the case of abstention, which is the percentage of total schedule holders.

[2]) Shifts indicated by the state electoral environment.

[3]) In this subtable, all shift-indicated schedules at the state level are non-shift-indicated at the national level. However, not all non-shift-indicated schedules at the state level are shift-indicated at the national level. We have subdivided those schedules by the indicated strategy at the national level. The division points up the importance of the national electoral milieu.

on the identity of the last-place candidate (congruent states) and those where Wallace ran first or second, we gain some insight into how informational congruence affected shift-voting decisions. Table 6 does this according to schedule type.

Table 6 suggests that additional corroborating information about the prospects of one's preferred candidate encouraged shift voting. Among holders of shift-indicated schedules, the percentage of sophisticated voters is more than four times higher in states with candidate rankings similar to the national outcome. Non-predicted shifts (from a stronger first-order to a weaker second-order preference or from a first-order preference for the runner-up to a second-order preference for the winner) also occurred with less frequency in congruent than in non-congruent states (2.7 versus 8.5 percent). The latter percentage, however, is the sum of the two sub-categories at the bottom of Table 6. A comparison of those figures with the data reported in category A illustrates the dominating influence of the national electoral environment on the selection of voting strategies. In comparison, the state electoral environment and the plurality rule exercised a secondary influence. Violations among all three types of schedules occur rarely in both groups of states.

Table 7 reveals that a greater likelihood of a last-place finish – induced by informational congruence and a dearth of fellow partisans[10]) – encouraged shifts to more viable second-order preferences. In states where Wallace finished in last place, his supporters were

Size of Wallace Vote in States in which Wallace Ran Third	Vote-Translation				
	Cases	First-Order	Shift	Violation	Abstention
0–14.4 %	45	26	8	1	10
Percent of all individuals included in survey		(56.8)	(17.8)	(2.2)	(22.2)
Percent of all voters in survey		(74.3)	(22.9)	(2.8)	–
14.5–28.5 %	28	17	1	0	10
Percent of all individuals included in survey		(60.7)	(3.6)	(0.0)	(35.7)
Percent of all voters in survey		(94.4)	(5.6)	(0.0)	–

Tab. 7: Voting Decisions of Shift-indicated *"P"* Schedules in States Congruent with the National Outcome

[10]) A simple "contact" thesis may be stated. Where the final vote for a candidate in the state is low, it is assumed that the prospective voter has, in the course of the campaign, encountered few of his partisans. Hence he finds little support for his preference and weak grounds for optimism about the candidate's chances. Controlling for candidate preference (because it was found to bias predictions), we found that when the states were separated into those in which Wallace received ten percent or less of the vote, those where he received 11 to 18 percent, and those where his percentage was 18 or more, the proportion of Wallace supporters who predict a national Wallace victory increases at each level of support. Where he received ten percent or less, 12.5 percent of Wallace partisans saw him as the likely winner. In the highest group, 28.3 percent made such a prediction. Only complete *"P"* schedules designating one of the three major candidates were analyzed. Of the entire sample, the percentage of respondents who were unable to predict the final victor was also greatest in the group of states giving Wallace 18 percent or more of the final vote.

more likely to shift to a second-order preference where the Wallace percentage of the total vote was small than in states where it was substantial. However, several reservations must be made. First, the number of respondents involved in this part of the analysis is relatively small. Second, when there is such a high percentage of shifts, the election returns provide a very distorted picture of intra-state first-order preferences. In spite of these reservations, the coercive effect of electoral rules on preference translation is clearly evident. The cases in Table 7 are at the "cutting-edge" of this coercion.

Although we are not directly concerned with voting turnout, it should be noted that the turnout rate is partially dependent upon the ability of individuals to differentiate and order their preferences. Non-voting is consistently higher among the three schedule types in noncongruent than in congruent states. Overall nationally, strong-order schedule holders were more likely to vote than weak-order schedule-holders; the latter exceed holders of incomplete schedules, and the highest percentage of non-voters is found among those tied on all three candidates. The highest percentage of non-voting among strong-order schedule-holders (36 percent) is found in the CBA group. Among R_1 schedules, those tied on the two front-running candidates in their states were least likely to vote. Among respondents who preferred the weakest candidate in their state, R_2 schedule holders with first-order preferences for C, i.e., C (AB), abstained with greater frequency than strong-order schedule holders who preferred one of the more viable candidates to the other, i.e., CAB or CBA. The respective percentages are 54 and 27. Table 8 summarizes these results and, in addition, provides the violation percentages for strong and weak-order schedules. Overall, the violation percentages were quite small: very few voters engage in "irrational" voting behavior.

Schedules	Violations	Abstentions
Strong-order	0.8 % (N = 783)	20.6 % (N = 986)
Weak-order	1.7 % (N = 174)	32.6 % (N = 258)
Incomplete	[1]	53.3 % (N = 30)
Indifferent	[1]	62.5 % (N = 24)

[1]) "Incomplete" and "indifferent" schedule-holders could not, by definition, violate their preference schedules. However, twenty percent of those voters holding incomplete preference schedules voted for a candidate they could not or would not place on the feeling thermometer. The percentages calculated in the "Violations" column are for voters only. The abstention figures are calculated for all respondents (including non-voters) in the survey.

Tab. 8: Violations and Abstentions by Schedule Type

Summary of Findings

A theory of candidate preference translation which outlines the influence of electoral rules on voting decisions has been presented here. This theory can be divided into two parts. The first specifies the degree of stability (in vote-translation) of individual preference orderings in a three-candidate race. Certain of these orderings are shift-prone or unstable. Other are inherently stable regardless of the strategic position of the voter within the electoral arena. The second part of the theory describes which strategic positions within the electoral arena encourage shift-prone or unstable voting. The distinction between the distribution of candidate preferences and the revealed electoral translation of that distribution has been emphasized throughout the argument. This distinction is of great importance for the analysis of third-party campaigns.

The theoretical argument for the influence of the Electoral College on presidential voting and third-party campaign strategies can be summarized as follows: In order to minimize the effect of the national media on perceptions of third-party viability (allowing a third-party campaign "to get off the ground"), a third-party candidate must capture enough individual untied first preferences such that he is a clear front-running or second-place contender within at least some states. The "capturing" of this support constitutes a necessary condition or threshold for a major third-party candidacy for two reasons. First, solid intra-state support disrupts the strong tendency of the electorate to view the election as a national plurality contest and, thus for third-party supporters to shift in their voting behavior to one of the major contenders. Second, the electoral college majority rule allows for an "issue" victory through third-candidate brokering (which is what Wallace attempted).

This theory and the findings seem to account for the "regional bastion" nature of third-party candidacies in the United States. In addition, since the threshold thesis requires the early development of first-order preferences (which in itself requires voter familiarity with the candidate), an important third-party candidate must have at least regional prominence before the general election campaign begins. The first weeks after the candidate choice-set is established constitutes the "pure" preference phase of an election period. During this stage of a campaign, the electorate articulates preferences straightforwardly without reference to strategic considerations. It is upon these preferences that the electoral rules later operate, paring down the candidate choice-set through perceptions of viability.

The strategic consequences of national polling on state-viability perceptions of intrastate candidate viability help to explain the Wallace campaign against the national media. An increased dependence by potential Wallace voters on state-bounded information would, interpreting the research results reported here, have decreased the percentage of shifts in some states; however, states mirroring the national distribution of first-order preferences would have remained the same.

The predictions derived from this theory are supported by the direction of the findings presented here. The rather low overall incidence of shift voting, however, indicates that some significant qualifications are in order. The most important of these concern perceptions of candidate viability. The decision to shift in vote-translation is heavily influenced by perceptions of candidate viability at the national level. In fact, the presidential election data reported here indicate a nearly overwhelming tendency to view presidential elections as national plurality contests. The data in Table 6 (particularly the lower half) clearly indicate that the rules of the Electoral College had little effect on supporters of the major party candidates. Regardless of the strategic position in which they found themselves, their voting decisions were straightforward translations of their candidate preference schedules. Such behavior is identical to that expected under a national plurality-determined contest.

However, the rules of the Electoral College seem to have greatly influenced the behavior of the Wallace supporters. The tendency of supporters of George Wallace to shift in their voting decisions was affected by the viability of Wallace within the state where the voter resided (see, in particular Table 7). The voting decisions of these Wallace supporters are consistent with that expected under the rules of the Electoral College (i.e., a disaggregated, majority-determined contest). In sum, then, the influence of the electoral college on individual voting decisions falls most heavily on third-party candidacies and lightly, if at all, on the voting decisions of major party adherents. These results are consistent both with the theoretical expectations of rational behavior developed in the body of this study and with the theoretical description of third-party candidacies set out above.

A few minor qualifications are also in order. The amount of strategically relevant information the electorate receives is probably quite small and haphazardly digested. In addition there may be a tendency to "reorder" candidate preferences once a shift is made. That is, once an individual has decided to shift from his unviable first-order preference, the seemingly incongruent preference distinction between his first-order preference and his intended vote could be eliminated by the revision of the original preference order. In the absence of other considerations, then, a large number of pre-election shifts would appear as changes in the distribution of first-order preferences. Thus, this reverse bandwagon ("jumping off") effect would account, to some extent, for the comparatively rapid decline in Wallace strength in the North and border state polls from his late August-early September peak.

Conclusion

These results suggest a number of possible comparative applications. First, while single-member plurality systems tend to reduce most elections to two candidate races, two-stage majority systems, multi-member districts, and proportional representation would all tend to increase the number of viable candidates. In two-stage majority systems, there would normally be three viable candidates in the first round. In effect, the perceived third-place candidate competes with the second-place contestant for a spot in the run-off. Similarly, in multi-member districts the number of viable candidates should, theoretically, be one more than the number of positions to be filled.[11]) Proportional electoral systems would depend on the representation threshold. For example, if fifteen percent of the total vote were necessary to win at least one seat, voter perceptions of candidate viability would center on the probable attainment of that threshold.

These speculative implications must be qualified by three considerations. First, the availability of strategic information is probably affected by the relationship of local races to the national result. In the United States, the most reliable and readily available information on voter preferences comes from national opinion surveys conducted by the major polling firms. The relative dearth of equivalent information at the state level probably encourages the voter to view his choice in a national context. Second, given electoral sys-

[11]) The type of multi-member district we are considering here must be described. In order for the above statement to hold, the system must give the voter the same number of votes as positions to be filled, bar bullet or cumulative voting, and provide for plurality, single-stage decisions. Such an arrangement or its theoretical equivalent would, of course, place significantly greater informational requirements on the individual voter than single-member, single-stage electoral systems.

tems of varying complexity and differing levels of strategic information, electorates will show widely differing propensities to shift-vote. Generally speaking, the more complex the electoral system and the less information about the electoral machinery possessed by the average voter, the lower the incidence of shift-voting. For example, two-stage proportional systems may impose information costs so high that shift-voting is a prohibitively expensive electoral strategy. Finally, intensely ideological political systems, in which many voters hold exclusive political allegiance to only one of a number of political parties, should exhibit little shift-voting. In these systems, the average preference ordering would 'tie' preferences for all but the voter's own party.

The logic of this argument suggests one additional conclusion. Electoral rules have often been regarded as a determining factor in the number of parties in a political system. Given the low incidence of shift-voting in the United States during the 1968 presidential race, it is clear that other systemic factors not directly related to electoral rules (for example, ideological intensity, the availability and cost of political information, and the educational level of the electorate) may be just as important.

References

Downs, A.: An Economic Theory of Democracy. New York 1957.

Duverger, M.: Political Parties. New York 1963.

Farquharson, R.: Theory of Voting New Haven 1969.

Ferejohn, J.A., and *M.P. Fiorina*: The Paradox of Non-Voting: A Decision Theoretic Analysis. American Political Science Review **68**, 1974, 525–536.

McKelvey, R., and *P.C. Ordeshook*: A General Theory of the Calculus of Voting. Mathematical Applications in Political Science, VI. Ed. by J. Herndon and J. Bernd. Charlottesville, Virginia, 1972.

Rae, D.: Political Consequences of Electoral Laws. New Haven 1967.

Riker, W.H., and *P.C. Ordeshook*: A Theory of the Calculus of Voting. American Political Science Review **62**, 1968, 25–42.

Sanders, E.: On the Costs, Utilities, and Simple Joys of Voting. Journal of Politics **42**, 1980, 192–201.

Weisberg, H.F., and *J.G. Rusk*: Dimensions of Candidate Evaluation. American Political Science Review **64**, 1970, 1167–1185.

4. Concepts of Power Measurement

Holler, M.J. (Ed.): Power, Voting, and Voting Power ©Physica-Verlag, Würzburg (Germany) 1981

The Problem of the Right Distribution of Voting Power

H. Nurmi, Turku[1])

1. Statement of the Problem

The principle of rule by the people is one of the basic tenets of democracy. At the heart of this tenet is the idea that everybody should have a say in the decision making taking place in the name of the people. The "say" in ancient polis was simply the right – indeed the duty – of being present in the meetings where public affairs were being discussed and decided upon. The principle of aggregating the individual wills into a collective one was in a way an obvious one. However, in the advent of the representational institutions the aggregation problem gained importance. The reason is clear: the representatives must necessarily be representatives of at least some *groups* as one of the main desiderata of representative institutions is to decrease the size of the decision making body. On the assumption that the citizens can be partitioned into mutually exclusive and exhaustive groups in a way that somehow "fairly" reflects their individual wills, one can ask: what is the right or just way of designing a collective decision making body so that the will of the people finds its expression in the workings of the body in the most faithful fashion?

In countries applying the proportional representation principle the problem has been solved by dividing the fixed number of parliamentary seats among parties or party coalitions roughly in the proportion of their support among the voters. Some variation in the accuracy of the proportionality can be observed due to variations in the computing formulae used in different countries. Nonetheless, the principle of aggregation of group wills into a collective will is the same: the groups (parties or party groupings) are treated as homogeneous units of which the society is composed. In one person electoral district systems the basic unit is the electoral district which for the purposes of aggregation is not subdivided into constituents but is treated as a block entitled to one representative.

Regardless of which of these aggregation procedures is resorted to, the design of the collective representational body is not yet completed. The most crucial of the remaining problems is the choice of the decision rule. The distribution of parliamentary seats in conjunction with the decision rule determines the voting power of the party. [See, e.g., *Laakso*, 1975; *Riker/Ordeshook*, 1973, 170–172]. Assuming that we want to distribute

---

[1]) This paper was written while the author was a British Academy Wolfson Fellow at the University of Essex. The comments of and discussions with Markku Laakso, Manfred J. Holler, Norman Schofield and Michael Taylor have been most helpful.

the legislative power – not seats simpliciter – according to the popular support, some new ways of designing the collective decision making bodies must be resorted to. This is one of the messages of the present paper. In the following I shall discuss some of the techniques of determining the power in voting bodies. If one aims at designing collective decision making bodies which are democratic in the sense of reflecting the popular support in terms of the voting power, we need indices of the latter which enable us to calculate for any given distribution of support and for any decision rule the distribution of seats that is "just". Alternatively, we may want to design decision rules that – given the distribution of seats and support – lead to a distribution of voting power which is identical with the distribution of support.

2. Power Indices

The indices most often used in measuring the voting power of groups in voting bodies are Shapley-Shubik index, Banzhaf index and two indices introduced by Coleman [see *Shapley/Shubik; Banzhaf*, 1965; *Coleman*]. The background of Shapley-Shubik index is the Shapley value of a player defined for players and groups of players in n-person games with a von Neumann-Morgenstern type of characteristic function [*Shapley*, 1953]. The intuitive justification of the Shapley value is that when joining a coalition a player makes a contribution to the value of the coalition. This follows from the superadditivity assumption of the von Neumann-Morgenstern characteristic functions of n-person games. The amount of pay-off that the player can reasonably expect to gain from the game should – according to Shapley – reflect the amount of contribution the player is able to make to various coalitions. Specifically, each player's Shapley value is a weighted sum of his contributions to all possible 2^n coalitions. The weights are computed as follows: the weight of player i in coalition S of size s equals

$$\frac{(s-1)!\,(n-s)!}{n!}.$$

The Shapley value of the player i is, thus, obtained as follows:

$$F_i^{Sh} = \sum_{S \subseteq N} \frac{(s-1)!\,(n-s)!}{n!}\,[v(S) - v(S-\{i\})].$$

Here N is the grand coalition comprising all n players, S is specific coalition of s players and v is the characteristic function of the game.

Now, the value of the player has been interpreted both as his reasonable payoff expectation and as his power (we encounter one more interpretation in this paper). Shapley-Shubik index is specifically designed for the latter interpretation. It is based on the assumption that only winning coalitions have value in decision making in collective bodies. Furthermore, the value of each winning coalition is assumed to be the same, viz. 1. The value of each losing coalition equals 0. With these assumptions the Shapley value concept can be extended to situations where no quantitative measure of a player's contribution to a coalition exists. We must, however, observe that the additional assumptions are simple analogs of the principle of insufficient reason. Their tenability must, thus, be assessed in casu.

Banzhaf index of voting power is based on similar assumptions as the Shapley-Shubik index, the only difference being that instead of counting the permutations of the members inside and outside any given coalition as indicated in the factorials of the weights, Banzhaf index takes account of each player's presence in and absence from winning coalitions only. Hence, whereas the Shapley-Shubik index can be interpreted as equating the voting power of player i with the relative number of times i has been pivotal in all $n!$ permutations of n players (i.e., i has been the last added member of a winning coalition which is assumed to be formed by adding members to it in all possible sequences), the Banzhaf index counts only the times i has been an essential or nonredundant member in a winning coalition. The index is made relative by dividing the number of "critical presences" of i in various winning coalitions by the number of all critical presences of the n players. In symbols

$$F_i^B = \frac{\sum_{S \subseteq N} [v(S) - v(S - \{i\})]}{\sum_{i=1}^{n} \sum_{S \subseteq N} [v(S) - v(S - \{i\})]}.$$

Following *Brams/Affuso* [1976] we can interpret F_i^B as i's proportion of critical defections in the voting game. The interpretation is obvious when one bears in mind that for all $T \subseteq N$ there is $v(T) = 1$ when T is winning and $v(T) = 0$ otherwise, according to the previous assumptions. Hence, in the denominator the expression in the brackets equals 1 if and only if i's presence is critical for S to be winning.

Another version of the index is the absolute or non-standardized Banzhaf index $F_i^{B'}$ defined as

$$F_i^{B'} = \frac{\sum_{S \subseteq N} [v(S) - v(S - \{i\})]}{2^{n-1}}.$$

Intuitively speaking the power of a player or a group of players may be of initiating or blocking nature. In particular, it may in some instances be the case that a party, though lacking the power to initiate collective action, has power to block it. The voting power seems thus to have two aspects. These are reflected in Coleman's two power indices. The index of initiative power is computed as follows:

$$F_i^{CI} = \frac{\sum_{S \subseteq N} [v(S + \{i\}) - v(S)]}{\sum_{S \subseteq N} [1 - v(S)]}.$$

Obviously the denumerator gives the number of losing coalitions among the 2^n coalitions. The numerator, in turn, indicates the number of times the presence of i has changed a losing coalition S into a winning one. Hence, F_i^{CI} gives the proportion of those coalitions which i has managed to turn into winning ones among all losing coalitions. The blocking power of i, on the other hand, is defined by Coleman as follows:

$$F_i^{CB} = \frac{\sum_{S \subseteq N} [v(S) - v(S - \{i\})]}{\sum_{S \subseteq N} v(S)}.$$

We notice that the denumerator counts the number of winning coalitions. Consequently, F_i^{CB} indicates the proportion among all winning coalitions of those coalitions in which the presence of i is critical.

It can readily be shown [see *Brams/Affuso*] that (*i*) the Coleman indices are linearly dependent on each other, and that (*ii*) the Banzhaf index is a proportional transformation of either one of the Coleman indices. In contradistinction, there does not seem to be any simple way of relating Coleman and Banzhaf indices to the Shapley-Shubik index. The reason for this is obvious: permutations of players play a crucial role in the calculation of the Shapley-Shubik index whereas both Banzhaf and Coleman indices completely overlook permutations concentrating instead exclusively on coalitions (or combinations) of players.

3. Power and Decision Rule

The fact that voting power depends on the decision rule seems prima facie obvious enough to need no further attention, all the more so as all of the previously introduced indices take account of this fact. What makes it still worthy of explicit scrutiny is the practice common in many representational bodies according to which seats are distributed among the parties roughly in proportion of their relative support, or in the winner-take-all fashion. This practice seems to be based on the idea that the relative power to influence the course of events in the legislature is reflected in the relative distribution of seats. In the case of single-member constituencies the assumption seems to be that the distribution of seats among the representatives of the constituencies gives the correct picture of the will of the people. It is clear that the assumption made in the majority principle systems is similar to the one made in proportional representation systems except for an implicit additional assumption made in the former systems: when elected, the representatives of the constituencies cease being representatives of their parties or groups and become instead representatives of the whole constituency. On this additional assumption the majority and proportionality principles amount to the same idea of representation. We shall not deal with this additional assumption in this context but focus on the common assumption of both proportionality and majority systems, viz. that the distribution of seats equals the voting strength. If not even this assumption is made, then it is really difficult to see what goals the proportionality is aimed to serve.

There is a number of studies suggesting that the voting power of parties in legislatures in general does not coincide with their share of the seats if the measure of voting power is any one of the aforementioned power indices [see *Banzhaf*, 1968; *Brams*, 1975; *Laakso*, 1975; *Shapley/Shubik*]. The discrepancy of the seat distribution and power distribution varies, of course, with the choice of the power index. This fact poses the problem of which index if any to choose. We postpone the discussion of this problem until later on in this paper. Let us instead focus on another one assuming that the index choice problem has been solved, viz. how to effect the change from a given electoral system to the one in which the distribution of support is identical with the distribution of voting power. This – I think – is a worthwhile goal to strive at because it is evident that the idea of representational democracy rests on this identity.

Now, an obvious answer to the problem just posed is to derive the seat distribution from the distribution of support so that the latter is first transformed into power index values of each party and, then, each party is given the share of seats that corresponds to its share of power. This procedure would technically work if just one decision rule is applied in the voting body. In most parliaments this is not the case; some issues require simple majority decisions, other 2/3 or even larger majorities. The problem now becomes that of weighting of different values of the chosen power index for different decision rules. In the case of the Finnish parliament where the decision rules to be applied are 1/2, 2/3 and 5/6, *Laakso* [1975] ends up with using an unweighted average of the Shapley value scores as the measure of the overall power of parties. This may, indeed, be a justifiable solution. As a matter of fact it is a variant of the principle of insufficient reason. Intuitively one could suggest that the issues requiring larger majorities are more important than others and that, consequently, the power index values for those decision rules should be given more weight than others. How much more weight, remains the problem. On the other hand, one could propose weighting the index values by the relative frequencies by which issues belonging to the domain of a given decision rule have in the past been put into the agenda of the voting body. This would, in most cases, mean putting the most of the weight on simple majority rule to the virtual neglect of large majority rules. Whether this is what voting power really means, remains to be shown. We may notice, however, that using relative frequencies as weights amounts to weighting power according to the relative number of situations in which it could have been exercised in the past.

The most obvious way of bringing voting power and a given seat distribution close to one another is to consider the number of votes of each party as a variable depending upon the decision rule to be applied. So, each party might, for instance, be given the number of seats that corresponds in terms of voting power the support it has been given if the decision rule is that of simple majority. For other rules the votes of the party would be changed according to changes in the voting power.

Computing the power index values assuming that the weighting problem is solved gives us a fairly straightforward way of allocating seats among parties so that the will of the people finds its expression in the power distribution. As the ensuing distribution of seats is likely to differ from the present one in any country, the change benefits some parties and hurts others. A more indirect way of ending up with the relative voting power distribution which is identical with the relative support resorts to manipulation of the decision rules. It was pointed out above that the voting power is a function of both the share of seats and the decision rule. Now, it would seem then that one can manipulate the latter keeping the seat distribution fixed and end up with power index values that correspond to the distribution of support. Indeed, in the case of the Shapley-Shubik index it is known that the average of the index values for all decision rules from 50 % to 100 % equals the share of the seats [*Laakso*, 1975; for proof, see *Shapley*, 1962]. Hence, if we want to keep the distribution of seats intact we can achieve the power distribution measured by Shapley-Shubik index which exactly corresponds the seat distribution by randomizing the decision rule so that each rule between 50 and 100 % is chosen with equal probability. The same result holds for the non-standardized Banzhaf index [see *Dubey/ Shapley*, p. 110]. Thus, on formal grounds a case can be built for using random decision rules in voting bodies.

The above "recipes" for institutional design are based on the crucial assumption that there is an unambiguous way of determining the voting power once the seat (or weight) distribution of parties is given. As was pointed out above the power indices do not in general give the same results when applied to a given seat distribution. Hence, before specific guidelines for the design of political institutions can be given, it is essential to know more about the properties of the power indices.

4. Which Index to Choose?

It has been pointed out by *Brams* [1975, 176–182] and *Brams/Affuso* [1976] that there are some paradoxical features related to the power indices introduced above. The first paradox, the paradox of size, consists of the fact that for some distributions of seats it may be beneficial for a coalition to split into parts in the sense that the sum of the powers of the constituent parts is greater than the power of the original coalition. Prima facie this seems to contradict both intuition and the super-additivity assumption of the characteristic function of n-person games. Upon closer inspection the contradiction with intuition disappears when one calls attention to the cases in which the split of a large heterogeneous group into small homogeneous ones increases the over-all power of the group. A case in point is the provision of collective goods for a large group by a "federalistic" arrangement whereby a large group (in the terminology of *Olson* [1965]) is turned into a collectivity of small ones in which the provision of collective goods presents no problems. Nor is the contradiction with the superadditivity assumption a real one: the calculation of power indices is based on the characteristic function. The number of times a party is pivotal or critical is a function of the coalition structure and may, consequently, quite consistently with the superadditivity assumption lead to the paradox of size. From the point of view of comparing the power indices it is worthwhile to notice that all of the aforementioned indices are subject to this apparently paradoxical feature for some distributions of seats.

This is also the case with respect to the second paradox discussed by Brams, viz. the paradox of new members. This occurs when a party is added to a collectivity so that its total membership is enlarged and yet the power of at least one of the parties of the original voting body is thereby increased. As in the previous case, this result is confirmed by many practical situations in which a party or grouping purposefully attempts to enhance its position in a voting body by proposing that new members be called upon. The third paradox in Brams' discussion is the paradox of quarrelling members, that is, a situation in which the refusal of two parties to get together in a coalition actually results, not in a loss of payoffs, but in an increase of them. It is easy to notice that this paradox is just a reinterpretation of the paradox of size.

Laakso [1978] has studied the variation of the power index values of certain parties in the Finnish parliament for different decision rules. He observes that the power indices exhibit somewhat irregular patterns of variation. So, for example, the maximum values of Banzhaf index for certain parties do not lend themselves to intuitively satisfactory interpretation. For all indices the variation seems irregular to the extent that Laakso feels justified to call this counter-intuitive behaviour "the paradox of the decision rule".

Startling as they may seem at first sight, the paradoxes do not represent truly disturbing situations when one compares them with the properties of our intuitive power concept. If power indices behave in a strange fashion, so does power itself in certain special circumstances. It remains to be shown, however, that the circumstances of "strange behaviour" coincide. We shall not dwell on this problem here, but focus instead on ways of differentiating the power indices by means of their underlying assumptions concerning the bargaining process which results in the distribution of power. As will become evident shortly these assumptions differ considerably.

Political scientists are very accustomed to speaking about coalitions of political actors. Therefore, they are not at all at odds with the idea of combination of members or parties as the basis for the computation of power index values. This intuitive familiarity may be considered as an advantage of Banzhaf and Coleman indices in contra-distinction to Shapley-Shubik index which makes use of permutations of actors instead of their combinations. Counter-intuitive as it may seem prima facie the permutations of players can be given a political interpretation; it has been argued by *Riker/Shapley* [1968] that any given permutation of players can be seen as an attitude dimension concerning some issue to be decided upon. At one end of the permutation we have actors having the most favourable attitude towards the issue with actors with indifferent attitudes in the middle and the opposed ones in the other end. In the computation of the Shapley-Shubik index it is assumed that the weight of each permutation is equal. This can be taken to mean that the a priori probability of each of the permutations is the same. As *Brams* [1975, p. 168] points out, this interpretation of permutations as attitude dimensions loses its intuitive plausibility when the number of actors increases. For instance, if we have five parties the number of equally probably "attitude dimensions" is 120 which makes it very difficult to figure out what sort of "attitudes" are in question.

Now the bargaining process underlying the above interpretation of Shapley-Shubik index is the following as outlined by Riker and Shapley: for any proposition to be decided there is supposedly a price that has to be paid by a person who wishes to obtain the necessary majority to support the proposition. Obviously the persons in favour of the proposition do not need any financial incentive to give their support. The highest price must obviously be paid for the pivotal actor if the actors are placed in the order of their willingness to support the proposition, as the pivotal actor is least favourable towards it and yet his support is necessary in order to get the proposition passed. Hence, the number of times an actor is pivotal reflects his "value" or power to decide issues. As nothing is known about the issues to be decided or the "attitudes" of the other actors, the principle of insufficient reason can be called upon to justify the assumption that each attitude dimension is equiprobable or of equal weight.

In Banzhaf index the bargaining process starts with the formation of minimal winning coalitions. The power of an actor ensues from his ability to threaten the other members of the minimal winning coalitions. In the computation of the index values one considers the distribution of actors into favouring and opposing groups. The computation takes into account minimal winning coalitions only, i.e. those opinion distributions in which the change of one actor's opinion changes the action taken in the name of the voting body as a whole. The "minimality" of the coalition is to be understood in the sense that for each minimal winning coalition there is at least one member whose removal would make the coalition non-winning. Obviously, this usage of the concept differs from Riker's "Size Principle" [*Riker*]. The equiprobability assumption is again made, but it concerns now the defections of actors: each defection from a minimal winning coalition is assumed to be equally probable. Analogous assumptions are made in Coleman indices.

If the intuitive justification of the Shapley-Shubik index is somewhat dubious, its game-theoretic background has recently been established much beyond that of the other indices. First, *Roth* [1977] has shown that the Shapley value is a utility function defined for games if certain conditions are met. This means that if we allow the notion of utility to be defined for games and not only for outcomes, the strategic utility $h(v) = (h_1(v), h_2(v), \ldots, h_n(v))$ – where $h_i(v) = h(v, i)$ $(i = 1, \ldots, n)$ indicates the utility of playing the position i in game defined by the characteristic function v – equals the vector of the Shapley values of the game v provided that the preference relation over games is risk-neutral both with respect ordinary and strategic risk. Neutrality towards ordinary risk amounts to the condition that for all games v and w under consideration the actors i make no difference between the following two options:

(1) $((pw + (1-p)v), i)$ and (2) $(p(w, i); (1-p)(v, i))$.

(1) means the option of playing position i in a game in which the characteristic function is a weighted average of w and v. (2) means the option of playing the position i in the game w with probability p and the position i in the game v with probability $(1-p)$.

In contradistinction to ordinary risk, a preference relation is said to be neutral to strategic risk if the player is indifferent between a game that gives him the utility t for certain and a game that gives to a k-member coalition to which be belongs the value of $k \cdot t$.

Now, Roth's result is, then, that if and only if all the actors are neutral to both kinds of risk mentioned, the vector of the Shapley values equals the vector of strategic utilities for all games. This result certainly gives the Shapley-Shubik index a fairly strong theoretical backing. What it says is that the index can be incorporated into the von Neumann-Morgenstern framework under certain additional assumptions. One should, however, bear in mind that the von Neumann-Morgenstern conditions for the utility function yield a unique function up to an affine transformation only. Hence, the fact that the Shapley value satisfied these conditions when the risk posture assumptions are made does not entail that it is the only index to have this nice theoretical property.

Shapley-Shubik index has recently been given another related type of theoretical justification by *Harsanyi* [1977]. Harsanyi is able to show that the Shapley value is in a way congruent with another solution concept of game theory, viz., with the Nash solution to co-operative games. More specifically, Harsanyi shows that in n-person games with transferable utility in which players of any forming coalition agree to co-operate in order to protect their common interests against the other players, the vector of the Shapley values of players is identical with the vector of payoffs in multilateral bargaining equilibrium. The multilateral bargaining equilibrium is an extension of the concept of bilateral bargaining equilibrium which, in turn, is defined as the Nash solution to two-person simple bargaining games, i.e., in bargaining games where for each player there is only one non-cooperative strategy whereby the levels of non-cooperation or threat are reduced to one. As is well known, the Nash solution of a two-person simple bargaining game is the outcome maximizing the following product:

$$N = (u_i - r_i)(u_j - r_r)$$

where u_i (u_j, respectively) is the payoff of player i (j) and r_i (r_j) is the payoff i (j) gets if no agreement between the players is achieved. Now, consider a situation where a bilateral equilibrium exists between every pair of players when the payoffs not subject to bargaining are fixed. That is, the situation is a Nash equilibrium for every two players on the assumption that the payoffs of the other players are constant. This situation is called the multi-lateral bargaining equilibrium. What Harsanyi shows then is that the payoffs of players in the multilateral bargaining equilibrium are equal to the Shapley values of the players.

5. What Should be Done?

The previous discussion has hopefully demonstrated that there is a need to revise our intuitions about the foundations of representation. Specifically I have made an attempt to show that one of the basic tenets of democracy, viz. that of representing the will of the people, is less straight-forward principle than is customarily thought. If we want to distribute the power in the legislature according to the distribution of support among the electorate, we must clearly change our methods of allocating the seats among parties or the decision rules if we accept some of the most common indices of power discussed in the literature.

The crucial issue now is whether the power indices are reliable enough to guide our process of institutional design. In the preceding I have made an attempt to address this problem by looking at the bargaining models underlying the power indices. I have also reviewed and assessed some recent results pertaining to the game-theoretic justification of the Shapley value. In conclusion it remains to be said that the results so far obtained do not suffice to settle the issue in favour of any particular index. What we now need is a measurement-theoretic approach to power. It is evident that this approach must be based on a careful conceptual analysis of the concept of power. This analysis should be particularly directed towards showing whether power can be related to observable features (e.g., seat distributions). Furthermore, the conceptual analysis should provide a suitable axiomatization of power because the measurement-theoretic analysis must be based on such an analysis. The result of the measurement-theoretic analysis is a characterization of the conditions under which we can measure power. Provided that the concept is measurable we need to know whether our measure – whatever it is – is unique or not. Specifically, the analysis should be capable of showing which one – if any – of the above power indices can be used as a measure of power.

References

Banzhaf, J.F. III: Weighted Voting Doesn't Work: A Mathematical Analysis. Rutgers Law Review **19**, 1965, 317–345.

– : One Man, 3.312 Votes. Villanova Law Review **13**, 1968, 304–332.

Brams, S.J.: Game Theory and Politics. New York 1975.

Brams, S.J., and *P. Affuso*: Power and Size: A New Paradox. Theory and Decision 7, 1976, 29–56.

Coleman, J.S.: Control of Collectivities and the Power of a Collectivity to Act. Social Choice. Ed. by B. Lieberman. New York 1971, 269–299.

Dubey, P., and *L. Shapley*: Mathematical Properties of the Banzhaf Power Index. Mathematics of Operations Research **4**, 1979, 99–131.

Harsanyi, J.C.: Rational Behavior and Bargaining Equilibrium in Games and Social Situations. Cambridge 1977.

Laakso, M.: Eduskunta koalitio- ja valtasuhderakenteena. The Finnish Parliament as a Coalition and Power Relation Structure. Helsinki 1975.

– : Valtaindeksien paradoksit. The paradoxes of the power indices. Research Reports. Institute of Political Science. University of Helsinki **Ser. A**, 1978, N49.

Olson, M.: The Logic of Collective Action. Cambridge 1965.

Riker, W.H.: The Theory of Political Coalitions. New Haven 1962.

Riker, W.H., and *P.C. Ordeshook*: An Introduction to Positive Political Theory. Englewood Cliffs 1973.

Riker, W.H., and *L. Shapley*: Weighted Voting. Representation Nomos X. Ed. by R. Pennock and J. Chapman. New York 1968.

Roth, A.: The Shapley Value as a von Neumann-Morgenstern Utility. Econometrica **45**, 1977, 657–664.

Shapley, L.: A Value for *N*-Person Games. Contributions to the Theory of Games. Ed. by H.W. Kuhn and A.W. Tucker. (Annals of Mathematical Studies **28**), Princeton 1953.

– : Values of Games with Infinitely Many Players. Recent Advances in Game Theory. Ed. by M. Maschler, Princeton 1962.

Shapley, L., and *M. Shubik*: A Method of Evaluating the Distribution of Power in a Committee System. American Political Science Review **48**, 1954, 787–792.

Holler, M.J. (Ed.): Power, Voting, and Voting Power ©Physica-Verlag, Würzburg (Germany) 1981

An Axiomated Family of Power Indices for Simple n-Person Games[1])

E. W. Packel, Lake Forest and *J.Deegan*, Jr., Rochester

1. Introduction

Over the last twenty-five years there has been considerable interest in attempting to assign a quantitative measure of power to players in simple n-person games. This interest stems from a desire to model the interaction and influence of participants in collective decision-making processes much as those found in legislative bodies, committees, and a variety of organizations. The packaging of each specific measure of power or power index usually consists of a motivating collection of modeling assumptions (i.e., a 'story') and an algebraic or combinatoric formula which reflects the assumptions and facilitates a numerical determination of individual power. An important third ingredient, sometimes present, is a set of 'reasonable' axioms that uniquely determine the index. Such a characterization often sheds light on the nature of the index in question, and provides a valuable basis for comparison with other similarly characterized indices. In that which follows we place a major emphasis on this axiomatic aspect of power indices.

The history of power indices essentially began with the index and axiomatic characterization proposed by *Shapley/Shubik* [1954]. The index of *Banzhaf* [1965] resulted from a significantly different model of power and has been used by the courts in questions involving fairness of representation in weighted voting situations. The efforts of *Dubey* [1975] subsequently provided an axiomization of the Banzhaf index, which revealed that it differs in surprisingly delicate fashion from a reworked set of axioms for the Shapley-Shubik index. In *Deegan/Packel* [1979] the authors presented and axiomatized a new power index for simple games based upon formation of minimal winning coalitions and equal distribution of payoffs among members of such coalitions. It should be noted that there is substantial similarity (in motivating concern) between the characterizing axioms for the Deegan-Packel index and the power indices of Shapley-Shubik and Banzhaf.

In the next section of this paper we generalize the power index of *Deegan/Packel* [1979] by abandoning the assumption that all minimal winning coalitions form with equal likelihood. By allowing such coalitions to form in accordance with varying probability functions we obtain a family of power indices and develop an accompanying axiomat-

---

[1]) Published in *Public Choice* 35, 1980, pp. 229–239; republished by permission of Martinus Nijhoff Publishers BV.

ic characterization. In comparing our approach with that of *Blair* [1976] and *Dubey* [1976], we observe that the indices of Shapley-Shubik and Banzhaf emerge from one particular type of construction, while our family of indices derives from a fundamentally different construction.

In the third section we consider a few examples, after which we discuss and compare proprieties, axioms, and paradoxes that obtain for the various indices discussed above. Finally, we introduce the notion of the dual of a simple game. We then develop a family of dual power indices and present the altered axioms which characterize this dual family.

2. Probabilistic Indices and their Characterization

A power index takes a class of simple games and assigns to each player i in a given game v a nonnegative real number $\rho_i(v)$ to represent the player's 'power'. Throughout this paper we focus specifically on the class C_N of *monotone* simple n-person games on the player set $N = \{1, 2, \ldots, n\}$. Formally, with 2^N denoting the power set of N,

$$C_N = \{v: 2^N \to \{0, 1\} \mid v(\phi) = 0; S \subseteq T \Rightarrow v(S) \leqslant v(T)\}.$$

We assume that n is fixed but arbitrary in that which follows. Since dummy players can always be adjoined to a game with fewer players, this is not a serious loss of generality.

To provide a concrete example of a power index on C_N and to set the stage for the generalization that follows, we briefly develop the index presented in *Deegan/Packel* [1979]. For $v \in C_N$, let $M(v)$ denote the set of *minimal winning coalitions*. Thus,

$$M(v) = \{S \subseteq N \mid v(S) = 1 \text{ and } v(T) = 0 \text{ for all } T \subset S\}.$$

If it is assumed that

1) Only *minimal* winning coalitions will form
2) Each such coalition has an equal probability of forming
3) Players in a (minimal) winning coalition divide the spoils equally,

then one is led inevitably to the following notion of power as represented by what player i can expect to 'get' from a game v:

$$\rho_i(v) = \frac{1}{|M(v)|} \sum_{\substack{S \in M(v) \\ i \in S}} \frac{v(S)}{|S|}.$$

While each of the assumptions listed above has limited domain of applicability, assumption (2) is probably the most difficult to accept and the most natural to generalize. We now proceed to do so. Let f: $2^N - \{\phi\} \to (0, 1)$ be a probability function on the set of coalitions. Thus $f(S)$ represents an a priori probability that coalition S will form. We assume that f is *symmetric* with respect to cardinality ($|S| = |T| \Rightarrow f(S) = f(T)$). Given such an f and any $v \in C_N$, we obtain a probability function $P^f(v)$ on the set of (minimal winning) coalitions in v by

$$P^f(v)(S) = [\alpha^f(v)]^{-1} \begin{cases} 0 & \text{if } S \notin M(v) \\ f(S) & \text{if } S \in M(v) \end{cases}$$

where

$$\alpha^f(v) = \sum_{S \in M(v)} f(S)$$

is the normalization factor for $P^f(v)$. Note that $P^f(v)$ has simply restricted the influence of f to the minimal winning coalitions in v.

We may now define a probabilistic power index $\rho^f: C_N \to \mathbf{R}^n$ by

$$\rho_i^f(v) = \sum_{S \ni i} [P^f(v)(S)]\, v(S)/|S|.$$

The rationale for this approach is based upon the modeling assumption that a coalition S, with a probability $P^f(v)(S)$ of forming, distributes its payoff $v(S)$ equally among its $|S|$ members. The fact that $P^f(v)(S)$ is nonzero if and only if S is a minimal winning coalition reflects the assumption that only minimal winning coalitions can successfully form. Discussion and possible justification of these assumption has been presented in *Deegan/Packel* [1979] and at greater length in *Deegan/Packel* [1976]. In these papers and in the index ρ defined earlier, the special case where

$$f \equiv 1/(2^n - 1) \quad \text{and} \quad \alpha^f(v) = |M(v)|\,/\,(2^n - 1)$$

is considered.

To proceed, we need the following definitions. A player i is a *dummy* in a game v if $v(S \cup \{i\}) = v(S)$ for all $S \subseteq N$ (equivalently, i belongs to no minimal winning coalitions). Players i and j are *symmetric* in v if $v(S \cup \{i\}) = v(S \cup \{j\})$ for all $S \subseteq N - \{i, j\}$.

Given $v, w \in C_N$, we define $v \vee w$ and $v \wedge w \in C_N$ as follows:

$$(v \vee w)(S) = \begin{cases} 1 \text{ if } v(S) = 1 \quad \text{or} \quad w(S) = 1 \\ 0 \text{ otherwise} \end{cases}$$

$$(v \wedge w)(S) = \begin{cases} 1 \text{ if } v(S) = 1 \quad \text{and} \quad w(S) = 1 \\ 0 \text{ otherwise.} \end{cases}$$

We say that, $v, w \in C_N$ are *mergeable* if

$$S \in M(v) \text{ and } T \in M(w) \Rightarrow S \not\subseteq T \text{ and } T \not\subseteq S.$$

This mergeability condition is equivalent to requiring that $|M(v \vee w)| = |M(v)| + |M(w)|$ and will be used in the characterization that follows.

Theorem 1. For a given symmetric function f: $2^N \to (0, \infty)$, the function $\rho^f: C_N \to \mathbf{R}^n$ is the unique power index satisfying the axioms:

A1: $\rho_i^f(v) = 0 \Leftrightarrow i$ is a dummy player.

A2: If i and j are symmetric in v, then $\rho_i^f(v) = \rho_j^f(v)$.

A3: $\sum_{i=1}^{n} \rho_i^f(v) = 1$ for all $v \in C_N$.

A4: If v and w are mergeable in C_N, then

$$\rho^f(v \vee w) = \frac{\alpha^f(v)\,\rho^f(v) + \alpha^f(w)\,\rho^f(w)}{\alpha^f(v) + \alpha^f(w)}.$$

Proof. Given

$$\rho_i^f(v) = \sum_{S \ni i} [P^f(v)(S)]\, v(S) / |S|,$$

we first show that A1 through A4 are satisfied. Property A1 holds since

$$\begin{aligned}\rho_i^f(v) = 0 &\Leftrightarrow P^f(v)(S)\, v(S) = 0 \text{ for every } S \text{ containing } i\\ &\Leftrightarrow P^f(v)(S) = 0 \text{ for every } S \in M(v) \text{ containing } i\\ &\Leftrightarrow \text{no } S \in M(v) \text{ can contain } i\\ &\Leftrightarrow i \text{ is a dummy.}\end{aligned}$$

The second axiom is satisfied by the symmetry between i and j and the symmetry of f. For A3 we have

$$\begin{aligned}\sum_{i=1}^{n} \rho_i^f(v) &= \sum_{i=1}^{n} \sum_{i \in S} [P^f(v)(S)]\, v(S) / |S|\\ &= \sum_{S \subseteq N} \sum_{i \in S} [P^f(v)(S)]\, v(S) / |S|\\ &= \sum_{S \subseteq N} P^f(v)\, v(S)\\ &= \sum_{S \in M(v)} [\alpha^f(v)]^{-1} f(S) = 1.\end{aligned}$$

Finally, A4 holds for ρ^f since, for each $i \in N$,

$$\begin{aligned}\rho_i^f(v \vee w) &= \sum_{S \ni i} [P^f(v \vee w)(S)]\,(v \vee w)(S) / |S|\\ &\quad [\alpha^f(v \vee w)]^{-1} \Big[\sum_{\substack{S \in M(v)\\ i \in S}} f(S)\, v(S) / |S| +\\ &\quad \sum_{\substack{S \in M(v)\\ i \in S}} f(S)\, w(S) / |S| \Big]\\ &= \frac{1}{\alpha^f(v) + \alpha^f(w)} [\alpha^f(v)\,\rho_i^f(v) + \alpha^f(w)\,\rho_i^f(w)].\end{aligned}$$

Conversely, suppose A1–A4 are satisfied by some function $\rho^f: C_N \to \mathbf{R}^n$. For any $v \in C_N$, enumerate the members of $M(v)$ as $S_1, S_2, \ldots, S_m$ and for each S_k let $v_k \in C_N$ denote the game for which

$$v_k(S) = \begin{cases} 1 \text{ if } S \supseteq S_k \\ 0 \text{ if otherwise.} \end{cases}$$

Since $M(v_k) = \{S_k\}$, a singleton set, the v_k are mergeable and $v = v_1 \vee v_2 \vee \ldots \vee v_m$.

For any $i \in N$ and v_k, axioms A1, A2, and A3 require that

$$\rho_i^f(v_k) = \begin{cases} 1 / |S_k| & \text{if } i \in S_k \\ 0 & \text{otherwise.} \end{cases}$$

Using A4 readily extended to a merge of m rather than 2 games, we have

$$\rho_i^f(v) = \frac{\sum_{k=1}^{m} \alpha^f(v_k)\, v_k\, \rho_i^f(v_k)}{\sum_{k=1}^{m} \alpha^f(v_k)}$$

$$= [\alpha^f(v)]^{-1} \sum_{k=1}^{m} \alpha^f(v_k)\, v_k(S_k) / |S_k|$$

$$= |\alpha^f(v)|^{-1} \sum_{k=1}^{m} f(S_k)\, v(S_k) / |S_k|$$

$$= \sum_{S \in i} [P^f(v)(S)]\, v(S) / |S|.$$

Q.E.D.

The intuitive content of and rationale behind the characterizing axioms A1 through A4 is straightforward and consistent with the desired properties of a power index. It is convenient to alter the normalization axiom A3 for certain indices (in particular, for an important version of the Banzhaf index), but we prefer to work exclusively with indices normalized to unity. This allows power index values to be viewed as probabilities and facilitates comparison between different indices. Axiom A4 says that power in a merged game is an appropriately chosen weighted mean of the powers of the component games. For the specific index ρ defined at the beginning of this section, the weights can be realized by using the number of minimal winning coalitions in each component game.

To illustrate the value of axiomatization, we note that [*Dubey*, 1975] replacing A4 by another additive type condition (specifically, $\rho(v + w) = \rho(v \vee w) + \rho(v \wedge w)$) leads to a characterization of the Shapley-Shubik index. If, in addition, A3 is replaced by a different 'normalization', the (nonnormalized) Banzhaf index is the unique result. By critically reviewing the particular axioms which seem appropriate for a given game situation, it may be possible to gain some insight into which power index might be most appropriate (see *Straffin* [1977] for a related discussion of these considerations).

The power indices of Shapley-Shubik and Banzhaf can be realized [see *Blair* or *Dubey*, 1976], as special cases of what Blair calls P-values, in a manner similar to our approach although their probability function P on the set of coalitions must be formulated in a slightly different manner. More significantly, the contributions to the 'payoff' of a player i in a coalition S are not determined by equal subdivision $[v(S) / |S|]$, but rather by what player i contributes to the coalition S $[v(S) - v(S - \{i\})]$. This difference in approach appears to be fundamental, placing our minimal winning coalition based indices in one category and the Shapley-Shubik and Banzhaf indices in another.

Other differences between the $v(S) - v(S - \{i\})$ approach and our $v(S) / |S|$ approach are noteworthy. The family of P-values has the class G_N of characteristic function form games as its natural domain. Restriction to C_N leads to a family of 'indices' whose members may require normalization to unity, and no coherent set of axioms seems to be available for these normalized indices. The *P*-value approach is somewhat more pleasing in that it generalizes smoothly to provide a family of linear 'values' on G_N without an *efficiency* axiom

$$(\sum_{i=1}^{n} \rho_i(\nu) = \nu(N)).$$

In contrast, our approach allows incorporation of the nature of each particular game in determining power (the probability function f is altered in accordance with the set $M(\nu)$), while extension to a value of G_N requires a generalization of the minimal winning coalition concept (see *Deegan/Packel* [1979] for some specialized results in this direction). Further differences between the two approaches discussed above can be inferred from the specific examples considered in the next section.

3. Examples, Properties, and Paradoxes

By looking at the indices of Shapley-Shubik (ϕ), Banzhaf (β) and Deegan-Packel (ρ) applied to specific games, we may gain further insight into the nature of the probabilistic families discussed previously. We start with the simplest nontrivial 3-person game, which can be defined in weighted voting game form by $w = [3; 2, 1, 1]$ (a quota of 3 with players having respective weights of 2, 1, and 1) and has $M(w) = \{\{1, 2\}, \{1, 3\}\}$. The various power index values for w, expressed in vector form, are

$$\phi(w) = (2/3, 1/6, 1/6)$$
$$\beta(w) = (3/5, 1/5, 1/5)$$
$$\rho(w) = (1/2, 1/4, 1/4).$$

Results of committee experiments in this 'veto for player 1' game are inconclusive regarding the 'empirical' power of the players; but, regardless of the empirical outcomes it is not clear that general models should be applied (or evaluated) with so few players. Nevertheless, we can draw some theoretical conclusions from the index values. It is readily determined that for any symmetric f: $2^N - \{\phi\} \rightarrow (0, 1)$ the probabilistic index $\rho^f(w)$ will agree with $\rho(w)$. It follows that for no general choice of f will ρ^f coincide with ϕ or β on C_N. This strengthens our contention that the indices to the family $\{\rho^f\}$ are fundamentally different in nature from the Shapley-Shubik and Banzhaf indices.

The index ρ, like ϕ and β, admits a variety of 'paradoxes' when considered in the domain of weighted voting games. The paradoxes of quarreling, added weight, and new members, documented for ϕ and β in *Brams* [1975] and *Brams/Affuso* [1976] can be exhibited for ρ [see *Deegan/Packel*, 1976]. While these paradoxes seem surprising to some, they appear to be present for all power indices and may [see *Raanen*, 1976] in a sense be inevitable.

For the sake of completeness, we feel obliged to point out another interesting paradox which occurs for ρ, but not for ϕ or β (and apparently not for the family of indices arising from Blair's approach). We illustrate by example with the weighted voting game

$v = [5; 3, 2, 1, 1, 1]$. It can be demonstrated that $\rho(v) = (18/60, 9/60, 11/60, 11/60, 11/60)$, showing that the '1 vote' players each have more power than the '2 vote' player. The impact of this paradox on the interpretation of ρ (and of the general $v(S) / |S|$ approach) as an a priori measure of power in certain political voting situations is open for discussion. We feel compelled to point out though that sociologists have, in fact, argued [for example, *Caplow*, 1968] that situations where minor players possess greater *potential* for power are not anomalous, but occur rather frequently in real-world situations.

We note, by way of balance, that the indices of Shapley-Shubik and Banzhaf can also be shown to exhibit counterintuitive properties. In particular, it has been shown by *Straffin* [1976] that both the Shapley-Shubik and Banzhaf indices are susceptible to alteration (in the context of weighted voting games) by players 'quarreling' with a dummy player (i.e., refusing to join the same coalition). This cannot happen in our minimal winning coalition approach. The differing assumptions underlying ϕ, β, and ρ naturally give rise to significantly different models of a priori power determination. While the relative merits of these indices might be debated at length, it seems likely that, as in so many aspects of n-person game theory, each index has a domain of more appropriate applicability. This is an area, however, where much work remains to be done.

4. Duality

Every $v \in C_N$ gives rise to a natural dual game $v^* \in C_N$ defined as follows:

$$v^*(S) = \begin{cases} 1 \text{ if } v(N-S) = 0 \\ 0 \text{ if } v(N-S) = 1. \end{cases}$$

Thus a coalition S is winning ($v^*(S) = 1$) in the dual game if and only if it can block any other coalition from winning in the original game v.

With f as in Section 2, we now define a family of dual indices $\rho^{*f}: C_N \to \mathbf{R}^n$ by $\rho^{*f}(v) = \rho^f(v^*)$. Intuitively, such indices measure (for a game v), the power of each player to block winning coalitions from forming (or to prevent passage of Motions). It is worth noting that the indices of Shapley-Shubik and Banzhaf are each equal to their duals, thus incorporating the power to initiate and the power to block equally. This is not generally the case for the family of indices we have developed. As a result, our family of indices has the capacity to provide a priori assessments of both 'power to initiate' and 'power to block' (see *Coleman* [1971] for related developments in this area).

The family of dual indices can also be characterized axiomatically. The following lemma sets the stage.

Lemma. $(v \wedge w)^* = v^* \vee w^*$ and $(v \vee w)^* = v^* \wedge w^*$.

Proof.
$$\begin{aligned} (v \wedge w)^*(S) = 1 &\Leftrightarrow (v \wedge w)(N-S) = 0 \\ &\Leftrightarrow v(N-S) = 0 \text{ or } w(N-S) = 0 \\ &\Leftrightarrow v^*(S) = 1 \text{ or } w^*(S) = 1 \\ &\Leftrightarrow (v^* \vee w^*)(S) = 1. \end{aligned}$$

The second equality follows from the first by the reflexive nature ($v^{**} = v$) of the dual.

Q.E.D.

Given f: $2^N \to (0, \infty)$ symmetric, and $P^f(v)$ a probability function on the coalitions of v, we define $\alpha^{*f}(v) = \alpha^f(v^*)$. Thus

$$\alpha^{*f}(v) = \sum_{S \in M(v^*)} f(S).$$

We then have:

Theorem 2. The function ρ^{*f}: $C_N \to \mathbf{R}^n$ is the unique power index satisfying the axioms:

A1*: $\rho_i^{*f}(v) = 0 \Leftrightarrow i$ is a dummy player.

A2*: If i and j are symmetric in v, then $\rho_i^{*f}(v) = \rho_j^{*f}(v)$.

A3*: $\sum_{i=1}^{n} \rho_i^{*f}(v) = 1$ for all $v \in C_N$.

A4*: If v and w have mergeable duals in C_N, then

$$\rho^{*f}(v \wedge w) = \frac{\alpha^{*f}(v)\,\rho^{*f}(v) + \alpha^{*f}(w)\,\rho^{*f}(w)}{\alpha^{*f}(v) + \alpha^{*f}(w)}.$$

Proof. The fact that our ρ^{*f} satisfies A1*–A3* follows directly from the corresponding results for ρ^f in Theorem 1. It suffices to observe that the sets of dummy players and symmetric pairs in v are unchanged in v^*. For A4* we use the Lemma and Theorem 1 as follows.

$$\begin{aligned}\rho^{*f}(v \wedge w) &= \rho^f((v \wedge w)^*) = \rho^f(v^* \wedge w^*)\\ &= \frac{\alpha^f(v^*)\,\rho^f(v^*) + \alpha^f(w^*)\,\rho^f(w^*)}{\alpha^f(v^*) + \alpha^f(w^*)}\\ &= \frac{\alpha^{*f}(v)\,\rho^{*f}(v) + \alpha^{*f}(w)\,\rho^{*f}(w)}{\alpha^{*f}(v) + \alpha^{*f}(w)}\end{aligned}$$

Finally, ρ^{*f} must be unique in satisfying the axioms on C_N since otherwise the uniqueness of ρ^f established in Theorem 1 would be contradicted. Q.E.D.

While the role of duality (note that A4* uses $v \wedge w$ while A4 used $v \vee w$) is aesthetically pleasing in the characterization provided by Theorem 2, the potential of the dual index is currently unclear. One can envision considering a political situation modeled by a game v and determining that for this situation the power to initiate should have weight t and the power to block weight $1 - t$. If f is the function describing probabilities of coalition formation, it would seem natural to define a combined index for this game as $t\,\rho^f(v) + (1 - t)\,\rho^{*f}(v)$. Unfortunately, there are various situations in which apparently unusual results are obtained. These results may relate to the 'failure to preserve weights' paradox described in Section 3. They are also partially explained by the fact that ρ^f acts peculiarly on improper games and that the dual of a proper game is often improper.

5. Some Concluding Thoughts

Does the world currently need another power index, let alone a large family of such, their duals, and a continuum of weighted combinations? The question is not unlike a more general one about the proliferation of solution concepts (none of them quite adequate) in cooperative game theory. We believe that there will always be room for simple, well-motivated models of individual and group behavior. If such models are accompanied by coherent schemes of characterizing axioms, they may simultaneously contribute meaningfully to the theory and carve out domains of practical applicability. Von Neumann and Morgenstern never said it would be easy.

References

Banzhaf, J.F.: Weighted Voting Doesn't Work: A Mathematical Analysis. Rutgers Law Review **19**, 1965, 317–343.

Blair, D.: Essays in Social Choice Theory. Unpublished Ph.D. Dissertation, Yale University, 1976.

Brams, S.J.: Game Theory and Politics. New York 1975.

Brams, S.J., and *P.J. Affuso*: Power and Size: A New Paradox. Theory and Decision **7**, 1976, 29–56.

Caplow, T.: Two Against One: Coalitions in Triads. Englewood Cliffs 1968.

Coleman, J.S.: Control of Collectivities and the Power of a Collectivity to Act. Social Choice. Ed. by B. Lieberman. New York 1971, 277–287.

Deegan, J., Jr., and *E.W. Packel*: To the (Minimal Winning) Victors Go the (Equally Divided) Spoils: A New Power Index for Simple n-Person Games. Module in Applied Mathematics, Mathematical Association of America. Cornell University, 1976.

– : A New Index of Power for Simple n-Person Games. International Journal of Game Theory **7** (2), 1979, 113–123.

Dubey, P.: On the Uniqueness of the Shapley Value. International Journal of Game Theory **4**, 1975, 131–139.

– : Probabilistic Generalizations of the Shapley Value. Cowles Foundation Discussion Paper No. 440, 1976.

Raanen, J.: The Inevitability of the Paradox of New Members. Department of Operations Research Technical Report 311, Cornell University, 1976.

Shapley, L.S., and *M. Shubik*: A Method for Evaluating the Distribution of Power in a Committee System. American Political Science Review **48**, 1954, 787–792.

Straffin, P.: Power Indices in Politics. Module in Applied Mathematics, Mathematical Association of America, Cornell University, 1976.

– : Homogeneity, Independence, and Power Indices. Public Choice **30**, 1977, 107–118.

Holler, M.J. (Ed.): Power, Voting, and Voting Power ©Physica-Verlag, Würzburg (Germany) 1981

Measuring Power in Voting Bodies: Linear Constraints, Spatial Analysis, and a Computer Program

H. Rattinger, Freiburg

1. Introduction

The purpose of this contribution is to present some extensions of an established method for measuring the distribution of power among the various groups within any voting body. If there are no formal alignments of individual voters – like parliamentary groups or fractions – within such a unit, and if voting occurs on a purely individual basis according to a "one man one vote" rule, all members obviously possess the same voting power in that they are all equally decisive for voting outcomes. If, on the other hand, voting patterns are mediated, so to speak, by a division of the voting body into several voting blocs with a fairly high probability of joint voting, as is the case for parliamentary groups within legislatures, then the voting power of individual members can vary between blocs depending upon the number of individuals in each bloc and the decision rule. In highly simplified economic terms this means that if one wants to "buy" the one decisive vote for a particular motion, then in the former case each member would be worth the same amount of money whereas in the latter case this amount would have to be weighted by the odds that an individual member will belong to the decisive voting bloc. In other words, the "price" paid for each voting bloc should covary with its probability of turning the outcome which is a straightforward measure of its power.

These basic notions about measuring power in voting bodies have received widespread acceptance and application following *Shapley's* [1953] and *Shapley's/Shubik's* [1954] seminal work. Their power index is presented as a standard tool for game-theoretical analysis of politics in textbooks [e.g., *Riker/Ordershook*, ch. 6], and it has been usefully applied to the analysis of the distribution of power in several legislatures [e.g., *Frey; Weiersmüller; Zerche; Holler/Kellermann*].

The intention of the present contribution is not to extend this series of applications of the "classical" power index but rather to attempt to overcome one of its serious deficiencies in empirical research. This shortcoming is the assumption implicit in calculations of the values of the index that all voting sequences within a given voting body are equally likely. After briefly discussing the conventional power index we will concern ourselves with various methods for avoiding this unrealistic assumption. We shall introduce either one-dimensional or spatial constraints on joint voting, or shall weight voting coalitions with the probability of joint voting of their participants. Finally, a computer program designed to perform this kind of modified computations of the power index will be presented together with an illustrative example.

2. Shapley's Power Index

If voting within a voting body is simply according to a "one man one vote" rule and if there are no voting blocs or alignments whatsoever, then there is no need for a power index. With N individual voters (and therefore N individual votes) each vote is equally likely to be decisive or "pivotal" for a given motion. Each voter clearly holds one N-th of the total voting power, i.e., in an infinite series of voting procedures his vote is expected to decide the outcome in one N-th of the total number of cases.

Empirically, voting bodies without any formal subdivisions are the exception rather than the rule. Whenever such subdivisions exist, then there is the problem of measuring their voting power. The simplest measure is the vote share commanded by each group or voting bloc, which is analogous to ascribing a power share of $1/N$ to each voter in the case of an unstructured voting body. The problem with this measure is that it is only in exceptional cases – e.g., if all voting blocs are of equal size – identical to the likelihood of each group to be decisive for voting outcomes. In most other circumstances vote shares and probabilities for being "pivotal" differ, the most extreme discrepancy occuring when one voting bloc commands just over half of the total number of votes.

This insight was the starting point for the development of Shapley's power index. It proceeds from the simple consideration that in a voting body with K units (fractions, parties, voting blocs), K blocs of votes are cast in any voting procedure if all units vote homogeneously. As blocs of votes are regarded as units, and not the individual votes, the weight of a unit is defined as the number of its individual votes.

If one assumes that in deciding on a particular motion the votes of all K units are homogeneously cast in a sequential fashion, unit after unit, there are $P_K = K!$ possible sequences of voting. If one further assumes that the votes of each bloc are homogeneously cast in identical direction (pro or con) to those of the previous blocs, one can for each of the P_K sequences determine which unit establishes a majority (pro or con) by adding its votes to those previously cast. For each unit i, let T_i denote the number of voting sequences in which i plays this pivotal role. Then obviously:

$$\sum_{i=1}^{K} T_i = P_K.$$

Shapley's power index S_i for each unit i is defined as $S_i = T_i/P_K$, so that naturally the values of S_i for all units sum to unity. This index can be substantially interpreted as the probability that unit i, by casting its votes, establishes a winning majority of minimum size in any voting sequence or, to put it differently, as the relative frequency with which unit i plays the pivotal role in an infinite number of random majority coalitions among the K units.

According to *Shapley* [1953] any attempt to measure the distribution of power among the units i in a voting body under his set of axioms either produces an index equivalent to S_i or leads to logical inconsistencies. It should be noted that Shapley's power index in its initial formulation is defined for the absolute majority rule, "majority" being the smallest integer greater than $N/2$. This restriction is not a logical necessity. In fact, it is possible to define any fraction of N as the required threshold of votes without affecting the logic of the power index itself or the logic of its computation. Therefore, the computer program to be presented below has been designed to compute the distribution of power, alternatively, for absolute and two-thirds-majority as the two most frequent decision rules for parliamentary voting.

The power index S_i represents an *a priori* distribution of power which does not take any restrictions on joint voting and on coalition formation into account – be they politically, sociologically, psychologically, or otherwise determined. Each numerically possible voting sequence which secures a majority is treated as equally likely. That is in many cases of course a gross distortion of reality. We will now turn to several strategies for avoiding this unrealistic assumption by introducing measures for the chances that various given units will jointly appear in a majority coalition into the computation of the power index. Let us start with linear constraints along a continuum.

3. One-Dimensional Constraints on Coalition Formation

In introducing linear constraints on coalition formation into the computation of the power index we proceed from the assumption of the existence of a one-dimensional ordinal policy space. This means that the K voting blocs can be arranged in an order conforming to their relative positions in this policy space. The obvious example naturally is an ideological left-right dimension where for any two voting blocs i and j the first unit i ideologically stands to the left of unit j if and only if $i < j$. With this kind of ordinal policy space it is assumed, of course, that the size of the intervals between positions has no relevance.

If such a transitive order of K voting blocs along any simple dimension of policy preferences exists, then obviously not all minimum winning coalitions are equally likely. The more dispersed a minimum winning coalition is along the relevant policy dimension the less likely is its formation, and vice versa, for the conflict of interest within a coalition depends upon its dispersion [*Axelrod*, p. 169]. The conflict of interest within a coalition is minimized – and therefore the coalition's utility for participating voting blocs is maximized – if dispersion along the policy dimension it kept to a minimum. Dispersion is lowest, however, if a coalition consists of adjacent voting blocs, or, to follow Axelrod's terminology, if it is connected.

More formally, the property of connectedness can be defined as follows: If K voting blocs have been arranged transitively along a one-dimensional policy space, then a coalition consisting of n voting blocs m is connected if and only if $\max(m) - \min(m) = n - 1$. If a minimum winning coalition is also connected, it is called a *minimum connected winning coalition.*

If we proceed from the basic logic of the Shapley-Shubik index and in addition assume that – given an ordinal policy space – *only* minimum connected winning coalitions will be formed, the voting power of any voting bloc i is clearly the share of all those coalitions in which it is pivotal. In order to find this share, all we have to do is find the number TA_i

of *connected* coalitions among the T_i minimum winning voting sequences in which i is pivotal. This can be easily performed by applying the numerical criterion given above [*Rattinger*, 1979]. We therefore obtain a modified power index for the units in a voting body which can be represented by an ordinal policy dimension:

$$SA_i = \frac{TA_i}{\sum_{i=1}^{K} TA_i}.$$

4. Spatial Constraints on Coalition Formation

The consideration that policy preferences along a policy dimension influence coalition formation, certainly represents an important step towards a more realistic measurement of voting power. However, one might argue that in many cases the assumption of a one-dimensional ordinal policy space still constitutes a gross oversimplification. It is conceivable that in a voting body dominated by ideological positions, coalitions among extremist voting blocs or factions from both left and right are more probable than coalitions comprising middle-of-the-road and extremist groups from either side. In such a situation certain minimum connected winning coalitions will *not* be formed whereas certain realistic coalitions are *not connected*.

Here generalizing the concept of connectedness for multi-dimensional ordinal policy spaces does not lead us any further. Instead, we have to assume that for each pair of two voting blocs i and j, out of the total of K voting blocs, we know whether or not i and j are willing to join forces in a coalition. Let $v_{ij} = 1$ if and only if i regards j as an acceptable partner in a coalition, and let $v_{ij} = 0$ otherwise. We then have a binary $K \times K$ adjacency matrix $V = [v_{ij}]$ with all entries v_{ii} on the main diagonal trivially being 1. Obviously matrix V does *not* have to be symmetrical as it is entirely conceivable that voting bloc i would accept j as a partner in a joint coalition, so that $v_{ij} = 1$, whereas j rejects i, so that $v_{ji} = 0$.

In this contribution we shall not concern ourselves with the problem of empirically arriving at the adjacency matrix V. We assume V to be given and demonstrate the opportunities for the measurement of voting power if information of the sort contained in V is available. Any minimum winning coalition can be formed if and only if for every pair of two voting blocs i and j in this coalition $v_{ij} = 1$, i.e., if each voting bloc is adjacent to all the other participants in this coalition. In graph-theoretical terms this means that if an empirical binary adjacency relation is represented by an adjacency digraph, then any empirically feasible minimum winning coalition has to correspond to a complete, reflexive, symmetric, and connected sub-digraph which, of course, is represented by a sub-matrix of V with entries of only 1. If at least one voting bloc i in a numerically possible minimum winning coalition is rejected by at least one other member j, i.e., $v_{ji} = 0$, then this coalition cannot be formed.

From these considerations the following concept of voting power constrained by spatial adjacency is derived: For each voting bloc i let TB_i be the number of those minimum winning coalitions for which i is pivotal *and* which are represented by a sub-matrix of V

containing only entries of 1, then a second modified Shapley-Shubik-type power index SB_i is given by:

$$SB_i = \frac{TB_i}{\sum_{i=1}^{K} TB_i}.$$

5. Policy Distance and Voting Power

The above concepts of adjacency or mutual acceptability between voting blocs within a voting body are obviously based upon a dichotomization of a more general concept of policy distance in multi-dimensional space. If policy distance between two units is *below* a certain threshold, they are said to be adjacent or mutually acceptable as partners in a joint coalition, and vice versa. All distances *above* the particular threshold are represented by an entry of zero in matrix V, entries of one correspond to distances *below* this threshold. Information on policy distance between i and j is reduced to information on whether or not they can appear together in one coalition. This logical relationship does not imply, however, that policy distances will have to be measured empirically before one can set up matrix V. In many cases it will be much easier to obtain the kind of categorical judgements contained in V, than to arrive at precise policy distance readings. Here SB_i is a useful improvement over Shapley's initial power index.

Let us now assume, however, that information on the policy distance between any two units i and j within a voting body is empirically available. Let $D = [d_{ij}]$ be a $K \times K$ distance matrix with $d_{ii} = 0$ and $0 \leqslant d_{ij} \leqslant Z$, where Z is any positive integer denoting the maximum value of the distance scale. d_{ij} is the policy distance perceived by unit i vis-à-vis voting bloc j. d_{ij} and d_{ji} can be equal empirically, but need not be identical for logical reasons.

If we assume coalition formation to be a process of policy distance minimization [*De Swaan*], then each numerically possible minimum winning coalition for which a given unit i is pivotal has to be weighted by its probability of occuring. This probability has to be an inverse function of the policy distances among the participating voting blocs. In order to arrive at appropriate probability weights, let us first define a $K \times K$ matrix $Q = [q_{ij}]$ with $q_{ij} = Z - d_{ij}$. $q_{ij} = 0$ if i sees j at maximum political distance from itself, and $q_{ij} = Z$ if i and j in i's judgement have identical policy positions. It should be noted that Q it *not* a probability matrix in the conventional sense. However, if we assume that the probability that i will join j in a coalition depends inversely and in a linear fashion upon the policy distance between i and j as perceived by i, and if we further assume that the maximum distance Z corresponds to a probability of zero then Q can be transformed into a probability matrix by an (unknown) similarity function $f(q_{ij}) = aq_{ij}$. But this kind of transformation is not required for the present purpose of weighting minimum winning coalitions, for which Q suffices.

Our problem now becomes how to assign weights to minimum winning coalitions which covary with their probabilities of formation. If such a coalition consists of only two voting blocs, the solution is fairly straightforward. But if there are more than two participants, there is no single compelling way of aggregating an overall probability weight. Instead, we have to rely on plausibility and face validity. One solution would be to compute a weighted mean of q_{ij} for all pairs of participants, weighting by n_i, the number of votes in each voting bloc i. Let us assume that a minimum winning coalition is established by voting blocs i, j, and k, with $n_i = n_j = n_k$, and $q_{ij} = q_{ji} = q_{jk} = q_{kj}$ with q_{ij} close to Z, and $q_{ik} = q_{ki}$ with q_{ik} close to zero. A weighted mean would yield a fairly high probability weight in the neighborhood of 2Z/3, whereas obviously this coalition is extremely unlikely as i and k, for all practical purposes, will not join in a coalition. A second solution, therefore, would be to take the *smallest* probability score of joint membership in a coalition for all pairs of its participants as the probability weight of a minimum winning coalition.

For this second solution it proves inconvenient that Q need not be symmetric. Before formally describing the two weighting procedures we therefore define a symmetric $K \times K$ matrix $P = [p_{ij}]$ with $p_{ij} = p_{ji} = (n_i q_{ij} + n_j q_{ji})/(n_i + n_j)$. For any two units i and j, P contains a probability weight for their joint appearance in a coalition which is derived as a weighted average from both units' evaluations of their proximity.

Given matrix P it is now possible to formally define the two strategies (as above) for assigning probability weights to minimum winning coalitions. We shall start with the first approach. Let M_{im} be the set of voting blocs which form the m-th minimum winning coalition for which unit i is decisive, and let a_{im} be the number of units in this coalition. Then the weighted average probability score, W_{im}, for this minimum winning coalition is:

$$W_{im} = \frac{\sum_{j=1}^{K} \sum_{k=1}^{K} p_{jk}(n_j + n_k)}{\sum_{j=1}^{K} 2(a_{im} - 1)\, n_j} \qquad \text{where: } j \in M_{im},\; k \in M_{im},\; j \neq k.$$

If T_i is the total number of minimum winning coalitions for which i is pivotal, TC_i is the sum of the probability weights of all those coalitions:

$$TC_i = \sum_{m=1}^{T_i} W_{im}.$$

Then obviously a third modified power index taking policy distances into account can be defined as:

$$SC_i = \frac{TC_i}{\sum_{i=1}^{K} TC_i}.$$

Following the second strategy we obtain the probability weight W'_{im} for the m-th minimum winning coalition for which i is pivotal:

$$W'_{im} = \min(p_{jk}) \qquad \text{where: } j \in M_{im},\; k \in M_{im},\; j \neq k.$$

Therefore:

$$TD_i = \sum_{m=1}^{T_i} W'_{im}.$$

Accordingly, our fourth and final modified power index, in which minimum winning coalitions are discounted by minimum proximity among participants is:

$$SD_i = \frac{TD_i}{\sum_{i=1}^{K} TD_i}.$$

Whether one prefers SC or SD, when information on policy distances is available, will depend upon personal judgement and upon empirical patterns of distances. If policy distances are highly "intransitive", so to speak, i.e., if within many minimum winning coalitions policy distances between participating voting blocs vary widely, then both indices will yield divergent results on voting power. Comparing the findings from both methods might lead to useful insights.

6. The Program

The five indices of voting power here described, can be computed within one FORTRAN-program.[1]) The basic idea of the program is to start with the votes of the first voting bloc and to add the votes of the second, third, etc. voting blocs until a minimum winning coalition is reached. This process is repeated for all the $K!$ logically possible permutations. Each minimum winning coalition is ascribed to the pivotal voting bloc. For each unit i there are five "accounts". In the first account, T_i, we have all minimum winning coalitions which i can establish. In the second and third accounts, TA_i and TB_i, only those minimum winning coalitions (established by i) which meet the appropriate numerical criteria are included. The final two accounts, TC_i and TD_i, sum the probability weights of the minimum winning coalitions for which i is decisive. Standardization across all i, finally yields the five measures of voting power described in this contribution.

A significant reduction of computing time is derived from the following consideration: If i is pivotal for a minimum winning coalition consisting of m voting blocs, then there are $(K-m)!$ permutations which contain exactly the same coalition in the first m places. We cannot only write one, but $(K-m)!$ minimum winning coalitions into the accounts of i and, therefore, take only a fraction of $K!$ loops to go through all permutations.

The program currently exists for a maximum of $K = 12$ voting blocs. As input it requires the number of voting blocs, the total number of votes, a vector of the numbers of votes in each bloc, a parameter which switches the program to absolute or to two-thirds-majority, an adjacency matrix V, and, finally, a distance matrix D. One has the option to rearrange voting blocs, as normally in the computation of SA their position in the input vector will be interpreted as their position in a one-dimensional ordinal policy space. The program's output will now be illustrated by the following example.

[1]) The program was written by Gertrud Steigmiller proceeding from a program written by myself for the purpose of analyzing voting power in the European Parliament [*Rattinger*].

7. An Example

In our example, K has the maximum value of 12. The program first prints back a symmetrized matrix V and matrix P. In the example these matrices look as follows:

Matrix V

1	1	1	1	1	1	1	1	0	1	1	0
1	1	1	1	1	1	1	1	0	1	1	0
1	1	1	1	1	1	1	0	0	1	1	0
1	1	1	1	1	1	1	0	0	1	1	0
1	1	1	1	1	1	1	1	1	1	1	1
1	1	1	1	1	1	1	1	0	1	1	0
1	1	1	1	1	1	1	1	1	1	1	0
1	1	0	0	1	1	1	1	1	1	1	1
0	0	0	0	1	0	1	1	1	1	1	1
1	1	1	1	1	1	1	1	1	1	1	1
1	1	1	1	1	1	1	1	1	1	1	1
0	0	0	0	1	0	0	1	1	1	1	1

Matrix P

5,0	3,9	3,6	3,0	3,0	2,4	2,1	2,1	1,2	2,1	2,1	0,1
3,9	5,0	3,9	3,6	3,3	3,0	2,7	2,4	1,5	2,1	2,1	0,5
3,6	3,9	5,0	3,6	3,0	2,4	2,1	1,8	1,2	2,4	2,1	0,9
3,0	3,6	3,6	5,0	3,9	3,3	2,4	1,8	1,5	2,7	2,4	1,5
3,0	3,3	3,0	3,9	5,0	3,6	3,3	3,0	2,7	2,4	2,1	2,1
2,4	3,0	2,4	3,3	3,6	5,0	3,9	3,0	1,8	3,0	3,0	1,8
2,1	2,7	2,1	2,4	3,3	3,9	5,0	3,6	3,0	2,4	2,1	1,8
2,1	2,4	1,8	1,8	3,0	3,0	3,6	5,0	3,9	3,6	3,3	3,0
1,2	1,5	1,2	1,5	2,7	1,8	3,0	3,9	5,0	3,6	2,7	2,4
2,1	2,1	2,4	2,7	2,4	3,0	2,4	3,6	3,6	5,0	3,9	3,6
2,1	2,1	2,1	2,4	2,1	3,0	2,1	3,3	2,7	3,9	5,0	3,6
0,1	0,5	0,9	1,5	2,1	1,8	1,8	3,0	2,4	3,6	3,6	5,0

We then receive information on the total number of permutations, the number of minimum winning coalitions satisfying the criteria of connectedness and of spatial adjacency, the number of program loops, the total number of votes, the number of independent votes not belonging to any voting bloc, and, finally, the requested type of majority and its numerical value. These figures are all presented below. Note that, on the average, slightly above 63 permutations per loop were dealt with. In spite of this reduction, more then 90 minutes CPU-time were required.

ΣT	ΣTA	ΣTB	Program-loops
479001600	4440960	45688320	7585920

Total votes	Independent votes	Absolute Majority
380	10	191

	1	2	3	4	5	6	7	8	9	10	11	12
Votes	30	10	20	30	40	50	60	10	40	40	20	20
Votes Share	.079	.026	.053	.079	.105	.132	.158	.026	.105	.105	.053	.053
T	37929600	11923200	24503040	37929600	51788160	67063680	83358720	11923200	51788160	51788160	24503040	24503040
S	.079	.025	.051	.079	.108	.140	.174	.025	.108	.108	.051	.051
TA	0	0	29376	380160	587520	1054080	1261440	241920	414720	207360	0	0
SA	0	0	.066	.086	.132	.237	.284	.055	.093	.047	0	0
TB	4510080	1330560	2592000	3732480	6238080	7758720	9383040	466560	207360	6238080	3231360	0
SB	.099	.029	.057	.082	.137	.170	.205	.010	.005	.137	.071	0
SC	.077	.025	.051	.079	.110	.142	.175	.025	.106	.109	.051	.049
SD	.067	.025	.052	.084	.116	.150	.185	.027	.099	.116	.056	.025

The final and most important segment of the program's output is a table which for each unit contains a column with the following data: absolute number of votes, vote share, number of minimum winning coalitions (T), of minimum connected winning coalitions (TA), and of spatially adjacent minimum winning coalitions (TB) for which this unit is decisive, and the five indices of voting power described in this contribution.

As our example is purely fictitious, it would not be very useful to analyze it in great detail. Let us, therefore, conclude with some very obvious observations. First, with just 12 voting blocs we already see vote shares and Shapley's basic index converging as there are no clearly preponderant units. Second, the assumption that only minimum connected winning coalitions will be formed leads to a substantial concentration of voting power in the middle of the underlying policy dimension. Third, as the matrices V and P also exhibit a moderate one-dimensional pattern of coalition preferences along the main diagonal, SB, SC, and SD do not deviate drastically from SA. With different matrices V and P, these discrepancies between the various power indices could be much stronger. If this were the case it would be a matter of substantive reasoning to decide which version of the index should be preferred.

References

Axelrod, R.: Conflict of Interest. Chicago 1970.

De Swaan, A.: An Empirical Model of Coalition Formation as an *N*-Person Game of Policy Distance Minimization. The Study of Coalition Behavior. Ed. by S. Groennings et al. New York 1970, 426–444.

Frey, B.S.: Eine spieltheoretische Analyse der Machtverteilung im schweizerischen Bundesrat. Schweizerische Zeitschrift für Volkswirtschaft und Statistik **104**, 1968, 155–169.

Holler, M.J., and *J. Kellermann*: Power in the European Parliament: What Will Change? Quality and Quantity **11**, 1977, 189–192.

Rattinger, H., and *H. Elicker*: Machtverteilung im Europäischen Parlament vor und nach der Direktwahl. Zeitschrift für Parlamentsfragen **10**, 1979, 216–232.

Riker, W.H., and *P.C. Ordeshook*: An Introduction to Positive Political Theory. Englewood Cliffs, N.J., 1973.

Shapley, L.S.: A Value for *N*-Person Games. Contributions to the Theory of Games. Ed. by A.W. Tucker and H.W. Kuhn. Annals of Mathematics Study **28**, Princeton 1953, 307–317.

Shapley, L.S., and *M. Shubik*: A Method for Evaluating the Distribution of Power in a Committee System. American Political Science Review **48**, 1954, 787–792.

Weiersmüller, R.: Zur Machtverteilung in den Gremien der EWG. Schweizerische Zeitschrift für Volkswirtschaft und Statistik **107**, 1971, 463–469.

Zerche, J.: Aspekte der Entscheidungstheorie und Anwendungsbeispiele in der Sozialpolitik. Aspekte der Friedensforschung und Entscheidungsprobleme in der Sozialpolitik. Ed. by H. Sanmann. Berlin 1971, 37–60.

Holler, M.J. (Ed.): Power, Voting, and Voting Power ©Physica-Verlag, Würzburg (Germany) 1981

Modification of the Banzhaf-Coleman Index for Games with a Priori Unions[1])

G. Owen, Monterey

1. Preliminaries

Owen [1977] suggests a modification of the Shapley value "so as to take into account the possibility that some players ... may be more likely to act together than others". We present in this paper a similar modification for the Banzhaf-Coleman power index.

We shall, in this paper, use N to denote the set $\{1, 2, \ldots, n\}$, and M to denote $\{1, 2, \ldots, m\}$. A game is a pair (v, N) where v is a function defined on the collection 2^N of subsets of N, satisfying $v(\emptyset) = 0$. For a game (v, N) we distinguish the two Banzhaf-Coleman indices, β and ψ, defined as

$$\beta_i[v] = \sum_{\substack{S \subset N \\ i \notin S}} [v(S \cup \{i\}) - v(S)] \tag{1}$$

and

$$\psi_i[v] = 2^{1-n} \beta_i[v]. \tag{2}$$

It is known [see *Owen*, 1978] that, if v is a simple game, $\beta_i[v]$ merely counts the number of *swings* for player i, where a swing is defined as a set S such that (a) S loses, (b) $i \notin S$, (c) $S \cup \{i\}$ wins. The normalized index ψ has many interesting properties [see *Owen*, 1978, *Dubey/Shapley*]. In particular, ψ is dummy-invariant, i.e., $\psi_i[v]$ will be unchanged for $i \in N$ if v is modified by the adjunction of one or more dummies to the set N.

2. A Priori Unions. The Modified Index

For a player set N, we define an *a priori union structure* as a partition

$$\mathfrak{J} = \{T_1, T_2, \ldots, T_m\}$$

i.e., a collection of disjoint sets whose union is N. These sets $T_1, \ldots, T_m$ are *a priori unions*, i.e., coalitions which have in some sense made a prior commitment to cooperate in playing the game.

[1]) This research was supported by the National Science Foundation Social Sciences Program, under a grant to the University of California/Irvine, grant # NSF-SES-80-079-15.

Let (u, N) be a game, and J an a priori structure on N. We define the *quotient game* u/J as a game (v, M) given by

$$v(S) = u\left(\bigcup_{j \in S} T_j\right) \tag{3}$$

for any $S \subset M$.

In effect, we assume that the several unions, T_j, will each choose a representative to act for the union in bargaining with the other unions. In that case, the several unions (or their representatives) will play the game v among themselves.

Let

$$\psi_j[v] = \sum_{\substack{S \subset M \\ j \notin S}} 2^{1-m} \left[v(S \cup \{j\}) - v(S)\right]$$

represent player j's power (as measured by the Banzhaf-Coleman index) in the game v. In some sense, this quantity should represent the total power of the union T_j in game u, given the a priori structure.

More generally, for fixed $j \in M$, let K be some subset of T_j, and let

$$K' = T_j - K$$

be its complement relative to T_j. We define the game $v_{T_j/K}$ as, in effect, what happens to v if the union T_j is replaced by K, i.e., if the members of K' were to be somehow excluded. Then, for $S \subset M$,

$$v_{T_j/K}(S) = u\left(\bigcup_{q \in S} T_q - K'\right). \tag{4}$$

Let us now define a new game, (w_j, T_j) by

$$w_j(K) = \psi_j[v_{T_j/K}]. \tag{5}$$

Thus $w_j(K)$ is the power of "player" j (in reality the subunion K) in the game $v_{T_j/K}$. In some sense, $w_j(K)$ measures the power of coalition K if it is to stand up alone (without its partners K') in bargaining with the other unions.

It is easy to see that, in the game $v_{T_j/\phi}$, player j is a dummy; hence, by a well-known property of the index,

$$w_j(\phi) = \psi_j[v_{T_j/\phi}] = 0$$

and thus w_j is indeed a game (though it may well be improper). That being so, we can compute its Banzhaf-Coleman index.

We define, now, for any $i \in T_j$,

$$\hat{\psi}_i[u; J] = \psi_i[w_j] \tag{6}$$

i.e., the *modified power* of player i in game u, given the a priori structure J, is the (ordinary) power of player i in the game w_j.

It is of interest to note that, even if u is a simple game, the several games w_j are usually non-simple. Thus it is important that the B-C index be defined also for non-simple games.

(Originally it was given only for simple games and some question arose as to the legitimacy of extending it to other games.)

Example 1. Consider the five-person simple game (u, N), where $N = \{1, 2, 3, 4, 5\}$ and the minimal winning coalitions are $\{1, 2\}, \{1, 3\}, \{1, 4\}, \{1, 5\}$ and $\{2, 3, 4, 5\}$. As is easy to verify, the ordinary B-C index for this game is

$$\psi[u] = \left(\frac{7}{8}, \frac{1}{8}, \frac{1}{8}, \frac{1}{8}, \frac{1}{8}\right).$$

Consider, now, the coalition structure

$$J = \{\{1, 2\}, \{3\}, \{4\}, \{5\}\}.$$

We see that $v = u/J$ is a simple game in which the first player (actually, the union $\{1, 2\}$) is a dictator.
Thus,

$$\psi_1[v] = 1$$

$$\psi_3[v] = \psi_4[v] = \psi_5[v] = 0.$$

Now, the game $v_{T_1/\{1\}}$ is a two-person game in which player 1 (the subunion $\{1\}$, i.e., real player 1) wins with the help of any other player and, in fact, holds a veto, i.e., the set $\{3, 4, 5\}$ loses. Thus 1 is extremely powerful, having power 7/8.

Finally, the game $v_{T_1/\{2\}}$ is a four-person game in which only the unaminous coalition can win; each player here has power 1/8.

We obtain thus the game w_1:

$$w_1(\{1\}) = \psi_1[v_{T_1/\{1\}}] = 7/8$$

$$w_1(\{2\}) = \psi_1[v_{T_1/\{2\}}] = 1/8$$

$$w_1(\{1, 2\}) = \psi_1[v] = 1.$$

This is an additive game and hence coincides with its power index. We obtain, thus, the modified index,

$$\hat{\psi}[u; J] = \left(\frac{7}{8}, \frac{1}{8}, 0, 0, 0\right).$$

3. An Alternative Formulation

As an alternative possibility, we might wish to define a modified value

$$\hat{\psi}[u; J]$$

as follows. Assuming u to be a simple game, $\beta_i[u]$ counts the number of swings for player i and $\psi_i[u]$ then normalizes this, dividing by 2^{n-1} which is the total number of coalitions

T which do not include player i. Thus $\psi_i\,[u]$ gives us the fraction of sets T, $i \notin T$, which are swings.

Suppose, however, the *a priori* union structure $\mathcal{J}$ exists. In this case, we might expect that there will be no coalitions "across union lines". In other words, player i, a member of the union T_j, would consider only joining sets which consist of some of his union members together with certain of the other unions, i.e., he would consider only sets of the form

$$Q = \bigcup_{q \in S} T_q \cup K$$

where $S \subset M$, $j \notin S$, $K \subset T_j$, $i \notin K$.

We might define

$$\hat{\beta}_i\,[u; \mathcal{J}]$$

as the number of such sets Q which are swings for i, or, equivalently,

$$\hat{\beta}_i\,[u; \mathcal{J}] = \sum_{\substack{S \subset M \\ j \notin S}} \; \sum_{\substack{K \subset T_j \\ i \notin K}} [u(\bigcup_{q \in S} T_q \cup K \cup \{i\}) - u(\bigcup_{q \in S} T_q \cup K)] \tag{7}$$

(which, of course, is meaningful also for non-simple games).

To normalize, we must divide this by the number of possible sets Q, and this is easily seen to be

$$2^{m-1}\,2^{t_j-1} = 2^{m+t_j-2}$$

since there are 2^{m-1} ways of choosing S, and 2^{t_j-1} ways of choosing K. (Here, t_j is the cardinality of T_j.) Thus we have, for $i \in T_j$,

$$\hat{\psi}_i\,[u; \mathcal{J}] = 2^{2-m-t_j}\,\hat{\beta}_i\,[u; \mathcal{J}], \tag{8}$$

as a possible alternative definition of the modified index.

Example 2. Let u be a simple seven-person majority game (all four-person coalitions, or larger, win), and let

$$\mathcal{J} = \{\{1, 2, 3\}, \{4, 5\}, \{6\}, \{7\}\}.$$

To analyze this game, we note that a swing set must have exactly three players. For player 1, there are eight swings: from 20 three-player sets, we must remove six which contain player four but not five, and six which contain five but not four. Thus, and by symmetry,

$$\hat{\beta}_1 = \hat{\beta}_2 = \hat{\beta}_3 = 8.$$

For player four, there are only two swings: sets $\{1, 2, 3\}$ and $\{5, 6, 7\}$. (This is due to the fact that the union $\{1, 2, 3\}$ cannot be split by any outside member.) Thus

$$\hat{\beta}_4 = \hat{\beta}_5 = 2.$$

In a similar manner

$$\hat{\beta}_6 = \hat{\beta}_7 = 2.$$

Next, we note that, for this partition, $m = 3, t_1 = 3, t_2 = 2, t_3 = t_4 = 1$. Thus

$$\hat{\psi}_1 = \hat{\psi}_2 = \hat{\psi}_3 = 2^{2\text{-}3\text{-}3}\,\hat{\beta}_1 = \frac{1}{2}$$

$$\hat{\psi}_4 = \hat{\psi}_5 = 2^{2\text{-}3\text{-}2}\,\hat{\beta}_4 = \frac{1}{4}$$

$$\hat{\psi}_6 = \hat{\psi}_7 = 2^{2\text{-}3\text{-}1}\,\hat{\beta}_6 = \frac{1}{2}$$

and hence

$$\hat{\psi} = \left(\frac{1}{2}, \frac{1}{2}, \frac{1}{2}, \frac{1}{4}, \frac{1}{4}, \frac{1}{2}, \frac{1}{2}\right).$$

As against, that, the ordinary power index is

$$\psi = \left(\frac{5}{16}, \frac{5}{16}, \frac{5}{16}, \frac{5}{16}, \frac{5}{16}, \frac{5}{16}, \frac{5}{16}\right).$$

It may be seen that the members of the three-player union gain in power; on the other hand, the two-player union has lost power, and the single players have gained power. Thus it is not clear that forming a union is, here, a profitable venture.

4. Equivalence of the Two Formulations

We have, above, formulated two alternative possibilities for a modified power index. The question obviously arises as to the relation between these two.

Theorem: The two modified indices, $\hat{\psi}\,[u;\,J]$ given by equations (6) and (8) respectively, are equal.

Proof: We will start with (6) and show that it equals (8). In fact, we will have

$$\psi_j\,[v_{T_j/K}] = 2^{1\text{-}m} \sum_{\substack{S\subset M\\ j\notin S}} [v_{T_j/K}(S \cup \{j\}) - v_{T_j/K}(S)]$$

or

$$w_j(K) = 2^{1\text{-}m} \sum_{\substack{S\subset M\\ j\notin S}} [u(\bigcup_{q\in S} T_q \cup K) - u(\bigcup_{q\in S} T_q)]$$

by the definitions of w_j and $v_{T_j/K}$.

In turn,

$$\psi_i\,[w_j] = 2^{1\text{-}t_j} \sum_{\substack{K\subset T_j\\ i\notin K}} [w_j(K \cup \{i\}) - w_j(K)]$$

and so

$$\psi_i [w_j] = 2^{1-t_j} 2^{1-m} \sum_{\substack{S \subset M \\ j \notin S}} \sum_{\substack{K \subset T_j \\ i \notin K}} \{[u(\bigcup_{q \in S} T_q \cup K \cup \{i\}) - u(\bigcup_{q \in S} T_q)] -$$

$$- [u(\bigcup_{q \in S} T_q \cup K) - u(\bigcup_{q \in S} T_q)]\}$$

or

$$\psi_i [w_j] = 2^{2-t_j-m} \sum_S \sum_K [u(\bigcup_{q \in S} T_q \cup K \cup \{i\}) - u(\bigcup_{q \in S} T_q \cup K)]$$

and this is precisely the value of $\hat{\psi}_i [u; J]$ according to (8). Thus our two formulations give the same modified power index.

5. Discussion

We have, through two different approaches, obtained the same modified power index. It would be of interest to determine whether this index can also be obtained axiomatically. In fact, we know that the (ordinary) B-C index can be defined by a system of axioms [see *Dubey* or *Owen*, 1978], while the modified Shapley value can be determined by a system of axioms [see *Owen*, 1977] very similar to Shapley's original system [*Shapley*].

It is not easy, however, to see how this axiomatization could best be done. In *Owen* [1977], the axiom A3:

"For any j, the quantity

$$\sum_{i \in T_j} \hat{y}_i [u; J]$$

depends only on the quotient game u/J,"

serves to tie the two values neatly together; unfortunately, no such simple analog is here apparent.

An alternative approach would be to state that $\hat{\psi}$ must be linear:

$$\hat{\psi} [\alpha u + \beta w; J] = \alpha \hat{\psi} [u; J] + \beta \hat{\psi} [w; J] \tag{A1}$$

and that for the unanimity game u_Q (the simple game for which S is winning if and only if $Q \subset S$),

$$\hat{\psi}_i [u_Q; J] = \begin{cases} 2^{2-m(Q)-q_j} & \text{if} \quad i \in T_j \cap Q \\ 0 & \text{if} \quad i \notin Q \end{cases} \tag{A2}$$

where $m(Q)$ is the number of unions T_k such that $T_k \cap Q \neq \emptyset$, and q_j is the cardinality of $T_j \cap Q$. The two axioms (A1) and (A2) serve to determine ψ uniquely, but (A2) does seem to beg the question.

Finally, we point out that there is no difficulty in generalizing the results of this paper, either to the case where sub-unions, sub-sub-unions, etc., exist, or to the case where *a priori* union structures are only given probabilitically. (The interested reader should see *Owen* [1977] for details.)

References

Banzhaf, J.R. III: Weighted Voting Doesn't Work: A Mathematical Analysis. Rutgers Law Review, 1965, 317–343.

Coleman, J.S.: Control of Collectivities and the power of a Collectivity to Act. Social Choice. Ed. by B. Lieberman. New York 1971.

Dubey, P.: Some Results on Values of Finite and Infinite Games. Ph.D. Thesis, Cornell University, Ithaca–New York 1975.

Dubey, P., and *L.S. Shapley*: Mathematical Properties of the Banzhaf Power Index. Mathematics of Operations Research, 1979, 99–131.

Owen, G.: Values of Games with A Priori Unions. Mathematical Economics and Game Theory. Ed. by R. Henn and O. Moeschlin. Berlin 1977, 76–88.

– : A Characterization of the Banzhaf-Coleman Index. SIAM Journal of Applied Mathematics, 1978, 315–327.

Shapley, L.S.: A Value for *N*-Person Games. Contributions to the Theory of Games, II. Ed. by A.W. Tucker and H.W. Kuhn (Annals of Mathematics Study **28**). Princeton 1953, 307–317.

Holler, M.J. (Ed.): Power, Voting, and Voting Power ©Physica-Verlag, Würzburg (Germany) 1981

Power and Satisfaction in an Ideologically Divided Voting Body

P.D. Straffin, Jr., Beloit, *M.D. Davis*, New York and *S.J. Brams*, New York

1. Introduction

In a voting body making dichotomous (for or against) decisions under a specified decision rule, there are two questions which are important to an individual member concerned with evaluating his or her position in the body. We will phrase these questions in probabilistic terms.

Question of Effect on Outcome: What is the probability that my vote will make a difference in the group decision? That is, what is the probability that changing my vote will change the outcome on a particular measure?

Question of Group-Individual Agreement: What is the probability that the group decision will agree with my decision? That is, what is the probability that the group will approve a measure I vote for, or reject a measure I vote against?

The first question is a question of *power*. How often will I be in a position to enforce my decision on the group? Indeed, we will see that the two best known measures of voting power in the literature of game theory and political science are precisely answers to the Outcome Question under particular probability assumptions.

The second question is a question of *satisfaction*. How often will I be satisfied with the group decision? This question concerns ends rather than means. It would be important to voters who would be pleased to have the group decision agree with theirs, whether or not their vote is actually crucial to the outcome.

It would seem that the answers to these two questions are related, but it is not clear exactly what the relationship is. On the one hand, one might think that the relationship is direct – the more power I have, the more often I can enforce my will on the group, the more often the group will agree with me. In fact, we will see that this is indeed true under the simplest possible assumption about voting behavior – that voters behave independently of each other. Under that assumption, satisfaction[1]) will be an increasing linear function of power.

---

[1]) When we refer to a member's "satisfaction" in this paper, we will always mean only the technical concept "the probability that the group decision will agree with that member's decision." This is satisfaction in a narrow sense. We are aware that the word has other connotations, but we were unable to come up with a more neutral word embodying as well the concept we wish to discuss.

On the other hand, it is easy to think of situations in which power and satisfaction are not directly related. For instance, *Blair* [1976] considers the possibility of having all family decisions made by his wife, with whom he almost always agrees. He would have no power under such an arrangement, but his high compatibility would assure him of high satisfaction. Subjects of a benevolent dictator might be in the same situation.

In a more democratic vein, consider the situation of voters in a strongly Republican small town in the United States. Since the Republican candidate almost always wins by large margins, individual voters have little chance to affect the outcome of elections. On the other hand, most of the voters (the Republicans) have high group-individual agreement. In a more heterogeneous large city, voters might actually have more power – they might be able to affect the outcome more often – but less chance of agreeing with the group decision.[2])

What differs in these situations is the ideological division, or lack thereof, in the voting body. This is precisely the question we wish to study in this paper: how does voting power and satisfaction vary with ideological structure in a voting body?

In section 2, we review the three best known measures of power and satisfaction from the political science literature. In section 3, we develop a simple model of a voting body and show how these three measures can be derived as answers to the Outcome and Agreement Questions under different probability assumptions. In section 4, we assume a particular kind of ideological division in the voting body and define measures of power and satisfaction in this case which generalize the earlier measures. Then, in section 5, we study how power and satisfaction vary with ideological structure in the simple example of a nine-member voting body acting under majority rule. From this example, we abstract some observations which we believe are worthy of study in more general contexts.

We continue the analysis of the nine-member body in section 6, looking at the effect of *caucuses* forming within the body. Among other findings, we show that under certain conditions *cross-ideological* caucuses may be more beneficial to their members than homogeneous caucuses. Finally, in the Appendix, we use the model of sections 3 and 4 to derive a suggestive result on the interrelationship of power, size, and ideological division in a voting body.

2. Classical Measures of Power and Satisfaction

The problem of obtaining suitable measures of voting power and satisfaction has received considerable attention over the past quarter century from mathematical game theorists, from political scientists interested in constitutional design, and from the United States courts. Two measures of power, due to *Shapley/Shubik* [1954] and to *Banzhaf* [1965], have received the most attention. The best known index of satisfaction is due to *Rae* [1969]. In this section, we will review the definitions of these indices. More details, especially on the power indices, can be found in *Brams* [1975], *Lucas* [1976] and *Straffin* [1976].

---

[2]) For a discussion of situations of this kind, see *Dahl/Tufte* [1973].

All three of the indices begin with a model of a voting body as a *simple game* $(N, \mathcal{W})$. $N = \{1, 2, \ldots, n\}$ is the set of *members* of the voting body, or *players* in the game. $\mathcal{W} \subset 2^N$ is the collection of *winning coalitions* of the voting body. The interpretation of $\mathcal{W}$ is that if a subset S of the players is the subset which votes "yes" on a given bill, then the bill will pass if $S \in \mathcal{W}$, fail if $S \notin \mathcal{W}$. The following assumptions are made about $\mathcal{W}$:

i) $\emptyset \notin \mathcal{W}$

ii) $N \in \mathcal{W}$

iii) If $S \in \mathcal{W}$ and $S \subset T$, then $T \in \mathcal{W}$.

Thus the empty set cannot pass a bill, the entire set can, and if S can pass a bill, any superset of S can also. The basic reference on simple games is *Shapley* [1962].

An easy example of a simple game is the *three-person veto game*, in which $N = \{1, 2, 3\}$ and $\mathcal{W} = \{\{1, 2\}, \{1, 3\}, \{1, 2, 3\}\}$. In this game notice that player 1 has a *veto*, in that no bill can pass without his assent. On the other hand, he needs the cooperation of either 2 or 3 to pass a bill.

The *Shapley-Shubik power index* [*Shapley/Shubik*] considers the members of the voting body as joining a coalition, in support of some bill, in some order. The unique (by properties i), ii), iii)) member who makes the forming coalition into a winning coalition is called *pivotal* for that ordering. Member i's Shapley-Shubik power index $\emptyset_i$ is simply his probability of being pivotal, given that all orders of coalition formation are equally likely.

For example, in the three-person veto game the six possible orderings, with the pivotal player underlined in each one are as follows:

$$1\underline{2}3 \qquad 1\underline{3}2 \qquad 2\underline{1}3 \qquad 23\underline{1} \qquad 3\underline{1}2 \qquad 32\underline{1}$$

Hence $\emptyset_1 = 4/6, \emptyset_2 = 1/6, \emptyset_3 = 1/6$. Notice that the Shapley-Shubik power index is *normalized,* in that the indices of the players always add to one. The Shapley-Shubik index has been so widely accepted and used by political scientists that it was known until recently as *the* power index [see for example *Riker/Ordeshook*]. In section 3 we will present an alternative definition of this power index in terms of a probability model which makes no mention of orderings of the players.

The Banzhaf power index was proposed in *Banzhaf* [1965] in connection with legal proceedings involving weighted voting in county governments in New York State. To determine the power of player i, one counts the number η_i of winning coalitions S which contain player i, and to which player i is *critical*, in the sense that $S - \{i\} \notin \mathcal{W}$. Player i's *unnormalized Banzhaf index* β'_i is then given by

$$\beta'_i = \eta_i / 2^{n-1}.$$

The 2^{n-1} is the total number of coalitions containing player i. In the three-person veto game, the three winning coalitions, with critical players underlined, are:

$$\underline{12} \qquad \underline{13} \qquad \underline{1}23$$

Thus $\beta'_1 = 3/4, \beta'_2 = 1/4, \beta'_3 = 1/4$.

Notice that the β'_i do not add to one. Banzhaf originally considered the corresponding normalized index

$$\beta_i = \beta'_i \Big/ \sum_{j=1}^{n} \beta'_j.$$

Many game theorists now believe that this normalization is unnatural, and results in the loss of valuable information [see *Dubey/Shapley*]. We concur with this view and believe that the probability model for the Banzhaf index in section 3 and the results of the following sections add strength to it. The Banzhaf index has been accepted by New York State courts as a basis for judging the constitutionality of weighted voting schemes [see *Imrie; Lucas*].

The Rae satisfaction index was proposed in *Rae* [1969] in connection with the problem of constitutional design. Rae proposed that we measure the satisfaction r_i of member i of a voting body as the probability that the group decision will agree with member i's decision (i.e., with the way he votes), given that each member is equally likely to vote "yes" or "no." The Rae satisfaction indices for players in the three-person veto game are calculated as follows. If each member is equally likely to vote "yes" or "no", all coalitions are equally likely to be the coalition voting "yes." Write out these coalitions, and see how often the corresponding decision agrees with member i:

Coalition voting "yes"	Outcome	Outcome agrees with member		
∅	No	1	2	3
1	No		2	3
2	No	1		3
3	No	1	2	
1, 2	Yes	1	2	
1, 3	Yes	1		3
2, 3	No	1		
1, 2, 3	Yes	1	2	3

Hence the Rae satisfaction indices are $r_1 = 7/8, r_2 = 5/8, r_3 = 5/8$.[3])

3. The Basic Model

In this section, we present a model which will enable us to represent the classical power and satisfaction indices of section 2 as answers to the Outcome Question and the Agreement Question, respectively, under different probability assumptions. We will then use the model to obtain generalized measures of power and satisfaction which take into account, in a simple way, ideological structure within the voting body.

In the basic model, we assume:

1) A voting body, represented as a simple game $(N, \mathcal{W})$.
2) A collection of bills on which the players will vote Yes or No. (We do not consider abstentions in the model.) Each bill is specified by a vector $(p_1, p_2, \ldots, p_n)$ with $0 \leqslant p_i \leqslant 1$. The interpretation is that p_i is the probability that player i will vote Yes on that bill.
3) A probability distribution on [0, 1] from which the p_i's will be chosen. We will assume that this distribution is the *uniform* distribution on [0, 1] – that is, it is equally likely that any number between 0 and 1 will be chosen.

---

[3]) Actually, Rae only applied his index to a limited class of symmetric simple games and concluded that, within this class of games, majority rule maximizes members' satisfaction. This result has been generalized in *Dubey/Shapley* [1977] and *Straffin* [1977b].

Notice that we have not specified in the basic model how the component p_i's for a given bill might be related to each other. Two alternative assumptions about this relationship both have some claim to simplicity and naturalness:

4I) (Independence Assumption) For each bill, the p_i's will be selected independently from [0, 1].

4H) (Homogeneity Assumption) For each bill, a number q will be selected from [0, 1], and then $p_i = q$ for all i.

Under the independence assumption, how one voter feels about a bill is unrelated to how any other voter feels about the bill. Since our p_i's are to be chosen from the uniform distribution on [0, 1] by 3), the independence assumption is equivalent to assuming that any voter will vote for any bill with probability 1/2. By contrast, the homogeneity assumption can be viewed as saying that voters judge bills by a common set of standards. The number q can be thought of as the "level of acceptability" of a bill according to those standards: all voters will vote for it with that probability.

The power and satisfaction indices of section 2 are related to the basic model and the probability assumptions by the following theorems, which are proved in *Straffin* [1977a, 1978]:

Theorem 1. The answer to player i's Question of Effect on Outcome under the Independence Assumption (4I) is given by his unnormalized Banzhaf index β_i'.

Theorem 2. The answer to player i's Question of Effect on Outcome under the Homogeneity Assumption (4H) is given by his Shapley-Shubik index ϕ_i.

Theorem 3. The answer to player i's Question of Group-Individual Agreement under the Independence Assumption (4I) is given by Rae's index r_i.

The "missing case" of a satisfaction index defined as the answer to player i's Question of Group-Individual Agreement under the Homogeneity Assumption (4H) is the index A_i studied in *Straffin* [1978].

A simple result is known about the relationship of a voter's power and his satisfaction when the Independence Assumption holds. The following is proved, for example, in *Brams/Lake* [1978] and *Dubey/Shapley* [1977]:

Theorem 4.

$$r_i = \frac{1}{2} + \frac{1}{2}\beta_i' .$$

Thus, in this case a voter's satisfaction is a linear function of his power. When we introduce an assumption that incorporates the possibility of ideological divisions in our voting body, we will see that the relationship is not so simple.

4. Ideologically Divided Voting Bodies

The special assumptions 4I and 4H in section 3 are alternative assumptions about how the p_i's of different voters might be related – they are chosen independently, or they are all equal to a common number q. A more general assumption might be a combination of these two – the voters might be partitioned into homogeneous groups, where all voters in one group would have a common probability-of-voting-yes q, but the q's for different groups would be chosen independently. This kind of composite assumption was called a "partial homogeneity" assumption in *Straffin* [1977a, 1978].

To model an ideologically divided voting body, we consider another possibility – namely, that two homogeneous groups of players may be ideologically opposed to each other. Specifically, we assume that if the common probability-of-voting-yes of members of one group is q, then that of members of the ideologically opposed group is $1 - q$. As before, over different bills q is chosen at random from $[0, 1]$. Thus, if q is near $1/2$, the associated bill will be controversial to members of both groups, but the more the members of one group are inclined to favor a bill, the more the members of the other group will be inclined to oppose it. Clearly, we could in general have several pairs of opposed groups, but the most common situation might be suitably modeled by the following assumption:

4D) (Ideological Division Assumption) The set N of voters is disjointly partitioned into three subsets, $N = Q \cup Q' \cup P$. For each bill, a number q, and numbers p_i for each $i \in P$, will be selected independently from $[0, 1]$. For $j \notin P$, set

$$p_j = \begin{cases} q & \text{if } j \in Q \\ 1 - q & \text{if } j \in Q'. \end{cases}$$

The set of voters thus consists of two groups Q and Q', homogeneous among themselves but ideologically opposed to each other, together with a collection P of independent voters. We will adopt this assumption and notation for the remainder of the paper.

For an ideologically divided voting body, we can define power and satisfaction indices as follows:

Definition 1. Player i's *power index* e_i is the answer to player i's Question of Effect on Outcome under the appropriate Ideological Division Assumption.

Definition 2. Player i's *satisfaction index* s_i is the answer to player i's Question of Group-Individual Agreement under the appropriate Ideological Division Assumption.

By the results cited in section 3, we have that if $Q = Q' = \emptyset$ and $N = P$ (all members are independent), then $e_i = \beta_i'$ and $s_i = r_i$. If $Q' = P = \emptyset$ and $N = Q$ (all members are in one group), then $e_i = \phi_i$ and s_i is the satisfaction index A_i discussed in *Straffin* [1978]. Thus e_i and s_i generalize the power and satisfaction indices due to Shapley and Shubik, Banzhaf, Rae, and Straffin.

For small games, the indices e_i and s_i can be computed as multiple integrals. For e_i, we first write the answer to player i's Outcome Question as a function f_i of q and $p_1, \ldots, p_m$ (where $m = |P|$). Then

$$e_i = \int_0^1 \ldots \int_0^1 f_i(q, p_1, \ldots, p_m)\, dq\, dp_1 \ldots dp_m.$$

For s_i, we first write the answer to player i's Agreement Question as a function g_i of q and $p_1, \ldots, p_m$. Then

$$s_i = \int_0^1 \ldots \int_0^1 g_i(q, p_1, \ldots, p_m)\, dq\, dp_1 \ldots dp_m.$$

For example, let us calculate e_1 for a five-person legislature acting under majority rule, with $Q = \{1, 2\}, Q' = \{3, 4\}, P = \{5\}$. Player 1's vote is crucial to the outcome only if the other four voters split two yes, two no. Thus

$$f_1(q, p_5) = \underbrace{2\cdot q\cdot(1-q)\,q\cdot(1-p_5)}_{2,\,3 \text{ or } 4 \text{ yes}} + \underbrace{q\cdot q^2\cdot p_5}_{2,\,5 \text{ yes}} + \underbrace{(1-q)\cdot(1-q)^2\cdot(1-p_5)}_{3,\,4 \text{ yes}} + \underbrace{2\cdot(1-q)\cdot(1-q)\,q\cdot p_5}_{3 \text{ or } 4,\,5 \text{ yes}}\,.$$

The p_5 and $(1-p_5)$ factors will integrate separately to 1/2. (This will always happen: independent behavior is equivalent to voting yes with probability 1/2.) We get

$$e_1 = \frac{1}{2}\int_0^1 [2q^2(1-q) + q^3 + (1-q)^3 + 2(1-q)^2 q]\,dq$$

$$= \frac{1}{2}\left[2\cdot\frac{1}{12} + \frac{1}{4} + \frac{1}{4} + 2\cdot\frac{1}{12}\right] = \frac{5}{12} \approx .417.$$

By symmetry, this is also the value of e_2, e_3, and e_4. On the other hand, we can calculate similarly that

$$e_5 = \int_0^1 [q^4 + 4q^2(1-q)^2 + (1-q)^4]\,dq = \frac{1}{5} + 4\cdot\frac{1}{30} + \frac{1}{5} = \frac{8}{15} \approx .533.$$

Hence, in this evenly divided voting situation, the independent voter is 28 % more likely to be crucial to the outcome than one of the group voters. We would say he has 28 % more power.[4])

The calculation for s_i is only slightly harder. For s_1 we must find the probability that the group will agree with player 1. This is the product of the probability q that player 1 will vote yes and the probability that two or more of the other players will vote yes, plus the product of the probability $1-q$ that player 1 will vote no and the probability that two or more of the other players will vote no. We then integrate between 0 and 1. By symmetry, the two terms in the sum will integrate to the same number, simplifying the calculation. For this example, we get that

$$s_1 = s_2 = s_3 = s_4 = \frac{19}{30} \approx .633$$

$$s_5 = \frac{23}{30} \approx .767.$$

The independent player has 21 % higher probability that the group will agree with him than each of the other players.

All expressions for e_i and s_i can be written as linear combinations of terms of the form

$$\int_0^1 q^a(1-q)^b\,dq = \frac{a!\,b!}{(a+b+1)!}\,.$$

---

[4]) Notice that the power index e_i is not normalized, just as β_i' was not normalized. In fact, normalizing it would destroy its probabilistic interpretation as the answer to player i's Outcome Question.

Hence we can also evaluate e_i and s_i combinatorially, or have a computer do it for us. A computer did the calculations in the next section.

5. Power and Satisfaction in a Nine-Member Body

As an example of how power and satisfaction vary with ideological division, we will study in detail a nine-member voting body operating under majority rule. The United States Supreme Court is one such body which has been widely studied, and the reader might find it interesting to interpret our results for that body. However, we will phrase the conclusions of our analysis in general terms, thinking of them as statements which might repay investigation in more general contexts.

In a symmetric voting body, such as one operating under majority rule, the nature of ideological division is completely specified by the triple of numbers $(|Q|, |Q'|, |P|)$. Similarly, the indices e_i and s_i will depend only upon whether i is in Q, Q', or P. Let e_Q be the common value of e_i for any i in Q, and define similarly $e_{Q'}$, e_P, s_Q, $s_{Q'}$, and s_P. Then the power of members of our nine-member body under all possible ideological division assumptions is given in Table 1, and the corresponding satisfaction figures are given in Table 2. (We have assumed without loss of generality that $|Q| \geqslant |Q'|$.)

A quick glance at Tables 1 and 2 shows that the indices e_i and s_i are not *conservative*: one player's gain in power or satisfaction need not be another player's loss. For instance, under ideological structure (0, 0, 9) *everyone's* power is higher than under (9, 0, 0), and *everyone's* satisfaction is lower. There is no reason, of course, that power and satisfaction should be conservative concepts. We will investigate this more thoroughly in the observations which follow.

Let us begin by looking at the relative positions of members of the larger ideological group Q, members of the smaller ideological group Q', and independent members P. Notice the following facts:

$$\text{If } |Q| > |Q'| + 1, \text{ then } e_Q > e_P > e_{Q'} \text{ and } s_Q > s_P > s_{Q'}.$$

$$\text{If } |Q| = |Q'|, \text{ then } e_P > e_Q = e_{Q'} \text{ and } s_P > s_Q = s_{Q'}.$$

These results are readily seen to be true for bodies of any size acting under a symmetric decision rule, and we phrase the conclusions as follows:

1) When one of two ideologically opposed groups is larger by more than one vote than the other, members of the larger ideological group have *both* higher satisfaction and more power than other voters. Independents are second, and members of the smaller ideological group are last.
2) When two ideologically opposed groups are of equal size, independent voters have *both* higher satisfaction and more power than members of either ideological group.

As regards *satisfaction*, these conclusions are intuitively clear, and show that our index does capture the most obvious commonsense notions of this concept. The conclusion about *power* in 1) is less obvious and hence more interesting. Although it seems clear that members of the larger ideological group should be more likely to get their way, it is not

Each entry is $(|Q|, |Q'|, |P|)$
$e_Q, e_{Q'}, e_P$

(0 , 0 , 9) – , – , .273									
	(1 , 0 , 8) .273, – , .273								
(1 , 1 , 7) .273, .273, .287		(2 , 0 , 7) .273, – , .260							
	(2 , 1 , 6) .287, .260, .287		(3 , 0 , 6) .260, – , .234						
(2 , 2 , 5) .287, .287, .304		(3 , 1 , 5) .287, .234, .269		(4 , 0 , 5) .234, – , .200					
	(3 , 2 , 4) .304, .269, .304		(4 , 1 , 4) .269, .200, .233		(5 , 0 , 4) .200, – , .167				
(3 , 3 , 3) .304, .304, .332		(4 , 2 , 3) .304, .233, .276		(5 , 1 , 3) .233, .167, .191		(6 , 0 , 3) .167, – , .143			
	(4 , 3 , 2) .332, .276, .332		(5 , 2 , 2) .276, .191, .220		(6 , 1 , 2) .191, .143, .161		(7 , 0 , 2) .143, – , .125		
(4 , 4 , 1) .332, .332, .406		(5 , 3 , 1) .332, .220, .258		(6 , 2 , 1) .220, .161, .183		(7 , 1 , 1) .161, .125, .139		(8 , 0 , 1) .125, – , .111	
	(5 , 4 , 0) .406, .258, –		(6 , 3 , 0) .258, .183, –		(7 , 2 , 0) .183, .139, –		(8 , 1 , 0) .139, .111, –		(9 , 0 , 0) .111, – , –

Tab. 1: Power as a Function of Ideological Structure in a Nine Member Voting Body

Each entry is ($|Q|$, $|Q'|$, $|P|$)
s_Q, $s_{Q'}$, s_P

(0 , 0 , 9) – , – , .637									
	(1 , 0 , 8) .637, – , .637								
(1 , 1 , 7) .591, .591, .643		(2 , 0 , 7) .682, – , .630							
	(2 , 1 , 6) .643, .539, .643		(3 , 0 , 6) .721, – , .617						
(2 , 2 , 5) .594, .594, .652		(3 , 1 , 5) .693, .484, .634		(4 , 0 , 5) .750, – , .600					
	(3 , 2 , 4) .652, .535, .652		(4 , 1 , 4) .733, .433, .617		(5 , 0 , 4) .767, – , .583				
(3 , 3 , 3) .597, .597, .666		(4 , 2 , 3) .707, .474, .638		(5 , 1 , 3) .760, .393, .595		(6 , 0 , 3) .774, – , .571			
	(4 , 3 , 2) .666, .528, .666		(5 , 2 , 2) .748, .420, .610		(6 , 1 , 2) .771, .366, .580		(7 , 0 , 2) .777, – , .563		
(4 , 4 , 1) .602, .602, .703		(5 , 3 , 1) .731, .454, .629		(6 , 2 , 1) .766, .385, .591		(7 , 1 , 1) .776, .347, .569		(8 , 0 , 1) .778, – , .556	
	(5 , 4 , 0) .703, .500, –		(6 , 3 , 0) .758, .409, –		(7 , 2 , 0) .774, .361, –		(8 , 1 , 0) .778, .333, –		(9 , 0 , 0) .778, – , –

Tab. 2: Satisfaction as a Function of Ideological Structure in a Nine Member Voting Body

as obvious that their votes are also more likely to be crucial to the outcome. That this is true means that power and satisfaction do covary in a voting body of fixed ideological structure operating under a symmetric decision rule.

Second, consider a member contemplating a change of values, or "party affiliation." Examination of Tables 1 and 2 reveals that if member i moves from Q' to P, from P to Q, or from Q' to Q (thus changing the ideological structure of the body), then s_i will increase but e_i *will not change*. (The only exception is that when $|Q| = |Q'|$, a movement from P to Q also does not change s_i.) Hence,

3) If a member changes his views in the direction of those of the larger ideological group, then his satisfaction will increase, but his power will remain constant.

Thus, any individual movement toward "conformity" (with the larger group) may be rationally motivated by a desire to side with the winners, but *not* by a desire to increase power. Although this may appear surprising, the fact that e_i does not change is quite easy to explain: it is a direct consequence of the fact that whether i's vote is or is not crucial to the outcome depends only on how the *other* members vote, not on how i votes.

Third, let us consider the effects of increasing ideological imbalance. Reading across the rows of Tables 2 and 1, respectively, yields the following conclusions:

4) As the ideological imbalance of a voting body increases, members of the larger ideological group gain satisfaction, while independent voters and members of the smaller ideological group lose satisfaction.
5) As the ideological imbalance of a voting body increases, *all* members lose power.

Conclusion 4) offers no surprises, but conclusion 5) underlines the non-conservative nature of power when it is measured by the Question of Effect on Outcome. As ideological imbalance increases, the probability of a close vote decreases, so all members have less chance of their votes' making a difference. Of particular interest is the situation of members of the larger ideological group: as their group becomes more dominant, they must pay for an increase in satisfaction by a decrease in power.

Finally, if we wish to make comparative judgments about social states, we might be interested in the average value of e_i or s_i across all voters i. We will call these values e_{av} and s_{av}. In Table 3, they are shown for the nine-member body. Moving from left to right in Table 3 (either directly across or along a diagonal), we see that

6) As the ideological imbalance of a voting body increases, the average level of satisfaction increases, while the average level of power decreases.

Again, therefore, we find evidence of a trade-off – this time, on average – between power and satisfaction.

On the other hand, this pattern of an inverse relationship between e_{av} and s_{av} is not strict. For instance, reading down columns five and six of Table 3 yields the interesting observation that

7) There are changes in ideological structure which can lower *both* average satisfaction and average power. This may occur, for instance, as the body becomes more *polarized*, i.e., as independent voters join the opposing ideological groups.

In other words, there are more and less desirable social states, as judged by both the

Each entry is $(|Q|, |Q'|, |P|)$
e_{av} s_{av}

(0, 0, 9) .273 .637									
	(1, 0, 8) .273 .637								
(1, 1, 7) .284 .631		(2, 0, 7) .263 .642							
	(2, 1, 6) .284 .631		(3, 0, 6) .243 .652						
(2, 2, 5) .296 .626		(3, 1, 5) .271 .637		(4, 0, 5) .215 .667					
	(3, 2, 4) .296 .626		(4, 1, 4) .245 .648		(5, 0, 4) .185 .685				
(3, 3, 3) .313 .620		(4, 2, 3) .279 .632		(5, 1, 3) .212 .664		(6, 0, 3) .159 .706			
	(4, 3, 2) .313 .620		(5, 2, 2) .245 .644		(6, 1, 2) .179 .684		(7, 0, 2) .139 .729		
(4, 4, 1) .340 .613		(5, 3, 1) .286 .627		(6, 2, 1) .203 .662		(7, 1, 1) .155 .705		(8, 0, 1) .123 .753	
	(5, 4, 0) .340 .613		(6, 3, 0) .233 .642		(7, 2, 0) .173 .682		(8, 1, 0) .136 .729		(9, 0, 0) .111 .778

Tab. 3: Average Power and Satisfaction as a Function of Ideological Structure in a Nine Member Voting Body

criteria of average satisfaction and average power.

Taken together, the conclusions above throw light upon the general relationship between power and satisfaction. If the ideological structure of a voting body remains constant and we look at how power and satisfaction vary among different voters in the body, we see in 1) and 2) the direct relationship between power and satisfaction discussed in the introduction and in section 2:

$$s_i \geqslant s_j \quad \text{if and only if} \quad e_i \geqslant e_j \, .$$

On the other hand, if we vary the ideological structure of the body, we see in 4), 5) and 6) the inverse relationship between power and satisfaction discussed in the examples of the introduction. Finally, 7) indicates that there are interesting subtleties to this relationship: some ideological structures may be socially better than others according to measures of both power and satisfaction.

6. The Effect of Caucuses

In conclusion 3) of section 4, we looked briefly at an individual member of a voting body trying to increase his power or satisfaction by changing his values. This, of course, is not how most change occurs. Usually groups of individuals, in order to increase their power or satisfaction, unite to form coalitions. Notice that in our model, Q and Q' are not coalitions of voters: they are simply groups of voters with common values. To model the effects of coalition formation, we introduce in this section the possibility that some voters may form a kind of coalition we shall call a *caucus*. The members of a caucus will agree to cast all of their votes as the majority of the members of the caucus prefer. The party caucuses of the United States Congress are examples of such coalitions.

We shall study two kinds of three-person caucuses in our nine-person voting body. The first kind is a *homogeneous caucus*, which consists of three members of Q. Thus the caucus consists of members with common values. This kind of caucus may be the most common kind of caucus in political situations. The second kind of caucus is a *cross-ideological caucus*, which consists of one member of Q, one member of Q', and one member of P. Thus, this kind of caucus cuts evenly across ideological cleavages. On a liberal-conservative ideological dimension, the Democratic caucus in the U.S. Congress could be thought of as a cross-ideological caucus, since it embraces members of very different persuasions in the Democratic Party.

For each kind of caucus, we will be concerned with the effects its formation has upon the power and satisfaction of the caucus members. Does forming the caucus, for instance, increase their power and satisfaction?

The results of the calculations for the three-member homogeneous caucus are shown in Table 4. They support the following generalizations:

8) Members of a homogeneous caucus always gain satisfaction.
9) Members of a homogeneous caucus *lose* power if the voting body is ideologically balanced. They *gain* power if the body is imbalanced.

The results of the calculations for the three-member cross-ideological caucus are shown in Table 5. They support the following generalizations:

Structure $(\lvert Q\rvert, \lvert Q'\rvert, \lvert P\rvert)$	e_Q without caucus	e_i of caucus members	s_Q without caucus	s_i of caucus members
(3, 6, 0)	.183	.183 same	.409	.444 up
(3, 5, 1)	.220	.202 down	.454	.494 up
(3, 4, 2)	.276	.224 down	.528	.571 up
(4, 5, 0)	.258	.222 down	.500	.544 up
(3, 3, 3)	.304	.242 down	.597	.642 up
(4, 4, 1)	.332	.245 down	.602	.649 up
(3, 2, 4)	.304	.254 down	.652	.696 up
(4, 3, 2)	.332	.260 down	.666	.712 up
(5, 4, 0)	.406	.268 down	.703	.754 up
(3, 1, 5)	.287	.260 down	.693	.734 up
(4, 2, 3)	.304	.267 down	.707	.750 up
(5, 3, 1)	.332	.274 down	.731	.775 up
(3, 0, 6)	.260	.260 same	.721	.760 up
(4, 1, 4)	.269	.267 down	.733	.773 up
(5, 2, 2)	.276	.274 down	.748	.788 up
(6, 3, 0)	.258	.279 up	.758	.796 up
(4, 0, 5)	.234	.260 up	.750	.787 up
(5, 1, 3)	.233	.267 up	.760	.796 up
(6, 2, 1)	.220	.274 up	.766	.801 up
(5, 0, 4)	.200	.254 up	.767	.800 up
(6, 1, 2)	.191	.260 up	.771	.804 up
(7, 2, 0)	.183	.268 up	.774	.806 up
(6, 0, 3)	.167	.242 up	.773	.804 up
(7, 1, 1)	.161	.245 up	.776	.806 up
(7, 0, 2)	.143	.224 up	.777	.805 up
(8, 1, 0)	.139	.222 up	.778	.806 up
(8, 0, 1)	.125	.202 up	.778	.804 up
(9, 0, 0)	.111	.183 up	.778	.802 up

Tab. 4: Effect on Power and Satisfaction of Forming a Three Member Homogeneous (Q) Caucus

Structure $(\lvert Q\rvert, \lvert Q'\rvert, \lvert P\rvert)$	$(e_Q, e_{Q'}, e_P)$ without caucus	$(e_q, e_{q'}, e_p)$ of caucus members	$(s_Q, s_{Q'}, s_P)$ without caucus	$(s_q, s_{q'}, s_p)$ of caucus members
(1, 1, 7)	(.273, .273, .287)	(.391, .391, .521) uuu	(.591, .591, .643)	(.630, .630, .760) uuu
(2, 2, 5)	(.287, .287, .304)	(.406, .406, .546) uuu	(.594, .594, .652)	(.633, .633, .773) uuu
(3, 3, 3)	(.304, .304, .332)	(.425, .425, .576) uuu	(.597, .597, .666)	(.637, .637, .788) uuu
(4, 4, 1)	(.332, .332, .406)	(.436, .436, .592) uuu	(.602, .602, .703)	(.640, .640, .796) uuu
(2, 1, 6)	(.287, .260, .287)	(.391, .391, .521) uuu	(.643, .539, .643)	(.656, .604, .760) uuu
(3, 2, 4)	(.304, .269, .304)	(.406, .406, .546) uuu	(.652, .535, .652)	(.656, .610, .773) uuu
(4, 3, 2)	(.332, .276, .332)	(.425, .425, .576) uuu	(.666, .528, .666)	(.650, .624, .788) duu
(3, 1, 5)	(.287, .234, .269)	(.375, .375, .496) uuu	(.693, .484, .634)	(.679, .575, .748) duu
(4, 2, 3)	(.304, .233, .276)	(.388, .388, .516) uuu	(.707, .474, .638)	(.681, .582, .758) duu
(5, 3, 1)	(.332, .220, .258)	(.414, .414, .560) uuu	(.731, .454, .629)	(.660, .608, .780) duu
(4, 1, 4)	(.269, .200, .233)	(.344, .344, .463) uuu	(.733, .433, .617)	(.702, .540, .735) duu
(5, 2, 2)	(.276, .191, .220)	(.350, .350, .455) uuu	(.748, .420, .610)	(.701, .544, .727) duu
(5, 1, 3)	(.233, .167, .191)	(.300, .300, .376) uuu	(.760, .393, .595)	(.729, .495, .688) duu
(6, 2, 1)	(.220, .161, .183)	(.286, .286, .349) uuu	(.766, .385, .591)	(.742, .482, .656) duu
(6, 1, 2)	(.191, .143, .161)	(.250, .250, .298) uuu	(.771, .366, .580)	(.756, .446, .648) duu
(7, 1, 1)	(.161, .125, .139)	(.214, .214, .246) uuu	(.776, .347, .569)	(.770, .413, .623) duu

Tab. 5: Effect on Power and Satisfaction of Forming a Three Member Cross-Ideological Caucus

10) Members of a cross-ideological caucus always gain power.
11) Minority and independent members of a cross-ideological caucus always gain satisfaction.
12) Members of a cross-ideological caucus from the larger ideological group can gain satisfaction if the voting body is ideologically balanced, but they *lose* satisfaction if the body is ideologically imbalanced.

Thus, the formation of caucuses exhibits another instance of the trade-off between power and satisfaction. If a homogeneous caucus forms within an ideologically balanced voting body, its members will gain satisfaction at the cost of power. If a cross-ideological caucus forms within an ideologically imbalanced voting body, at least some of its members (those from the larger ideological group) will gain power at the cost of satisfaction.

If members do not wish to make this trade-off – if all members insist on losing neither power nor satisfaction from the formation of the caucus – then a homogeneous caucus should form when the voting body is imbalanced, but a cross-ideological caucus should form when the body is balanced. Perhaps somewhat rashly, we could generalize this observation to the following rule of thumb: to avoid trade-offs between power and satisfaction, *the ideological structure of the caucus should roughly match the ideological structure of the voting body as a whole.*

Insofar as the most natural caucuses in political bodies are probably homogeneous caucuses, their members may often accept a decrease in power for an increase in satisfaction. On the other hand, political parties in the United States tend to be more like cross-ideological caucuses – microcosms of an ideologically divided electorate. Hence their members may gain both power and satisfaction. Although many analysts have deplored their lack of ideological consistency, our analysis reveals a possible rational reason for the existence of ideologically diverse parties.

7. Summary and Conclusions

The two questions of Effect on Outcome and Group-Individual Agreement are basic concerns to members of voting bodies and to political scientists analyzing those bodies. The Outcome Question has been the basis of the most widely used power indices for voting bodies. The Agreement Question has been studied as a measure of the responsiveness of decision rules to individual values. The interesting relationships between the answers to these two questions have not, to our knowledge, previously been the subject of formal analysis.

We defined a model of a voting body with an elementary kind of ideological structure, which enabled us to define precisely a member's power index as the answer to his Question of Effect on Outcome, and a member's satisfaction index as the answer to his Question of Group-Individual Agreement. These indices generalize classical indices in the political science literature. We were then able to study the effect of varying ideological structure on members' power and satisfaction in the case of a nine-member voting body operating under majority rule. We formulated our observations from this case as tentative general statements 1)–7).

As a contribution toward understanding the dynamics of coalition formation in voting bodies, we analyzed the effect on power and satisfaction of the formation of two different types of caucuses – homogeneous caucuses and cross-ideological caucuses. Data from the nine-member example supported tentative general statements 8)–12), and a rule of thumb that caucus members could avoid making a trade-off between power and satisfaction by matching the ideological structure of their caucus to the ideological structure of the voting body as a whole.

Appendix

We can use the model in this paper to say something interesting about the interrelationship between ideological structure, size, and the power of members in a voting body. This kind of question is discussed, for instance, by *Dahl/Tufte* [1973]. Consider a voting body of odd size $n = 2k + 1$ operating under majority rule. If the body is homogeneous, with ideological structure $(2k + 1, 0, 0)$, then each member has power equal to $1/n$. This follows immediately, for instance, from Theorem 2 of section 3 and properties of the Shapley-Shubik power index.

On the other hand, suppose the body is evenly ideologically divided, with ideological structure $(k, k, 1)$. Using the combinatorial approach sketched at the end of section 4, one can show that the power of a committed member (Q or Q') is

$$e_Q = \frac{1}{2k\binom{2k-1}{k-1}} \sum_{i=1}^{k} \binom{2i-2}{i-1}\binom{2k-2i+1}{k-i}$$

$$= \frac{1}{2k\binom{2k-1}{k-1}} \cdot \frac{1}{2}\left[4^k - \binom{2k}{k}\right] \quad \text{by a combinatorial identity}$$

$$= \frac{1}{2k}\left[\frac{4^k}{\binom{2k}{k}} - 1\right]$$

$$\approx \frac{\sqrt{\pi k} - 1}{2k} \quad \text{using Stirling's approximation.}$$

For large n, this value of e_Q is approximately $\sqrt{\pi/2n}$. In other words, the power of members of an evenly ideologically divided voting body of size n decreases only like $1/\sqrt{n}$, whereas the power of members of a homogeneous body of size n decreases like $1/n$.

One interesting way to formulate this result is to say that a member of an evenly ideologically divided body of size N has as much power as a member of a homogeneous body of size n, where

$$\sqrt{\frac{\pi}{2N}} = \frac{1}{n}, \text{ i.e., } N = \frac{\pi}{2} n^2.$$

For instance, by this model a member of an evenly ideologically divided body of size 15,000 has about as much power as a member of a homogeneous body of size 100.

References

Banzhaf, J.F.: Weighted voting doesn't work: a mathematical analysis. Rutgers Law Review **19**, 1965, 317–343.

Blair, D.H.: On a class of power measures for voting rules. University of Pennsylvania Department of Economics Discussion Paper #361, 1976.

Brams, S.J.: Game Theory and Politics. New York 1975.

Brams, S.J., and *M. Lake*: Power and satisfaction in a representative democracy. Game Theory and Political Science. Ed. by P.C. Ordeshook. New York 1978, 529–562.

Dahl, R.A., and *E.R. Tufte*: Size and Democracy. Stanford 1973.

Dubey, P., and *L.S. Shapley*: Mathematical properties of the Banzhaf power index. Rand Paper P-6016. Santa Monica 1977.

Imrie, R.W.: The impact of the weighted vote on representation in municipal governing bodies of New York State. Annals of the New York Academy of Sciences **219**, 1973, 192–199.

Lucas, W.F.: Measuring power in weighted voting systems. Case Studies in Applied Mathematics. Mathematical Assoc. of America, 1976, 42–106.

Rae, D.: Decision rules and individual values in constitutional choice, American Political Science Review **63**, 1969, 40–56.

Riker, W.H., and *P.C. Ordeshook*: An Introduction to Positive Political Theory. Englewood Cliffs 1973.

Shapley, L.S.: Simple games: an outline of the descriptive theory. Behavioral Science **7**, 1962, 59–66.

– : A comparison of power indices and a non-symmetric generalization. Rand Paper P-5872. Santa Monica 1977.

Shapley, L.S., and *M. Shubik*: A method for evaluating the distribution of power in a committee system. American Political Science Review **48**, 1954, 787–792.

Straffin, P.D.: Power Indices in Politics. Modules in Applied Mathematics. Mathematical Assoc. of America. Cornell University 1976.

– : Homogeneity, independence and power indices. Public Choice **30**, 1977a, 107–118.

– : Majority rule and general decision rules. Theory and Decision **8**, 1977b, 351–360.

– : Probability models for power indices. Game Theory and Political Science. Ed. by P.C. Ordeshook. New York 1978, 477–510.

Holler, M.J. (Ed.): Power, Voting, and Voting Power ©Physica-Verlag, Würzburg (Germany) 1981

Power in an Ideological Space

D. Wittman, Santa Cruz

1. Introduction

Power and satisfaction are often seen as two unrelated concepts: power being, the ability to change an outcome and satisfaction being the utility derived from an outcome [see, e.g., *Straffin/Davis/Brams* (in this book)]. Here we combine the two concepts with power being the means to satisfaction. Power is defined as the ability to increase one's own utility. This approach to power makes sense on empirical grounds. We will be unlikely to observe power being exercised unless it ultimately increases the person's own welfare. Even the use of threats to decrease other's welfare are best understood within the context of increasing one's own welfare. Power thus depends critically on each person's preference function. Different preference relationships would indeed change the relative power configurations of the players.

2. Power in a k-Dimensional Space

1) Let Mi be a vector of preferred positions of player i in Euclidean K space Rk, $i = 1, 2, \ldots, N$. (Refer to Figure 1 where a 2-dimensional space is drawn.)
2) Player i has a preference ordering over the points in Rk represented by circular indifference curves. I.e., i strictly prefers v to w if and only if $\| v - Mi \| < \| w - Mi \|$ where $\| z \|$ is the Euclidean distance.
3) Let X be the outcome when all N players are in the game.[1]) Let Xi be the outcome when all N players except i are in the game.
4) The power of player i is $Pi = \| Mi - Xi \| - \| Mi - X \|$.

With additional notation we could redefine power, Pi, to encompass situations where outcomes occur with probability less than one.

Player i is more powerful than j if $Pi > Pj$.

---

[1]) For our purposes it does not matter whether the game is a cooperative or non-cooperative game. Under certain circumstances we might want to define power in terms of these alternatives. Game theory might not be able to predict an outcome in certain games. We ignore this problem. One way of getting around this problem is to observe the outcome.

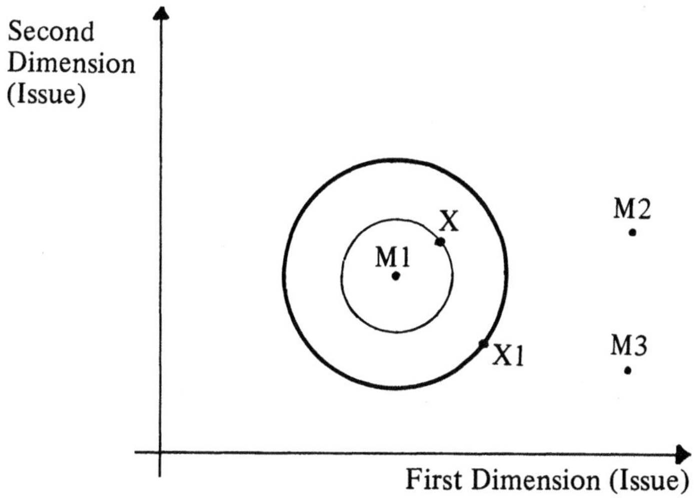

X – outcome when all three players are in the game,
$X1$ – outcome when players 2 and 3 are in the game, but not player 1

3. Power in a One Dimensional Election Game

Much of the work on candidate strategies has assumed a single ideological dimension. In this section we will analyse voting power within the familiar left-right continuum. For practical reasons we will slightly alter our definition of power. An unaltered version would compare the outcome of the election whenever i abstained from voting to the outcome when voter i voted for his most preferred candidate. Unfortunately this involves both an odd and an even number of voters voting. When there is an even number of voters voting, then the possibility of a tie and some kind of random mechanism being used to break ties arises. To avoid this unnecessary complication we will assume that the number of voters is odd and that there are no abstentions.

5) The power of *voter i* (as opposed to player i in the n space game) is the change in the winning platform when voter i switches his vote from the candidate who is farthest away from his most preferred position to the candidate who is closest to his preferred position. (When the candidates have identical positions the voter votes for either with probability one half.)
6) The power of k voters acting in concert is the change in the winning platform when each of the k voters switches his vote from the candidate who is farthest away from the particular voter's most preferred position to the candidate who is closest to the particular voter's most preferred position.[2])

We will assume that the candidates are solely interested in winning. Under this assumption the result will be that both candidates will be at the median voter's most preferred

[2]) Note that if k is an even number we could then allow abstentions (instead of having voters vote against their preferred positions) without having to consider ties.

position. The power of a voter is thus his ability to redefine who is the median voter when the voter changes from voting against his preferred candidate to voting for his preferred candidate.

Proposition 1: If there are $2 + k$ or more voters who have a most preferred position at the median voter position and an equal number of voters strictly to the left and strictly to the right, then no set of k voters acting in concert has any power.

It is clear that even if k voters switch their votes (or abstain), the median position will remain the same. Therefore no set of k voters has any power when these conditions hold.

Proposition 2: If the $(N + 1 - 2k)/2$ voter from the left is closer to the median $[(N + 1)/2]$ voter than the $(N + 1 + 2k)/2$ voter is, then k voters to the left of the median voter acting in concert are more powerful than k voters to the right of the median voter.

When a voter on the left votes against his preferred position, the new candidate equilibrium will move one voter to the right. Thus the power of a voter on the left is the distance between the $(N + 1)/2$ voter's preferred position and the $(N + 3)/2$ voter's preferred position. By assumption this is larger than the distance between the preferred positions of voters $(N + 1)/2$ and $(N - 1)/2$. The analysis readily extends to k voters acting in concert. Proposition 2 demonstrates that more extreme coalitions have less power than less extreme coalitions (where the measure of "extreme" is the distance of the farthest member from the median voter).

Proposition 3: If k voters on the left and l voters on the right act in concert (k greater than or equal to l), then the power of the set of voters is equal to $k - l$ voters on the left. In particular, when $k = l$, the power of the group is zero.

The voter on the left is cancelled out by a voter on the right. When the left votes for, the right votes against; and when the left votes against, the right votes for. The median voter does not change when the antagonistic pair change their votes simultaneously or (jointly abstain). Thus, electoral coalitions in a unidimensional ideological space must have consistent ideological preferences in order to be effective.

This paper has demonstrated that in ideological space not all voters are equally powerful even though all players have one vote each.

Holler, M.J. (Ed.): Power, Voting, and Voting Power ©Physica-Verlag, Würzburg (Germany) 1981

Measuring Power

H. Nurmi, Turku[1])

1. Introduction

The subject of this paper is the measurement of power. The specific problem discussed is whether power as we intuitively understand it can be measured. It is debatable whether the intuitive power concept is unambiguous enough to give guidelines for measurement. We shall adopt an approach which as much as possible avoids the thorny conceptual problems related to power and instead takes its point of departure in an analogy which – if fruitful – allows us to outline the structure of the power concept in detail without going very deep into its substantial aspects. Of course, some commitments concerning the content of the power concept must be made but as said, these shall be kept to a minimum.

The analogy exploited in this paper comes from the probability theory for the obvious reason that probability as a concept has been subject of a good many measurement-theoretic analyses. I intend to utilize the example provided by the probability concept to the fullest possible extent:

1) as an example of the application of the measurement-theoretic analysis, and
2) as a basis for the axiomatization of the structure of the power concept.

The main goal of this paper is to show to what extent an approach stemming from measurement theory can be useful in the assessment of power indices that have been used to measure power in collective voting bodies. We start with some elementary pre-requisites.

2. Preliminaries

Intuitively speaking, measurement consists of attaching numbers to the entities being measured. It is, however, obvious that not just any method of assigning numbers to things or phenomena will do. Some additional conditions must be fulfilled. What these additional conditions are and how we can ascertain their presence or absence is what the theory of

---

[1]) This paper was written while the author was a British Academy Wolfson Fellow at the University of Essex. The author wishes to thank Manfred J. Holler for perceptive comments on an earlier draft.

measurement is about. In the theory the concept of measurement is assigning numbers to entities in a "plausible" or "natural" way. Plausibility, in turn, means that the numbers be assigned to such entities only for which there exists a measure. Measurement, then, quite obviously means applying a measure. It presupposes, therefore, the existence of the latter.

Given the problem of measuring something, one shows that there exists a measure for it by proving a representation theorem. The theorem says that there is a plausible way of attaching numbers to entities under certain conditions. The conditions restrict the applicability of measurements by indicating the conditions which must be fulfilled by the entities if the measurement is to be meaningful. We notice that the representation theorem presupposes a kind of "theory" of the phenomenon under study in the sense that the conditions of meaningful number assignment refer to the properties of the phenomenon. By proving a representation theorem one shows that the properties of the entities investigated can be represented by the numbers, so that the relational structure of the numbers preserves the relational structure of the empirical properties.

Having proven the representation theorem one still faces another problem related to measurement, viz. that of determining whether the number assignment is unique. In other words, one must determine whether the given rule of assigning numbers to phenomena is the only one under the conditions listed in the representation theorem. If it is unique, one can, with no risk of being misunderstood, talk about the results of measurement without having to mention which one of the measures was actually applied.

The above remarks can more precisely be presented as follows [*Scott/Suppes*]. Let A be a finite set and $R_1, \ldots, R_n$ a sequence of relations on A. Consider now a sequence of positive integers $s = \langle m_1, \ldots, m_n \rangle$. The $n+1$-tuple $U = \langle A, R_1, \ldots, R_n \rangle$ is called a relational system of type s if

$$\forall i = 1, \ldots, n \colon\ R_i \subset A^{m_i}$$

where A^{m_i} is the m_i-fold Cartesian product set of A.

Let there be two relational systems U and V of the type s. U is defined as above and V as follows:

$$V = \langle B, S_1, \ldots, S_n \rangle.$$

Assume that there is a function $f\colon A \to B$ (onto). Let $\langle a_1, \ldots, a_{m_i} \rangle$ be an arbitrary sequence of m_i elements of A. $\langle f(a_1), \ldots, f(a_{m_i}) \rangle$ is then the sequence of the images of $\langle a_1, \ldots, a_{m_i} \rangle$ in B under f. Function f is called a homomorphic mapping or homomorphism if

$$\forall i = 1, \ldots, n \colon \langle a_1, \ldots, a_{m_i} \rangle \in R_i \text{ iff } \langle f(a_1), \ldots, f(a_{m_i}) \rangle \in S_i.$$

If furthermore $a_i \neq a_j$ implies $f(a_i) \neq f(a_j)$, $\forall\, a_i, a_j \in A$, then f is called an isomorphism.

Consider the special case where $A \subseteq B$ and R_i is the restriction of S_i to A for all $i = 1, \ldots, n$. U is then called a subsystem of V. Let V' be a subsystem of V. If there is a homomorphism $g\colon U \to V'$, U is said to be embeddable in V. If finally A or B in the above definitions is the set Re of real numbers, U or V is called a numerical relational system.

Let V be a numerical relational system and U an empirical system. Then a homomorphism $g\colon U \to V'$ is called a numerical assignment for U. Clearly it makes it possible to assign numbers to objects in a way that is natural in preserving the relations between the empirical properties. One can then say that the numerical system represents the empirical one.

3. Probability and Power

We now proceed to give an overview of the main results in the measurement of probability. As was pointed out above the probability concept has two roles in this paper, one of which is to exemplify the nature of the measurement-theoretic approach. This approach when applied to the analysis of probability takes its point of departure in the following question: under which conditions an intuitively given empirical relation of "being at least as probable as" is measurable? In other words, one starts with an intuitive notion of comparative probability. This notion is of entirely qualitative nature. It is not self-evident that there is a plausible or natural way of assigning numbers to it. We must put somewhat more structure into the intuitive notion in order to restrict the numerical assignments so as to hopefully end up with the plausible or natural ones only.

To claim that there is a measure of probability is tantamount to claiming that we can order the subsets of the set of elementary events – assuming that the entities the probabilities of which we investigate are called composite events – in a way that given an additive probability value assignment to each subset, the ordering of the subsets corresponds to the order of probability values [*Kraft/Pratt/Seidenberg*, p. 408]. Specifically, let X be a nonempty set of elementary events and let $\mathcal{A}$ be a Boolean algebra on X. Assume now that $\geqslant$ is a binary relation in $\mathcal{A}$ interpreted as "is at least as probable as." To say that $\geqslant$ is measurable is tantamount to saying that there is a function P: $A \rightarrow \mathrm{Re}$ such that
$\forall A, B \in \mathcal{A}$:

(1) $P(A) \geqslant 0$,
(2) $P(X) = 1$,
(3) $A \cap B = \emptyset$ implies $P(A \cup B) = P(A) + P(B)$, and
(4) $A \geqslant B$ iff $P(A) \geqslant P(B)$ [*Niiniluoto*].

To be more specific the fulfillment of the above conditions guarantees that P is an additive probability measure, the additivity being due to (3). If $A \geqslant B$ implies $P(A) \geqslant P(B)$ we also say that the ordering according to $\geqslant$ arises from the measure P.

Now the question arises as to under which conditions such a measure exists. In particular, what are the structural properties of the event set that are necessary and/or sufficient for the existence of the measure? In order to answer this question we have to set up the set of structural properties or axioms characterizing the relation $\geqslant$. We assume that X is a finite set and $\mathcal{A}$ a set algebra on it. Following *de Finetti* [1931] we require that
$\forall A, B, C \in \mathcal{A}$:

(a) $\geqslant$ is transitive
(b) $\geqslant$ is complete (or comparable)
(c) $A \geqslant \emptyset$
(d) it is not the case that $\emptyset \geqslant X$, and
(e) $A \cap B = C \cap B = \emptyset$ implies that $A \geqslant C$ iff $A \cup B \geqslant C \cup B$ [*Niiniluoto*].

It can be verified that these axioms can also be set upon the relation $\geqslant$ when interpreted as "has at least as much power as" or "is at least as powerful as." Under this interpretation – which can be called the weak power relation – it is natural to take all A, B and C ($\in \mathbb{A}$) to be coalitions of players in voting game consisting of players represented by the set X. In this interpretation the requirement that $\mathbb{A}$ be a set algebra on X simply means that for all $A, B \in \mathbb{A}$, there are $\bar{A} \in \mathbb{A}$ and $A \cup B \in \mathbb{A}$, where $\bar{A}$ is the complement of A, i.e., the set of players not belonging to A. In other words, we require that $\mathbb{A}$ is a collection of coalitions (i.e. subsets of X) such that for each coalition in the set, also its complement is in the set, and that for each pair of coalitions in the set, also their union belongs to the set. Of course, there may be reasons related to the specific circumstances that make it practically impossible for some types of coalitions to form, but on a general level we cannot take these reasons into account. Axiom (a) comes to mean that the weak power relation has the property that $\forall A, B, C \in \mathbb{A}$: $A \geqslant B$ and $B \geqslant C$ imply $A \geqslant C$. This is to say that if A is at least as powerful as B and B at least as powerful as C, then it follows that A is at least as powerful as C. Completeness property (b) now means that we are able to compare any two coalitions in terms of their power, i.e. $\forall A, B \in \mathbb{A}$: either $A \geqslant B$ or $B \geqslant A$ (or both). The axioms (c) and (d) have a natural meaning in our interpretation: the former says that any coalition is at least as powerful as an empty one (that is, one consisting of no players); the latter, in turn, saying that the empty coalition cannot be more powerful than the grand coalition (i.e. the coalition consisting of all players).

In the case of probability it has been shown that the axioms (a)–(e), although each necessary are not jointly sufficient to guarantee the existence of a probability measure [*Kraft/Pratt/Seidenberg*]. In other words, it has been shown that each ordering of subsets of X which arises from a measure has the above properties (a)–(e), but that there are orderings having these properties without arising from a measure. What additional properties, then, one must impose upon X and $\mathbb{A}$ in order to guarantee the existence of a probability measure? The earliest answers to this question – due to Savage and de Finetti – were based on the (implicit) assumption that X be infinite [see *Luce*]. As we are interested in the sufficient conditions only in so far as they may be applied to the measurement of power, we omit these solutions because power indices obviously are being applied to finite cases only.

Scott [1964] gives a reformulation of the necessary and sufficient conditions for the existence of the probability measure for a finite $X = \{x_1, \ldots, x_k\}$ such that the ordering $\geqslant$ arises out of it. These conditions were originally presented by *Kraft/Pratt/Seidenberg* [1959]. As Scott's algebraic approach requires less preliminary definitions than the original one, we present the result in the form Scott gave to it [cf. *Niiniluoto*].

Let $\mathbb{A}$ be the set of all subsets of the set X. We can, then, define the set $A \in \mathbb{A}$ either by listing the elements of it or by means of the characteristic function $f_A : X \to (0, 1)$ so that

$$f_A(x_i) = 1, \quad \text{if } x_i \in A$$

$$f_A(x_i) = 0 \ \text{ otherwise, for all } i = 1, \ldots, k.$$

Under these conditions the relation $\geqslant$ in $\mathbb{A}$ arises from a measure if and only if the axiom (c) above holds along with the axiom (d) slightly strengthened, viz.:

(d′) $X \geqslant \emptyset$ and not: $\emptyset \geqslant X$, in conjunction with the following condition:

(f) for all f_A and f_B such that

$$\sum_{i=1}^{k} f_A(x_i) = \sum_{i=1}^{k} f_B(x_i), \text{ the following holds:}$$

$$f_A(x_i) \geqslant f_B(x_i), \text{ for } i = 1, \ldots, k-1 \text{ implies that}$$

$$f_B(x_k) \geqslant f_A(x_k).$$

Returning to our reinterpretation of the measurement-theoretic results we can easily see that the condition (d′) lends itself quite naturally to the interpretation in terms of power. The condition (f) does so equally naturally, viz. what it says is that if the number of people in two different coalitions A and B is the same and if the number of those belonging to A among $k-1$ persons is larger than or equal to the number of those belonging to B, then it cannot be the case that the remaining k-th person belongs to A without belonging to B. Indeed, our intuition would no doubt warrant a stronger condition than this. Let us, however, restate the result: these conditions are necessary and sufficient for the existence of an additive probability measure in A.

4. Additive Measures and Power Indices

What bearing do the above remarks have upon the measurement of power in voting bodies? I intend to restrict the discussion to the most common power indices only in an effort to find out their measurement-theoretic properties. The research motivation stems from practical considerations as many representative voting bodies are based on an (explicit or implicit) idea that the power should be distributed according to support. However, as the bodies are collective decision making units in which fixed decision rules are applied, the method of distributing votes or seats strictly according to the distribution of support does not simpliciter guarantee that the desired power distribution is achieved. This at least is the conclusion if some of the most common power indices is used as a measure of power.

On the other hand, the power indices – being based on somewhat differing views concerning the bargaining processes underlying the coalition formation in voting bodies – by no means give identical results when applied to voting bodies. Therefore, it would be important to know whether a measurement-theoretic analysis could show that some of them is a measure of power, or failing that, that none of them is under the above axiomatization of $\geqslant$. In the following I shall briefly present the definitions of the three most common power indices. For the discussion of their properties the reader is referred to *Brams/Affuso* [1976], *Coleman* [1971], *Banzhaf* [1968], *Shapley* [1953], *Shapley/Shubik* [1954]. The underlying bargaining models are discussed in *Brams* [1975], *Riker/Shapley* [1968] and *Nurmi* [1978].

Let an n-person game be defined by means of a characteristic function $\nu: \mathsf{A} \to (0, 1)$, where A is the set of all 2^n subsets of the set N of players. ν assigns to each subset $A \in \mathsf{A}$ the value 1 or 0 depending on whether A is a winning coalition or not, respectively. We notice that we are dealing with a special case of the von Neumann/Morgenstern type characteristic functions in that the winning coalitions and only they are assumed to have non-zero value. Furthermore, the value of each winning coalition is assumed to be the same, viz. 1.

On these assumptions the Shapley-Shubik power index value of player i is defined as

$$F_i^{\mathrm{Sh}} = \sum_{\substack{S \subseteq N \\ i \in S}} \frac{(s-1)!\,(n-s)!}{n!} \, v(S) - \sum_{\substack{S \subseteq N \\ i \notin S}} \frac{s!\,(n-s-1)!}{n!} \, v(S).$$

The first summation is, thus, taken over all coalitions S consisting of s members in which i belongs, whereas the latter summation is over all the remaining coalitions, i.e. those to which i does not belong. F_i^{Sh} can, consequently, be expressed more briefly as follows:

$$F_i^{\mathrm{Sh}} = \sum_{S \subseteq N} \frac{(s-1)!\,(n-s)!}{n!} \, [v(S) - v(S - \{i\})].$$

The crucial role in the computation of the Shapley-Shubik index is played by permutations of players. For the determination of F_i^{Sh} we have to compute for all 2^n coalitions the number of permutations of the remaining $n-s$ members. In practice, however, the task is somewhat simpler as we have to count those cases only in which $[v(S) - v(S - \{i\})] \neq 0$, i.e. precisely those cases in which i is 'pivotal'.

As permutations do not in general lend themselves to a straightforward interpretation in terms of bargaining process [see, however, *Riker/Shapley; Brams*, p. 168], whereas the combinations do seem to have "natural" counterparts in coalitions of players, the remaining power indices are based on combinations rather than permutations. The starting point is still the characteristic function defined above. The (*standardized*) Banzhaf index value F_i^{B} of i is calculated as follows:

$$F_i^{\mathrm{B}} = \frac{\sum_{S \subseteq N} [v(S) - v(S - \{i\})]}{\sum_{i=1}^{n} \sum_{S \subseteq N} [v(S) - v(S - \{i\})]}.$$

The numerator expresses the number of times the departure of i from a coalition S makes it losing while i's presence would enable S to be winning. In other words, the numerator counts the number of i's critical defections [*Brams*, p. 165]. Consequently, the denumerator obviously counts the number of all critical defections among the n players. F_i^{B} is then the relative number of i's critical defections among all critical defections.

Coleman's two power indices, power to initiate and power to block collective action, are based on coalitions rather than permutations as well. The definitions are as follows:

$$F_i^{\mathrm{CI}} = \frac{\sum_{S \subseteq N} [v(S + \{i\}) - v(S)]}{\sum_{S \subseteq N} [1 - v(S)]}$$

for the power to initiate, and for the blocking power we have:

$$F_i^{\mathrm{CB}} = \frac{\sum_{S \subseteq N} [v(S) - v(S - \{i\})]}{\sum_{S \subseteq N} v(S)} .$$

The denumerators count the total number of losing and winning coalitions, respectively, in the voting game. It is easy to recognize the affinity of the numerators of these formulae to one another and to the Banzhaf index. Indeed, it has been shown by *Brams/Affuso* [1976] that the Coleman indices are proportional transformations of each other and of the Banzhaf index.

Let us now see whether these indices satisfy the conditions of measurability set forth in the preceding section. Assuming that the necessary conditions of measurability put forward by de Finetti hold and that the binary relation $\geqslant$ can be read as "is at least as powerful as," we notice that each power index satisfies the following requirements: (1) $F_A^r \geqslant 0$, $r =$ Sh, B, CI, CB and $A \in \mathbb{A}$. In other words, each index takes values greater than or equal to zero. Thus, the first condition of measurability is satisfied by all indices.

In the case of probability measurement the second requirement is that $P(X) = 1$. This clearly holds for the Shapley-Shubik index as well as for the Banzhaf index because

$$\sum_{i \in N} F_i^r = 1, \quad \text{for } r = \text{Sh, B}.$$

This property does not, simpliciter, hold for the Coleman indices. The sum taken over the number of critical defections of each player is not necessarily equal to the number of losing coalitions in Coleman's first index. Nor does the property hold in general for the second index of Coleman. Upon closer inspection, however, this is more or less a matter of standardization. For Banzhaf and Coleman indices there are both standardized and non-standardized version s. For example, *Holler* [1978] uses a standardized Coleman index while *Straffin* [1978] utilizes a non-standardized Banzhaf index. From the point of view of interpreting what "power" means in various situations, the non-standardized indices seem to be more useful than the standardized ones.

The third requirement for measurability was that for all $A, B \in \mathbb{A}$: $A \cap B = \emptyset$ implies that $P(A \cup B) = P(A) + P(B)$. The translation for our purposes would be the following: for any distinct coalitions $A, B \in \mathbb{A}$:

$$F_{A \cup B}^r = F_A^r + F_B^r, \; r = \text{Sh, B, CI, CB}.$$

This property of additivity does not hold for any of the indices. As a counterexample, consider the following one taken from *Brams* [1975, 177–178]. In a voting body of seven members each with one vote, the parties A and B have 2 seats each and party C 3 seats. The decision rule is 4. The power of each party both in terms of the Shapley-Shubik index and the Banzhaf index is 1/3. If now the party C is split into three "fractions" D, E and F, each with one member, the power distribution in the voting body changes. In terms of the Banzhaf index A and B now have the power of 2/7 each while D, E and F have each 1/7. In terms of the Shapley-Shubik index the new distribution is $A = 36/120$, $B = 36/120$, $D, E, F = 16/120$. The sum of powers of D, E and F is in terms of the Banzhaf index $3/7 = 9/21$ whereas the power of C in the original body is 7/21. Similarly, in the case of the Shapley-Shubik index the sum of powers of D, E and F equals 48/120, whereas the power of C is only $1/3 = 40/120$. Thus, for both the Shapley-Shubik and Banzhaf index it is *not* the case that for all $A, B \in \mathbb{A}$: $F^r_{A \cup B} = F^r_A + F^r_B$; $r =$ Sh, B.

It is straightforward to verify that the same applies to the Coleman indices as well. As was pointed out above the Coleman indices can be obtained as proportional transformations of the Banzhaf index. Hence,

$$F^{\mathrm{CI}}_{A \cup B} = c \cdot F^{\mathrm{B}}_{A \cup B},$$

with c constant given the seat distribution and decision rule of the body. Similarly,

$$F^{\mathrm{CI}}_A = c \cdot F^{\mathrm{B}}_A$$

and

$$F^{\mathrm{CI}}_A = c \cdot F^{\mathrm{B}}_B.$$

If

$$F^{\mathrm{B}}_{A \cup B} \neq F^{\mathrm{B}}_A + F^{\mathrm{B}}_B$$

as in the previous example, then obviously

$$c \cdot F^{\mathrm{B}}_{A \cup B} \neq c \cdot F^{\mathrm{B}}_A + c \cdot F^{\mathrm{B}}_B$$

or

$$F^{\mathrm{CI}}_{A \cup B} \neq F^{\mathrm{CI}}_A + F^{\mathrm{CI}}_B.$$

Hence, the nonadditivity holds also for the Coleman indices.

As a conclusion from the previous observations we may state that none of the power indices outlined above is an additive measure of power. In other words, none of the indices can be used to realize the relation "is at least as powerful as" which was discussed in the preceding section. Stated still in another way, there is no way in which we can assign numbers to coalitions of $\mathbb{A}$ so that the ordering of coalitions according to the $\geqslant$ relation would coincide with the order of the numbers. And yet I have argued that the necessary and sufficient conditions for the realizability of $\geqslant$ are quite plausible if the relation is interpreted as "is at least as powerful as." Consequently, this relation is realizable under the stated conditions, but none of the above power indices realizes it.

In a sense the failure of the power indices to realize $\geqslant$ is justified as one can readily construct a measure realizing $\geqslant$ which, however, would be implausible on other grounds. One can define F: $\mathbb{A} \rightarrow \mathrm{Re}$ so that $\forall A \in \mathbb{A}$:

$$F(A) = \frac{n_A}{n}$$

where n_A is the number of members in the coalition A and n is the number of members in the voting body. This would, however, be a trivial measure although a formally correct one. It is trivial and unacceptable as a power index on the grounds that the decisions are made under fixed rules and these rules give obviously some coalitions more and others less power than their vote share would indicate. The above power indices try to capture this feature. One notices that the problem of just allocation of seats given the distribution of support is in the systems of proportional representation being solved (roughly) in a way that presupposes the additive measure of power.

5. Nonadditive Measures

If the power indices are not additive measures of power, one may turn to nonadditive measurability for rescue. Obviously, if some real valued function fails to be an additive measure it can certainly be a nonadditive one. Let us now take a look at a nonadditive measure which comes otherwise close to the above defined probability measure [see *Terano/Sugeno*]. Consider a finite set X and a sigma-algebra H on it. If the subsets of X are coalitions, we can obviously assume that the set algebra of subsets of X is closed under union, i.e., a sigma-algebra. The function g: $H \rightarrow$ Re with the following properties:

(1) $g(\emptyset) \neq 0$, $g(X) = 1$, and
(2) $A, B \in H$ and $A \subset B$ imply $g(A) \leqslant g(B)$,

is an example of a measure which instead of being additive is monotonic. We notice that according to (2) whenever a set is a proper subset of another set, the measure g assigns at least as large value to the latter as to the former. Hence, the measure allows the assignment of numbers in a manner that imposes a different type of relation upon the elements of H. It allows a partial ordering of the elements of H. Obviously, the property (2) is a reasonable one if we consider the comparative power measurement: it is plausible to require that if a coalition splits into a set of subcoalitions, ceteris paribus none of these has more power than the original coalition. Clearly then our measures of power should reflect this property. And indeed both the Shapley-Shubik index and the Banzhaf index are special cases of the monotonic measures as one can readily verify by looking at the computation formulae of the indices. In the case of the Shapley-Shubik index, a subset of players cannot possibly be more often pivotal than a larger set of which it is a subset. Similarly, looking at the Banzhaf index it cannot be the case that a set A of players can turn more coalitions from winning ones into losing ones by defecting than a set B of players if $A \subset B$. The non-standardized Coleman indices and the non-standardized Banzhaf index fail to satisfy the property (1) as was pointed out earlier.

The fact that the Shapley-Shubik index and the Banzhaf index are monotonic measures implies that they are two special cases of an infinite family of similar functions satisfying (1) and (2). Their justification must then be based on substantial considerations. More important implication is, however, this: the power indices which are of monotonic type cannot be used to make quantitative comparisons of power. In other words, by looking at the index values one cannot meaningfully say that the power of A is x times larger than the power of B. If we interpret the $\geqslant$ relation as has been done earlier, the monotonic measures give an infinite number of possible value assignments for each $A \in H$ such that the above conditions (1) and (2) are fulfilled.

Would it then be advisable to make more assumptions concerning the measures so as to eliminate implausible alternative monotonical measures? Yes, it would and that has often been done by the scholars who have devised the power indices. The strategy has often been to set more and more restrictions upon the measure so as to end up with just one. From the viewpoint of the present paper it is, however, important to bear in mind that the failure of being additive measure is a very crucial limitation of the above power indices because via additivity only we can be sure of the uniqueness of the realization of the $\geqslant$ relation axiomatized above. Indeed, the resorting to monotonic instead of additive measures entails that much of the rationale of measurement is lost because in monotonic measures the numbers (i.e., the values of the measurement function) do not have the same meaning as in the additive measures.

6. Concluding Remarks

In the preceding we have given a new interpretation to the $\geqslant$ relation defined over a set algebra. We have observed that the conditions or axioms that guarantee the existence of an additive measure can be given a plausible interpretation in terms of the relation "is at least as powerful as" defined over the set algebra of coalitions. We have, however, noticed that none of the non-standardized power indices discussed is an additive measure. On the other hand, it turns out that the non-standardized versions of two of them satisfy the conditions of monotonicity. This is a much more general property than additivity and consequently substantial assumptions are needed in order to guarantee the uniqueness of measures. But even with these additional assumptions the numbers assigned to coalitions to represent their power lose much of their importance; indeed, only partially ordinal significance can be given to the values of monotonic measurement functions.

In the light of the preceding discussion one can see why the power indices sometimes produce counter-intuitive results. Some of these have been called paradoxes [see *Brams*, 176–182; *Brams/Affuso*]. The so-called paradox of size appears in situations of the type discussed in section 4 where the split of a party into constituent parts actually increases the sum of the power of the constituents. This is an obvious consequence as well as an indication of non-additivity of the indices. The same applies to another "paradox", the paradox of new members which consists of the fact that the power index values of some of the members of a collectivity may increase when new members are called upon to join the collectivity. Again this is a straight-forward case of non-additivity. What we have done above is to provide a measurement-theoretic explanation for these "paradoxes".

It seems then that the issue of which power index to choose must be settled on substantial grounds if the choice must be made between the Shapley-Shubik and Banzhaf indices. But, of course, one can always construct other indices. Without clear criteria of admissibility this process may, however, go on indefinitely. What is called for, therefore, is a view of the collective decision making that goes beyond the surface of seat and support distributions to an analysis of the political actor. Especially a decision oriented view of power seems to have an important place in the theory of power. By this I mean a perspective that takes into account in addition to the objective features of seat distribution, decision rule etc., also the subjective ones related to rationality and risk posture. Some theoretical background and justification for the Shapley-Shubik index has been found in the theory of bargaining games [see *Harsanyi; Roth; Nurmi*]. Similarly, the Banzhaf index of power has recently been given an extensive mathematical analysis by *Dubey/Shapley* [1979]. Probabilistic interpretations of both the Shapley-Shubik and Banzhaf indices have been discussed by *Straffin* [1977, 1978]. An important property of the power indices is the stability of the outcomes which assign the power index valued payoffs to each player. I have elsewhere discussed this property of the indices [*Nurmi*, 1980]. These studies have uncovered important theoretical properties of the indices. It seems that instead of arguing for the superiority of any one of the indices in general terms, it is advisable to look at the theoretical properties of them in the effort to assess their applicability in concrete cases.

References

Banzhaf, J.F., III: One Man, 3.312 Votes. Villanova Law Review **13**, 1968, 304–332.
Brams, S.J.: Game Theory and Politics. New York 1975.
Brams, S.J., and *P. Affuso*: Power and Size: A New Paradox. Theory and Decision **7**, 1976, 29–56.
Coleman, J.S.: Control of Collectivities and the Power of a Collectivity to Act. Social Choice. Ed. by B. Lieberman. New York 1971, 269–299.
Dubey, P., and *L.S. Shapley*: Mathematical Properties of the Banzhaf Power Index. Mathematics of Operations Research **4**, 1979, 99–131.
de Finetti, B.: Sul significato soggettivo della probabilita. Fundamenta Mathematicae **17**, 1931, 298–329 (quoted from *Niiniluoto* [1975]).
Harsanyi, J.C.: Rational Behavior and Bargaining Equilibrium in Games and Social Situations. Cambridge 1977.
Holler, M.J.: A Priori Party Power and Government Formation. Munich Social Science Review **4**, 1978, 25–41.
Kraft, C., *J. Pratt*, and *A. Seidenberg*: Intuitive Probability on Finite Sets. Annals of Mathematical Statistics **30**, 1959, 408–419.
Luce, R.D.: Sufficient Conditions for the Existence of a Finitely Additive Probability Measure. Annals of Mathematical Statistics **38**, 1967, 780–786.
Niiniluoto, I.: Todennäköisyyden lajeista (On the kinds of probability) Yhteiskuntatieteiden eksakti metodologia. Ed. by P. Tuomela. Helsinki 1975.
Nurmi, H.: Power and Support. Munich Social Science Review **4**, 1978, 5–24.
– : Game Theory and Power Indices. Zeitschrift für Nationalökonomie **40**, 1980, 35–58.
Riker, W.H., and *L. Shapley*: Weighted Voting. Representation: Nomos X. Ed. by R. Pennock and J. Chapman. New York 1968.
Roth, A.: The Shapley Value as a von Neumann-Morgenstern Utility. Econometrica **45**, 1977, 657–664.
Scott, D.: Measurement Structures and Linear Inequalities. Journal of Mathematical Psychology **1**, 1964, 233–247.
Scott, D., and *P. Suppes*: Foundational Aspects of Theories of Measurement. Journal of Symbolic Logic **23**, 1958, 113–128.
Shapley, L.: A Value for *N*-Person Games. Contributions to the Theory of Games. Ed. by H.W. Kuhn and A.W. Tucker. (Annals of Mathematical Studies vol. 28), 1953.
Shapley, L., and *M. Shubik*: A Method of Evaluating the Distribution of Power in a Committee System. American Political Science Review **48**, 1954, 787–792.
Straffin, P.D.: Probability Models for Power Indices. Game Theory and Political Science. Ed. by P.C. Ordeshook. New York 1978.
– : Homogeneity, Independence, and Power Indices. Public Choice **30**, 1977, 107–118.
Terano, T., and *M. Sugeno*: Conditional Fuzzy Measures and Their Applications. Fuzzy Sets and Their Applications to Cognitive and Decision Processes. Ed. by K.-S. Fu, K. Tanaka and M. Shimura. New York 1975.

5. The Empirical Approach

Holler, M.J. (Ed.): Power, Voting, and Voting Power ©Physica-Verlag, Würzburg (Germany) 1981

Party Power and Government Formation: A Case Study[1])

M.J. Holler, Munich

1. Introduction

This is a report of an analysis of voting power in the Finnish Parliament. The purpose of the analysis was (a) to reveal some characteristics of the indices for measuring a priori voting power, (b) to discuss the descriptive power of the chosen indices with respect to the composition of government, (c) to gain additional insight in the parliamentary system of Finland. Various power indices were calculated and compared to seat ratios and participation in Government. The numerical results indicate that some characteristics of Government formation, which are thought to be caused by an ideological bias, may as well be "explained" by the power indices. Two parties, the left-wing Democratic Union of the Finnish People (SKDL), and the right-wing Conservative Party (Kok), seem to be the victims of the numerical structure of the Finnish Parliament.

2. The Concept of Power and Power Measurement

This paper analyzes power in the context of a weighted majority game, picturing hypothetical collective decisions in a non-hypothetical parliament. Power is understood, following Max Weber's definition, as "the *probability* that one *actor* within a social relationship will be in a position to carry out his own will despite *resistance*" [*Weber*, p. 152]. The *actors* this paper deals with are political parties. They are considered to be teams formed to carry out the common will of their members through parliamentary decision making, i.e., by introducing motions and by voting on introduced motions. To simplify we will assume that the party representatives vote as a bloc. Thus, the number of votes of a party is given by the number of party members holding a seat. The *resistance* originates from the rivalry of the actors (i.e., parties and coalitions) who try to carry out opposing wills through voting in parliament. If the decision rule implicates some majority rule, only one of the opposing motions on a certain issue will be passed. The higher the likelihood

[1]) This article is a revised version of the author's article "A Priori Party Power and Government Formation" published in Munich Social Science Review 4, 1978. The author is grateful to Jürgen Schielke for the collection of data, to R.J. Johnston for his computer program, to Robert Koll for aid in operating the computor program, and to Jacqueline Mitchell for editorial work on the paper.

for a party to win a ballot, the higher its probability to enforce its will and hence the more powerful it is [see *Wittman*]. This is the underlying concept of the various indices used in measuring power. A profound theoretical discussion of the indices is to be found elsewhere.[2]) I shall restrict this analysis to the usage of (a) a minimum winning coalition index (MWC), and (b) the (normalized) Banzhaf index. (Precise definitions are given later.) For the analyzed seat distributions, the values of the well-known Shapley-Shubik power index are almost identical with the values of the Banzhaf index, when calculated under the simple majority rule. I have chosen the normalized version of the Banzhaf index to make the values comparable to the seat ratios.

The calculation of power indices may give information about the inner structure of hypothetical voting bodies and the impact of various decision rules. This might be helpful for designing efficient collective decision units. Power indices may also help us to understand the process which determines the seat distribution and decision rules of voting bodies.[3]) Furthermore, the usage of power indices may reveal to what extent the coalition actually formed (and therefore the formation of government) is based on ideological (programmatic) consensus of the colluding units, and to what extent it is pure arithmetic that fulfills the condition of a given decision rule. Whether this arithmetic is better represented by the seat distribution or by power indices, which measure the a priori voting power by combining the seat distribution and the voting rule, is a question open to discussion. This is illustrated by the following analysis.

3. The Political Frame

Most of the parliaments of the western parliamentary democracies are either two or "deux et demi" [see *Attali*, p. 156] voting bodies (FRG, Austria, Britain, Canada, Australia). Others show the dominance of one party opposed by a comparatively strong coalition of smaller parties (Sweden, Norway), or the rivalry of two ideologically bound coalitions (France). In all these cases the power indices are quite obvious, which certainly does not mean that they are of no analytical value. On the contrary, it is not difficult to list arguments which are used in daily discussion and which show that people are aware of voting power that deviates from seat distribution.

Multi-party systems seem to be a much more fascinating and difficult test for power indices. However, most of these multi-party systems are very unstable. Some change completely within a period of thirty years. Others, as in Italy, show a basic asymmetry. Following the footsteps of *Axelrod* [1970] I thought about including Italy into the analysis, as Italy shows a rather stable party system. As the communists, a nonmarginal frac-

---

[2]) See *Coleman* [1972], *Allingham* [1975], *Brams* [1975], and *Straffin* Jr. [1977]. See also the contributions of Hannu Nurmi in this volume.

[3]) On July 12th, 1976, the nine heads of state of the member countries of the European Community agreed to increase the number of seats in the European Community from 198 to 410, thereby considerably modifying the relative ratios of representatives per state. However, there is no majority coalition in the decided seat distribution, given bloc voting, which could not be formed in accordance with the old seat distribution and vice versa. Thus the Coleman-Banzhaf index, as well as the Shapley value, must be the same in both distributions [see *Holler/Kellermann; Johnston*].

tion, have been excluded from incumbency, the a priori voting power will not be directly reflected by the historical facts. Only the proverbial instability of Italian government coalitions may reflect the communists' (voting) power in the Italian parliament. In Finland no party which has had more than 5 % of the seats in two subsequent legislative periods has been excluded from government during the past thirty years. Thus members of seven different political parties, excluding nonparty experts, have held a position as minister. Neutrality might be one reason for this ideological variety in the selection of government members. However, Austria, Sweden, and other countries are also neutral, and do not experience this variety. It seems more reasonable to assume that the intermediary function of the Finnish government, tying the executive as represented by the President to parliamentary control, allows for its greater ideological variety. This can be understood by taking a closer look at the political system of Finland.[4])

The supreme executive power is vested in the President of the Republic. He is elected by the Finnish people for a term of six years through an electoral college of 300 members. The president determines Finland's relations with foreign powers. He is Commander-in-Chief of the armed forces. He appoints the members of the Council of State which is identical with the Government. In the exercise of his authority, the President is bound to cooperate with the Parliament through the Council of State. For enforcement, the decisions of the President must be countersigned by the Minister concerned (member of the Council of State). Thus the cabinet becomes responsible for the President's decisions. Since the cabinet and each of its individual members must enjoy the confidence of the Parliament, the executive power is responsible to the Parliament. A statement of no-confidence by a majority of Parliament leads to the resignation of the Council or the members concerned.

The legislative power is vested in the Parliament, although the President participates in legislation not only by sanctioning laws, on which he may exercise a suspensive veto, but also by issuing decrees. Both, Parliament and President have the right to introduce motions in legislative affairs.

Matters other than legislative ones as well as legislative ones which are not constitutional law (or a bill with the character of a constitutional law) must be approved by at least a simple majority. In enacting a constitutional law two modes of procedure can be followed. The bill may be declared as being urgent by a 5/6 majority, and then be approved by a 2/3 majority in the same parliament. The second method is such, that the bill is approved for being held by a majority. Then, after elections, it must finally be approved by the new parliament through a 2/3 majority.

4. The Execution of Party Power

In analyzing party power which is exercised in competition with the will of other parties, the simple majority rule is of a far more delicate interest than the 5/6 and 2/3 major-

---

[4]) That which follows is more or less an excerpt from two brochures, "the Finnish Parliament" and "Finland: Facts and Figures" both published in Helsinki 1976, and an excerpt from the Constitution of Finland (in force). I have selected the paragraphs and details with regard to the subject under examination. The presentation is therefore somewhat superficial.

ity rules which presume a large consensus among the Members of Parliament anyhow. This analysis will therefore exclusively concentrate on the simple majority rule.

As far as I know, there is no complete registration as to which motions were brought in by which party (member) and which party carried them or not. I shall simply take the composition of the Governments (Councils of State) as an indicator of party collusion. The Government is viewed automatically as enjoying the confidence of Parliament until the Parliament specifically expresses its lack of confidence. Therefore, it may be assumed as long as there is no statement of no-confidence, that the government is supported by a coalition of at least half of the Members of Parliament. This support may also be indirect. If no alternative government can be expected to have the confidence of Parliament, it could be that the Government in power is accepted by parties which are not represented in the Council of State. However we cannot really count them as exercising (indirect) governmental power.

In order to evaluate the role of the Finnish Government we must restate its dependence on the President who appoints its members, as well as its dependence on the Parliament which may dismiss each single member. Under such circumstances, a change in the party composition of the members of the Council of State introduces a different ideological pattern, and has but a rather moderate impact on the political, social, economic, and cultural system. Thus, in general, Government is open to all parties. Frequent changes of government as well as changes in ideological dedication do not greatly disturb either the efficiency of the political apparatus or the basic trends in Finnish society. Given the Downsian hypothesis that parties strive for incumbency [*Downs*, pp. 24ff.], the composition of Government reflects the voting power of the parties holding seats in Parliament.

5. The Measurement of Power

The Banzhaf index refers to the concept of the essential (or critical) coalition member. In the context of our analysis, this implies the following. If the remaining coalition still is a winning coalition after subtraction of the votes of a certain party fraction, then this party is not essential for this coalition. However, if after subtraction a swing from a winning to a loosing coalition occurs, the party is essential. The number of coalitions n_i, in which a party i is essential, is divided by the total number of all possible swings. For a given seat distribution and a given decision (voting) rule the normalized Banzhaf index of a party i thus is:

$$\beta_i = \frac{n_i}{\sum_{i=1}^{N} n_i}, \quad N \text{ being the number of parties.} \tag{1}$$

The calculation of this power index shall be illustrated by the following simple example: Given a set of three parties (1, 2, 3) and a seat distribution $V(1) = 50$, $V(2) = 40$, and $V(3) = 10$. If a simple majority is acquired (case (a)), the set of all winning coalitions is given by C_1 (1, 2); C_2 (1, 3); C_3 (1, 2, 3). In coalitions C_1 and C_2 all party fractions are essential. In coalition C_3 only the defection of 1 would be critical. If party 1 or party 2 (but not both) leave C_3, this will not cause a swing. Thus party 1 is essential in all three coalitions: $n_1 = 3$. Party 2 is essential in only one coalition and so is party three: $n_2 = n_3 = 1; n_1 + n_2 + n_3 = 5$. From this result we derive: $\beta_1 = 3/5, \beta_2 = 1/5$, and $\beta_3 = 1/5$ as power indices.

If we forget the simple majority rule (case (a)) and introduce the 50 %-rule (case (b)) we have, given the above seat distribution, the following winning coalitions: C_1 (1); C_2 (1, 2); C_3 (1, 2, 3); and C_4 (2, 3).

Party 1 is essential in C_1 and C_2, whereas party 2 and 3 are essential in C_4. In C_3 no individual party is essential. The power indices therefore are: $\beta_1 = 1/2; \beta_2 = 1/4$; and $\beta_3 = 1/4$. We see that for identical seat distributions different power distributions may result for different decision rules.

Since the vote distribution has changed during the thirty years on which we shall base our analysis, we shall weight the power indices β_i with e_t. "e_t" is the time share of each seat distribution which is equal to the relative time between two subsequent elections. Since nine legislative periods shall be analysed, we have nine different e_t (t=1, . . . , 9). Hence the weighted power index of a party i may be expressed as:

$$P_i = \sum_{t=1}^{9} e_t \beta_{it}. \tag{2}$$

Criticism of the Banzhaf index is focused on the assumption that all coalitions are equally likely. This assumption is expressed through the equal weighting of all essential elements of a coalition. There are many theories which say that some coalitions are more likely to be formed than others. *Riker's* "Size Principle" [1962, pp. 32ff.] claims that if 50 seats are required as a minimum, then the winning coalition which comes closest to having this minimum of 50 seats will be formed. *Leiserson's* bargaining theory [1968] says that the coalition which is initiated by a minimum of bargaining partners is more likely to be formed than others. Thus, if a winning coalition can be initiated by 2, 3, or 4 parties, the 2-party coalition shall result. *Axelrod* [1970] tested the hypothesis of closed range minimum coalitions through use of the Italian parliamentary history. This hypothesis claims that coalitions which consist of a minimum of ideologically neighbouring parties are more stable and therefore longer in power than others.

There is no doubt that size and ideological homogeneity are relevant factors for coalition formation. However, these dimensions cannot be accepted without interpretation. There is not always agreement on a one dimension ideological scale among voters as well as among political parties.[5]) Even the size is a vague dimension. We have to define the "size of a party," the "size of a coalition," and so forth. We also have to analyse whether the claim of a party concerning its coalition surplus (cabinet positions, prestige, executive power) is related to its membership size, to the number of seats held in parliament, or to the number of seats forming the coalition.

---

[5]) The Swedish People's Party of Finland, for instance, is often seen as a conservative right-wing party, although some of its members consider themselves very close to the left. Conservative voters blame the party for its cooperation with the Social Democratic Party in many governments. Nevertheless, about 80 % of all Swedish speaking Finns vote for this party. They do not see it as representing a certain ideology, but rather as an expression of the interests of a national (or cultural) minority.

Nevertheless, a minimum winning coalition index (MWC) was calculated for reference. A MWC was hereby defined as a coalition formed only by essential party blocs.[6]) Each MWC is equally likely. Since by definition, each coalition can be destroyed by each individual member (party bloc), the voting power can be plausibly defined as the frequency with which a party fraction was part of potential minimum winning coalitions. As in the calculation of the P_i-index, we multiply the MWC-index (that was due to a certain seat distribution) with the time share e_t during which the seat distribution was valid. The MWC-index M of a party i thus is:

$$M_i = \sum_{t=1}^{9} e_t \cdot \mathrm{MWC}_{it}. \tag{3}$$

Hereby MWC_{it} is the index of the specific seat distribution of party i for the legislative period t.

The MWC-index has the noteworthy property that a party 1 which has more seats in a voting body than party 2 might have a smaller MWC_{it} than party 2. For example, after the elections of 1951 the "Democratic Union of the Finnish People" (SKDL) had 43 seats in Parliament, and the "Finnish Social Democratic Party" (SDP) had 53. The corresponding index for the SKDL is 0.214, whereas the $\mathrm{MWC}_{SDP/1961}$ is only 0.179. The reversal of the power / seat ratio is due to the neglect of all non-minimum winning coalitions. If the larger SDP-party-fraction is added to a non-winning proto-coalition which thereby becomes winning it is quite likely that one of the smaller member parties becomes unessential. The coalition as a whole does thereby not contribute to the power ratio of any of the participating parties like the SDP.

This property of the MWC_{it}-index causes doubt concerning its validity. Here this index is used to picture an alternative to the Banzhaf index which seems more adequate in the context of this analysis.

6. The Measurement of Participation

The empirical performance of a party i with respect to participation in Government will be measured by the following formula:

$$G_i = \sum_{r=1}^{62} t_r \cdot m_{ir}. \tag{4}$$

There have been 62 different Governments during the analyzed time span: we thus label the various Governments "r", whereby $r = 1, \ldots, 62$. Correspondingly, t_r indicates each Government's time ratio. (From a legal point of view, a Finnish Government is in power until the nomination of the succeeding Government.) m_{ir} represents the relative number of chairs which members of party i held in the Government r, $i = 1, \ldots, 11$.

The latter factor, m_{ir}, gives equal weights to each chair in the cabinet. This assumption

---

[6]) This definition of a minimum winning coalition is not in accordance with *Riker's* Size Principle [1962, pp. 32ff.]. It is in accordance with the game theoretical analysis of *v. Neumann/Morgenstern* [1953] concerning coalition formation.

is open to criticism, however, it is by no means clear what the better choice concerning weights would be. Because of the strong executive position of the President, some of the classical chairs (like foreign affairs) imply less executive competence than in other parliamentary systems. The executive competence of a minister seems to be largely determined by (a) his (or her) personality, (b) the composition of the cabinet, i.e., the composition of the coalition, (c) the interest of and the relation to the President, and (d) the factual contemporary political needs. Because of the large fluctuations in Government, it seems justified to assume that these factors are, in the course of time, balanced out for each cabinet chair.

The empirical performance of party i with respect to its representation in Parliament will be measured by its seat ratio, i.e., the relative number of seats held by members of party i, s_{it}, multiplied by the time share e_t. Both correspond to the duration of the legislative period t ($t = 1, \ldots, 9$). From this we obtain the formula:

$$S_i = \sum_{t=1}^{9} e_t \cdot s_t. \tag{5}$$

7. The Numerical Results

The following Table 1 shows the values of the Banzhaf index as calculated from the seat distributions of the nine legislative periods from 1948 to 1979. The calculation corresponds with the above formula (1).

The relative voting power values PR indicate that the seat shares are a rather poor proxy for the voting power as defined by the Banzhaf index. We can now use the values of Table 1 to calculate P_i from formula (2) and S_i from formula (5). The corresponding values as well as the values of M_i and G_i are shown in Table 2.

If we abstract from the minimum winning coalition index M_i (which needs further interpretation because of the indicated nonmonotonic relation to seat ratios), we obtain the ordering of the values as pictured on the right hand side of Table 2. We realize that the power indices P_i describe the empirical power as expressed by the index G_i more adequately than the seat ratio does if we consider only the six parties ($i = 1, \ldots, 6$) which were represented in all parliaments since 1948. This is confirmed by comparison of the numerical differences:

$$D_{PG} = \sum_{i=1}^{11} |P_i - G_i| \text{ and } D_{SG} = \sum_{i=1}^{11} |S_i - G_i|.$$

D_{PG} is about .446 and D_{SG} about .539. We see that $D_{PG} < D_{SG}$. This indicates that the power indices P_i may give a better description of the historical (and perhaps also the future) composition of Government than the seat ratios S_i.

We also realize from Table 2 that the government indices G_i of the parties $i = 2$ and 3 are smaller than their power indices (P_2 and P_3) and their seat ratios (S_2 and S_3). Their participation in Government was much less than the seat ratio would indicate. However, since P_2 and P_3 are smaller (although not by very much) than S_2 and S_3, the shortcoming in participation might be due to the unfavourable a priori voting power of the two parties. All the other parties which have participated in Government during the last thirty

Year		1 SDP	2 SKDL	3 Kok	4 Kesk	5 RKP	6 LKP	7 SMP	8 SKL	9 SKYP	10 SPK	11 SPSL	Others	e_t
1948	s_i	27.00	19.00	16.50	28.00	7.00	2.50							
	β_i	28.57	14.29	14.29	28.57	14.29	0.0							
	PR	1.0583	0.7519	0.8658	1.0204	2.0408	–							0.096
1951	s_i	26.50	21.50	14.00	25.50	7.50	5.00							
	β_i	28.57	21.43	7.14	28.57	7.14	7.14							
	PR	1.0782	0.9967	0.5102	1.1204	0.9524	1.4286							0.088
1954	s_i	27.00	21.50	12.00	26.50	6.50	6.50							
	β_i	28.57	21.43	7.14	28.57	7.14	7.14							
	PR	1.0582	0.9967	0.5952	1.0782	1.0989	1.0989							0.142
1958	s_i	24.00	25.00	14.50	24.00	7.00	4.00					1.50		
	β_i	24.14	27.59	6.9	24.14	6.9	6.9					3.45		
	PR	1.0057	1.1034	0.4756	1.0057	0.9852	1.7241					2.2989		0.118
1962	s_i	19.00	23.50	16.00	26.50	7.00	6.50					1.00	.5	
	β_i	17.37	23.31	10.59	30.08	8.05	6.36					2.97	1.27	
	PR	0.9144	0.9917	0.6621	1.1353	1.1501	0.9778					2.0661	2.5424	0.135
1966	s_i	27.50	20.50	13.00	24.50	6.00	4.50	.5				3.50		
	β_i	31.70	21.88	6.7	25.45	6.7	4.02	0.45				3.13		
	PR	1.1526	1.0671	0.5151	1.0386	1.1161	0.8929	0.8929				0.8929		0.131
1970	s_i	26.00	18.00	18.50	18.00	6.00	4.00	9.00	.5					
	β_i	28.69	16.39	17.21	16.39	9.02	0.82	10.66	0.82					
	PR	1.1034	0.9107	0.9304	0.9107	1.5027	0.2049	1.1840	1.6393					0.056
1972	s_i	27.50	18.50	17.00	17.50	5.00	3.50	9.00	2.00					
	β_i	30.08	17.07	14.63	16.26	6.5	3.25	8.94	3.25					
	PR	1.0939	0.9229	0.8608	0.9292	1.3008	0.9292	0.9937	1.6260					0.122
1975	s_i	27.00	20.00	17.50	19.50	5.00	4.50	1.00	4.50	.5	.5			
	β_i	32.92	17.08	12.92	17.08	6.25	5.42	1.67	5.42	0.63	0.63			
	PR	1.2191	0.8542	0.7381	0.8761	1.2500	1.2037	1.6667	1.2037	1.2500	1.2500			0.113
1979	s_i	26.00	17.50	23.50	18.00	5.00	2.00	3.00	5.00					

s_i = Relative number of seats (seat share) of party i
β_i = Banzhaf index of party i
PR = Relative voting power (β_i/s_i)
e_t = Time share of the legislative period t

Tab. 1

Party i	(1) S_i	(2) M_i	(3) P_i	(4) G_i	Orderings of the various measures
1 SDP	.257	.180	.277	.295	$S_1 < P_1 < G_1$
2 SKDL	.213	.171	.205	.047	$G_2 < P_2 < S_2$
3 Kok	.152	.149	.103	.037	$G_3 < P_3 < S_3$
4 Kesk	.236	.167	.243	.403	$S_4 < P_4 < G_4$
5 RKP	.064	.132	.078	.080	$S_5 < P_5 < G_5$
6 LKP	.046	.102	.049	.056	$S_6 < P_6 < G_6$
7 SMP	.017	.036	.019		
8 SKL	.007	.028	.011		$G_i < S_i < P_i$
9 SKYP	.000	.002	.001		but $G_i = 0$, $i = 7, 8, 9, 10$
10 SPK	.000	.002	.001		
11 SPSL	.008	.027	.012	.009	$S_{11} < G_{11} < P_{11}$
	1.000	.996	.099	.927[1])	

[1]) These ratios do not add up to 1 because of the "administrative governments." These were not composed of party members.

S_i = Seat ratio, i.e., relative number of seats held by members of party i multiplied by the time share e_t,

M_i = Minimum winning coalition index, weighted with the time share e_t,

P_i = Banzhaf index for party i weighted with the time ratios of the various governments (as defined by (2)),

G_i = Government (participation) index of party i (as defined by (4)).

Tab. 2

years have power indices which exceed their seat ratio. If we decode the numerical label, we realize that party 2 is the Democratic Union of Finnish People (SKDL), which is considered to occupy the left wing of the ideological scale of the parties in Parliament. We also see that party 3 is the Conservative party (Kok) which is considered to be the strongest right-wing party. Although the ideological scale is a rather dubious instrument for classifying party positions, it is widely accepted for the classification of these two parties. At first, the underrepresentation of SKDL and Kok might be attributed to their "extreme" ideological position. However, our calculation, which is not based on any ideological scaling at all, indicates that these two parties might be "victims" of their unfavourable a priori voting power.

8. Conclusion

Although the concepts used to measure voting power in this analysis are rather crude, the results advise us to consider the numerical structure of the voting body (as determined by the seat distribution *and* the decision rule) before claiming discrimination against or favouritism for a certain political group. It is evident that the concept of a priori voting power is a better tool for handling this problem than the concept of seat distribution.

References

Allingham, M.G.: Economic Power and Values of Games. Zeitschrift für Nationalökonomie **35**, 1975, pp. 293ff.

Attali, J.: Analyse economique de la vie politique. Paris 1972.

Axelrod, R.: Conflict of Interest: A Theory of Divergent Goals with Application to Politics. Chicago 1970.

Brams, S.J.: Game Theory and Politics. New York 1975.

Coleman, J.S.: Control of Collectivities and the Power of a Collectivity to Act. Social Choice. Ed. by B. Lieberman, New York 1972, 269–300.

Downs, A.: An Economic Theory of Democracy. New York 1957.

Holler, M.J., and *J. Kellermann*: Power in the European Parliament: What Will Change? Quality and Quantity **11**, 1977, pp. 189ff.

Johnston, R.J.: National Sovereignty and National Power in European Institutions. Environment and Planning **9**, 1977, pp. 569ff.

Leiserson, M.A.: Fractions and Coalitions in One-Party Japan: An Interpretation Based on The Theory of Games. American Political Science Review **62**, 1968, pp. 770ff.

Neumann, J.v., and *O. Morgenstern*: Theory of Games and Economic Behavior. 3rd ed. Princeton 1953.

Riker, W.H.: The Theory of Political Coalitions. New Haven 1962.

Straffin, P.D. Jr.: Homogeneity, Independence, and Power Indices. Public Choice **30**, 1977, pp. 107ff.

Weber, M.: The Theory of Social and Economic Organization. Ed. by T. Parsons. New York 1947.

Wittman, D.: Power in Electoral Games. Foundations and Applications of Decision Theory, Vol. II. Ed. by Hooker, Leach, and McClennen. Dordrecht 1978, 185–206.

Holler, M.J. (Ed.): Power, Voting, and Voting Power ©Physica-Verlag, Würzburg (Germany) 1981

The Distribution of Power in Specific Decision-Making Bodies

E. Bomsdorf, Köln

1. Introduction

In discussions regarding possible coalitions in the West-German Bundestag or similar bodies, attention is usually focused on the distribution of seats but rarely on the qualified majorities. Considering, for example, the 8th German Bundestag[1]), one can see that – if only the absolute majority is considered necessary for making decisions – the FDP, like all the other factions, can establish a majority with any other faction. If a coalition is to form not only an absolute majority, but rather a qualified majority of 2/3 there is no such majority which the FDP could establish with just one other parliamentary group. For the CDU/CSU and the SPD however, such a coalition does exist. Obviously the FDP's power depends on the qualified majority. On the other hand, it becomes clear that in a decision-making body like the German Bundestag the distribution of seats, or rather the distribution of votes, is not sufficient to characterize the distribution of power but that information about the qualified majority must be taken into consideration.

2. The Index

A number of approaches are available to measure the power of several groups or persons in decision-making bodies [cf. e.g., the juxtaposition in *Nurmi*].

In this paper we shall use a measure from Game Theory which can, in its application to decision-making bodies, from the view of statistics be interpreted in two ways. In the field of cooperative n-person-games the Shapley value [cf., e.g., *Shapley*] $\phi_i(v)$ is well known, which defines for the player i a value to measure in a certain way the power of this player. Applied to decision-making bodies, the Shapley value may be interpreted as an a-priori power index, measuring the power of the i-th member of a certain body by the expected winnings. All possible coalitions are regarded, whereby the sequence in which the players join the coalition is taken into account, and for each player the difference of the coalition's winnings with and without him is calculated.

---

[1]) The distribution of seats in the 8th Bundestag of 1976 to 1980 was CDU/CSU 244, SPD 213, FDP 39.

The formula is:

$$\phi_i(v) = \sum_{\substack{A \subseteq N \\ i \in A}} \frac{(n-|A|)!\,(|A|-1)!}{n!} (v(A) - v(A - \{i\}) \qquad i = 1, 2, \ldots, n.$$

N is the set of all n members of the decision-making body, A is a subset of N.

The application of the Shapley value for decision-making bodies is rather simply if these can be interpreted as weighted majority games[2]), i.e., if a number of votes r_i $(i = 1, 2, \ldots, n)$ can be assigned to each faction i (party i, player i), with $r = \sum_{i=1}^{n} r_i$,

$$v(A) = \begin{cases} 1 \text{ for } \sum_{i \in A} r_i \geqslant w \\ 0 \text{ for } \sum_{i \in A} r_i < w \end{cases} \qquad \text{and } w > \frac{1}{2} r,$$

thereby w is the threshold for a winning coalition as given by the decision rule.

The standardization which is carried out by setting $v(A) = 1$ resp. $v(A) = 0$ leads to a simple interpretation of the results. The Shapley value ϕ_i can then be interpreted as the probability for i to deliver the necessary votes for a qualified majority.

3. Numerical Results

In the following, the quantitative approach introduced above will be applied to some political bodies. It will illustrate the low relevancy, at times, of the distribution of votes, as well as the importance of a qualified majority or other rules for the decision-making possibilities of several groups in political life [cf. *Mann/Shapley; Shapley/Shubik*].

1st Application: The Chairman

Before the above approach is applied to special bodies – like the German Bundestag – a general situation shall be considered. In decision-making bodies, stalemates are frequent, i.e. the number of votes in favor of or against a proposal are equal. To prevent such a situation, it is often the chairman's vote which decides. What are the consequences of this rule for the chairman's power?

With an uneven number of members present in a body, a stalemate-situation is impossible.[3]) With an even number of members present, the chairman's voting power, in cases where he decides if the votes are tied, depends on the number of members in the body. In order to calculate the Shapley value, we assume, first of all, that the one-man-one-vote rule holds. Since it is only if the chairman belongs to this half, that exactly half of all

---

[2]) In the following we refrain from using v as an argument of ϕ since only decision-making bodies will be regarded which can be interpreted as weighted majority-games. As there are for all other approaches, there are also objections to the use of the Shapley-value. However this index is useful, because, as *Shapley* [1953] has shown, only this index fulfills certain conditions which can be reasonably expected of a power-index.

[3]) Abstinence from voting is counted with the refusals.

members of a specific body are able to carry through a motion, one can state that the chairman's importance be greater than that of each other member. Based on this situation, one can construct a weighted majority game.

Table 1 gives the Shapley values for the chairman (1st member) and all other members for the total of 2, 4, . . . , 14 members. As can be seen, the chairman's importance declines in absolute and relative terms as the number of members increases.[4])

Number of members	2	4	6	8	10	12	14
ϕ_1	1,0000	0,5000	0,3333	0,2500	0,2000	0,1667	0,1429
$\phi_{i\neq 1}$	0,0000	0,1667	0,1333	0,1071	0,0889	0,0758	0,0659

Tab. 1: Shapley values (ϕ_i) for members in a decision-making body with an even number of members, assuming that the one-man-one-vote rule holds. One exception is that, if votes are tied, the chairman (i = 1) has the deciding vote.

2nd Application: The 1st Bundestag of 1949 and the 8th Bundestag of 1976

In the following the above approach will be applied to the composition of the Bundestag for 1949 and for 1976.[5]) The computation of the power-indices for parties leads to the results given in tables 2, 3 and 4, depending upon the qualified majorities.[6]) The results in Table 2 show that in the case of an absolute majority, the power of the FDP in the 1st Bundestag of 1949 is obviously much greater than its number of seats reveals. If the qualified majority is a 2/3-majority, then each of the two large parties has an overwhelming importance, a 2/3-majority cannot be established without the CDU/CSU. Each of the other parties has less power.

Party	Distribution of Seats absolute	relative	Power-Index (absolute majority)	Power-Index · 402 (absolute majority)	Power-Index (2/3-majority)	Power-Index · 402 (2/3-majority)
CDU/CSU	139	0,3457	0,3256	130,9	0,5138	206,5
SPD	131	0,3259	0,2744	110,3	0,3890	156,4
FDP	52	0,1294	0,2253	90,6	0,0138	5,5
DP	17	0,0423	0,0363	14,6	0,0138	5,5
BP	17	0,0423	0,0363	14,6	0,0138	5,5
KPD	15	0,0373	0,0305	12,3	0,0138	5,5
WAV	12	0,0299	0,0274	11,0	0,0138	5,5
Zentrumspartei	10	0,0249	0,0220	8,8	0,0138	5,5
DRP	5	0,0124	0,0096	3,9	0,0138	5,5
SSW	1	0,0025	0,0032	1,3	0,0002	0,1
Notgemeinschaft	1	0,0025	0,0032	1,3	0,0002	0,1
Parteilos	1	0,0025	0,0032	1,3	0,0002	0,1
Parteilos	1	0,0025	0,0032	1,3	0,0002	0,1

Tab. 2: 1st Bundestag of 1949. Total Number of Seats: 402

[4]) In general, $\phi_1 = 1/n$ and $\phi_i = (n-1)/(n \cdot (2n-1))$ for $i = 2, 3, \ldots, 2n$, if $2n$ is the total number of members of the body under consideration.

[5]) Without the representatives from Berlin.

[6]) It is assumed that all members of a certain party vote as a bloc.

For the 1976 Bundestag we will, in addition to the current case of three factions, also discuss that of four factions, which was a topic of lively debate for a certain period of time. In the first case (Table 3) the situations arising are very different, depending on the qualified majorities. In the case of a simple majority decision rule all factions have the same power-index. Any two factions can establish an absolute majority, if they form a coalition. In the case of a 2/3-majority, the FDP plays no role, since the two other factions are needed in order to establish such a majority and together they already establish this majority. So the power index of the FDP in the case of an absolute majority makes it clear why the FDP held more and more important cabinet posts than one would have expected from its number of parliamentary seats.

Party	Distribution of Seats absolute	relative	Power-Index (absolute majority)	Power-Index · 496 (absolute majority)	Power-Index (2/3-majority)	Power-Index · 496 (2/3-majority)
CDU/CSU	244	0,4919	0,3333	165,3	0,5000	248,0
SPD	213	0,4294	0,3333	165,3	0,5000	248,0
FDP	39	0,0786	0,3333	165,3	0	0

Tab. 3: 8th Bundestag of 1976 (3 factions). Total Number of Seats: 496

This simple presentation points out that the a priori voting power of the various parties depends on a qualified majority. However in the case of an absolute majority, all parties have the same power as measured by their Shapley values – the votes of two factions are enough for an absolute majority but no party is able to establish this majority on its own. In the case of a 2/3-majority the FDP lacks importance since it can only establish a winning coalition with the two other parties; on the other hand, these parties can however establish a qualified majority together without the FDP.

How the situation would have been if we had had four instead of three factions is shown in Table 4. It reveals that the position of the SPD would have been stronger in the case of four factions. Without the SPD the other factions can establish an absolute majority only if they all form a coalition together. The SPD on the other hand could form such a majority with any other single faction in the Bundestag. The importance of the FDP diminishes, the CDU and the CSU divide the power index they held in the three-factions-case into two equal indices. For the achievement of a 2/3-majority the CSU obviously plays no role.

Party	Distribution of Seats absolute	relative	Power-Index (absolute majority)	Power-Index · 496 (absolute majority)	Power-Index (2/3-majority)	Power-Index · 496 (2/3-majority)
CDU	191	0,3851	0,1667	82,7	0,5000	248,0
CSU	53	0,1069	0,1667	82,7	0	0
SPD	213	0,4294	0,5000	248,0	0,5000	248,0
FDP	39	0,0786	0,1667	82,7	0	0

Tab. 4: 8th Bundestag of 1976 (4 factions). Total Number of Seats: 496

3rd Application: The 6th Reichstag of July 1932 and the 8th Reichstag of March 1933

In this example the power index shall be applied to the German Reichstag of July 1932 and of March 1933.

Party	Distribution of Seats absolute	relative	Power-Index (absolute majority)	Power-Index · 608 (absolute majority)	Power-Index (2/3-majority)	Power-Index · 608 (2/3-majority)
NSDAP	230	0,3783	0,5066	308,0	0,5183	315,1
DNVP	37	0,0609	0,0066	4,0	0,0340	20,7
Christlich Sozialer Volksdienst	3	0,0049	0,0023	1,4	0,0029	1,7
Landbund	2	0,0033	0,0015	0,9	0,0020	1,2
Landvolkpartei	1	0,0016	0,0008	0,5	0,0008	0,5
Bauernpartei	2	0,0033	0,0015	0,9	0,0020	1,2
Volksrechtspartei	1	0,0016	0,0008	0,5	0,0008	0,5
DVP	7	0,0115	0,0063	3,8	0,0069	4,2
Wirtschaftspartei	2	0,0033	0,0015	0,9	0,0020	1,2
BVP	22	0,0362	0,0066	4,0	0,0098	5,9
Zentrum	75	0,1234	0,1540	93,7	0,1070	65,1
DDP	4	0,0066	0,0034	2,1	0,0038	2,3
SPD	133	0,2188	0,1540	93,7	0,2026	123,2
KPD	89	0,1464	0,1540	93,7	0,1070	65,1

Tab. 5: 6th Reichstag of July 1932. Total Number of Seats: 608

The calculations show that the NSDAP was more important in the 6th Reichstag (Table 5) than could have been assumed from the number of seats which it had held. The NSDAP could have entered many possible coalitions in order to establish a qualified majority, independent of the type of majority, (disregarding the fact that some coalitions are unlikely for political reasons). The 8th Reichstag composition (Table 6) shows that some parties were of no importance with regard to the possibility of establishing an absolute majority.

Party	Distribution of Seats absolute	relative	Power-Index (absolute majority)	Power-Index · 647 (absolute majority)	Power-Index (2/3-majority)	Power-Index · 647 (2/3-majority)
NSDAP	288	0,4451	0,6000	388,2	0,5798	375,1
DNVP	52	0,0804	0,1000	64,7	0,0563	36,5
Christlich Sozialer Volksdienst	4	0,0062	0	0	0,0052	3,3
Landbund	1	0,0015	0	0	0,0008	0,5
Bauernpartei	2	0,0031	0	0	0,0016	1,0
DVP	2	0,0031	0	0	0,0016	1,0
BVP	19	0,0294	0	0	0,0385	24,9
Zentrum	73	0,1128	0,1000	64,7	0,0817	52,9
DStP	5	0,0077	0	0	0,0063	4,1
SPD	120	0,1855	0,1000	64,7	0,1385	89,6
KPD	81	0,1252	0,1000	64,7	0,0897	58,0

Tab. 6: 8th Reichstag of March 1933. Total Number of Seats: 647

The results illustrate, that the NSDAP was a priori of greater importance than one would imagine to be possible due to its share of votes, and, therefore, that it had a greater potential influence on the other parties. Carrying out these calculations for all Reichstags from 1919 to 1933 only after the election to the 6th Reichstag a party did emerge with a power index of more than 0.5, whereas, before, it seems that the multitude of relatively weak parties had complicated the formation of a coalition.

The power index used in this paper permits an approach to the quantitative analysis of the distribution of power in a decision-making body by taking qualified majorities into account. It can help to reveal the strategic position and the negotiating leverage of the parties in coalition talks.

The above examples assumed that all members of a party vote as a bloc. This assumption may not always be realistic, but very often reasonable. A further breakdown into groups within a party allows for additional analyses. It should be stressed once more that the application of this index to decision-making bodies gives only an a priori value and does not take possible preferences into account. It can however demonstrate the difficulty in coming to an agreement (i.e., in establishing a majority) when many members constitute the body, each member having thereby only a small degree of power.

Acknowledgement

Errors appearing in sums due to rounding are not corrected. The tables also show the values of all power indices multiplied with the total number of seats in the specific body. This facilitates the comparison between the distribution of power and the absolute distribution of seats.

References

Mann, J., and *L.S. Shapley*: Values of Large Games IV: Evaluating the Electoral College by Montecarlo Techniques. RAND RM 2651, Sept. 1960, and RM 3158, Mai 1962.

Nurmi, H.: Power and Support: The Problem of Representational Democracy. Munich Social Science Review **4**, 1978, 5–24.

Shapley, L.: A Value for *N*-Person Games. Contribution to the Theory of Games Vol. I. Ed. by H.W. Kuhn and A.W. Tucker. (Annals of Mathematical Studies Vol. 28), Princeton 1953, 307–317.

Shapley, L., and *M. Shubik*: A Method of Evaluating the Distribution of Power in a Commitee System. American Political Science Review **48**, 1954, 787–792.

Holler, M.J. (Ed.): Power, Voting, and Voting Power ©Physica-Verlag, Würzburg (Germany) 1981

Political Geography and Political Power[1])

R.J. Johnston, Sheffield

1. Introduction

With the widespread adoption of universal adult franchise in the 'Western' world, it would seem that the democratic ideal of 'one man, one vote; one vote, one value' has been achieved. This is not the case, however; 'one man, one vote' may be a reality, but 'one vote, one value' is not, at least in a large number of countries. The reason for this can be summarised briefly as: although votes have been given to people, it is 'people in places' who have power [*Johnston*, 1978a]. The aim of the research work, of which this paper reports one segment only, is to analyse the extent to which power is unequally distributed between people within a political system because of where they live. The nature of the analyses, and the insights which they offer, indicates the value of a political geographical contribution to the social sciences.

The presentation here is in three sections. In the first, I look briefly at the nature of electoral systems with a strong geographical component, with particular emphasis on the plurality method and one of its variants. The second section looks at the measurement of power in weighted voting systems and at some of the implications of such power. The final section moves the geographical scale downwards, to look at the power of individual voters and groups of voters within single territories.

2. Electoral Systems

Almost all elections for national Parliaments and similar bodies are conducted in a lattice of constituencies: Israel is one of the few exceptions, with the members of the Knesset being voted for in a national contest. Thus in many countries, a person's vote is relevant to the result in a single constituency, and only indirectly to the national result; as a consequence, there are often major discrepancies between the percentage of the national vote which a party wins and its percentage of the constituencies [*Lakeman; Rae*, 1971].

There are three main ways of conducting elections by constituencies [*Taylor/Johnston*, 1978a]: the plurality, or first-past-the-post, method; the party list method; and the preferential method. Of these, the first tends to produce the greatest discrepancies between

---

[1]) An earlier version of this article was published in Munich Social Science Review 3, 1978, 5–31.

votes and seats [*Rae*, 1971; *Johnston*, 1978b], and it is on that system – which is used in the United Kingdom and the United States – that I shall concentrate here.

Operation of the plurality system is extremely simple. The relevant territory is divided into a number of constituencies, and in each of these the candidate (or party) receiving most votes is declared the winner, irrespective of whether his vote total comprises a majority of those cast. This means that, over all the constituencies, for each party many of the votes cast for it have no influence at all on the number of constituencies (and thus Parliamentary seats) which it wins. In a constituency which it loses, all of its votes are wasted: in a constituency which it wins, all of those votes extra to the number needed to defeat the second-place getter are in excess of requirements, and they too are wasted [*Gudgin/Taylor*]. The greater the proportion of its votes which are wasted, the less successful a party will be in converting those votes into seats, a fact well-recognised by those politicians who are able to design constituency lattices (as in the United States, where both malapportionment and gerrymandering have been widespread for a long time: *Johnston* [1978b]).

Because of the distribution of voters of different political attitudes and persuasions across the lattice of constituencies, some groups in a population have greater power over election results than others. Thus in a two-party state – in which the parties are labelled *A* and *B* – one can have three types of constituency. The first comprises the safe seats for *A*, in which it commands the support of a large majority of the voters: the second comprises the similar safe seats for *B*. In neither of these types does any particular voter, or relatively small group of voters, have much power: whichever way they cast their vote (which includes abstaining) their action is unlikely to influence the constituency result. In the third type, however, are the marginal constituencies, in which *A* and *B* are fairly evenly matched; in these, the decisions of small groups, even of a few individuals, may be crucial in determining the outcome of an election. Thus although it is the residents of the first two types who determine the outcome of many of the contests, their votes are assured; it is the voters in the marginal constituencies who can affect the overall result, and who therefore have considerable political power. Policies are likely to be directed at them in particular [*Johnston*, 1976] so that the geography of who lives where in the constituency lattice can influence not only the electoral geography of a country but also the direction, in a spatial sense, of political policy.

In some constituency lattices, different weight is given to different constituencies, usually to reflect differences in constituency populations. Three examples can be quoted: the Electoral College used to elect United States' Presidents, in which the candidate winning each state gets a number of votes reflecting the state's population; the E.E.C. Council of Ministers, in which each of the nine countries has a bloc of votes [*Johnston/Hunt*]; and the European Parliament, whose composition was determined in 1976 [*Taylor/Johnston*, 1978b]. It is with the distribution of power among such weighted constituencies that much of the remainder of this paper is concerned.

3. The Measurement of Power in Weighted Constituencies

There are two basic ways of looking at the distribution of power which results from a particular distribution of votes. In the first, the focus is on the formation of governments, formal coalitions of voting blocs which have a permanent majority and in which the different contestants are in conflict over the allocation of 'spoils', such as cabinet seats [*Browne/Franklin; de Swaan*]. In the second, permanent government formation is irrelevant, and instead the focus is on the bargaining between the contestants over individual issues. Bargains are made between contestants on the basis of 'who can be most useful to whom' in getting pet projects passed. It is the latter type of power – the number of favourable bargains an individual contestant can make – which is the focus of attention here.

3.1 A Power Index

Several methods of indexing power in a weighted voting situation have been proposed, with the main choice being between that devised by *Shapley/Shubik* [1954] – whose base is the distribution of spoils in a game that comprises all possible orderings of voters – and that used, in a variety of forms, by *Banzhaf* [1968], *Coleman* [1972], and *Rae* [1972], in which the basis is the number of winning coalitions of which an individual voter is a crucial member. The latter is chosen here [see *Laver; Johnston*, 1978c].

Distribution of Votes				
	A	B	C	D
	40	20	20	20
Majority 51				
Coalitions				
Potential Coalition	Votes	Viable?	Destroyers	
AB	60	Yes	A, B	
AC	60	Yes	A, C	
AD	60	Yes	A, D	
BC	40	No		
BD	40	No		
CD	40	No		
ABC	80	Yes	A	
ABD	80	Yes	A	
ACD	80	Yes	A	
BCD	60	Yes	B, C, D	
The Power Index				
	A	B	C	D
Coalitions can destroy	6	2	2	2
Proportion = Power Index	.5	.167	.167	.167
Proportion of Votes	.4	.2	.2	.2
Power: Vote Ratio	1.25	0.835	0.835	0.835

Tab. 1: Derivation of the Power Index

Table 1 illustrates how this index is derived for a very simple voting system of four members; one has forty votes and the other three have twenty votes each. Every possible coalition of voters is considered. If its total of votes exceeds the set majority needed to win in the voting body, the coalition is deemed viable. It is then analysed to find those members who could destroy it, by a unilateral withdrawal (i.e. their withdrawal from the coalition would make it non-viable). The number of potential coalitions which an individual can destroy, as a proportion of the total available destructions, is its power index; in Table 1, individual A has half of the power with only 40 per cent of the votes. The two proportions can then be combined to give a power: vote ratio – a ratio exceeding 1.0 indicates that the individual has relatively more of the power than of the votes, whereas less than 1.0 indicates less power than votes. The power index, thus, is a measure of potential bargaining strength, whereas the power: vote ratio relates such strength to the distribution of votes.

The index has been used in a series of recent papers to evaluate the distribution of power between countries in two institutions which are part of the E.E.C.: the Council of Ministers and the European Parliament [*Johnston*, 1977a; *Johnston/Hunt; Taylor/Johnston*, 1978b]. The results show that in those institutions the distribution of power – as defined here – must of necessity be very different from the distribution of votes: some countries will be relatively powerful (relative, that is, to their number of votes) whereas others will be relatively powerless.

In certain circumstances, the distribution of power is extremely sensitive to changes in the distribution of votes, as is indicated in the following four hypothetical situations:

1. In the first, there are four voters: A and B have 30 votes each, and C and D share another 30, in varying proportions. As Figure 1 shows, once a voter gets less than 15 votes in this situation, he becomes totally powerless whilst as the other approaches the vote total of A and B his bargaining strength approaches unity (same proportion of power as of votes), which characterises those two throughout.

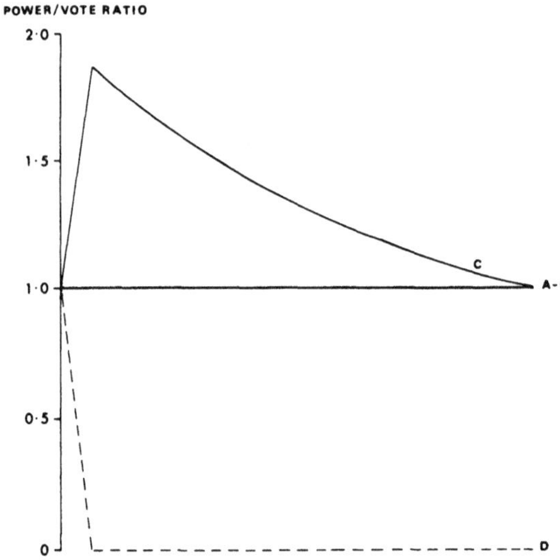

A	30	30	30	30	30	30	30	30	30	30	30	30	30	30	30	30
B	30	30	30	30	30	30	30	30	30	30	30	30	30	30	30	30
C	15	16	17	18	19	20	21	22	23	24	25	26	27	28	29	30
D	15	14	13	12	11	10	9	8	7	6	5	4	3	2	1	0

Fig. 1

2. In this case, A and B have 25 votes each, and C and D share another 50. Fewer votes for D do not mean powerlessness in this configuration, however; instead, his power: vote ratio increases after an initial fall from when all four have 25 votes each (Figure 2), and with fewer than 8 votes his power: vote ratio exceeds 1.0 whereas C's, with more than 42 votes, falls below unity.

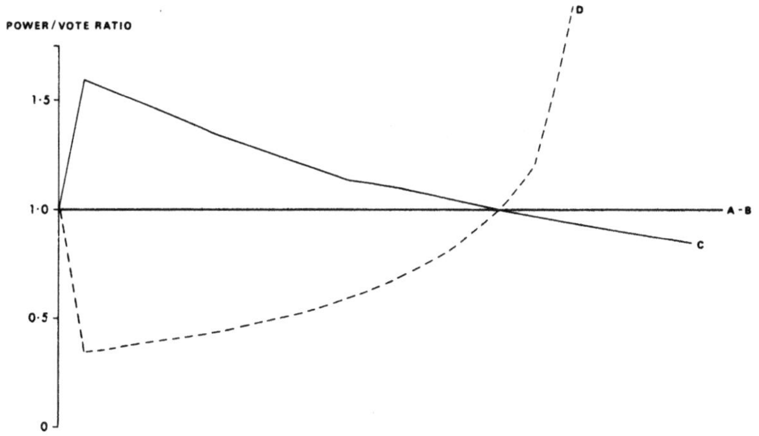

A	25	25	25	25	25	25	25	25	25	25	25	25	25	25	25	25	25	25	25	25	25	25	25	25	25	25
B	25	25	25	25	25	25	25	25	25	25	25	25	25	25	25	25	25	25	25	25	25	25	25	25	25	25
C	25	26	27	28	29	30	31	32	33	34	35	36	37	38	39	40	41	42	43	44	45	46	47	48	49	50
D	25	24	23	22	21	20	19	18	17	16	15	14	13	12	11	10	9	8	7	6	5	4	3	2	1	0

Fig. 2

3. In this third example, A has 40 votes, B has 30 votes, and C and D share a further 30 votes between them. Here the trace of power: vote ratios (Figure 3), as the number of votes held by C and D varies, is quite complex, with the power of A and B being changed even though there is no alteration in their number of votes.

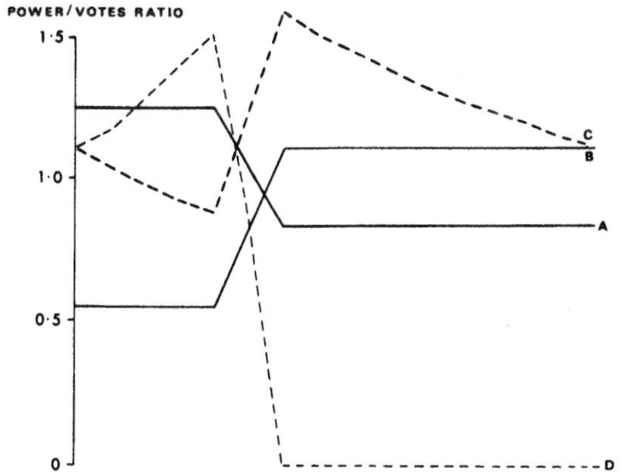

A	40	40	40	40	40	40	40	40	40	40	40	40	40	40	40	40
B	30	30	30	30	30	30	30	30	30	30	30	30	30	30	30	30
C	15	16	17	18	19	20	21	22	23	24	25	26	27	28	29	30
D	15	14	13	12	11	10	9	8	7	6	5	4	3	2	1	0

Fig. 3

4. This final example is based on a possible percentage distribution of seats in a Welsh Assembly between the four major parties there (Lab-Labour: Con-Conservative: Lib-Liberal: PC-Plaid Cymru). In the left-hand graph (Figure 4), Labour and Conservative retain their same shares of the seats, and have constant power: vote ratios; the ratio for Liberal increases as its share of votes falls. In the right-hand graph, Conservative gains seats from Labour, and the relative distribution of power oscillates quite considerably.

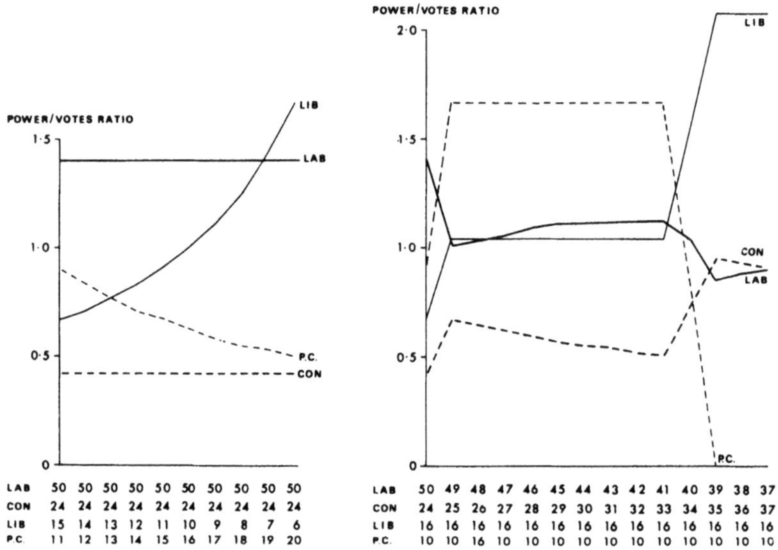

Fig. 4

These four examples are intended as illustrative of the sensitivity of power distributions to vote allocations and indicate the strength of the general thesis advanced in this research that 'one man, one vote' – i.e. an equitable allocation of votes in a weighted system – does not ensure, in fact almost certainly fails to ensure, 'one vote, one value'. (This finding applies whatever the majority required in the 'Parliament': *Johnston/Hunt* [1977]; *Taylor/Johnston* [1978b].)

Application of this method to European institutions produces the result given in Table 2. In the Council of Ministers, it will be seen, the relative distributions of votes and of power deviate markedly from unity power: vote ratios in the three smallest countries only. In the Parliament, the distribution of power between the nine countries is exactly the same as in the Council (assuming that the latter operates on an absolute majority: *Johnston/Hunt* [1977]), but because the distribution of votes differs (the four largest countries have eight times as many Parliamentary as Council votes, whereas four of the other have five times as many and the last – Luxembourg – has three times) the power: vote ratios vary considerably. Clearly in this latter case, although the distribution of Parliamentary representatives may meet the 'one man, one vote' criterion it does not also meet 'one vote, one value'.

Country	Council of Ministers Power Index	Council of Ministers Power: Vote Ratio	European Parliament Power Index	European Parliament Power: Vote Ratio
United Kingdom	0.174	1.01	0.174	0.88
France	0.174	1.01	0.174	0.88
Germany	0.174	1.01	0.174	0.88
Italy	0.174	1.01	0.174	0.88
Belgium	0.087	1.01	0.087	1.49
Netherlands	0.087	1.01	0.087	1.43
Luxembourg	0.043	0.84	0.043	2.97
Denmark	0.043	0.84	0.043	1.11
Ireland	0.043	1.26	0.043	1.19

Source: various tables in *Johnston* [1977a].

Tab. 2: Power Indices and Power: Vote Ratios in European Institutions

3.2 A Two-Level Analysis

The form of analysis just reported and illustrated is more valuable for the study of bodies such as the American Electoral College and the European Council of Ministers, in both of which votes are cast en bloc, than for the investigation of institutions such as the European Parliament, where each country's votes can be cast individually, although they are distributed among parties. If we assume that parties vote as blocs, then how is power distributed? This calls for a two-level analysis.

In Table 3, the four countries of Table 1 now have their votes divided between four political parties: country A, for example, has 16 of its 40 votes allocated to party IV, 12 to party III, and so on panel 1 in Table 3. The left-hand matrix in this panel shows the inter-party distribution of votes for each country whereas that on the right-hand side expresses those distributions as proportions of the raw (country) totals. The latter is termed the *interest matrix*, as it shows the relative interest of each country in the various parties.

1. Interest in Party Groups (distribution of country's votes)[1])

Countries	Parties I	II	III	IV			I	II	III	IV
A	4	8	12	16		A	.1	.2	.3	.4
B	8	6	4	2	→	B	.4	.3	.2	.1
C	2	2	8	8		C	.1	.1	.4	.4
D	12	4	2	2		D	.6	.2	.1	.1

2. Power over Party Groups (coalitions in each party that country can destroy)

Parties	Countries A	B	C	D			A	B	C	D
I	2	2	2	6		I	.17	.17	.17	.50
II	5	3	1	3	→	II	.42	.25	.08	.25
III	6	2	2	2		III	.50	.17	.17	.17
IV	7	0	0	0		IV	1.00	0	0	0

[1]) The right-hand matrix in the panel indicates proportional distribution of each country's votes.

Tab. 3: Power over Party Groups

We can now work out the power of each country in each party, using the method of Table 1. This produces the matrices in panel 2 in Table 3: that on the left-hand side shows the number of potential coalitions in each party which each country could destroy; that on the right-hand side expresses those data as power indices. Thus country A, with 16 of the 28 seats, has complete control over party IV; it shares control of party III with B and C and D; and so on.

In the Parliament in which the four countries are represented, the four parties have the following number of votes:

I.	26	II.	20	III.	26	IV.	28

It is these, and not the countries, which bargain in the Parliament, so using the method of Table 1 their relative power is worked out as:

	Party			
	I	II	III	IV
Coalitions can destroy	4	0	4	4
Power index	0.33	0	0.33	0.33

From these indices, we can then inquire into the power of the countries through the parties. This is calculated by pre-multiplying the intra-party power indices (panel 2 of Table 3) by the above vector of inter-party power indices. It gives the following intercountry distribution of power:

	Country			
	A	B	C	D
Power index	0.551	0.112	0.112	0.221
Power: vote ratio	1.378	0.561	0.561	1.105

Thus A is the most powerful country, largely because of its hegemony over party IV, which shares power in the Parliament with parties I and III.

Analysis of power in the Parliament can be modified by suggesting that parties will only bargain and form coalitions with what we will term their 'ideological neighbours'. Assume that our parties are distributed along an ideological continuum from left to right [*Downs; Budge/Crewe/Fairlie*], with I at the extreme left and IV at the extreme right. We then constrain the coalition-formation process by saying that a party will not join a coalition with another party if an intervening party on the continuum is not also in the coalition. Two different power indices can thus be calculated:

1) the power to destroy a viable coalition; and
2) the power to initiate a coalition, by joining a non-viable grouping.

Table 4 illustrates how these are derived for the four parties.

From each, an inter-country distribution of power, as mediated through the party system, is derived as follows:

	Country			
	A	B	C	D
Power to Destroy	0.585	0.133	0.108	0.181
Power to Initiate	0.566	0.232	0.166	0.034

Distribution of Votes							
I	26	II	20	III	26	IV	28
Majority 51							

Coalitions Potential Coalition	Votes	Viables?	Destroyers of Viables	Initiators of Non-Viable
I	26	No		
II	20	No		
III	26	No		IV
IV	28	No		III
I, II	46	No		III
II, III	46	No		I, IV
III, IV	54	Yes	III, IV	
I, II, III	72	Yes	I, II, III	
II, III, IV	74	Yes	III, IV	

Power Indices	I	II	III	IV
Power to Destroy				
Coalitions can destroy	1	1	3	2
Power Index	0.143	0.143	0.429	0.286
Power to initiate				
Coalitions can initiate	1	0	2	2
Power Index	0.2	0	0.4	0.4

Tab. 4: Power Indices for Ideologically-Constrained Coalitions

Compared to the analysis previously reported – in which parties are free to make bargains with all others, irrespective of ideology – countries A and B are more powerful, while C and D, especially D, are less so.

Finally in the two-level analysis we can ask what influence the countries have over each other, what the parties have in common, and how inter-country influence is reflected in the distribution of power. Such questions have been attacked by *Coleman* [1973] and *Batty* [1976] in their works on the mathematics of collective action. The answers are provided by deriving two interaction matrices from those on the right-hand side of Table 3. If the power matrix is premultiplied by the interest matrix, the result is the inter-country interaction matrix given in part 1 of Table 5.

The proportions in the principal diagonal of this matrix indicate the degree of control each country has over all of the parties in which it is represented: clearly A is much more independent of other countries in this respect than are D, B and C. The off-diagonal elements indicate the degree to which the country named in the row has its representatives controlled by the country named in the column, so that the column sums are indices of total power. The greatest degrees of control shown are that of A over the parties in which C is represented and of both A and D over B.

The second interaction matrix is derived by pre-multiplying the interest matrix by the power matrix: this gives the interparty interactions shown in panel 2 of Table 5. In this, the elements on the principal diagonal show the degree to which power in each party is controlled by countries with the greatest interest in that party. Party II has the smallest value. The off-diagonal elements show the degree to which the power in one party (that

1. Inter-Country

Countries	A	B	C	D
A	0.651	0.118	0.084	0.151
B	0.394	0.177	0.126	0.309
C	0.659	0.110	0.093	0.143
D	0.336	0.169	0.135	0.367
Total	2.040	0.574	0.438	0.970

2. Inter-Party

Parties	I	II	III	IV
I	0.402	0.202	0.203	0.203
II	0.300	0.217	0.233	0.250
III	0.237	0.202	0.269	0.302
IV	0.100	0.200	0.300	0.400
Total	1.037	0.821	1.005	1.155

Tab. 5: Interaction Matrices

named in the row) is located in countries with interests in the other party (that named in the column). Assuming that representatives from the same country, irrespective of party, will have some common interest, these values suggest the likely strength of inter-party bargaining.

One last power index which can be derived from those already produced involves pre-multiplying the inter-country interaction matrix by the vector showing the inter-country distribution of power, as mediated by the party system. As the former matrix shows the influence of the countries over each other whereas the latter vector shows their influence in the Parliament, the vector resulting from their multiplication can be interpreted as a Total Power Index combining influence over others with parliamentary influence. Using the unconstrained power vector (0.551, 0.112, 0.224) produces:

	Country A	B	C	D
Total Power Index	0.548	0.133	0.098	0.211

which when combined with the distribution of votes (Table 1) gives:

	Country A	B	C	D
Total Power: Vote ratio	1.37	0.67	0.49	1.06

in which A turns out to be, relatively, the most powerful and C the least.

3.3 Two-Level Analyses of the European Parliament

The method of two-level analysis just described can be applied to the European Parliament. In such analyses, it is necessary to simulate what the party representation will be from each country. Two simulations are used here. The first is by *Johnston* [1977b], which allocates national parties to six 'party groups', the same as those in the pre-direct

Country	Communist	Socialist	Liberal	Progressive Democrat	Christian Democrat	Conservative
			Party Group			
United Kingdom	0	34	16	0	0	31
France	21	18	19	23	0	0
Germany	0	37	7	0	37	0
Italy	25	13	8	0	35	0
Belgium	0	8	5	0	11	0
Netherlands	0	12	6	0	7	0
Luxembourg	1	2	1	0	2	0
Denmark	0	5	5	3	0	2
Ireland	0	˙2	0	7	6	0
Total	47	131	67	33	98	33

Source: as used in *Johnston* [1977b].

Tab. 6: Party Group Representation in the European Parliament

elections Parliament, which are located on an ideological continuum based on the work of *Inglehart/Klingemann* [1976]: the distribution is given in Table 6.

The second simulation is by *Rattinger/Zangle/Zintl* [1977], which places the parties into a four-group continuum (Table 7). Power indices have been computed, along with inter-country and interparty interaction matrices.

Country	Left	Left-Centre	Centre-Right	Right
		Party Group		
United Kingdom	0	36	43	2
France	17	31	9	24
Germany	0	42	39	0
Italy	33	8	37	3
Belgium	0	9	11	4
Netherlands	2	9	11	3
Luxembourg	0	3	2	1
Denmark	2	8	4	2
Ireland	0	2	13	0
Total	54	148	169	39

Source: from *Rattinger/Zangle/Zintl* [1977]

Tab. 7: An Alternative Composition for the European Parliament

Table 8 shows the power indices for the party groups in the Parliament, according to the compositions predicted by the two simulations. Combined with the power indices for the countries over the individual parties, we get the measures of national power in the Parliament, as mediated through the party system (Table 9).

Not surprisingly, in all six of the analyses reported, the bulk of the power lies in the four largest countries. Between them, these have 79 per cent of the Parliamentary seats: amongst them, in the Johnston simulation, Italy has complete control over the Communist party group, France over the Progressive Democrats, and the U.K. over the Conservatives; in the Rattinger et al. simulation, Italy has complete control over the Left and France over the right. A major difference between the two simulations is that in the Johnston one, there are occasional power: vote ratios exceeding unity for the five smaller

1. Johnston Simulation

	Party Group					
	Communist	Socialist	Liberal	Progressive Democrat	Christian Democrat	Conservative
Unconstrained						
Power Index	0.143	0.357	0.143	0.071	0.214	0.071
Constrained Indices						
Power to Destroy	0.083	0.333	0.250	0.067	0.083	0.083
Power to Initiate	0.148	0.278	0.278	0.148	0.000	0.148

2. Rattinger et al. Simulation

	Party Group			
	Left	Left-Centre	Centre-Right	Right
Unconstrained				
Power Index	0.167	0.167	0.500	0.167
Constrained Indices				
Power to Destroy	0.000	0.500	0.500	0.000
Power to Initiate	0.000	0.333	0.500	0.167

Tab. 8: Power Indices for the European Parliament

countries, but no such ratios in the Rattinger et al. simulation. Between the various indices in each simulation, the main differences reflect the relative power of the 'extreme' party groups. In the Rattinger et al. simulation, Italy, for example, is extremely powerful in the unconstrained index, largely because of its power over the Left group: in the constrained solutions, however, the Left is totally powerless, and Italy's power: vote ratio ratios fall accordingly.

Simulation	Johnston			Rattinger		
Index[1])	U	D	I	U	D	I
Country						
United Kingdom	0.19(1.0)	0.23(1.1)	0.28(1.4)	0.19(1.0)	0.26(1.3)	0.24(1.2)
France	0.17(0.9)	0.20(1.0)	0.28(1.4)	0.24(1.2)	0.16(0.8)	0.28(1.4)
Germany	0.18(0.9)	0.15(0.7)	0.11(0.5)	0.19(1.0)	0.30(1.5)	0.24(1.2)
Italy	0.26(1.3)	0.17(0.9)	0.21(1.1)	0.31(1.6)	0.15(0.8)	0.14(0.7)
Belgium	0.06(1.0)	0.04(0.7)	0.03(0.5)	0.02(0.4)	0.03(0.5)	0.03(0.5)
Netherlands	0.08(1.2)	0.07(1.1)	0.05(0.9)	0.02(0.4)	0.03(0.5)	0.03(0.5)
Luxembourg	0.01(0.7)	0.01(0.6)	0.05(3.0)	0.01(0.3)	0.01(0.3)	0.01(0.3)
Denmark	0.02(0.5)	0.03(0.7)	0.03(0.7)	0.01(0.3)	0.02(0.5)	0.02(0.4)
Ireland	0.03(0.9)	0.02(0.4)	0.04(1.1)	0.02(0.8)	0.02(0.6)	0.02(0.6)

[1]) Key: U – unconstrained power index; D – power to destroy in constrained situation; I – power to initiate in constrained situation; Power: vote ratios in brackets.

Tab. 9: National Power in the European Parliament (as mediated by the party system)

Turning to the inter-country interaction matrices (Table 10), two conclusions immediately stand out: the first is that only the four largest countries have any real independent influence over the parties which represent them; the second is that these same countries, not surprisingly, have most power over the others. No detailed comparison of the two simulations is presented here: the greater hegemony of the four largest countries in the Rattinger et al. simulation, however, suggests that the smaller the number of parties

1. Johnston Simulation

	U.K.	France	Germany	Italy	Belgium	Netherlands	Luxembourg	Denmark	Ireland
U.K.	0.547	0.143	0.138	0.000	0.040	0.055	0.018	0.047	0.011
France	0.129	0.392	0.073	0.259	0.035	0.048	0.014	0.044	0.006
Germany	0.138	0.123	0.238	0.193	0.117	0.094	0.033	0.033	0.030
Italy	0.070	0.060	0.136	0.491	0.101	0.074	0.025	0.021	0.021
Belgium	0.147	0.126	0.198	0.194	0.125	0.104	0.034	0.045	0.027
Netherlands	0.192	0.167	0.212	0.118	0.101	0.097	0.033	0.056	0.024
Luxembourg	0.134	0.116	0.174	0.308	0.097	0.083	0.028	0.039	0.022
Denmark	0.320	0.358	0.110	0.000	0.051	0.069	0.021	0.063	0.009
Ireland	0.032	0.496	0.121	0.169	0.083	0.054	0.019	0.006	0.019
Total	1.709	1.981	1.400	1.732	0.750	0.678	0.225	0.354	0.169

2. Rattinger et al. Simularion

	U.K.	France	Germany	Italy	Belgium	Netherlands	Luxembourg	Denmark	Ireland
U.K.	0.280	0.171	0.288	0.151	0.032	0.032	0.005	0.018	0.023
France	0.143	0.408	0.153	0.249	0.014	0.014	0.002	0.011	0.006
Germany	0.287	0.165	0.298	0.140	0.032	0.032	0.005	0.019	0.022
Italy	0.158	0.083	0.157	0.530	0.021	0.021	0.003	0.009	0.019
Belgium	0.239	0.291	0.246	0.130	0.027	0.027	0.004	0.015	0.020
Netherlands	0.229	0.239	0.236	0.205	0.026	0.026	0.004	0.015	0.019
Luxembourg	0.240	0.321	0.251	0.100	0.025	0.025	0.004	0.017	0.016
Denmark	0.206	0.310	0.218	0.193	0.021	0.021	0.004	0.015	0.012
Ireland	0.284	0.072	0.280	0.233	0.038	0.038	0.005	0.015	0.035
Total	2.066	2.060	2.127	1.931	0.236	0.236	0.036	0.134	0.172

Tab. 10: Inter-Country Interaction Matrices

in the Parliament, the greater the powerlessness of the small countries. They would probably be more influential if their parties stayed outside the major party groupings.

The inter-party interaction matrices, again not surprisingly, show that most power resides in the centre parties: those of the extremes have representatives from too few countries (Table 11).

1. Johnston simulation

	Communist	Socialist	Liberal	Progressive Democrat	Christian Democrat	Conservative
Communist	0.309	0.160	0.099	0.000	0.432	0.000
Socialist	0.063	0.375	0.165	0.085	0.210	0.098
Liberal	0.071	0.355	0.232	0.100	0.101	0.142
Progressive Democrat	0.259	0.222	0.235	0.284	0.000	0.000
Christian Democrat	0.137	0.293	0.134	0.018	0.420	0.000
Conservative	0.000	0.420	0.198	0.000	0.000	0.382
Total	0.839	1.825	1.063	0.487	1.163	0.622

2. Rattinger et al. Simulation

	Left	Left-Centre	Centre-Right	Right
Left	0.407	0.099	0.457	0.037
Left-Centre	0.172	0.440	0.374	0.103
Centre-Right	0.121	0.329	0.483	0.044
Right	0.210	0.383	0.111	0.296
Total	0.910	1.251	1.425	0.480

Tab. 11: Inter-Party Interaction Matrices

	Solution[1])		
1. Johnston Solution			
	Unconstrained	Power to Destroy	Power to Initiate
U.K.	0.201 (1.02)	0.216 (1.09)	0.251 (1.27)
France	0.163 (0.82)	0.179 (0.90)	0.227 (1.15)
Germany	0.153 (0.77)	0.137 (0.69)	0.148 (0.75)
Italy	0.231 (1.17)	0.186 (0.94)	0.236 (1.19)
Belgium	0.081 (1.37)	0.068 (1.15)	0.074 (1.25)
Netherlands	0.073 (1.20)	0.066 (1.08)	0.076 (1.25)
Luxembourg	0.024 (1.60)	0.020 (1.33)	0.024 (1.60)
Denmark	0.035 (0.90)	0.036 (0.92)	0.041 (1.05)
Ireland	0.017 (0.46)	0.016 (0.43)	0.016 (0.43)
2. Rattinger et al. Simulation			
U.K.	0.210 (1.06)	0.232 (1.17)	0.224 (1.13)
France	0.205 (1.04)	0.196 (0.99)	0.233 (1.18)
Germany	0.219 (1.11)	0.189 (0.95)	0.233 (1.18)
Italy	0.295 (1.49)	0.220 (1.11)	0.233 (1.18)
Belgium	0.026 (0.44)	0.031 (0.52)	0.027 (0.46)
Netherlands	0.026 (0.43)	0.031 (0.51)	0.027 (0.44)
Luxembourg	0.003 (0.20)	0.003 (0.20)	0.003 (0.20)
Denmark	0.013 (0.33)	0.014 (0.36)	0.013 (0.33)
Ireland	0.016 (0.43)	0.020 (0.54)	0.018 (0.49)

[1]) Power: vote ratios in brackets.

Tab. 12: Total Power Indices for the European Parliament

Finally, Table 12 shows the Total Power Indices for the nine countries, computed for both the simulations and for each of the three ways of calculating the inter-party distribution of power in the Parliament (unconstrained; power to destroy; power to initiate). Comparison of the two sets of results, in particular their power: vote ratios, shows that with a smaller number of party groups the Rattinger et al. simulation places most of the power in the four large countries; only two of the fifteen power: vote indices for the other five countries even exceed 0.5. Among the four largest, in general it is Italy and the United Kingdom which receive the largest 'over-proportions' of power; in the Johnston simulation, however, there are much larger power: vote ratios for some of the smaller countries – notably Luxembourg.

All of the indices presented here for the European Parliament are based on single-sample simulations, and so their substantive validity is open to considerable doubt. *Johnston* [1977b] showed, for example, that his predicted distribution of Parliamentary seats for the United Kingdom – Conservative 34, Labour 31, Liberal 16 – produced the 'worst possible' power: vote ratios for that country.

Thus further discussion of the results reported in Table 6–12 is not justified here. The major aim of the presentation has been to introduce and illustrate a linked series of methods which can provide some insight into the extremely tricky problem of measuring political power in a body such as the European Parliament.

4. Power within Constituencies

The focus of the analyses so far has been on the use of weighted blocs of votes in political bargaining. The same methods can be employed to estimate the relative power of the groups of voters who produce these weighted blocs, and they can be illustrated using the same data.

	Class			
Constituency	I	II	III	IV
A	4	8	12	16
B	8	6	4	2
C	2	2	8	8
D	12	4	2	2

Tab. 13: Data for Analysing the Power of Classes in Constituencies

In Table 13 the same matrix that appeared in Table 3 is repeated, with different titles for the rows and for the columns. Each row is a constituency whose voters have been divided into four social classes. To win each constituency, a party must put together a majority of the voters, so it bargains with the various social classes, attempting to bring them together into winning coalitions. What power has each social class in each constituency? Clearly in constituency D class I is all-powerful since no winning coalition could be formed without it, but in the other three some combination of classes is necessary. Inter-class power distributions can then be calculated for all constituencies, using one of the three methods outlined above (unconstrained, with all classes bargaining with all others;

constrained, power to destroy; and constrained, power to initiate: the last two assume that the classes can be ordered along an ideological continuum).

Detailed arguments have already been published to show how different constituency sizes and different class distributions influence inter-class power [*Johnston*, 1977c]. Of particular interest is the way in which the use of constituencies allocates power differently from how it would be if there were no constituencies – i.e., if elections were held for a single, national constituency, as in Israel. Table 14 illustrates this with data taken from the 1971 Census for England; it shows the power: vote ratios for power to initiate and power to destroy.

	Class	Number	Power to Initiate Constituency Mean	Power to Initiate National	Power to Destroy Constituency Mean	Power to Destroy National
I	Employers, managers	2,404,240	0.19	0	0.02	0
II	Professionals	838.000	0.33	0	2.59	1.81
III	Intermediate, non-manual	1,795,840	0.31	0	1.92	1.69
IV	Junior, non-manual	5,014,840	0.86	0.52	1.05	0.97
V	Skilled manual	5,626,260	2.61	3.70	1.27	1.29
VI	Semi-skilled manual	4,545,940	0.78	0.57	1.10	1.07
VII	Unskilled manual	1,783,370	0.24	0	1.93	1.70
VIII	Own account (non-professional)	1,004,560	0.16	0	1.78	1.51
IX	Other	3,042,950	0.14	0	0.02	0

Tab. 14: Inter-Class Power: Vote Ratios – England, 1971

The 26 million members of the working population are allocated to one of nine social classes, which are assumed to be on a single ideological continuum from I–IX, and classes are assumed to bargain only with their neighbours on this continuum. If a campaign were held nationally, use of the power to initiate method shows (in the final column of that part of the table) that only three classes would have any power, with almost all of it (0.8) going to the central one on the continuum – the skilled manual workers. On the other hand, if the campaign were fought separately in each of the country's 516 constituencies, each class would have some power even though, as the other columns in that part of the table shows, class V would still win most (on average, 0.563). Using the power to destroy method, there is no obvious hegemony for class V and power is relatively widely distributed: as with the power to initiate, however, the consequence of bargaining separately in 516 constituencies is a wider dispersion of power.

As yet, methods of analysis at this level have not been developed very far. Those reported here [as in *Johnston*, 1977c] make the unreal assumption that the classes vote as blocs and the somewhat unrealistic assumptions that classes can be arranged along an ideological continuum and only bargain with their neighbours. The methods promise avenues of advance, however, which allow them to be integrated with those reported earlier. It should eventually be possible to write a whole system of mathematics of collective action which links voters in constituencies with parties and other blocs of votes which are used to bargain over policies in Parliaments and elsewhere. This will give much better appreciation of how power is distributed.

Alternative methods of measuring such power are available, which include extensions of *Coleman's* [1973] mathematics of collective action [*Batty*]. It can also be measured simply by identifying the size of a particular group in each constituency relative to the size of the majority there at the last election [*Keech; Johnston*, 1978b], and more detailed analyses relate size of group in a constituency to their attitudes (including strength of feeling) on various issues, indicating where campaigning, and on what, is most likely to pay off [*Pool/Abelson/Popkin*]. The range of possible procedures for looking at the distribution of power is considerable, therefore.

5. Conclusions

The implication of 'one man, one vote' is 'one man, one value', that every enfranchised individual has the same influence, or potential influence, over Parliaments through his participation in the election process. In almost all electoral systems this is not so, however. Some voters in some places are of much greater potential value to the parties seeking their support than are both others in the same place and all voters in other places. The focus of the research reported here is the measurement of the value of a voter; the results obtained so far suggest that the value varies very considerably, and that 'one vote, one value' is far from secured.

In most electoral systems, the political actors competing for voter support are parties, and it is these bodies which yield the political power in Parliaments, not the individual elected members.

Parliaments comprise weighted blocs of votes, and the various simulations reported here, especially those relating to, the European Parliament, indicate that in such situations power is far from equitably distributed according to the 'one vote, one value' norm, even if it meets 'one man, one vote'.

The whole focus here has been on the measurement of power, and as yet a full mathemathics has not been developed. At present, therefore, the sorts of analyses presented here can only be used as illustrative indicators both of how power can be measured and of who holds it. Eventually, the test of the measures must be in their predictive ability, of who wins in bargaining processes and what places get most policy benefits. General systems frameworks have been developed for this [*Johnston*, 1978b], and much supporting anecdotal evidence adduced, but much more work remains to be done before fullyintegrated analyses can be reported.

References

Banzhaf, J.F., III: One man, 3.312 votes: a mathematical analysis of the Electoral College. Villanova Law Review **14**, 1968, 304–332.

Batty, M.: A Political Theory of Planning and Design. Geographical Papers No. 45, Department of Geography, University of Reading, Reading, 1976.

Browne, E.C., and *M.N. Franklin*: Aspects of coalition payoffs in European parliamentary democracies. American Political Science Review **67**, 453–469.

Budge, I., I. Crewe, and *D. Fairlie* (eds.): Party Identification and Beyond. London 1976.

Coleman, J.S. Control of collectivities and the power of a collectivity to act. Social Choice. Ed. by B. Lieberman. New York 1972, 269–300.
– : The Mathematics of Collective Action. London 1973.
de Swaan, A.: Coalition Theories and Cabinet Formation. Amsterdam 1973.
Downs, A.: An Economic Theory of Democracy. New York 1957.
Gudgin, G., and *P.J. Taylor*: Electoral bias and the distribution of party voters. Transactions, Institute of British Geographers **63**, 1974, 53–73.
Inglehart, R., and *H. Klingemann*: Party identification, ideological preference, and the left-right dimension among Western mass publics. Party Identification and Beyond. Ed. by I. Budge, I. Crewe and D. Fairlie. London, 1976, 243–276.
Johnston, R.J.: Resource allocations and political campaigns: notes towards a methodology. Policy and Politics **5**, 1976, 181–199.
– : National sovereignty and national power in European institutions. Environment and Planning A **9**, 1977a, 569–577.
– : National power in the European Parliament as mediated by the party system. Environment and Planning A **9**, 1977b, 1055–1066.
– : Population distributions and electoral power: preliminary investigations of class bias. Regional Studies **11**, 1977c, 309–321.
– : People, places and votes: an introduction. People, Places and Votes: Essays on the Electoral Geography of Australia and New Zealand. Ed. by R.J. Johnston. University of New England, Department of Geography, Armidale, 1978a, 1–10.
– : Political, Electoral and Spatial Systems. London 1978b.
– : On the Measurement of power: some reactions to Laver. Environment and Planning A **10**, 1978c.
Johnston, R.J., and *A.J. Hunt*: Voting power in the E.E.C's Council of Ministers: an essay on method in political Geography. Geoforum **8**, 1977, 1–9.
Keech, W.R.: The Impact of Negro Voting. Chicago 1968.
Lakeman, E.: How Democracies Vote. London 1974.
Laver, M.: The problems of measuring power in Europe. Environment and Planning A **10**, 1978.
Pool, I. de S., *R.P. Abelson*, and *S.L. Popkin*: Candidates, Issues, and Strategies. Cambridge, Mass., 1964.
Rae, D.W. The Political Consequences of Electoral Laws. New Haven, Conn., 1971.
– : An estimate for the decisiveness of election outcomes. Social Choice. Ed. by B. Lieberman. New York 1972, 379–392.
Rattinger, H., *M. Zangle*, and *R. Zintl*: The distribution of seats in the European Parliament after direct elections: a simulation study. European Journal of Political Research **5**, 1977, 201–218.
Shapley, L.A., and *M. Shubik*: A method of evaluating the distribution of power in a committee system. American Political Science Review **48**, 1954, 787–792.
Taylor, P.J., and *R.J. Johnston*: Geography of Elections. Harmondsworth 1978a.
– : Population distributions and political power in the European Parliament. Regional Studies **12**, 1978b, 61–68.

Holler, M.J. (Ed.): Power, Voting, and Voting Power ©Physica-Verlag, Würzburg (Germany) 1981

Regional Power Allocation: The Problem of British Devolution

P.S. Goodrich, Leeds

1. Introduction

Most previous analyses of public opinion on devolution have focused on cross national comparisons. Opinion has been grouped according to the English, Welsh and Scottish dimensions. Yet, nationality represents but one meaningful context for the analysis of this opinion. Regional variations may be more strongly affected by economic and cultural factors. As a result, intra-national attitude variations may be larger than international differences. In short, previous opinion analyses may have obscured, by their design, important underlying dimensions for devolution.

The primary data to be analysed will be that of the June 1970 poll carried out for the Commission on the Constitution by Social and Community Planning Research ("Kilbrandon poll"). Because of the large sample size of this report, regional analysis is feasible. This poll, however, is eleven years old. Many new political developments may have changed the structure of opinion. Yet, these have occurred principally in Scotland and to some extent in Wales. Because there was little likelihood of devolution to the English regions, these data are probably still valid.

The major problem with the inquiry is that the poll was designed with a national focus. Thus, sample sizes may be insufficient for extensive regional breakdowns with statistical significance. Still, statistical significance is not synonymous with theoretical significance. Hopefully, this paper will provide some tentative hypotheses which might be tested in subsequent polls designed specifically to tap regional diversity.

2. Constitutional Change

The next few years are crucial to the constitutional development of the United Kingdom. As *Jennings* [1965, p. 35] has pointed out, "the constitutional lawyer can, by appropriate drafting, solve any constitutional problem *if people are willing to accept a solution.*" It is vitally important, therefore, that the policy-makers heed public opinion. In complex issues such as devolution popular attitudes generally do not play a *leading* role but rather a *limiting* one. Public opinion defines the limits to the various options in the devolution debate. A key problem in analysing public opinion lies in asking the correct questions of the people. This requires precise definitions of terms and concepts in the political debate. Unfortunately, both politicians and academics alike have been unable to agree on these key issues. Because of this confusion, public opinion has tended to narrowly reflect the questions posed by the pollsters. *Smith* [1977] has noted that the Kilbrandon Commission attitude survey is based on the proposal of a single remedy (devolution) to cure the ills of government. In these conditions, the responses must be biased toward a more favourable answer than if open-ended or alternative proposals were provided.

The main issues that this paper hopes to address are those about administrative power and sovereignty (Unionist, Quasi-Federalist, Confederalist, and Separatist), power, (Centralist, Decentralist), and territorial identity/inequality (National, Regional).

The devolution debate had been fuelled primarily by the threat of the Scottish Nationalist Party (S.N.P.) rendering the U.K. Parliament at Westminster unable to field a majority government in perpetuity. In order to appease the S.N.P., the British government had proposed devolving certain powers to Scotland. The problem is that the real desire is to maintain essentially a strengthened Unionist government. However, many political theorists have felt that devolution as presently planned is but a stepping stone to Separatism.

(The Devolution Process ---→------→------→-------→---------→

Levels of Sovereignty	Unionist	Quasi-Federalist	Federalist	Confederalist	Separatist
U.K.	maximum	very high	equal	subordinate	nominal
England (whole)	minimum	low	equal	very high	maximum
Scotland	minimum	moderate	equal	very high	maximum
Wales	minimum	low	equal	very high	maximum
Regions[1])	minimum	low	equal	very high	minimum

[1]) Assuming the possible devolution along regional lines with all three nations having regions.

Tab. 1: Sovereignty Alternatives

In essence, the government would like to have the minimal devolution process that would still yield effective government. The devolution plans in the Scotland and Wales Acts stopped short of any real sharing of sovereignty because they did not share the revenue raising function. Basically a quasi-federal form having shared tasks at regional and local government levels was to remain. Only Scotland was to get legislative devolution but without the crucial financial devolution.[1]) The minimal concessions by the Labour Government to the devolutionists created confusion in the referendum. Should those favouring devolution vote for the Scotland/Wales Bill because it was a stepping stone or reject it because it did not go far enough?

[1]) Let there be no mistake about the crucial nature of controlling the "purse strings." To cite a recent example from a federal government, the U.S.A., the 1973 imposition by the central government of a 55 mile per hour speed limit throughout America appears to infringe on the constitutional right of the various states to control their own highways. Previously, each state had set its own speed limits; each still has a separate, distinct highway code. In theory, then, each state has jurisdiction. Yet, bills introduced in Congress to challenge the edict have failed to overturn the law because the federal government retains a powerful lever in the allocation of sizable portions of state highway budgets, so vital for maintenance throughout the fifty states. Of course, since the states have jurisdiction over speeders, enforcement of the limits have been haphazard. The 5 February 1977 *Autocar* reported that Louisiana bumper stickers proclaim – "Drive 65 and Freeze a Yankee." The October 1977 *Car* magazine reports that only a few states like Ohio and Maryland strictly enforce the statute. Most everywhere the limits remain unenforced.

3. The Locus of Power

The locus of power is the key to the centralist-decentralist argument. Should the central government have the power to impose sanctions on the various regions/nations or not? These controls would be primarily fiscal. Within the centralist camp, the social democrats argue that the allocation of resources should be centrally controlled; the socialists hold that the basic economy should be centrally planned. Decentralists state that small governmental units are more efficient and that control rightly belongs closer to the people.

Because of the preponderance of England in a federal U.K. based on the nations, a truly federal Britain should have about ten to twenty sub-national units. The number and size of these units is very important in determining the power and influence of the central authority and its relationship to the periphery. As Vile noted, the fewer the number of regional units and, as a result, the larger the size of these units, the more power for each unit. The greater the number of units, the less power they can attain (given relative equality). In the United States, fifty sub-national units have resulted in limited overt bargaining between the various levels of government with the resulting independence of federal government.

Yet, it is important that the boundaries of these regions be drawn in conformity with "genuine community interest, whether economic, racial, linguistic or social differences, if the local regional units are to become effective politically" [Royal Commission, Vile (ed.), 1973b, p. 31].

Vile also pointed out that if the boundaries are arbitrary rather than reflective of true regional differences the central government has a much better chance of maintaining effective control thereby minimising the danger of separatist movements. He concludes his discussion of the character of regional units with a provocative paragraph:

> "However, the question naturally arises, to what extent should any future boundaries of decentralised units in Great Britain be allowed to follow historical and cultural divisions. The dangers of establishing only four units, England, Scotland, Wales and Ireland are very great, for if they become the genuine object of political allegiance they could begin to foster those very attitudes which nationalists would wish to see develop – indeed the present situation in Northern Ireland points this up very clearly. To divide England alone would not be a solution to the problem, for it is, in Wales and Scotland, that the potential for separatist movements exists. The conclusion would seem to be a set of boundaries which did not coincide with, or reflect in any significant sense, the historical boundaries of the 'nations'. One further word of warning, however, the creation of such regional units *could* simply be a step to a further reorganisation along more historic lines at a later date. One would not wish to push too hard the lessons of a country as distinct as that of India, but in that country the attempt to establish a federal system on the basis of administrative divisions which did not reflect communal reality was soon subject to a basic revision." [Royal Commission, Vile (ed.), 1973b, p. 31.]

In short, there is a real problem for the future of British devolved government. If, on the one hand, the central government truly tries to allocate power more effectively, then it should set up regions based on true differences rather than arbitrary bureaucratic divisions. On the other hand, to do so is risky since giving more power to the decentralised regions leaves less power for the centre to divert threatened fragmentation. But, if the division of the country is too arbitrary, government may not only be inefficient but also unworkable.

4. Regional Identity

Most analyses of opinion towards devolution have used a national focus. Because the plans for devolution in England, Scotland and Wales are different, this has been a reasonable approach. However, it begs the question by assuming that a national breakdown is the best way to subdivide popular attitudes. Further, it assumes that attitudes *within* the nations exhibit no significant differences.

One of the problems with determining regional identity is the fact that respondents owe their allegiance to many territorial areas, both distinct and overlapping – the nation, the region, the county, the town, even the neighbourhood. So, when the Kilbrandon Commission asked respondents what they thought of as their region of the country – only in the South West did a majority identify their region in accordance with the map the interviewers displayed. (See Appendix 1 for the map.)

On their own initiative, people were confused about their regional identification, but were quite agreeable to the acceptability of the regions on the map as being a sensible way to run the country [Royal Commission, 1973a, p. 43]. For Britain as a whole, 71 % thought the map "sensible". Regionally, this ranged from a high of 81 % in East Anglia to a low of 59 % for Scotland. A plurality of the Scots felt that their "region" was too large. Thus, there might be acceptability for a regional division for Scotland as well as for England. The Kilbrandon report noted that "the attitude survey indicates that there is a substantial minority of people in Wales who tend to identify themselves with North or South Wales rather than with Wales as a whole . . . In Scotland, there are distinctive traditions in the Highlands and Islands, and a greater tendency than elsewhere in Britain to think in terms of a town or county. It cannot be assumed that all people living in North Wales or in the Highlands of Scotland would view with equanimity the prospect of government from Cardiff or Edinburgh; there may even be some who would regard rule from London as a lesser evil" [Royal Commission, 1973c, 104–105].

In fact, these regional dimensions within Wales and Scotland were evident in the March 1979 referendum result. In Scotland, distance from Edinburgh was positively associated with the 'No' vote (Spearman's Rank Correlation Coefficient $R = .70$). In Wales, however, distance from Cardiff was positively associated with the 'Yes' vote (Spearman's Rank Correlation Coefficient $R = .59$). This is explained by the fact that the North-West countries comprise the largest proportion of Welsh speakers.

In the Kilbrandon polls people readily accepted their regional designation as appropriate [Royal Commission, 1973a, p. 43]. On average, 82 % felt it to be correct. This ranged from a low of 72 % in the West Midlands to 94 % in Scotland. Thus, the people appeared quite willing to accept the present regional arrangements as valid, but not spontaneously.[2])

With regard to the issue of inequality, there is widespread variation of feeling about government understanding of regional needs. On the whole, 21 % of the respondents felt that government understood their own regional needs worse than others. But this varied

[2]) I hope to pursue this avenue of "spontaneous regions" by subjecting the Kilbrandon survey to an in-depth, primary analysis using both factor and variance analysis to sort the 120 constituencies into compatible regions.

from a low of 5 % in Greater London to a high of 49 % in Scotland. This perception of "distance" strongly correlates to a regional breakdown along a centre-periphery dimension. As the regions are more distant from London, they are less likely to feel properly understood by government. (Spearman rank correlation $R = .81$; statistically significant at .05.)

5. Methodology

The poll for the Royal Commission on the Constitution was conducted by Social and Community Planning Research in June 1970. The large sample size of 4,892 allows for regional breakdowns with satisfactory statistical confidence. Still, there are four standard regions that had less than 200 respondents – the North, the East Midlands, East Anglia, and the South. Interpretation of individual percentages within these small regions must be treated with some caution.[3]) Added care should be applied to the East Anglian data. Of the four sampled constituencies, as reported in the Commission document, one, Ashfield, lies adjacent to Nottingham and thus appears misplaced.

One of the main advantages of this particular poll is the over-representation of Wales and Scotland. As a result, these countries can readily be divided into sub-national regions for analysis. In this study, the regions to be analysed are the standard regions. This creates a problem in that two of these standard regions are also nations – Wales and Scotland. Thus, differences of attitudes *within* Wales and Scotland may be obscured.

The basic problem, of course, is determining the most viable regions. Any definition must be somewhat arbitrary and open to question. In a future analysis, data will be gleaned from the polled Parliamentary constituencies and aggregated into homogeneous regions for analysis.

Another difficulty is that of the age of the survey. While the Kilbrandon poll is eleven years old, as far as Scotland is concerned, it represents a stage in the debate when the Scottish Nationalist Party had not gained its present ascendancy. As a result, the effects of lengthy political campaigns on attitudes to devolution had not taken their toll in Scotland. It is not to be asserted that the opinions of Scotland (to a large extent) or of Wales (to a lesser extent) are of the same order today as they were eleven years ago. Yet the level of devolution debate in the three British nations was far more similar in 1970 than today. A newer poll would, therefore, be affected by the much higher level of debate in Scotland and Wales as compared to England in recent years. Therefore, the 1970 poll may better tap the "harder" underlying values of the British towards devolution than would a more recent poll. In short, one might hypothesise that if the English were offered similar options regarding devolution as the Welsh and the Scots, the attitudes would probably follow similar patterns.

The method of the research involves the use of secondary analyses of combinations of regional aggregates of the standard regions to determine which combinations are most ex-

---

[3]) The maximum margin of error at the 95 % confidence level for a random sample of 150 is +/– 8 %.

planatory of the variables of sovereignty, power, and identity/inequality.[4])

Most political scientists have minimised regional cleavages in British politics. Despite the composition of the U.K. into four distinct nationalities, England, Ireland, Scotland and Wales, it has been posited that, over time, regional differences in British politics are insignificant. Finer has attributed this regional homogeneity of culture to demography [5]) frequent inter-marriage between nationalities, and inter-dependent industrialisation [*Finer*, p. 137].

In general, this perception of the minimal role of regional splits in British politics seems reasonably accurate. However, for certain questions and at certain times, regionalis. feelings are important. Devolution is just such a question. Several regional cleavages seem especially important for this issue. These are the centre-periphery split, the difference in economic potential, a Northwest (Scotland, North, Wales) versus Southeast (Anglia, Midlands, South) division, and the conventional separation of England, Scotland and Wales.

6. Class Distinctions

One must recognise that regional differences may be due to class differences. Finer has asserted that "it has been shown that the political preferences of the various regions is not due to local national or religious factors but to local *class* structures" [*Finer*, p. 135; see also *Alford*, pp. 289f.]. With this caveat in mind, let us consider the class composition within the standard regions.

	Middle Class %	Working Class %
London and Southeast	42	58
Southwest	37	63
East Anglia	36	64
South Central	35	65
Yorkshire	30	70
Scotland, Lancashire/Cheshire	29	71
West Midlands	28	72
Wales	26	74
East Midlands	25	75
Northeast	22	78

Source: Adapted from *Butler/Stokes* [1969, 178–179]; quoting numerous National Opinion Polls.
Tab. 2: Class Composition by Region, 1963–1966

[4]) In the future, the data will also be analyzed as soon as possible in the primary mode to cross-check the findings and organize the data in other than standard regional breakdowns. Fortunately, the *Devolution Attitudes* survey [Royal Commission, 1973a] lists the constituencies that were polled. Thus, the responses may be compared with the characteristics of the constituencies directly. There were 120 separate constituencies each with about 40 respondents in two wards. By using the actual sample constituencies as the base for comparison rather than the more arbitrary standard regions, it should be possible to reformulate regions into homogeneous units of theoretical interest. One of the great advantages of using this poll is the higher number of constituencies sampled in both Wales and Scotland. Thus, it will be possible to sub-divide both Wales and Scotland. It is deemed that an N of 400 using 12 regions of 10 constituencies each would provide a good target. This sample size yields a +/– 4.9 % margin of error.

[5]) The English represent 80 % of current U.K. population; in the nineteenth century, only 50 %.

In order to see if class will be an excessive influence on the regional analysis, each of the regional cleavages to be analysed was compared to the regional class composition using Spearman's rank correlation coefficient analysis. There were no significant correlations between class composition of the regions and core-periphery, economic potential or areas of assistance. Only the Northwest-Southeast axis seems to be strongly associated with class composition. Northwest Britain tends to have a predominance of working class. Only Yorkshire has 30 % or more middle-class; while Scotland, Wales, and the Northeast are all below 30 % in middle class composition. It would seem, therefore, that any differences along this dimension *may* be due to class – it will be difficult to sort out. Differences with regard to core-periphery, economic potential, and assistance areas, however, should be due to region rather than class due to the lack of correlation between the two dimensions.

7. Sovereignty

With regard to the question of sovereignty, several questions from the Kilbrandon poll are appropriate. The most important question asked, 'For running the region as a whole, which of these five alternatives would you prefer?' the responses were: (1) "Leave things as they are at present", (2) "Keep things much the same as they are now but make sure that the needs of the region are better understood by the government", (3) "Keep the present system but allow more decisions to be made in the region", (4) "Have a new system of governing the region so that as many decisions as possible are made in the area", and (5) "Let the region take over complete responsibility for running things in the region" [Royal Commission, 1973a, p. 62].

The Royal Commission's analyses of the attitude data defined devolution as positive responses to alternatives (3), (4) and (5) – each of which involves the giving of more decision-making responsibility to the regions. Alternative (3) stops short of any significant change from the present unitary system. As a result of this, the Royal Commission tended to exaggerate the popular desire for devolution. Only alternatives (4) (maximum regional decisions) and (5) (complete regional responsibility) provide for a new system such as the devolved governments in the Scotland and Wales Bill. As a result, the Commission may have overstated the desire for devolution.

Alternative (4) might be termed quasi-federalism. Alternative (5) is very difficult to analyse because it could be merely quasi-federalism, federalism, confederalism, or even separatism. Given the wording of the question with regard to system change, alternatives (1), (2) and (3) all opt for the present system; alternatives (4) and (5) for a new system. Yet, the Royal Commission chose to dichotomise these alternatives by grouping alternative (3) (present system/more regional decisions) with alternative (4) (new system/maximum regional decisions) and (5) (new system/complete regional responsibility) rather than with alternatives (1) (leave present system) and (2) (present system/better understanding).

The North-West/South-East dichotomy has certainly been important in British voting behaviour. As Steed has noted, in North-West Britain Labour attained a 78 seat majority in the February 1974 election; in South-East Britain, the Conservatives had a contrasting 88 seat majority [*Steed*, p. 23]. It has already been pointed out that this may be due to the underlying class bias in these areas. Whereas 27 % of the population is middle class in North-West Britain, 37 % is middle class in South-East Britain [*Steed*, pp. 20ff.]

Alternative Chosen	North-West Britain	South-East Britain
(1) + (2) + (3)	60 %	62 %
(4) + (5)	39 %	36 %
Don't know	1 %	2 %
	100 %	100 %
Sample *N* (unweighted)	2730	2162
Chi-Square	27.7	
Significance (.05)	yes	
Contingency Coefficient	.08	

Source: Royal Commission [1973a, Table 45, p. 62]; and *Steed* [1977, 21–23].

Tab. 3: Desire for a New System (NW/SE Britain)

Despite the fact that the above finding is "statistically" significant, it would seem that this significance is primarily due to the large sample size. Note that the association is very low indeed. Thus, the North-East/South-West dichotomy does not seem to be very helpful in explaining the desire for a change to the British system of government. While the Scots most favour radical change, the Welsh are among the least likely to call for complete responsibility over their own affairs.

Steed has presented a very useful outline of the geographical and historical background to this core-periphery dimension. The basic outline is as follows:

Inner Core:	Southeast
Outer Core:	Anglia, Midlands, and Wessex to include southern Hampshire.
Inner Periphery:	North, Wales, and the Southwest Peninsula to include Devon, Cornwall, and West Somerset.
Outer Periphery:	Scotland, Ireland.

Let us look at the aggregate percentages for those alternatives calling for a new system (4 + 5) as well as the more radical change (5).

	(4) Maximum Regional Decisions	(5) Complete Regional Responsibility	(4) + (5) New Regional System
Inner-Core	20 %	16 %	36 %
Outer-Core	21 %	18 %	37 %
Inner-Periphery	22 %	15 %	37 %
Outer-Periphery	24 %	23 %	47 %
Spearman's Rank Correlation	.57	.02	.44
Significance (.05)	no	no	no

Source: Royal Commission [1973a, Table 45, p. 62].

Tab. 4: Desire for a New System (Core-Periphery)

The core-periphery dimension seems, therefore, to explain the desire for a new system which stops short of devolving complete responsibility to the regions. It does not seem to be an adequate explanation of a more radical desire for the regional assumption of complete responsibility. The core-periphery dimension, therefore, does not include a call for confederation or separation, but rather a quasi-federal or perhaps a federal level of devolution.

Another regional factor that is closely linked to the core-periphery concept is the different levels of economic potential. Each region of a country exhibits a certain level of accessibility to the markets of that country. By using data on mileage, cost of transport, population, total income, and market size in each region, one is able to assess the economic potential of the region. Figure 1 represents a map of economic potential of Britain.

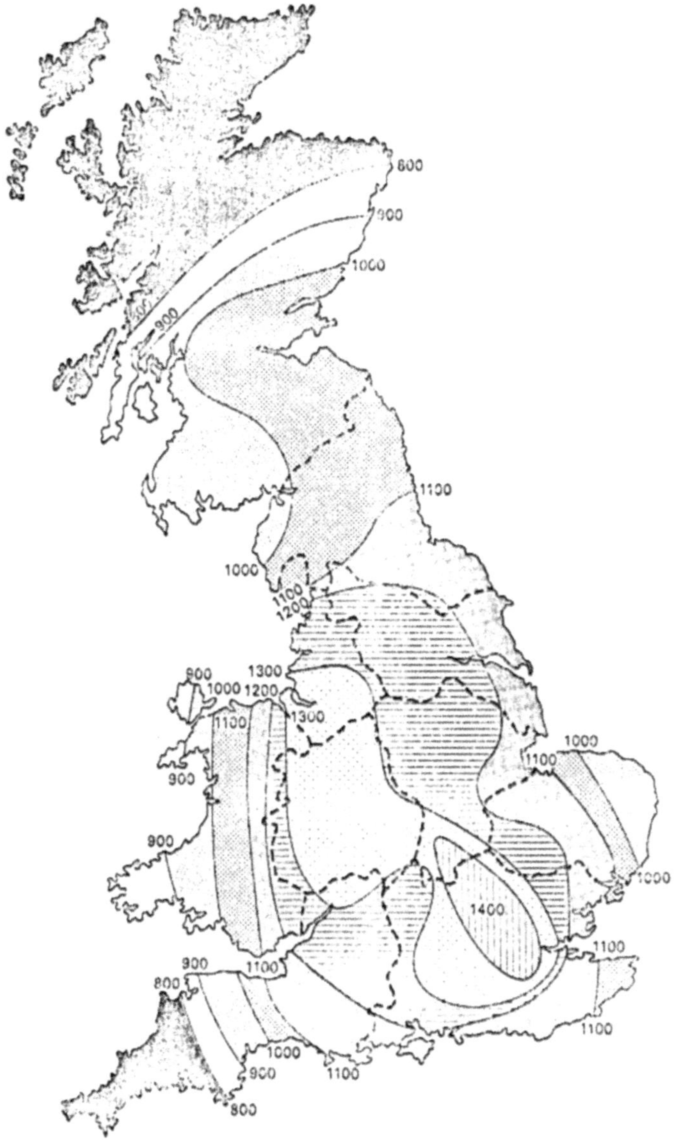

Source: *Sant* [1974, p. 21]. Reprinted by permission of the publishers.

Fig. 1: Economic Potential in Great Britain

This econo·nic potential data was related to the standard regions. The regions were then rank ordered and compared with the sovereignty question. There was hardly any correlation at all between economic potential and selection of alternatives (3) + (4) + + (5) (Spearman's rank correlation R = .01, not significant). Nor was there much association between economic potential and a call for the regions taking over complete responsibility for running their own affairs as stated in alternative (5). Just as was noted in the analysis of the centre-periphery dimension above, the combination (4) + (5) which call for a system change resulted in the strongest connection. This was principally due to the fact that alternative (4) calling for a new system making as many decisions in the area as possible displayed the strongest links of all. Those regions with the greatest economic potential – the Southeast and the West Midlands were least in favour of systematic change. Scotland, the area with the least economic potential, wanted change the most. (It must be noted that this analysis does not include the potential value of the North Sea oil.)

Level of Potential	(4) Maximum Regional Decisions	(5) Complete Regional Responsibility	(4) + (5) New Regional System
1400	19	15	34
1300	18	17	35
1200	22	16	38
1100	21	16	37
1000	21	19	40
Spearman's R	–.50	–.30	–.57
Significance (.05)	no	no	no

Source: Derived from *Sant* [1974, 20–21]; and Royal Commission [1973, Table 45, p. 62].

Tab. 5: Desire for a New System (Economic Potential)

This economic potential is evaluated by the U.K. government and certain regions are assisted to help equalise employment and production over wider areas. Thus, certain areas are deemed to be worthy of assistance. Figure 2 presents a map of the special development areas, development areas, intermediate areas, and derelict land clearance areas. Each of these areas was related to the standard regions and compared to the sovereignty question.

There was a fairly strong positive association between the degree of assistance and the desire for a new governmental system. Contrary to the classic Roman notion of government by *panem et circenses*, modern-day Britain is prone to what might be termed the "dole hypothesis". That is, the more hand-outs the British citizen receives, the less likely he is to appreciate "the hand that feeds him." In this case, the more assistance a region is receiving, the more likely that that region desires a change from the present system. This may be due to a lack of communication from the government to the people or it may be that the assistance is generally ineffective or it may be that the help offered is of the wrong type. There is, of course, enormous potential for both national and supra-national governments to gain in prestige by well-structured, highly publicised development schemes for the deprived regions. Ionescu has urged the European Community to be aware of the opportunities for direct intervention at the regional level throughout the

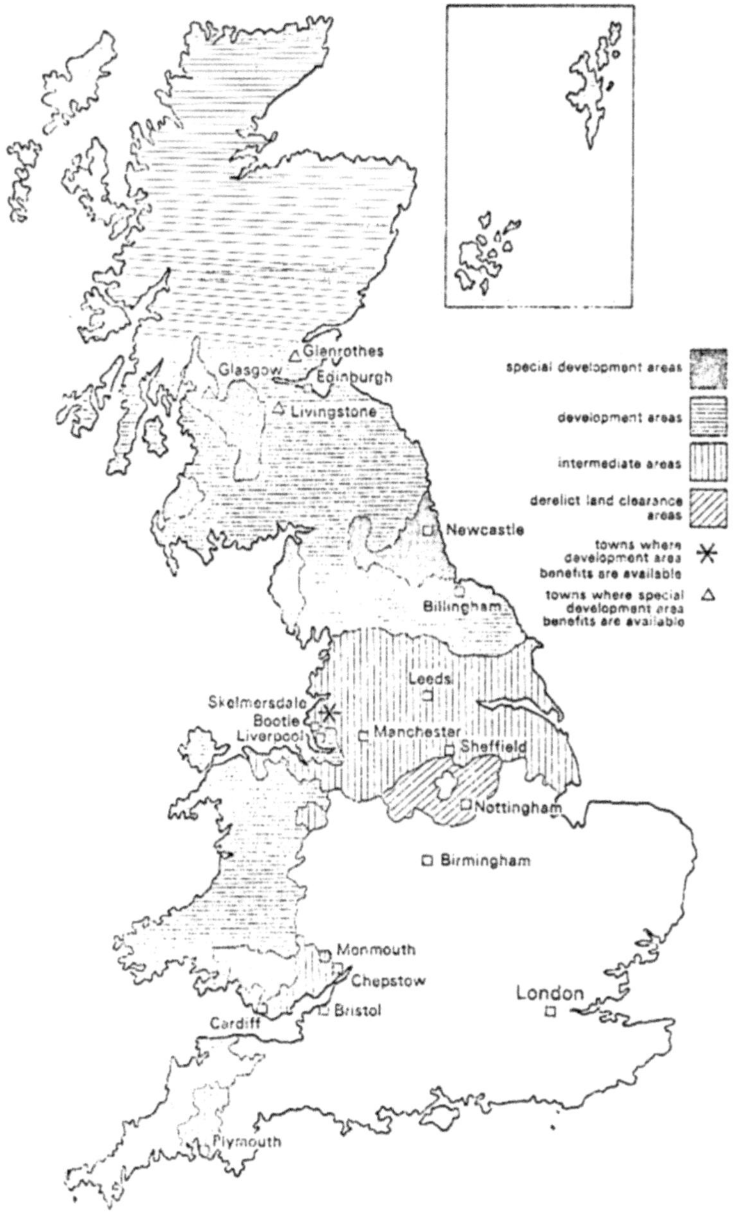

Source: *Sant* [1974, p. 34]. Reprinted by permission of the publishers.

Fig. 2: Assisted Areas: Great Britain 1972

E.C. In the battle for public opinion, the E.C. Regional Development Fund could be crucial to the popularity and power of the Common Market in Britain [*Ionescu*, pp. 197f., 208].

Table 6 illustrates the relationships between the sovereignty question and the development areas.

	Sovereignty Alternatives		
Type of Area	(4) Maximum Regional Decisions	(5) Complete Regional Responsibility	(4) + (5) New Regional System
Unassisted	20	19	39
Intermediate/Derelict Land	22	15	37
Development	23	19	42
Spearman's R	.52	−.20	.25
Significance (.05)	no	no	no

Source: Derived from *Sant* [1974, 34–35]; and Royal Commission [1973a, Table 45, p. 62].

Tab. 6: Desire for a New System (Development Areas)

Let us now compare the traditional national analysis to the foregoing. Does the aggregation of the English regions in order to contrast these with Wales and Scotland help or hinder the analysis of the underlying attitudes towards devolution? Here the extremely close similarity between England and Wales is contrasted with the distinctive Scottish case. Yet, in the choice of alternative (4) (a new system with maximum regional decisions), Wales and Scotland are closely aligned. The Welsh, it seems do want real change but not total responsibility.

Alternative Chosen	England	Wales	Scotland
(1) + (2) + (3) (Present system)	63 %	64 %	52 %
(4) (New system/Maximum decisions)	20 %	23 %	24 %
(5) (New system/Complete responsibility)	16 %	13 %	23 %
Don't know	1 %	0 %	1 %
Total	100 %	100 %	100 %
Sample *N* (unweighted)	3274	726	892
Chi-Square	56.3		
Significance (.05)	yes		
Contingency Coefficient	.11		

Source: Royal Commission [1973a, Table 45, p. 62].

Tab. 7: Desire for a New System (Nations)

While the relationship is statistically significant, it is almost exclusively due to the differences between Scotland and England/Wales. The association again is low. Nationality seems to be overrated as an indicator of attitudes to devolution (except for Scotland).

It is interesting to note the remarkable stability of Scottish opinion here. The difference between the 52 % – 47 % response to the June 1970 poll for retention of the present system and the March 1979 referendum result of 52 – 48 % is within the statistical margin of error. The Welsh referendum result was also remarkably stable. The closest alternative for Wales was alternative (4) (a new system with maximum regional decisions). The Wales Act stopped short of alternative (5) (a new system with complete responsibility). In the June 1970 poll, 23 % of the Welsh respondents favoured alternative (4); in the March 1979 referendum, 24 % of Welsh voters favoured the Wales Act.

With regard to sovereignty, then, the most promising regional breakdown for analysis appears to be that of the core-periphery. In second place, is the development areas but these strongly overlap the core-periphery itself. Third, the economic potential breakdown is a relatively good indicator of regional feelings. Neither the North-West/South-East nor the National division seem as likely to provide much explanation. Because of these findings, a federal regional solution encompassing the standard regions of England, a two-way split of Wales, and a three-way split of Scotland might provide a more viable solution to the core-periphery dissatisfaction that the 1979 Scotland and Wales Act which fail to come to grips with such problems as the West Lothian Question.

The question that best delineates the struggle for power between the centralists and the decentralists is as follows – "I asked you just now about things like the health service, schools, the roads, the police and so on. In general do you think it is better that the standards for such services be the same in every part of Britain, or do you think each region should be allowed to set its own standards?" [Royal Commission, 1973a, p. 103].

The relationship between the regional dimensions of core-periphery, economic potential, and assisted areas with that of the feeling that each region should be allowed to set its own standards is negligible. These regional breakdowns do not seem to provide much explanation of the dencentralist quest for power. The calculations of Spearman's rank correlation coefficient are as follows:

	Core-Periphery	Economic Potential	Assisted Areas
Spearman's R	–.15	.14	.15
Significance (.05)	no	no	no

Source: Royal Commission [1973a, Table 74, p. 103]

Tab. 8: Decentralisation by Regional Typology

With regard to the geographic cleavages of North-West/South-East Britain and the national breakdown, provide hardly any explanation at all. In fact, amazingly, the North-West/South-East dichotomy offers no explanation at all!

Responses	North-West/South-East		England	Wales	Scotland
Same in every part of Britain	53 %	53 %	53 %	61 %	50 %
Each region sets own standards	44 %	44 %	44 %	36 %	45 %
Don't Know	3 %	3 %	4 %	3 %	4 %
	100 %	100 %	100 %	100 %	99 % (rounding)
Sample N (unweighted)	2730	2162	3274	726	892
Chi-square	0.0		22.6		
Significance (.05)	no		yes		
Contingency Coefficient	.00		.07		

Source: Royal Commission [1973, Table 74, p. 203].

Tab. 9: Decentralization by NW/SE and National Cleavages

In summary none of the regional dimensions seem to explain the centralist-decentralist power struggle.

Regional identity is tapped by the following question – "If someone called you a (regional name) would you accept it as reasonable or would you want to correct them?" [Royal Commission, 1973, p. 47]. All the British regions had strong positive responses to this question. On average 82 % felt they could accept the regional designations as stated. Scotland, the North, and Yorkshire all exceeded 90 %; Greater London, the Southwest and the West Midlands fell below 75 %.

The regional breakdowns of core-periphery, assistance areas, and economic potential all display strong associations with the identity variable. Both core-periphery (and assistance areas have statistically significance correlations of .66 and .69 respectively. Much of this is probably due to the fact that there is much less physical mobility in the periphery. While 62 % of the respondents stated that they had lived in their region all their lives, over 70 % in Wales, the North, and Scotland had done so. By contrast less than half of the people in the Southeast had lived there all their lives [Royal Commission, 1973a, p. 46].

Both the North-West/South-East Britain split as well as the National division are highly explanatory of the sense of identity in the regions. Along the NW/SE dimension, there is a difference of 10 % in accepting the regional designation. Along national lines, the Scots are 15 % more likely to accept the regional designation than the English (though it must be noted here that one is comparing a regional designation with a national one).

Responses	North-West/South-East		England	Wales	Scotland
Accept regional name	88 %	78 %	79 %	85 %	94 %
Correct the person	11 %	20 %	19 %	15 %	6 %
Don't know	1 %	2 %	2 %	0 %	1 %
	100 %	100 %	100 %	100 %	101 % (rounding)
Sample N (unweighted)	2730	2162	3274	726	892
Chi-Square	38.3		110.6		
Significance (.05)	yes		yes		
Contingency Coefficient	.09		.15		

Source: Royal Commission [1973a, Table 35, p. 47].

Tab. 10: Identity by NW/SE and National Cleavages

In summary, all the dimensions have shown a strong linkage with the identity facet of regionalism. The farther from the centre, the greater the assistance, the less the economic potential, the more northerly, and the less English that respondents are, the more likely they are to have strong senses of identity and attachments to their regions.

Core-Periphery, Economic Potential, and Assistance Areas all are strongly related to feelings of inequality. Both core-periphery and economic potential are highly and significantly correlated to the inequality variable. Spearman rank correlation coefficients R are .81 and –.75 respectively. The government is perceived to fail to understand regional needs along these dimensions.

The North-West/South-East dichotomy and the national dimension are also explanatory of feelings of inequality. All the North-West regions are above the average of 21 % of the respondents who feel that government understanding of regional needs is worse in comparison with other parts of Britain. The North (40 %) and Wales (39 %) nearly double the average; Scotland more than doubles it (49 %).

Responses	North-West/South-East		England	Wales	Scotland
Better/About same	60 %	79 %	75 %	56 %	44 %
Worse	33 %	12 %	17 %	39 %	49 %
Don't know	7 %	9 %	8 %	5 %	6 %
Total	100 %	100 %	100 %	100 %	100 % (rounding)
Sample N (unweighted)	2730	2162	3274	726	892
Chi-square	295		457		
Significance	yes		yes		
Contingency Coefficient	.24		.29		

Source: Royal Commission [1973a, Table 37, p. 51].

Tab. 11: Inequality by NW/SE and National Cleavages

The strength of the regional dimensions both for feelings of identity and for inequality indicate that there is a real need for the British government to consider how it might best improve the situation. Unfortunately, the people offer little guidance with regard to the centralisation or decentralisation of power. It would seem that the people desire a changed system of government that falls short of offering complete responsibility to the regions. There seems to be very little sentiment for either confederalism or separatism.

As *Smith* [1977, p. 28] has stated, "Regionalism cannot work unless the region or nation can be shown to be the optimum area for a range of services." Bogdanor has pointed out that one of the most important factors to consider in the determination of the size of the administrative units within a country is the expressive function denoted by these units. These administrative units are seen to "express the society's normative view as to how political power should be organised" [*Bogdanor*, p. 165]. He points out that regionalism and devolution has not been fully explored in Britain because of the implicit nature of the British constitution: it is hoped that, by highlighting some of the regional dimensions with respect to the question of sovereignty, power, identity, and inequality, the differences between the various regional groupings can be developed and amplified. Bogdanor's assertion that the British public, generally speaking, accept the high concentration of centralised power has been confirmed in this paper. Devolution effectively challenges the centralist philosophy. Because of this and the uncodified nature of the British constitution, fundamental constitutional principles are attacked. The regional dimensions that have been analysed indicate that the public desires change for the betterment of their regional interests. The government is accorded considerable leeway on the path to effective government for the regions. The citizenry is not specific in calling for a specific method, level of sovereignty, or locus of power. But, the citizenry is dissatisfied with the present manner of conducting the government's affairs.

The government must seek a workable solution – not an expedient one which, for short-term gain, could spell long-term chaos. The Scotland and Wales Bills were recognised as such.

Appendix I

Map Depicting Regions for use in the Survey for the Royal Commission on the Constitution.

Source: Royal Commission on the Constitution [1973, p. 44].

References

Alford, R.: Party and Society. London 1964.

Bogdanor, V.: Regionalism: The Constitutional Aspects. Political Quarterly, April–June 1977, 164–174.

Butler, D., and *D. Stokes*: Political Change in Britain. Harmondsworth, Middlesex, 1969.

Finer, S.E.: Comparative Government. Harmondsworth, Middlesex, 1970.

Goodrich, P.S.: British Attitudes Toward the European Community, October 1971 to February 1974. London 1979.

Ionescu, G.G.: Centrepetal Politics. London 1975.

Jennings, Sir Ivor: The Queen's Government. Harmondsworth, Middlesex, 1965.

Royal Commission on the Constitution: Devolution and Other Aspects of Government: An Attitudes Survey. Research Paper Number 7, London 1973a.

– : Federalism in the United States, Canada and Australia. Research Paper Number 2. Ed. by M.J.C. Vile. London 1973b.

– : Report, Volume I. London 1973c.

Sant, M.E.C.: Regional Disparities. London 1974.

Smith, B.: Confusions in Regionalism. Political Quarterly, January–March 1977, 14–27.

Steed, M.: Devolution – What English Dimension? Paper presented to the PSA Conference. University of Wales at Aberystwyth, 1977.

Holler, M.J. (Ed.): Power, Voting, and Voting Power ©Physica-Verlag, Würzburg (Germany) 1981

The Paradox of Redistribution: Some Theoretical and Empirical Results

A. Schotter, New York[1])

1. Introduction

It is widely known among game theorists that the voting weight a member has in a voting body is not a good proxy for his voting power or influence within the body. This fact is easily illustrated. For instance, consider the voting body $V = (50\ \%; 35\ \%; 45\ \%; 20\ \%)$ where 50 % is the voting rule used in the organization – if any members form a coalition with 50 % or more of the votes, they are winning and can make decisions that are binding on the entire body – and 35 %, 45 % and 20 % are the voting weights of voters 1, 2 and 3, respectively. In this body then, although the weights are not distributed equally, it is easy to see that all the members are indeed equally powerful under the 50 % majority rule, since any voter cannot win a vote by himself and any coalition of two or more voters is winning. Consequently, it is clear that voting weights are not perfect proxies for voting power. The question that arises, however, is how bad a proxy are they? In other words, if we were to increase (or decrease) a voter's voting weight within a voting body would his resulting influence within the organization always increase (or decrease), although possibly not in proportion to the increase in his weight, or could his influence within the organization actually decrease (increase)?

This paper presents the results of two previous studies of this question done by *Fischer/Schotter* [1978] and *Dreyer/Schotter* [1980]. Our results are simple:

a) Voting weights are extremely bad proxies for voting power. In fact, they are so bad that it may be possible to increase a voter's voting weight within an organization and actually decrease his power when power is measured by both the Banzhaf and Shapley-Shubik power in indices. In addition, it is possible to decrease a voter's voting weight within a voting body and increase his power. This later result was termed the "Paradox of Redistribution" by *Fischer/Schotter* [1978].
While the result is interesting, it would only be of empirical significance if the likelihood of such an occurance were great. In other words, if the paradox were merely a theoretical possibility, it may not cause a problem from a policy point of view. To this end, Fischer/Schotter have proved the following.

[1]) The author would like to thank Dietrich Fischer and Jacob Dreyer for their previous collaboration on the idea presented here. In addition, the support of the Office of Naval Research, Contract Number N0014-78-C-0598 is gratefully acknowledged.

b) Not only is the "Paradox of Redistribution" possible, but such a paradox is inevitable (for $n \geqslant 6$ in the case of the Banzhaf index and $n \geqslant 7$ in the case of the Shapley-Shubik index) in the sense that for any voting body $V = (d; w)$ where d is a decision rule and w is a voting weight distribution, there always exists another voting body, $V' = (d; w')$, where d is held constant and w changed to w', in which at least one voter has his percentage of the vote decreased and his percentage of the power increased. This result is not quite satisfactory, however, because while it proves that there exist some other voting distribution w' which gives rise to our inverse relationship between voting power and voting weight, it gives us no indication as to how likely the paradox really is. To try to settle this question, Fischer/Schotter performed a Monte Carlo experiment. These results are summarized by Figure 1 of the appendix and can be stated as follows: The paradox of redistribution has a surprisingly high likelihood of occurrence. In fact, for voting bodies with 6 voters using either a 50 or a 90 percent voting rule, the probability of occurrence was 30 %.

All of these results would still be of no significance if the organizers of national and international organizations clearly understood the relationship between voting weight and voting power and acted accordingly. However, when one observes the real world, one realizes that in most major institutions the organizers of those institutions act as if voting weights were indeed perfect proxies for voting power. Consequently, it is not surprising to find institutions whose true power relationships are far different from the power relationships desired by the institution's planners.

To demonstrate this point, *Dreyer/Schotter* [1980] examined the power changes that occurred when some changes were made in the voting rules and voting weight distribution of the International Monetary Fund. They found that in the recent redistribution of the votes:

c) 38 countries had their percentage of the votes in the organization decreased and yet had their percentage of the power within the organization increased, while,
d) 4 countries had their percentage of the power within the organization increased and yet suffered decreases in their power within the organization.
e) Finally, the Dreyer-Schotter results indicate that smaller countries within the I.M.F. have power that is out of proportion to their percentage of votes and that the recent voting changes at the Fund exacerbated this fact.

This paper tries to synthesize these theoretical and empirical results. We will proceed as follows:

Section 2 will briefly present a simple 3-person example illustrating the paradox of redistribution. Section 3 will present some simple theorems demonstrating the inevitability of the "paradox of redistribution." Section 4 will discuss the voting procedures of the International Monetary Fund and present some results indicating the extent to which voting weights are poor proxies for voting power. Finally, Section 5 will offer some conclusions and present some problems that might arise when we try to adjust the voting weights in a voting body to better represent the desired power relationships of the voting body.

2. The Paradox of Redistribution for a Three-Member Voting Body

Consider the following voting body:

$$\nu = (70\ \%; 55\ \%, 35\ \%, 10\ \%)$$

where 70 % is the decision rule and (55 %, 35 %, 10 %) is the vote distribution. The Banzhaf and Shapley-Shubik power indices associated with this voting body are both (1/2, 1/2, 0). Now let us redistribute the votes, keeping the decision rule the same, so that the following voting body is determined:

$$\nu' = (70\ \%; 50\ \%, 25\ \%, 25\ \%).$$

Here the Banzhaf index is (3/5, 1/5, 1/5), while the Shapley-Shubik index is (2/3, 1/6, 1/6), showing that although member 1's voting weight decreased from 55/100 to 50/100, his power increased.

Now it might be interesting to ask whether in a three member voting body there exist vote distributions which are paradox proof in the sense that any redistribution of the votes which starts at one of these distributions must give a voter less voting power if it gives him less weight. The answer is yes, and as a matter of fact there are an infinite number of such vote distributions. For the purpose of illustration, however, consider the following voting body, $\nu = (70\ \%; 55\ \%, 25\%, 20\%)$. Here the power distribution is (3/5, 1/5, 1/5) if the Banzhaf index is used, and (2/3, 1/6, 1/6) if the Shapley-Shubik index is used. The reader can check for himself that it is not possible to give a voter more power by diminishing his voting weight.

3. The Inevitability of the Paradox of Redistribution

The question we investigate in this paper, then, is the circumstances under which the paradox illustrated above is inevitable. To do this, we must demonstrate how, given a vote distribution $w = (w_1, \ldots, w_n)$ and a voting rule d, we can construct a new vote distribution $w' = (w'_1, \ldots, w'_n)$ which gives at least one voter a smaller proportion of the vote yet gives him more power, when power is measured by either the Banzhaf or the Shapley-Shubik power index. The following propositions do just that.

Proposition 1: For voting bodies with $n \geqslant 6$, a paradox is always possible no matter what initial vote distribution exists, when power is defined by the Banzhaf index.

Proof of Proposition 1.

1. For any voting rule d and any weight w_1, of voter 1, his maximum power is at least 1/5, no matter how small w_1 is. He can achieve this power by assigning weight $w_2 = d - w_1/2 - \delta/2$ to voter 2, $w_3 = 1 - d - w_1/2 - \delta/2$ to voter 3, and $w_4 = \ldots = w_n = \delta/(n-3)$ to the remaining voters where δ is arbitrarily small but smaller than w_1. In particular $w_4 + \ldots + w_n = \delta < w_1/2 + \delta/2$, that is, $\delta < w_1$, so that the voters $4, \ldots, n$ are all dummies with zero voting power.
2. If there are 6 voters, the weakest of them has at most power 1/6 (since the power indices add up to 1). By point 1 of the proof, the weakest voter can now redistribute the

weights of the other voters and increase his power to 1/5, keeping his voting weight constant. However, since he can achieve a power of 1/5 with an arbitrarily small voting weight, he can in fact decrease his weight to any small positive value and still achieve this power. Q.E.D.

Proposition 2: For voting bodies with $n \geqslant 7$, a paradox is always possible no matter what initial vote distribution exists, when power is defined by the Shapley-Shubik index.

Proof of Proposition 2. Analogous to the proof of Proposition 1.

The import of these theorems is that for any voting body $v = (d; w_1, \ldots, w_n)$ – where $n \geqslant 6$ for the Banzhaf case and $n \geqslant 7$ for the Shapley-Shubik case – any initial vote distribution is subject to the paradox of redistribution in that there always exists another vote distribution such that in the redistribution of voting weights at least one player's weight is decreased while his voting power is increased. It is in this sense that the paradox is inevitable.

One shortcoming of our results is that they do not give us any indication of the minimum size of the redistribution necessary to create the paradox. Clearly our results would be more disturbing if for any given initial distribution of votes there was another distribution within a small neighborhood of the original which would create the paradox. It is interesting to note that in the case of the International Monetary Fund (to be discussed in the next section), the redistribution of voting weights was not a "drastic" one. Also, our simulation results given in the appendix demonstrate that the occurrence of the paradox is not a rare event.

Our results so far are rather general in that we do not constrain the decision rule used in our voting bodies in any way. However, the most common voting rule is the simple majority voting rule and when this rule is used, it is possible to show that both for the Banzhaf and the Shapley-Shubik power indices no paradox proof vote distributions exist for $n \geqslant 4$.

Proposition 3: If the voting rule used is the simple majority voting rule (i.e., if $d = 1/2$), then for $n \geqslant 4$ a paradox is always possible.

Proof of Proposition 3. Let 1 be the weakest voter. (Every voter's weight is always positive, thus $w_1 > 0$.) Voter 1 can now achieve a power of 1/3 by distributing the weights as w_1, $w_2 = w_3 = (1 - w_1 - \delta)/2$, $w_4 = \delta/(n-3) = \ldots = w_n$ with $\delta > w_1$. Then voters $4, \ldots, n$ all have zero voting power and voters 1, 2 and 3 have power 1/3 each. This is true both for the Banzhaf and the Shapley-Shubik power indices.

With four or more voters in a voting body, the weakest voter has, at most, power 1/4 (in general $1/n \leqslant 1/4$). But the weakest voter can increase his power to 1/3 by redistributing the voting weights of the remaining players as indicated while keeping his voting weight the same. However, since voter 1 can achieve a power of 1/3 even with an arbitrarily small voting weight, he can in fact decrease his voting weight and still achieve this power. Thus a paradox of redistribution always exists for $n \geqslant 4$ and $d = 1/2$. Q.E.D.

Instead of restricting the voting rule as we did in Proposition 3, we could have placed a restriction on the vote distribution. One restriction would be to constrain the weight of the smallest voter. If we make the restriction that the voter with the smallest voting weight (say voter i) has a weight $w_i > 2d - 1$ initially (which in the case of $d = 51$ % merely requires that he has more than 2 % of the vote), then it is possible to prove that no paradox proof vote distributions exist for $n \geqslant 4$ for both the Banzhaf and Shapley-Shubik power indices.

Proposition 4: If the decision rule is d and if the voter with the smallest voting weight in the voting body $v = (d; w_1, \ldots, w_n)$ has a weight greater than $2d - 1$, then with $n \geqslant 4$ (and either the Banzhaf or the Shapley-Shubik index), a paradox is always possible.

Proof of Proposition 4. The weakest voter (say voter 1) has at most power $1/n \leqslant 1/4$. We can increase his power to 1/3 by assigning weights w_1, $w_2 = w_3 = (1 - w_1 - \delta)/2$, $w_4 = \ldots = w_n = \delta/(n-3)$, with $w_1 + w_2 = (1 + w_1 - \delta)/2 > d$ or $\delta < w_1 - (2d - 1)$, where it is always possible to choose $\delta > 0$, by assumption. Q.E.D.

4. Power in the International Monetary Fund

As was stated in the introduction, all of the results derived so far would be of no significance if the types of phenomena we are discussing never occurred in the real world. However, at least in the International Monetary Fund, the planners of that organization seem to ignore the fact that voting weights are not perfect proxies for voting power. Consequently, when they desire to change the power relationships within the fund to reflect the changing importance of their members in international trade, they rely totally on changes in voting weights without giving any consideration to the effects these new weights actually have on the members' power.

Probably the best example of this myopia can be found in the recently ratified "Second Amendment to the Articles of Agreement of the International Monetary Fund" which along with the sixth review of the Fund's quota distribution was instituted to make the fund better reflect the changing importance of its members in the world trade. These amendments and quota revisions altered the voting rules and vote distribution among the members of the fund and the consequences of these revisions were analyzed by *Dreyer/Schotter* [1978]. Their conclusions were as follows:

1. Under the proposed changes 38 countries in the IMF had their percentage of the total vote decreased and yet their voting power within the organization increased when power is measured by the Banzhaf power index.
2. With the new vote distribution and voting rules, four major countries – Belgium, Holland, West Germany and Japan – had their percentage of the total vote increased and yet had their percentage of the total power decreased.
3. Under the previous distribution of votes and voting rules, smaller countries had a voting power that was out of proportion to their voting weights, and the newly introduced changes would generally aggravate this disproportion.
4. The power of the United States within the Fund increases substantially on issues where most countries vote through their Executive Directors (as groups), as opposed to issues where they vote through their Governors (individually).
5. Under both the previous and current voting system, significant diminishing returns to

voting weights exist and the tendency is more pronounced under the new system. In most voting situations power is a concave function of voting weight with large linear segments.

6. Although these results are in many instances not quantitatively substantial, qualitatively they indicate a noticeable discrepancy between what one would think the consequences of the voting changes would be and what they actually are.

Before we formally present these results, let us briefly discuss the voting rules and procedures at the International Monetary Fund.

4.1 Voting in the IMF

The organization of the IMF is very simple. All powers of the Fund are vested in its Board of Governors which is composed of the Fund's 131 member countries. Each country has 250 votes plus one additional vote for each part of its quota which is equivalent to one hundred thousand Special Drawing Rights (S.D.R.'s). The Board of Governors may, however, delegate certain decisions to be made to the Fund's body of Executive Directors which is composed of one representative from each of the five members of the Fund having the largest quotas plus 15 other representatives each of whom represents a certain subset or coalition of countries. There are then twenty Executive Directors, each one having the number of votes equal to the sum of the votes contained in the subset of countries it represents. Thus, voting by the Directors is, in fact, a two stage process. First each coalition meets and agrees (using a simple majority rule) on how its representative (Executive Director) will cast his vote in the body of Executive Directors. Then the Executive Directors themselves meet and, using a decision rule that is not necessarily a simple majority rule, cast their votes.

Essentially, decisions binding on all IMF members can be taken either by the required majority of votes cast by the voting body of Governors or the required majority of votes cast by the voting body of Executive Directors. The majorities required by these two bodies depend upon the type of issue to be decided. One type (which for want of a better description we shall denote as issues of procedure) requires a 70 percent majority in both voting bodies. This rule was left unchanged by the new amendments. Another class of issues (which we shall denote as issues of substance), however, required in any of the two voting bodies an 80 percent majority under the old rules and requires an 85 percent majority under the new ones. The required majority for deciding issues of substance was raised from 80 to 85 percent at the insistence of the United States to retain its veto power: the U.S. made this change a pre-condition for its agreement to having its voting share lowered from above to below 20 percent of the total vote.

One apparent curiosity that needs to be mentioned is that, in fact, no decisions within the Fund are made by means of formal balloting. It is an institution operating on the basis of consensus reached through informal consultations among members. In this context, possession by a member, or a group of members, of a given share of the total vote has to be viewed as an indication of its strength during the process of informal negotiations when a compromise among differing views on a certain issue is being forged. It is the threat by a country (or a group of countries) of bringing an issue to a formal vote in which its view would prevail that renders the actual vote unnecessary and decision making by consensus roughly approximate to decision making by actually counting ballots.

4.2 Previous Power Distribution

Before we investigate the consequences of the recent changes in the voting rules, distribution of voting weights, or the shares of the members of the IMF, let us first investigate the power relationship existing prior to April 1, 1978.

This data is illustrated in Diagrams 1 through 4 (upper solid curves) of the appendix. From these diagrams, several interesting features appear. First, from Diagram 1 (upper solid curve), we see that when individual countries voted on issues employing the 70 percent decision rule, the relationship between power and voting weights was practically log-linear except for the two largest countries, the United States and the United Kingdom, for which the relationship flattened out considerably. Put differently, while all members had a voting power proportional to their voting weights, the United States and the United Kingdom had voting powers considerably below their shares of the total vote. For issues involving the 80 percent rule (see upper solid curve in Diagram 2), the linear relationship failed to hold for the ten countries with largest voting shares: the United States, the United Kingdom, Germany (Federal Republic), France, Japan, Canada, Italy, India, Netherlands, Australia. This result is interesting since, in the Fund, votes are allocated on the basis of a country's contribution to the Fund. Consequently, say in the 70 percent case, while all countries may have claimed to be getting their "money's worth" in terms of power, this could not be said for the United States and the United Kingdom. For instance, while the United States contributed almost 16 percent more to the Fund than West Germany, it only received approximately 4 percent more of the power, as measured by the Banzhaf index, for that contribution.[2])[3])

Similar results hold for issues which were voted upon by Executive Directors (see upper solid curves in Diagrams 3 and 4), again with the concavity more pronounced for issues involving the 80 percent decision rule than for issues involving the 70 percent rule. In this voting body, however, the United States had relatively more power than it did in the voting body consisting of Governors; e.g., on issues involving the 70 percent decision rule, the U.S. had 13.54 percent of voting power as opposed to 9.07 percent when the same rule was used by the Board of Governors. In other words the United States' power within the Fund increased when the other countries voted in blocks rather than separately. This seems somewhat counter-intuitive, of course, since one would expect that a "large" member would be hurt by the formation of syndicates, each of which would act in unison on particular votes. However, as several recent studies in game theory have

---

[2]) *Olson/Zeckhauser* [1966] demonstrate, through a model that describes the services of international organizations such as NATO or the UN, as public goods, that in most organizations of this type larger countries (notably the U.S.) wind up making a disproportionately large contribution to the financing of the organization.

[3]) It should be pointed out, however, that the United States has a veto on all issues at The International Monetary Fund and that these power indices fail to incorporate that fact.

shown [see *Aumann; Postlewaite/Rosenthal;* and *Schotter*], syndication need not always be advantageous for the members who syndicate and here is an example of that phenomenon.

To present a picture of past power relationships in the IMF from a different angle, consider the "power Lorenz curves" (lower solid curves in Diagrams 5 to 8), constructed to represent the degree of inequality of the distribution of power in the IMF among Executive Directors and individual Governors for issues involving the 70 percent and 80 percent voting rules.

In all of these diagrams, the cumulative percentage of the voting weights is plotted against the cumulative percentage of the voting power. As we might expect from our previous discussion, since large countries had voting powers that were less than proportional to their voting weights, the resulting Lorenz curves should demonstrate a certain overrepresentation for smaller countries. This was more pronounced on issues requiring 80 percent of the total vote than on issues calling for a 70 percent majority. As we would expect, the inequality diminished when countries voted through their Executive Directors instead of individually which is easily explained by the increase in power of large countries on issues requiring Executive Directors.

4.3 Consequences of Quota Changes

1. *Some Surprises.* When we analyze the consequences of the recent quota changes, we find some surprises and some expected results. Among the surprises are the paradoxical results described before. Specifically, some of the power relationships resulting from the changes contradict the intentions of their initiators. These paradoxical results are summarized in Tables 1 and 2 where we see (in Table 1) that, as a result of the quota changes, 38 countries have their percentage of power increased within the Fund even though their voting share decreases, while four countries (Table 2) have their percentage of power decreased even though the new vote distribution awards them a larger share of the total vote.[4]) This result is not surprising to students of voting power since, as we have seen, the power of a member depends not only on the number of votes or percentage of the total vote that he has, but also on the way the remaining votes are distributed amongst the other $n - 1$ voters and the decision rule used.

2. *Power Effects.* If we were to give a general assessment of the recent changes, we could state that under the new distribution of voting weights larger countries have unquivocally less power than they had under the old distribution. This fact is demonstrated in Diagrams 1 through 4 below, where we superimpose the voting power/voting weights relationship under the new scheme over the relation we found under the previous scheme.

The overall impression from these diagrams is that the voting changes did not drastically alter the basic relationship between voting weight and voting power. There is a universal tendency for the power of the large countries to be less than proportional to their

[4]) Since we are dealing with a very large voting body, it is not surprising that many of our results hold true at a third decimal place; many countries have virtually no power to start with. However, the qualitative result still holds: increases or decreases in voting percentages do not necessarily imply increases or decreases in corresponding voting powers.

voting shares and this tendency is more pronounced for issues of substance (the 80 % and 85 % decision rules) than it is for issues of procedure (the 70 % decision rule).

When we superimpose our power Lorenz curves constructed for the new rules and distribution of voting shares over the Lorenz curves previously presented (see Diagrams 5 through 8), we see that there is practically no change in the degree of power inequality in the Fund except for issues of substance voted upon by Governors. In fact, for the body of Executive Directors, the Lorenz curves for the 70 percent voting rule under the new system coincides with the Lorenz curve generated under this rule for the old system (see Diagram 7). For issues of substance, however, power is further redistributed in favor of the smaller countries.

To summarize our results, the recent changes in the voting rules and distribution of voting shares in the International Monetary Fund have somewhat increased the power of its smaller members. In addition, in many instances, these changes have produced outcomes opposite to the intentions of the drafters of the Amendments.

There is one more question that deserves investigation. It is whether or not the power relationships in the Fund fairly reflect the relative economic importance of its members. This question will be discussed in the following section.

4.4 World Trade Shares and Power within the IMF

One purpose of periodic adjustments in the IMF members' quotas is to bring in line a member's importance in the fund with its importance in world trade. To see if this purpose was achieved, *Dreyer/Schotter* [1978] investigated the relationship between the share of any particular country in total exports of all IMF members with its power within the organization. These relationships are presented as a set of two-power Lorenz curves (Diagrams 9 and 10) for 80 percent decision rules.

For the purpose of comparison, we have superimposed these Lorenz curves over the power Lorenz curves presented before. These diagrams demonstrate that for small countries, trade shares are even worse proxies for power within the Fund than are their voting weights, that is, the distribution of power is even more biased in favor of the smaller countries when the members' trade shares, instead of voting weights, are used as a yardstick. In addition, if we compare power Lorenz curves under previous rules and quotas with the ones that result from the recent change, we see that this inequality is magnified (Diagrams 11 and 12).

5. Conclusions and Implications

Our conclusions are simple. First, voting weights are extremely poor proxies for voting power as one might have expected. However, as was seen by our example of the International Monetary Fund, real world organizations seem not to want to realize this fact. If they did, however, the problem would not be solved, since it would then be mandatory for the planners of these institutions to prescribe the power distribution they desire and the analyst's problem would then be to choose a vector of voting weights whose associated power distribution was the prescribed one. This is not easy for two reasons:

1) First, it would assume that the members could decide on one power index as the one they were going to use to measure power and there is nothing that says that they will be able to agree on one unanimously. If they do not, then with what voting weights are they going to decide on one?
2) Second, even if the index could be agreed to, the mapping from voting weight distributons to voting power distributions is a many-to-one mapping. Consequently, for any power distribution, there may exist many vote distributions yielding it. The choice among these distributions will also have to be decided and while each of these distributions yield identical power distributions, some may involve veto powers for members while others may not.

Consequently, it would appear that more work is needed in this area which would apply some results from the social choice literature and allow the members in voting bodies to rationally choose among alternative vote distributions.

Appendix

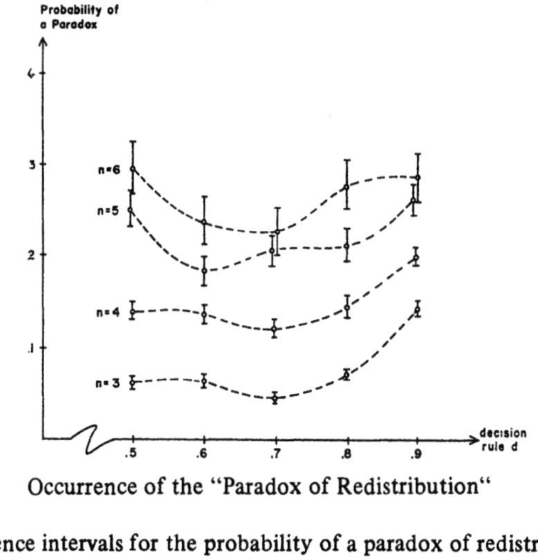

Occurrence of the "Paradox of Redistribution"

Fig. 1: 95 % confidence intervals for the probability of a paradox of redistribution for the Banzhaf power index, for various-numbers n of voters and decision rules d

	The Voting Body of Governors			
	Previous Voting System d = .80		Current Voting System d = .85	
Country	% of Vote	% of Power	% of Vote	% of Power
Luxembourg	.14	.20	.13	.22
Papua New Guinea	.14	.20	.13	.25
Jordan	.15	.21	.13	.22
Honduras	.15	.22	.14	.23
Cyprus	.16	.22	.14	.23
Malagasy Republic	.16	.22	.14	.23
Ethiopia	.16	.23	.14	.23
Liberia	.17	.24	.14	.24
Yemen (P.D.R.)	.17	.24	.16	.25
Costa Rica	.18	.25	.16	.25
Cameroon	.19	.27	.17	.27
Guatemala	.19	.27	.18	.30
Panama	.19	.27	.17	.27
Bahamas	.14	.20	.13	.22
Dominican Republic	.21	.30	.19	.31
Kenya	.23	.33	.22	.37
Tunisia	.23	.33	.21	.34
Syria	.23	.33	.21	.34
Jamaica	.24	.35	.23	.39
Burma	.26	.38	.23	.39
Trinidad and Tobago	.27	.39	.25	.41
Uruguay	.29	.42	.26	.43
Sudan	.30	.43	.27	.44
Ghana	.35	.50	.31	.51
Sri Lanka	.38	.55	.34	.56
Iraq	.41	.60	.39	.64
Morocco	.43	.61	.41	.68
Zaire	.43	.61	.42	.69
Ireland	.45	.64	.43	.69
Peru	.46	.66	.45	.73
Bangladesh	.46	.67	.42	.66
Turkey	.54	.78	.53	.86
Egypt	.66	.94	.60	.97
Romania	.66	.95	.64	1.03
Pakistan	.80	1.14	.73	1.17
Norway	.82	1.17	.76	1.20
Denmark	.88	1.25	.79	1.26
Austria	.91	1.29	.84	1.32

Tab. 1: Occurence of the Paradox of Redistribution in the International Monetary Fund [from *Dreyer/Schotter*] (where decreasing voting share leads to increasing power)

The Voting Body of Governors

Country	Previous Voting System d = .80 % of Vote	% of Power	Current Voting System d = .85 % of Vote	% of Power
Belgium	2.08	2.76	2.17	2.62
Netherlands	2.24	2.92	2.30	2.68
Japan	3.78	4.06	3.99	2.99
Germany (Fed. Rep.)	5.01	5.39	5.16	3.01

Tab. 2: Occurence of the Paradox of Redistribution in the International Monetary Fund [from *Dreyer/Schotter*] (where increasing voting share leads to decreasing power)

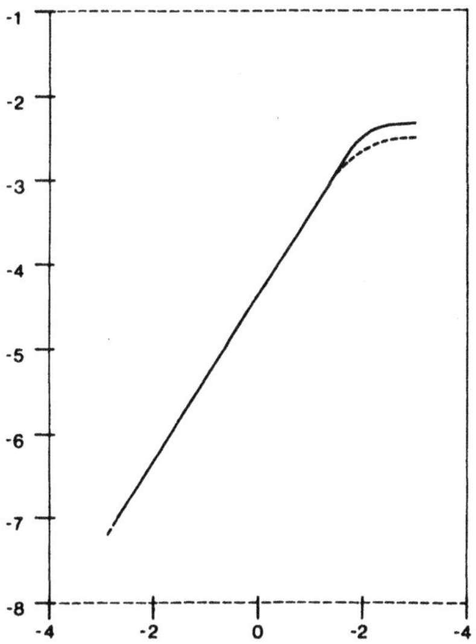

Diagram 1:
The relationship between voting weight and voting power under previous (——) and current (– –) quotas. Logs of weights (horizontal axis) vs. logs of Banzhaf power indices (vertical axis). The body of Governors voting on issues requiring a majority of 70 percent.

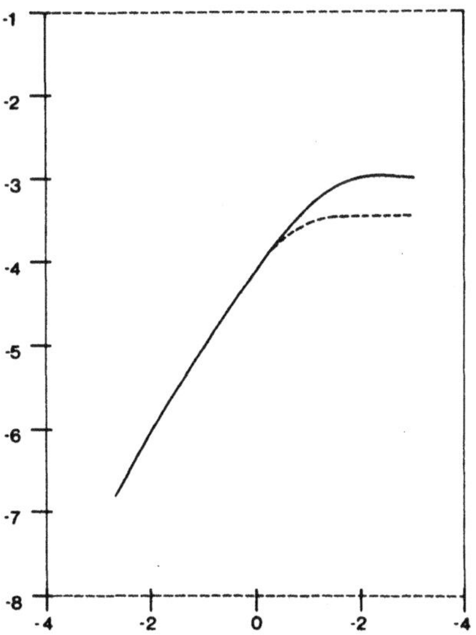

Diagram 2:
The relationship between voting weight and voting power under previous (——) and current (– –) quotas. Logs of weights (horizontal axis) vs. logs of Banzhaf power indices (vertical axis). The body of Governors voting on issues requiring a majority of 80 and 85 percent under previous and current rules, respectively.

Note: On the horizontal axis of Diagrams 1–4 is the voting weight of a country as represented by its *natural* logarithm. If, as in Diagram 1, a country like the United States has 21 % of the votes the horizontal axis would place the logarithm of 21 (which is about 3.044) and not the log of .21. On the vertical axis we measure the voting power of a country again in terms of the natural logarithm. However, here, as in the case of the United States in Diagram 1, if a country has a voting power of 9 % we would place the log of .09 (which is about –2.3).

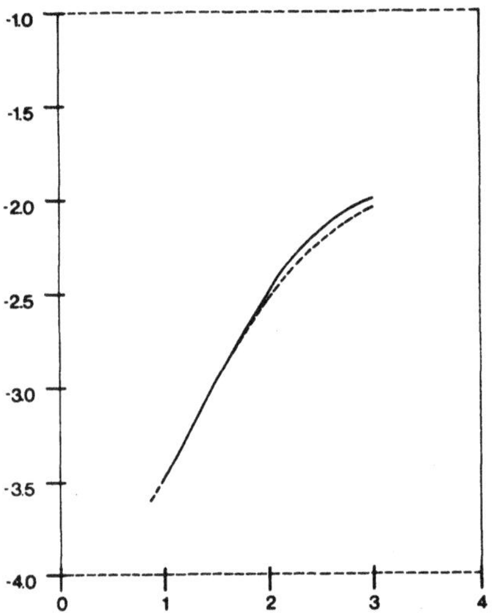

Diagram 3:
The relationship between voting weight and voting power under previous (——) and current (– –) quotas. Logs of weights (horizontal axis). vs. logs of Banzhaf power indices (vertical axis). The body of Executive Directors voting on issues requiring a majority of 70 percent.

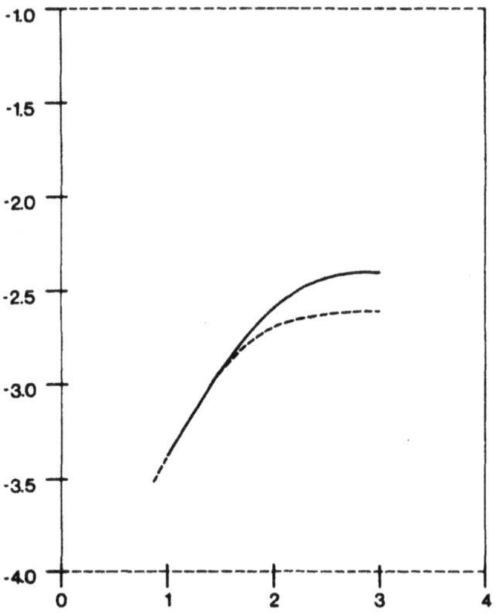

Diagram 4:
The relationship between voting weight and voting power under previous (——) and current (– –) quotas. Logs of weights (horizontal axis) vs. logs of Banzhaf power indices (vertical axis). The body of Executive Directors voting on issues requiring a majority of 80 and 85 percent under previous and current rules.

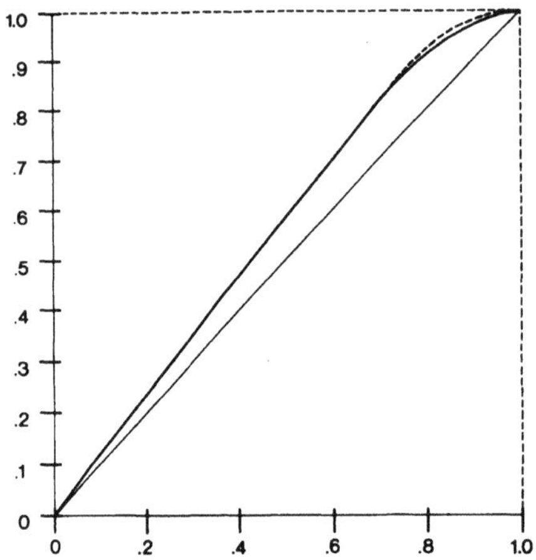

Diagram 5:
Power Lorenz curves. Cumulative voting weights (horizontal axis) vs. cumulative Banzhaf power indices (vertical axis) under previous (——) and current (– –) quotas. The body of Governors voting on issues requiring a majority of 70 percent.

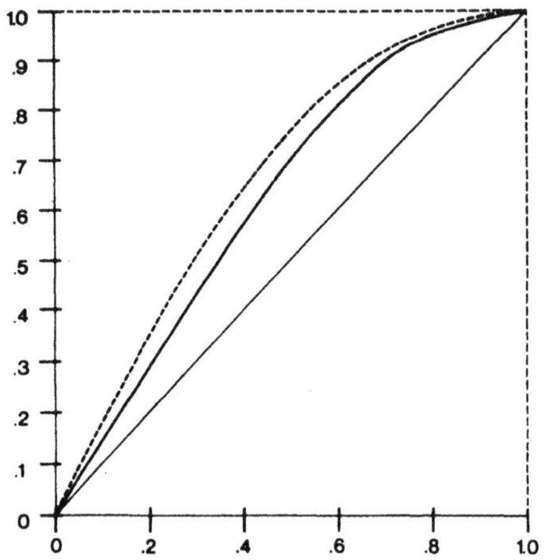

Diagram 6:
Power Lorenz curves. Cumulative voting weights (horizontal axis) vs. cumulative Banzhaf power indices (vertical axis) under previous (——) and current (– –) quotas. The body of Governors voting on issues requiring a majority of 80 and 85 percent under previous and current rules, respectively.

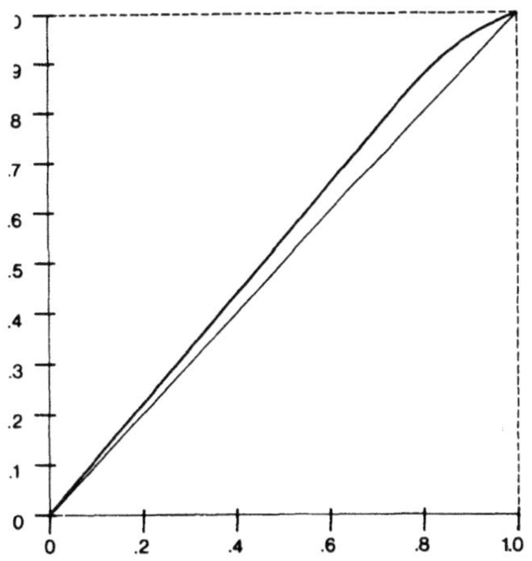

Diagram 7:
Power Lorenz curves. Cumulative voting weights (horizontal axis) vs. cumulative Banzhaf power indices (vertical axis) under previous (—) and current (– –) quotas. The body of Executive Directors voting on issues requiring a majority of 70 percent under previous and current rules, respectively.

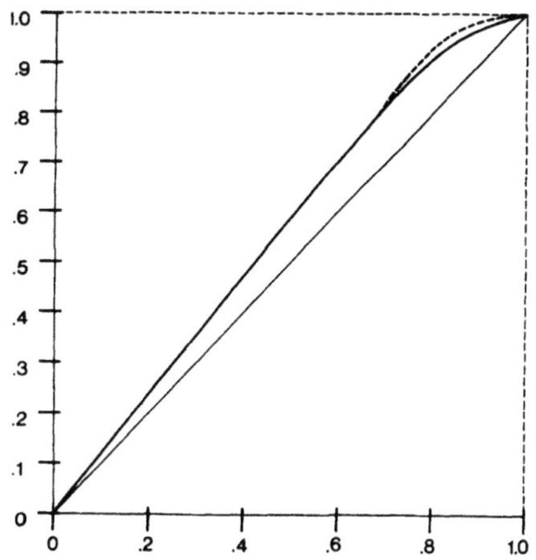

Diagram 8:
Power Lorenz curves. Cumulative voting weights (horizontal axis) vs. cumulative Banzhaf power indices (vertical axis) under previous (—) and current (– –) quotas. The body of Executive Directors voting on issues requiring a majority of 80 and 85 percent under previous and current rules, respectively.

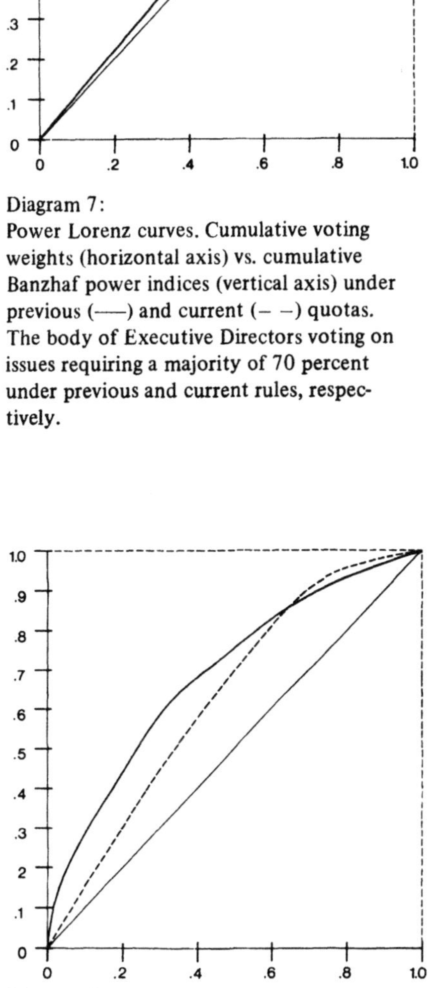

Diagram 9:
Power Lorenz curves. Cumulative export shares (—) and cumulative voting weights (– –) vs. cumulative Banzhaf power indices (vertical axis) under previous quotas. The body of Governors voting on issues requiring a majority of 80 percent.

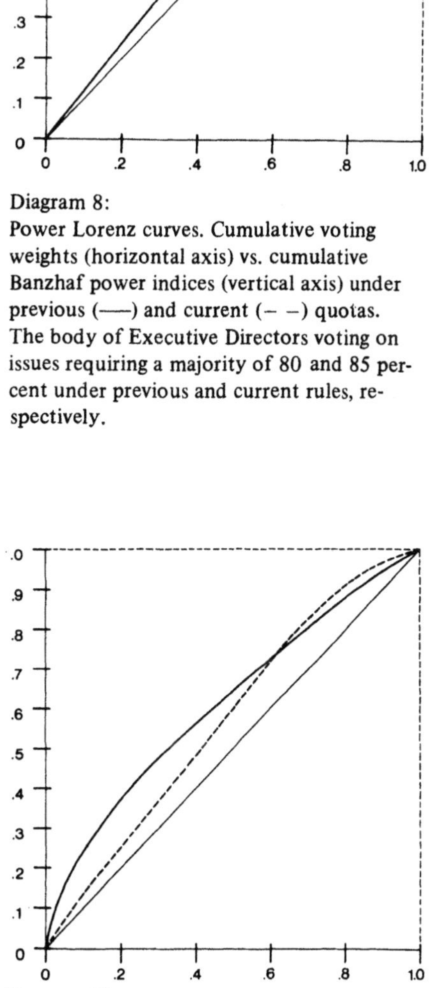

Diagram 10:
Power Lorenz curves: Cumulative export shares (—) and cumulative voting weights (– –) vs. cumulative Banzhaf power indices (vertical axis) under previous quotas. The body of Executive Directors voting on issues requiring a majority of 80 percent.

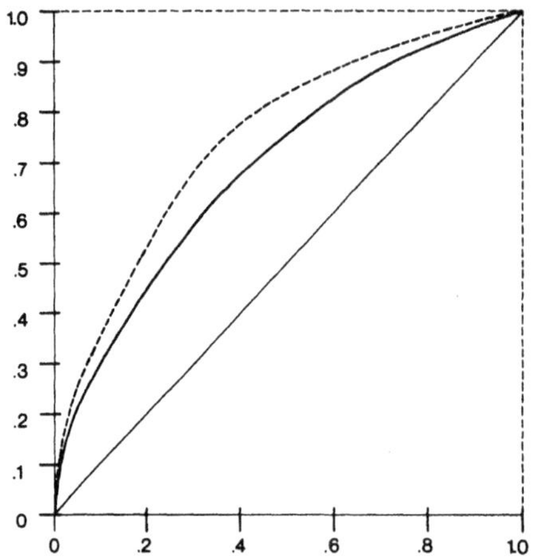

Diagram 11:
Power Lorenz curves. Cumulative export shares (horizontal axis) vs. cumulative Banzhaf power indices (vertical axis) under previous (——) and current (– –) quotas. The body of Governors voting on issues requiring a majority of 80 and 85 percent under previous and current rules, respectively.

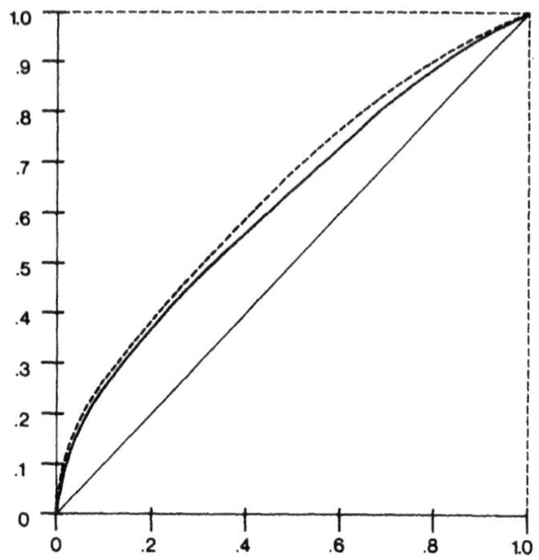

Diagram 12:
Power Lorenz curves. Cumulative export shares (horizontal axis) vs. cumulative Banzhaf power indices (vertical axis) under previous (——) and current (– –) quotas. The body of Executive Directors voting on issues requiring a majority of 80 and 85 percent under previous and current rules, respectively.

References

Aumann, R.: Disadvantageous Monopolies. Journal of Economic Theory **6** (1), 1973, 1–12.

Brams, S., and *M. Lake*: Power and Satisfaction in a Representative Democracy. Game Theory and Political Science. Ed. by P. Ordeshook. New York 1978.

Dreyer, J., and *A. Schotter*: Power Relationships in the International Monetary Fund: The Consequences of Quota Changes. Review of Economics and Statistics **62** (1), 1980, 97–106.

Fischer, D., and *A. Schotter*: The Inevitability of the Paradox of Redistribution in the Allocation of Voting Weights. Public Choice **33** (2), 1978, 49–67.

International Monetary Fund: A Report by the Executive Directors to the Board of Governors. Washington, D.C., March 1976.

Lucas, W.: Measuring Power in Weighted Voting Systems. Technical Report #227, School of Operations Research and Industrial Engineering, Cornell University, September 1974.

Olson, M., and *R. Zeckhauser*: An Economic Theory of Alliances. Review of Economics and Statistics **48** (3), 1966, 266–279.

Owen, G.: Multilinear Extensions and the Banzhaf Value. Nav. Res. Log. Quart. 22, 1975, 741–750.

Postlewaite, A., and *R. Rosenthal*: Disadvantageous Syndicates. Journal of Economic Theory **9**, 1974, 324–326.

Raanan, J.: The Inevitability of the Paradox of New Members. Technical Report #311, School of Operations Research and Industrial Engineering, Cornell University, September 1976.

Schotter, A.: Disadvantageous Syndicates in Public Goods Economies. American Economic Review **69** (5), 1979, 927–933.

GPSR Compliance

The European Union's (EU) General Product Safety Regulation (GPSR) is a set of rules that requires consumer products to be safe and our obligations to ensure this.

If you have any concerns about our products, you can contact us on ProductSafety@springernature.com

In case Publisher is established outside the EU, the EU authorized representative is:

Springer Nature Customer Service Center GmbH
Europaplatz 3
69115 Heidelberg, Germany

Batch number: 10726298

Printed by Printforce, the Netherlands